Global Journal

Vera Slavtcheva-Petkova & Michael Bromley

Global Journalism

An Introduction

First published 2019 by
RED GLOBE PRESS

Red Globe Press in the UK is an imprint of Springer Nature Limited,
registered in England, company number 785998, of 4 Crinan Street,
London N1 9XW.

Red Globe Press® is a registered trademarks in the United States,
the United Kingdom, Europe and other countries.

ISBN 978–1–137–60404–0 hardback
ISBN 978–1–137–60403–3 paperback

A catalogue record for this book is available from the British Library.

A catalog record for this book is available from the Library of Congress.

For
Tsvetan, Zoya, Nadia and Jordan, and Zoya and Yordan
and kdhb

Contents

Acknowledgements

No book-length project is completed by the authors alone without a great deal of assistance – provided both consciously and unwittingly – from others. As academics, our main source of support is from colleagues in our own and other institutions. We have met, discussed and exchanged ideas on campuses, in conferences and over coffee with too many to acknowledge them all individually. However, there is also another group with whom we engage routinely but who usually remain unacknowledged – students. These have been domestic students in Australia, the UK and the US (many of them multi-lingual and of international backgrounds) with an interest in the global nature of journalism, and so-called international students from dozens of places around the world, many of them practising journalists, who have not simply taken on board the Western ways of doing journalism but have generously shared their wide range of experiences as journalists and with journalism. They have inspired this work. Even if they have to remain anonymous, we thank them all.

More specifically, we are grateful for the assistance of current and former colleagues and students in the Department of Media, University of Chester, the Department of Communication and Media at the University of Liverpool, and the Department of Journalism and Centre for Law, Justice and Journalism at City, University of London.

Many individuals have helped us develop our interest in global journalism, including Omar Al Ghazzi, Judith Clarke, Thomas Hanitzsch, Zahera Harb, Claudia Mellado, Hillel Nosseck, James Rodgers, Howard Tumber and Silvio Waisbord.

We wish specifically to thank Sara De Vuyst, Merete Jansen, Juha Rekola and Joe A. Vella for their assistance in compiling some of the data used in

Chapter 7, and Lis Howell for supporting the idea. Our thanks, too, to the anonymous peer reviewers of the text, and to Lloyd Langman, commissioning editor at Red Globe Press, who responded enthusiastically to the idea for this book, and our editor Nicola Cattini, who sympathetically guided it to completion.

We are grateful to the World Journalism Education Council for permission to reproduce the Declarations of Principles of Journalism Education, to the Worlds of Journalism study for allowing us to use their data and to Elana Beiser from the CPJ for sharing their data with us.

Finally, we acknowledge all journalists around the world who, despite the challenges they experience on a daily basis, do an excellent job of informing the public and upholding freedom of expression as a fundamental human right.

Abbreviations

(Note: some entities are known only by their initials; for example, CBS, CNBC, RT and TMZ. We have included these with their previous names.)

ABC(Aus)	Australian Broadcasting Corporation
ABC(US)	American Broadcasting Company
AFP	Agence France-Presse
AP	Associated Press
ASNE	American Society of News Editors
AWM	Alliance for Women in Media
BBC	British Broadcasting Corporation
BRIC(S)	Brazil, Russia, India, China (and South Africa) group of nations
CBS	formerly Columbia Broadcasting System
CCTV	China Central Television (operating as CGTN internationally)
CGTN	China Global Television Network
CNBC	formerly Consumer News and Business Channel
CNN	Cable News Network
CPJ	Committee to Protect Journalists
ESPN	formerly Entertainment and Sports Programming Network
EU	European Union
FoI	freedom of information
HRW	Human Rights Watch
IACHR	Inter-American Commission on Human Rights
ICIJ	International Consortium of Investigative Journalists
ICT	information and communication technology
IFJ	International Federation of Journalists
IMC	Independent Media Center
IMF	International Monetary Fund
IPS	Inter Press Service

IS	Islamic State (Daesh)
IWMF	International Women's Media Foundation
MENA	Middle East and North Africa
NANA	Non-Aligned News Agency
NATO	North Atlantic Treaty Organization
NBC	National Broadcasting Company
NDTV	New Delhi Television
NGO	non-governmental organization
NHK	Japan Broadcasting Corporation
NJM	New Jewel Movement (Grenada)
NPPA	National Press Photographers Association
NWICO	New World Information and Communication Order
OAS	Organization of American States
PANA	Pan-African News Agency
PNA	Philippine News Agency
PRG	People's Revolutionary Government (Grenada)
PSB	public service broadcasting
RT	formerly Russia Today
RWB	Reporters Without Borders/Reporters Sans Frontières
SADC	Southern African Development Community
SPJ	Society of Professional Journalists
TeleSUR	La Nueva Televisora del Sur
TMZ	thirty-mile zone
UAE	United Arab Emirates
UGC	user-generated content
UK	United Kingdom (sometimes (Great) Britain)
UN	United Nations
UNESCO	United Nations Educational, Scientific and Cultural Organization
UNHCR	United Nations High Commissioner for Refugees
UPI	United Press International
US	United States (of America)
WAN-IFRA	World Association of Newspapers and News Publishers
WHNPA	White House News Photographers Association
WIBS	Windward Islands Broadcasting Service
WJEC	World Journalism Education Congress
WJWC	Women Journalists Without Chains/Munaẓẓamat Ṣaḥafiyāt Bilā Quyūd
WoJ	Worlds of Journalism
WTB	Wolffs Telegraphisches Bureau
WTO	World Trade Organization

List of Case Studies

List of Figures

List of Tables

Preface

Over many years, and most especially since the late 1940s, journalism has evolved into a global idea; that is, demands for freedom of expression as a human right, based in freedom of the press ('information disseminated in word and image' freely available to all) principally captured in the production of news by journalists, have emerged in more and more societies, and continue to do so promoted by organizations such as the United Nations Educational, Scientific and Cultural Organization (UNESCO) (Berger, 2017, pp. 17–18). Moreover, this movement has been facilitated – and accelerated – by the uptake of digital information and communication technologies (ICTs) since c. 1990s. As Ward (2017, p. 212) has pointed out, pre-digital journalism, from its formation in the seventeenth century to its professionalization in the twentieth century, was largely 'parochial' in nature, oriented chiefly around the nation-state. By the beginning of the twenty-first century it was both increasingly global and less specialized, embracing movements such as citizen journalism. This diffusion of journalism supposedly made it more difficult to control and, in some people's minds, less reliable. This led to concerns about misinformation, so-called fake news and the post-truth era. Others, however, regarded these developments as democratizing, giving voice to the previously voiceless and circumventing elite state, commercial and professional domination of journalism.

As the concepts of *journalism*, *freedom of expression* and *free press* spread in both place and time from the global West where they emerged, they had to negotiate different cultural contexts. One of the main premises of this book is that we cannot fully understand what role journalists play in their societies and worldwide unless we take into account the wider contexts in which they work and the range of factors that influence their work. Even within the global

West, attitudes to journalism have never been quite the same everywhere, and profound changes have occurred over time. Therefore, while the single (and in English, singular) word *journalism* is used more or less universally, it may actually carry different meanings and involve varying practices. One apparent difference is between so-called 'quality' journalism and tabloid journalism. Another may be between journalism practised in state-controlled environments and that practised in commercial conditions or by public service media. Many recognized journalists blog as part of their work; but are bloggers journalists? Should journalists be professionals with appropriate credentialing, or should journalism be an 'open' practice given the universal right to freedom of expression? What is the role of the ordinary person in journalism – citizen, consumer, participant?

Such questions point to the key issue of the relationship between journalism as a universal concept and aspiration, and the world's various cultures (defined by the *Cambridge Dictionary* (2017) as 'the way of life, especially the general customs and beliefs, of a particular group of people at a particular time'). This book aims to address this by scoping the contemporary global situation of journalism and by bringing into focus debates about journalism in its global context now and into the foreseeable future. It provides a comparative perspective of the contexts and challenges in which journalists operate across the world as well as an overview of global news reporting. We acknowledge that to date it remains impossible to canvass the entire world in relation to journalism: if nothing else, the information is simply not always available. However, there are more data now than there have ever been. It is also the case that most analyses of journalism originate in the global North. That does not mean that they are not more widely applicable. Yet as journalism appears in more varied cultural contexts, new ways of evaluating it are being produced. Finally, we recognize that interest in journalism exists in overlapping groups of those who seek to analyse it critically through scholarship, through everyday discussion and through the kind of 'shop talk' that journalists and other communication practitioners engage in. At the centre of this is the seemingly ever-expanding community of students who bring to the study of journalism a general interest which prompted them to study journalism in the first place, and who are introduced to both scholarship through higher education and 'shop talk' through interaction with practitioners. This community is itself global, situated in many cultures with many commonalities as well as differences, and often supported by international exchanges.

This book is an invitation to explore not just journalism as a single entity in the world, but equally the multiple worlds (cultures) that host journalism and the varieties of journalisms which exist across the world. It suggests a simple (somewhat journalistic) approach: first, identify, access and collect the data (information/facts) and concepts (ideas/principles); then explain and understand those data and concepts, and assess their application and appropriateness in varying contexts. To do so means not automatically accepting preconceptions, orthodoxies or received wisdom but identifying assertions for what they are and putting them to the test.

Therefore this is not a practical handbook or 'how to' text. Vocational learning may be undertaken in parallel, and may inform readings of this book. But journalism is not just about doing: it involves thinking, too – a working blend of theory and practice which enables practitioners not only to produce journalism, but also to understand it as a cultural form and to contribute centrally to debates about its role in our lives. In this regard we do not privilege the exceptional (the accomplishments of journalism's elites) over the routine and mundane (the everyday experiences of the majority of journalists). We address the role of non-governmental organizations (NGOs) and other global institutions which are increasingly playing a part in journalism, including guarding the safety of journalists; and, where relevant, we consult reports, working papers, online resources, etc. – the so-called 'grey literature' – where much of the contemporary global concern with journalism is expressed.

Our objective is to stimulate evidence-based analysis; comparison; questioning; evaluation; and argument. We aim for you to be able to marshal the evidence to answer a range of questions about global journalism, including:

* *What* is journalism? (The definitions used in multiple contexts, as well as universally.)
* *Who* are journalists? (Who is recognized as a journalist and by whom?)
* *Where* is journalism practised? (Both social locations and the instruments carrying journalism.)
* *When* does journalism emerge? (The favourable conditions for it to flourish, and those which curtail its development.)
* *How* does journalism develop? (The processes and trends involved both externally – the contexts – and internally within journalism.)
* *Why* does journalism manifest itself? (The reasons and arguments for journalism.)

Of course, these somewhat macro questions beg even more questions at the mezzo and micro levels. Each chapter in the book aims to introduce more focused issues for analysis.

The global proliferation of journalism and uptake of digital ICTs have given rise to more questions and will continue to do so. The text which follows aims to provide a foundation for thinking about today's and tomorrow's global journalism.

Approaches to the Book

The main text of this book provides an analytical introduction to global journalism which can be read on its own as such. However, the expansion of journalism globally has been accompanied by vastly increased numbers of people studying journalism formally in vocational and academic programmes in universities and colleges. This text is designed to support those studies. Therefore, each chapter is introduced by an overview which summarizes the content which follows, and learning outcomes to identify the range of knowledge, comprehension, application, analysis, synthesis and evaluation which should be developed through reading the chapter.

A third dimension to the evolution of journalism and its study globally has been the proliferation of scholarship, research and publication in the field. At the end of each chapter we list between six and eight items of suggested further reading. These lists are by no means exhaustive and can be easily supplemented with other readings. Our suggestions come with the usual caution to use a range of sources and to question all sources in a critical way.

Finally, we have made an effort to provide the most up-to-date account of the state of journalism around the world but journalism is fast changing so some of the trends we describe might have changed by the time the book comes out.

Note: where an item appears in the suggestions for further reading but is not cited in the main text, it is not included in the References. If web addresses given in the text are not listed in the References with their own access date, their date of last access can be taken to be 10 April 2018.

MSB
VS-P
September 2018

1

Introduction

Global Journalism in the Digital Age:
Key Concepts and Issues

Chapter overview

This chapter introduces the key topics covered in the book and the overall aims it serves. It is also a first attempt to identify the main issues facing global journalism at present and to define the book's key terms and concepts. The chapter is structured around three main topics: (1) What is global journalism? (2) Key terms and developments in journalism (studies). (3) The future of journalism.

Learning outcomes

After having read this chapter you will be able to:

1. Discuss what global journalism is and recognize the importance of context
2. Identify some of the key terms used in journalism studies as well as recent developments in the field such as the proliferation of fake news
3. Outline the main questions facing the future of journalism.

More than 68.5 million people were forced to flee their homes by the end of 2017 because of war and military conflicts. The United Nations (UN) announced in June 2017 that the number of refugees in the world had reached the highest level ever recorded and by June 2018 there were 25.4 million refugees, over half of whom were under the age of 18. In their pursuit of a better future, hundreds of thousands of people attempted to seek asylum in Europe.

The UN Refugee Agency (2016) reported that between January 2015 and August 2016 an estimated 6,940 people had drowned or had gone missing while 'trying to reach safety in Europe'. 'On average 11 men, women and children have perished across Europe every single day over the last 12 months' (UNHCR, 2016). The refugee crisis understandably attracted heightened media attention but the most iconic image was undoubtedly of a 3-year-old boy who was found washed up on a beach in Turkey in September 2015. The family of Aylan Kurdi, a Syrian of Kurdish origin, was trying to cross the Mediterranean Sea when their inflatable boat capsized. Aylan, his mother and brother drowned while his father survived. The photos of Aylan, shot by a Turkish journalist, reached the computer 'screens of almost 20 million people across the world in the space of 12 hours and via thirty thousand tweets' (D'Orazio, 2015, p. 12), and were headline news for numerous media outlets. D'Orazio (2015) claimed, however, that the story was not picked up by legacy media outside Turkey until five hours after it was first published.

Did the photos have a truly global reach (the world's total population exceeded seven billion people), and were they eventually published by journalists from all continents? This question does not have an easy answer. Vis and Goriunova's (2015) edited report suggested that the audience of the photos became 'truly global' only after the *Washington Post* Beirut bureau chief shared a tweet. However, the report indicated that nearly half of the shared images on social media were from accounts in Europe; 28 per cent from the US; 11 per cent from the Middle East and North Africa; 7 per cent from Asia; 2 per cent from Latin America, and 4 per cent from other locations. Why were Asian, African and Latin American journalists and audiences not as interested in the poignant photographs as their European and American colleagues? Did they actually see them? Can we realistically expect journalists and audiences in Africa to have picked up the photos, given that the internet penetration rate in 20 countries and territories on the continent was below 10 per cent (it was 35.2 per cent for Africa as a whole on 31 December 2017 according to Internet World Stats (2018))? Or could it be that those who saw the photos were actually interested in Aylan's story but Western researchers had not really succeeded in capturing their reactions? While answering this question in full is beyond the scope of this book, we investigate some of the key factors that explain the global flows and contra-flows of news: namely, how news stories are produced and then disseminated not just within individual nation-states but also across borders, and more broadly how news flows globally. The example of the photos of Aylan clearly demonstrates the shifting dynamics in the ways news travels in the digital age, and the changing relationship between journalists and their audiences. More importantly, the differences in coverage and 'shares' illustrates the close interconnectedness between the relevant political, economic and cultural contexts and journalistic values and practices. The refugee crisis was dominating the news headlines in Europe for months, but did it feature at all in the news in other continents, and if it did, was that because people from these countries were directly affected by the refugee crisis or simply because journalists relied mainly on agency copy? We cannot fully understand what role journalists play in their societies and worldwide unless we ask these types of questions, which require us to take into account the broader context journalists work in and the range of factors that influence their work. The texts written by journalists cannot be isolated from the conditions in which they are produced.

As already indicated in the Preface, this appreciation of the importance of context is a core principle of this book, together with an attempt to avoid media- and Western-centrism. Media do not exist in a vacuum, and evaluating the factors and processes that influence the work of journalists is of crucial importance. All too often, however, when attempting to explain certain developments or how media messages are received by audiences, media and journalism scholars focus almost exclusively on the role of the media, thus often ignoring the importance of all other actors, factors and social structures that play a role in the process. Our aim is to avoid this trap of media-centrism. Similarly, while most of the theories used and the empirical contexts discussed in journalism textbooks are from the developed democracies of the West that have 'free' media, only 13 per cent of people in the world live in countries with media which are designated as free (Freedom House, 2017a).[1] Our aim, therefore, is to offer a comprehensive overview of the state of journalism around the world, not just Western countries, and of global news reporting in the digital age by also exploring the impact of a range of contributing factors – local, national, international and global.

---

[1] Although it is important to acknowledge the sources of such judgements – Freedom House is a US government-funded NGO whose origins lay in propagating the US involvement in the Second World War and the Cold War – the findings should not be overlooked. Our evaluations of how well journalists serve the public and do their job are often based on idealistic (normative) expectations, whereas the reality on the ground can be very different and should certainly be investigated in more depth before any judgements are passed.

What is 'Global' Journalism?

We have also been concerned particularly with what constitutes the 'global'. At its simplest, the word means nothing more than 'the whole world'. However, that implies crossing, if not ignoring, spatial and temporal boundaries, and navigating multiple cultures, established both naturally and by human activity. Thus, 'global warming' refers to overall climate change affecting the entire planet Earth, although it may manifest itself differently in different places. In journalism, one of the earliest uses of the concept of the global was in Marshall McLuhan's 'global village'. McLuhan argued that the electronic media (especially television) provided instantaneous connections across time and space, and the sharing of the same information, as if we were all living in a village with face-to-face human contact (McLuhan & Fiore, 1967, p. 63). Even prior to that, the wire services (news agencies) – Reuters, Associated Press (AP), Havas and Wolff – were 'global media organizations' trading news across the world (Boyd-Barrett & Rantanen, 1998, p. 1). Before the internet, television or radio, the telegraph (almost exclusively under British control with US support) formed a 'global media system' which linked the world with cables and later wireless radio telegraphy (Winseck & Pike, 2009, p. 34). These were building blocks in the construction of globalization in which all activities (political, economic, social and cultural) were potentially undertaken on a global scale. This implied three things: (1) the relegation of the distinctiveness of the national and the local, and, directly related to that, (2) linguistic domination and (3) the inbuilt advantage of more economically developed countries, such as the US and UK, in establishing global presences. However, notwithstanding the existence of large global news businesses, such as News Corp, or the domination of the World Wide Web by the English language, national and local media in many languages have proven to be quite resilient. In line with our desire not to see the global from a Western and Northern perspective we agree with Stevenson (1999, p. 4) who argued that globalization 'has asked us to think again about projecting our own backyard onto the rest of the world'.

These developments impacted on journalism in four main ways:

1. Journalists were part of an increasingly globalized labour force characterized by more flexible working, greater precarity of employment and off-shoring (Bromley et al., 2015, pp. 289–90; Bunce, 2010).
2. Journalists' work was more consciously directed at global users (for example, UK national newspapers the *Daily Mail* and the *Mail on Sunday* had print circulations largely confined to Britain of 1.5m and 1.375m respectively, whereas the MailOnline website with its global reach attracted close to 14m browsers).

3. At the same time, journalists interpreted global events and issues for local users (their retreat from this led to anxieties over how ill-informed Americans were about the world, especially after the 9/11 attacks (Rash, 2011)).
4. There was a residual corps of foreign correspondents reporting from one or more countries to another (home) country (see Chapter 5).

There has been a resurgence of interest in global/international journalism in recent years even as the numbers of foreign correspondents appeared to decline (Keller, 2013). A growing number of universities around the world offer postgraduate programmes and undergraduate courses/modules in both global and international journalism – from universities in the West which wish to expose students to diverse experiences to those in the global South which are looking to test Western models and evaluate their own indigenous practices. However, despite the increasing number of courses, there is no single overview that provides a comprehensive understanding of journalism within the context of media globalization in the digital era. A few texts on related topics have appeared in recent years but most tended to focus narrowly on specific topics and themes. On the one hand, some authors focused on the exceptional – the reporting of global crises and the role of foreign correspondents. Berglez (2013) structured his analysis around the notion of 'global journalism', defined as 'a new form of journalism that is increasingly needed in global times' (back cover), concentrating on the exceptional – the coverage of global crises. Cottle (2008) similarly offered insights into international journalism which skirted its mundane existence. Williams (2011) and Owen and Purdey (2009) focused almost exclusively on the role of foreign correspondents. A few studies published (mainly) in the US concentrated predominantly on the mundane – the contexts in which journalists around the world work, organized by regions and/or countries (de Beer, 2008; Weaver & Willnat, 2012).

Global journalism concerns the routine as much as the exceptional – the comprehensive coverage of its mundane as well as exceptional aspects, features and processes. We broadly define *the exceptional* as the coverage of global crises and conflicts, and *the mundane* as comprising the challenges, pressures and conditions journalists face and work in across contexts and platforms. We explore three key topics:

1. *Contexts:* The different journalistic cultures – 'worlds of journalism' (Hanitzsch et al., 2011) – across the world; the importance of context and the interactions between the global, national and local levels across a range of media.

2. *Theories:* Key trends and theories in the field, including globalization of professional practices, transnational/global news flows and contra-flows.
3. *Journalistic practices:* The history and current state of international/foreign news reporting.

We start by discussing the importance of context, then move on to relevant theories that attempt to conceptualize the relationship between context and journalistic practices, and finally explore in detail some of these practices – on both a transnational/international and a national/local level, including the role of the big news organizations, foreign correspondents and citizen journalists.

A key aim is to investigate the state of global journalism by being truly global in our scope and coverage. As already indicated, the conditions in which journalists around the world work and the challenges and pressures they face as well as the conventions they follow are likely to differ significantly. Journalism studies as an academic field is dominated by Western scholars and as a result the majority of books, textbooks and journal articles focus on the Western world. The hysteria provoked by Donald Trump's election as the 45th US President allegedly facilitated by the unprecedented spread of 'fake news' is a case in point. If we define fake news as the opposite of 'true' news, namely completely made-up stories, then how new is this phenomenon, especially for the 87 per cent of the world's population who live in countries where the media are not free? Have these people ever lived in an age of truth?

Examples of fake news proliferate in most of these countries; for example, the Ukrainian website stopfake.org began exposing fake news about Ukraine in 2014. It even had a section with tips on 'How to identify a fake' and an 'Are you easily fooled?' test. The most notorious fake news story exposed was a report about the alleged crucifixion of a 3-year-old boy by Ukrainian soldiers. The report was included in the prime-time news bulletin of the most popular Russian TV channel, Первый канал (Channel One – the report was still available on YouTube in 2017). The co-founder of the website, Yevhen Fedchenko, argued that this story and numerous other 'fake news' items were 'an integral part of information warfare' orchestrated by the Russian prop-aganda machine. Its increased efforts in that respect during the conflict in Ukraine clearly paid off because Russian President Vladimir Putin's popular-ity soared from a 63 per cent approval rating in June 2013 to a record 89 per cent in June 2015 (Levada-Center, 2015). Similarly, 87 per cent of Russians supported the annexation of Crimea.

In an attempt to avoid Western-centrism, we offer a comprehensive and up-to-date account of the current state of media freedom and journalistic practices across national contexts and cultures – from traditional democracies in Western Europe and North America to repressive dictatorial regimes in Asia and Africa. It is important to do this prior to introducing the key theories in the field, because it helps us better interpret and question these key theories. We draw a distinction between journalistic practices and challenges that media professionals experience in the traditional and emerging democracies and industrialized economies of the global North (Europe, Northern America and Oceania) in contrast to the situation in the largely non-democratic countries or young democracies and industrializing countries of the global South (Asia, Africa, Latin America and the Caribbean). Another commonly used distinction is between the East and the West; however, the global North/ South distinction has become more pertinent following the fall of the Berlin Wall, presaging a shrinking gap in journalistic practices and contributing factors between the East and the West, while the gap between the North and the South appears to be widening (the digital age and post 9/11 political developments have to an extent contributed to this development).

Prior to the fall of the Berlin Wall, there was a clear distinction between the East and the West. The ideological battle between the US and the Soviet Union (USSR) was fought on every single front – political, social, cultural and economic. While in the West there was a clear commitment to democracy, liberalization of media markets and free media, in the East the mass media were used as propaganda tools in the hands of the communist regimes and dictators. The fall of the Berlin Wall and the subsequent rapid democratization of some Central and Eastern European countries and former Soviet republics led to a very quick transformation of these societies and their media systems. Eleven of the 30 countries became members of the European Union (EU) and the North Atlantic Treaty Organization (NATO) (a twelfth, Albania, joined NATO only), and embraced democratic values. Others had aspirations to join the EU. However, a number of former Soviet republics have eschewed democratization, and the commitment to press freedom in some Eastern and Central European countries has been questioned (Garcia, 2015). Some of the distinctions among European countries are explored in Chapter 2. Moreover, journalism and the media play significantly different roles in emerging and transitional democracies than in established liberal democracies (Jebril et al., 2012, p. 7). Therefore, occasionally we have found it useful to refer to Western countries which are ideologically liberal democratic but not necessarily industrialized, and to industrialized nations which are not liberal.

The UN has now classified the majority of countries in the global North as 'developed', while the majority of countries in the global South are 'developing' or 'least developed'. This distinction between the global

North and the globalSouth, while geographic on the surface, is based on a range of factors – economic, political and developmental, including 'levels of industrialization, economic progress, science and technology, standards of living and political-economic power in the global arena' (Guttal, 2016). There are noticeable differences between and within countries, and we further acknowledge these differences in the next chapters, but as a whole, as Guttal (2016) points out, 'structural differences in living conditions, human and societal capabilities and economic and political power, are still prevalent between the North and South'. Needless to say, these distinctions are indeed social 'constructs' and as such are useful only to an extent – as a means of drawing out key differences and similarities, and common challenges. We provide examples from different contexts to more clearly illustrate some of the general points that we make. Similarly, categories such as democratic/undemocratic and free/not free have their limitations but they are widely adopted by global audits so it is worth considering them in a critical way.

Key Terms and Developments in Journalism (Studies)

While fascinating in their own right, the case studies we use throughout the book also tell a wider story about journalism as a profession and the role journalists play in their societies and globally. Hence, we explore a range of key theories and concepts of global journalism that help us make sense of past and recent intriguing developments. The conceptualization of journalism as a profession is just as much a moving target as is the practice of journalism itself. In their review of theories used in journalism studies in the digital age, Steensen and Ahva (2015, p. 2) claimed that the field was 'not marked by a specific and shared academic culture', namely 'a shared set of theories and methodologies'. They counted more than a hundred different theories in use – mainly from political science, sociology, and language and critical studies. Steensen and Ahva (2015, p. 13) disagreed with Zelizer's (2009, p. 34) claim that 'journalism studies still has not been able to "produce a coherent picture of what journalism is"', because they argued that 'such coherence' was not necessarily desirable or possible 'in the digital era, where multiple journalisms coexist and the practice of journalism is dispersing'.

Various terms and theories have been used to explain how flows and contra-flows take place – among them, 'globalization', 'glocalism' and 'glocalization'. These terms were coined with the aim of explaining the interrelation between the global and the local. Put simply, globalization has inevitably brought about a range of changes but the process is not linear and global flows impact local societies and communities differently depending on the relevant context. These global events and developments can in turn be affected by local products, events and developments. This is a constant process with a range of implications for journalism that we consider in this book. Wasserman's (2006) study on the glocalization of journalism ethics in African countries is an interesting case in point. Although when apartheid ended South African journalists initially adopted Western ethical codes, they later came up with an African code of ethics after facing societal pressure to report 'as Africans' and to be loyal to their 'African values'. While we do indeed review a range of theories, we should make it clear from the onset that we do not endorse one specific theoretical framework or indeed an overarching theory of journalism, not only because such a theory does not exist but also because the conceptualization of journalism is an ongoing process we should all get involved in. Critically reflecting upon our practice is an essential skill for all journalists, journalism scholars and students.

A key ideological debate in the field is what direction journalism is moving in – is it an instrument in the hands of dominant corporate media, or is it ushering in an expansion of the public sphere? The process of aligning journalism with democracy, the norm in the theorization of journalism for decades, is becoming problematic. As journalism, as a modern concept, became more global it necessarily interacted with multiple contexts and their social, cultural, economic and historical, as well as political, specificities. On the one hand this allowed the flow of the same journalistic content globally, but on the other hand, with the advent of the internet we have also witnessed a proliferation of national, local and hyperlocal news and increased fragmentation of the news. Recent studies even suggest that the digital era has made Habermas's (1989) public sphere concept redundant, because most academic attempts to find evidence of online democratic deliberation have proved futile (for a summary, see Slavtcheva-Petkova, 2016a, 2016b). Put simply, the cyberoptimistic expectation that the advent of the internet would lead to an opening up of the public sphere or even potentially the emergence of a virtual public sphere has not really materialized. The flow of news is not a linear process and we investigate both the key milestones in this process and the various terms and theories used to explain how flows and contra-flows of news take place.

The term 'international journalism' is often associated with the work of a particular group of journalists – foreign correspondents. Being a foreign correspondent is a very prestigious profession because, as Hamilton and Jenner (2004b) argued, 'correspondents talk to heads of state and dine on the Via Veneto, while colleagues back home toil under the watchful eye of editors' (p. 98).

The stereotypical image of foreign correspondents created during the so-called 'golden age' of the 1930s was captured by Alfred Hitchcock in his 1940 movie *Foreign Correspondent*, based loosely on the biography of Vincent Sheean of the *Chicago Tribune* and part-scripted by another former US foreign correspondent of the period, Ben Hecht. The main protagonist was portrayed as a 'reflective, interpretive' journalist, a heroic figure upholding the public's right to know (Cozma & Hamilton, 2009, pp. 499–500; Ehrlich, 2010, pp. 80, 176). Cozma and Hamilton (2009, p. 500) argued that such films 'often verged on popular propaganda' as American journalists were represented as solving the world's problems. In post-colonial times such characterizations were unrealistic and less acceptable. Foreign correspondence in the later twentieth and early twenty-first centuries comprised less 'fun and glamour', reporting revolutions, war and espionage (the exceptional), and more routine politics, economics, entertainment, travel (the mundane) (Cottle, 2009, p. 347; Terzis, 2015, p. 305). Nevertheless, in the spirit of the trailer for *Foreign Correspondent* which focuses on the assassination of a high-profile European leader, 'a camera with gun attachment, trick windmills and a mid-ocean plane crash' (Turner Classic Movies at www.tcm.com), foreign correspondents remained popularly associated with reporting from war and conflict zones with bombs and gunshots exploding in the background (Simpson, 2016).

However, when the first foreign stories appeared in European newspapers they were not necessarily all about wars and conflicts nor were they written by 'professional' journalists. 'Seafarers' often sent letters back home with 'phantasmagoria' such as 'tales of monsters', serpents and other scary creatures born out of 'fear of the unknown, of lands unexplored and peoples undiscovered' (Williams, 2011, p. 47). We provide a brief history of foreign correspondents by focusing on the main periods and the lives and careers of a few of them, because their experience also shows how the profession has evolved – from reporting hearsay and phantasmagoria to interpreting complex cultural issues for cosmopolitan audiences (Turnbull, 2014).

As the majority of countries with foreign correspondents have not been formally at war for most of the period since the 1940s – the bulk of the world's foreign correspondents in 2017–18 came from and were based in the US, the UK and the rest of the EU – for some the distinction between foreign and war correspondents has eroded. In contemporary times war reporting from dangerous zones in third-party locations has been assigned chiefly to foreign correspondents who have borne the associated risks. Although at the beginning of the 2003 invasion of Iraq the casualty rate among journalists was greater than that among US soldiers (Seib, 2004, p. 58), deaths among journalists continued after the invading forces left. Between 2012 and 2016 Iraq and

Syria were the two deadliest countries for journalists with up to 75 per cent of those who died covering war. In 14 months more journalists were killed in the civil war in the former Yugoslavia than in 14 years of the Vietnam War or the whole of the Second World War (Santora & Carter, 2006; Simpson, 1995). However, the numbers of journalists killed since 1992 in crossfire or combat (296) and 'on dangerous assignment' (165) was only a fraction of the number simply murdered (844) (Committee to Protect Journalists, 2018a). (We note here that deaths among journalists while doing their job seemed to continue to rise almost monthly.)

A persistent theme is whether foreign correspondents are an 'endangered' (Willnat & Martin, 2012, p. 495) or 'vanishing' (Lewis, 2010, p. 121) species. Reports on the state of foreign correspondence (Enda, 2011; Hamilton & Jenner, 2004b; Moore, 2010; Sambrook, 2010) suggested that foreign correspondents might indeed be becoming redundant because of the impact of new technologies, the global economic downturn and the diminishing interest in foreign news. The number of countries, regions and continents with no permanent correspondents based in them was growing – ironically at a time when there appeared to be an increase in disturbing developments with global repercussions, including public health threats (the 2014–16 Ebola outbreak in West Africa), humanitarian emergencies (famine in Nigeria, South Sudan, Somalia and Yemen in 2017), and military conflicts (in Syria, Iraq, Libya, Yemen). Mainly stringers and parachute journalists covered Africa, Latin America and parts of Asia. By contrast, the European beat was growing – there were more than 1,000 accredited journalists in Brussels, mainly from countries outside Europe – Asia and North America.

Foreign correspondents were not the only ones who contributed to the transnational flow of news, and we also explore the role of 'big global media' – news agencies such as Reuters, AP and Agence France-Presse (AFP), and hegemonic and counter-hegemonic TV stations such as Cable News Network (CNN), Al Jazeera and RT (formerly Russia Today). While there was evidence of a transformation of business models and a drop in advertising revenues in a lot of European and North American countries, Asia was one of the fastest growing media markets in the world. We explore the extent to which we are likely to experience global journalism flows from this market – in particular from China and India as 'the economic giants of the future'.

The vacuum left by legacy media has been filled in some contexts by non-professional/citizen journalists. We delve deeper into the role citizen and alternative journalists, activists, NGOs and social media have played not only in relation to foreign correspondence but also more broadly. Social media played an unprecedented role during the Arab Spring but what role, if any, has alternative/citizen journalism played in both 'hard' and 'soft' authoritarian regimes? We use a number of case studies – from Occupy New York City bloggers and Brazilian ninja citizen journalists to activists posting YouTube videos of the atrocities in Syria and North Koreans sharing their videos about the regime in the country by smuggling them into South Korea. Legacy media have also successfully launched some projects exclusively dedicated to promoting citizen journalism projects (CNN iReport is a case in point), and we investigate the role they have played. Convergence has become the buzzword in the industry and some big companies such as the British Broadcasting Corporation (BBC) show how journalists and news media have adapted or changed their practices in response to these recent developments.

The Future of Journalism?

What does the increased blurring of the boundaries between citizen and professional journalists mean for the future of global journalism and global journalists? Will there be one, universal journalism – and if so, will it be based on any particular existing model? Or will many journalisms flourish, each responsive to and serving its particular wider context – and will this constitute an end to any shared global concept of journalism? Or will something in-between emerge? Accounts of journalism differ: on the one hand, some argue that journalism around the world is fundamentally similar but glossed by different cultural and social situatednesses; on the other hand, it is suggested that journalism shares no more than a veneer of sameness underpinned by cultural and social specificities. These positions have manifested themselves in pragmatic projects. A liberal (North Atlantic, or Anglo-Saxon) model of journalism has been strongly promoted globally through both liberal economics and education (epitomized by UNESCO curricula). This has appeared to overwhelm alternatives, such as the established (European) democratic corporatist and polarized pluralist models, let alone other variants evident elsewhere. However, other practices have arisen both spontaneously (out of existing cultural traditions) and with state support. Examples include development, participatory and Asian values journalisms.

Whether the view of journalism's future is of a homogenized (converged), heterogenized (diverged) or hybridized (mixed) practice is in large part determined by the configurations of units of analysis – political and economic systems, history, culture, geography and social structures. A key dimension of this is whether the larger context is taken to be the nation-state or a globalized world. Digitization has tended to foster more globalized, transnational and intranational practices, and as such has been associated with 'the end of journalism' insofar as, in this context, privileging professionalized practice based on national cultures has been more difficult, as access to the means of mass creation and dissemination has allowed the development outside of spatial boundaries of novel practices such as citizen journalism. Thus the structured education of journalists has become a marker of 'professionalism', as well as a vehicle for fostering varieties of journalisms. It now plays a key, if somewhat hidden, role in shaping expectations of journalism. As such, journalism education is a contested area in the development of practice in which assumptions about the identity and role of journalism in the global future are shaped, reproduced and transmitted.

The wider, global challenge for journalism is not as much its continued relevance to the 13 per cent of the world's population living in cultures with a 'free' press (although as the consumption of mainstream journalism in these domains continues to decline, this is an issue) as its status elsewhere and in the interstices between 'the West and the rest'. At the same time, media development is uneven across the world in terms of both decline and growth and the popularity of platforms. While it is evident that Web 2.0 has stimulated a global expansion of the use of the internet and in particular social media, newspaper reading has increased significantly in China and Japan; television usage has grown in India, and both commercial and community radio stations have proliferated in Africa. Furthermore, the internet has facilitated access to the journalisms of legacy media through mechanisms such as pod- and vod-casts, apps, branded websites and aggregation sites, alongside and sometimes in conjunction with the likes of Facebook and Twitter. The future of global journalism is by no means clear – will it be a US-led, a Chinese- or BRICS-led or a hybrid future?

Another question we pose is: will journalism (and journalism studies) benefit if freed from platform determinism? Despite some common changes journalists experience in the global news environment, they also face context-dependent challenges – the work of BBC's Europe editor who has huge resources and a support network at her disposal is very different from the work of an Eritrean journalist who is not allowed to travel abroad, does not even have access to the internet (only 1.4 per cent of the population in Eritrea have internet access) and faces the threat of spending the rest of his/her life in a prison camp. We also discuss the role that activists and NGOs such as Freedom House, the Committee to Protect Journalists (CPJ), Reporters Without Borders (RWB), Article 19 et al. play in their efforts to promote press freedom and to end impunity. The UN adopted in 2012 a plan of action on the safety of journalists with the aim of ending impunity. What difference have these activists made? Have we witnessed any short-term and long-term changes? We conclude by making suggestions for a more effective approach to tackling some of these issues, while also recognizing the importance of relevant societal, political and economic developments.

Further Reading

1. Freedom House (2016; 2017) 'Freedom of the press: country reports', https://freedomhouse.org, accessed 17 August 2018.
2. McLuhan, M. & Fiore, Q. (1967) *The Medium is the Massage* (London: Penguin).
3. Steensen, S. & Ahva, L. (2015) 'Theories of journalism in a digital age,' *Journalism Practice* 9(1), 1–18.
4. Stevenson, N. (1999) *The Transformation of the Media: Globalisation, Morality and Ethics* (Harlow: Longman).
5. Vis, F. & Goriunova, O. (2015) *The Iconic Image on Social Media: A Rapid Research Response to the Death of Aylan Kurdi* (Sheffield: Visual Social Media Lab).
6. Weaver, D.H. & Willnat, L. (eds) (2012) *The Global Journalist in the 21st Century* (New York: Routledge).

2

Journalism – the Global North and the Global South

Chapter overview

This chapter explores the current state of media freedom and journalistic practices around the world – from traditional democracies in Western Europe and North America to repressive dictatorial regimes in Asia and Africa.

We draw a distinction between the situation in the traditional and emerging democracies of the global North (Europe, Northern America and Oceania) and the largely non-democratic countries or young democracies of the global South (Asia, Africa, Latin America and the Caribbean). Our comprehensive and up-to-date comparison is based on four key indicators: (1) Safety threats, including violence against journalists. (2) Legal restrictions. (3) State and political pressures. (4) Economic pressures.

Learning outcomes

After having read this chapter you will be able to:

1. Discuss the current state of media freedom and journalistic practices around the world and outline the main differences between the global North and the global South
2. Identify the main factors that influence journalists' work, the roles they play and the practices they engage in, both in the global South and in the global North
3. Evaluate the use of key comparative indicators in major investigations of media systems and journalistic cultures conducted by NGOs and academics.

Journalism is 'a noble profession and one of unequalled importance for its influence upon the minds and morals of the people'. These words belong to the American journalist and newspaper publisher Joseph Pulitzer who endowed the most prestigious awards for US journalists – the Pulitzer Prizes. The winners of the awards were announced for the 100th time in April 2016. While American journalists were celebrating their 'excellence' with centennial events around the country, British journalists were fighting a privacy injunction in the English courts imposed at the request of a famous celebrity couple. The celebrity couple did not want the English public to know that they had an open relationship and that one of them had had a long-term affair with a businessman, involving a threesome with his partner, even though details of the affair were already published by newspapers and magazines around the world and online, including in Scotland. Meanwhile, also in April 2016, yet another Syrian journalist was murdered by Islamic State (IS). Zaher al-Shurqat was the fourth Syrian journalist killed in Turkey in six months. As many as 1,310 killings of journalists had been confirmed since 1992 (Committee to Protect Journalists, 2018a). The actual number was probably considerably higher, and continued to grow into mid-2018.

What these examples show is that journalists around the world work in different environments, and the challenges and pressures they experience differ. The greatest threat to the lives of journalists came not from war but from covering politics: 47 per cent of journalists killed were reporting on politics (Committee to Protect Journalists, 2018a). Exploring the everyday, as well as the exceptional, contexts in which journalists work is key to understanding what role they play in their respective societies. In terms of media freedom Freedom House (2017a) suggested that the most extreme differences were between European countries such as Finland, Norway and the Netherlands that traditionally topped the press freedom rankings and some states in Asia and Africa such as North Korea, Turkmenistan and Eritrea, usually ranked last out of 199 countries and territories. The latter, according to Reporters Without Borders (2014) were 'news and information black holes and living hells for the journalists that inhabit them'.

To facilitate this appreciation of the importance of context and draw out key differences and similarities in journalistic practices in a systematic way, this chapter makes a distinction between journalistic practices and challenges that media professionals experienced, according to reports, in the traditional and emerging democracies of the global North in contrast to the situation in the largely non-democratic countries or young democracies of the global South. There were considerable variations recorded between and within countries and regions so it is important for us to clearly outline what were identified as some of the broader challenges, pressures and opportunities. In order to avoid mere description and/or unnecessary opposition between the two key regions, we first outline the key indicators and factors that NGOs and academics have used when comparing media systems and journalistic cultures. Based on these indicators and a few key studies that offered typologies of media systems and journalistic cultures, separate sections are devoted to Asia, Africa, Latin America and the Caribbean (the global South), and Europe, Northern America and Oceania (the global North). This grouping of countries is based on the United Nations' (2013) geoscheme classification, which is not the only one in use (even by the UN) but is widely accepted. We also present case studies and examples of journalistic practices from each of these regions with the aim of revealing the broader trends. Drawing distinctions is also very important because oversimplifications and generalizations can be counterproductive when attempting to understand the range of practices journalists engage in. Thus, in Asia some journalists were recorded as working in 'living hells' (as noted above), such as North Korea where they faced daily the threat of political prison camps or even death sentences, but there were also practitioners in the Middle East who were found to be forced to work 'under the exclusive supervision of the Isis media offices' (Dearden, 2014). Asia is also home to a few economic giants with huge media markets (but facing very different political and cultural issues) such as China, India and Japan. Comparisons made between these countries reveal aspects of the hybridity of journalistic experiences and practices.

The broader distinction we draw between the global North and the global South is not the only distinction used in the academic literature. As indicated in Chapter 1, some commentators differentiated between the East and the West but we have mainly adopted the global North/South distinction because after the fall of the Berlin Wall in 1989 the gap in journalistic practices and contributing factors between the global North and the global South appears to be widening while that between Eastern and Western countries (particularly in Europe) is shrinking, although not in every case. A range of political, economic and technological factors such as the democratization of Eastern and Central Europe, the advent of the digital age and post 9/11 developments have contributed to this phenomenon. We further explore their significance in this and subsequent chapters.

Comparing the Global North and the Global South – Key Indicators

What in the second decade of the twenty-first century were the main pressures and challenges that journalists faced around the world? The most recent reports released by the leading NGOs in the field (Freedom House, RWB, CPJ) suggested that 'there has been a deep and disturbing decline in respect for media freedom at both the global and regional levels' (Reporters Without Borders, 2016). Freedom of expression appeared to be 'in retreat around the world' (Dunham, 2016). This steady downward trend has been observed for the past decade with only a minority the world's population living in 'countries where coverage of political news is robust, the safety of journalists is guaranteed, state intrusion in media affairs is minimal, and the press is not subject to onerous legal or economic pressures' (Dunham, 2016). Reporters Without Borders (2016) also warned that Islamist armed groups such as IS, al-Qaeda, al-Shabaab and Boko Haram had waged a global 'jihad against journalists'. Two main factors have contributed to this decline in press freedom: 'heightened partisanship and polarization', and 'the degree of extra-legal intimidation and physical violence faced by journalists' (Dunham, 2016). Freedom House identified six dangerous topics for journalists: organized crime, corruption, environment and land development, religion, disputed sovereignty, and laws against the state or top officials (Dunham, 2016). In 2012 the UN endorsed a Plan of Action on the Safety of Journalists and the Issue of Impunity. According to the document, 'there has been disquieting evidence of the scale and number of attacks against the physical safety of journalists and media workers as well as of incidents affecting their ability to exercise freedom of expression', and the perpetrators of these crimes were not prosecuted in nine out of ten cases (UN, 2012). Yet, as the UN Plan (2012, p. 1) said:

> The safety of journalists and the struggle against impunity for their killers are essential to preserve the fundamental right to freedom of expression, guaranteed by Article 19 of the Universal Declaration of Human Rights. Freedom of expression is an individual right, for which no one should be killed, but it is also a collective right, which empowers populations through facilitating dialogue, participation and democracy, and thereby makes autonomous and sustainable development possible. Without freedom of expression, and particularly freedom of the press, an informed, active and engaged citizenry is impossible.

The main pressures and challenges journalists faced fell into a few core categories (the list is not exhaustive and there are some overlaps):

1. Safety threats, including violence against journalists – physical attacks and murders; (informal/'para-legal') threats and harassment.
2. Legal restrictions – a range of laws regulating the work of journalists in different areas: national security, secrecy and surveillance; hate speech, blasphemy and obscenity; restrictions in relation to freedom of information requests; defamation; privacy; copyright; court reporting restrictions; press and broadcast regulatory laws, including laws specifying quotas for domestically originated media content; culture/country-specific restrictions such as lese-majesty laws (Thailand), genocide revisionism laws (Rwanda), apartheid laws (South Africa).
3. State and political pressures – censorship; threats of closure; propaganda; media regulation (licensing and spectrum allocation, regulatory authorities, accreditation of journalists); access to information; partisanship; repressive practices such as lawsuits, arrests, detentions in prisons and/or prison camps; informal editorial interference by politicians.
4. Economic pressures – ownership; state funding; advertising policy; infrastructural capacity, including access to modern technical facilities and penetration. (UNESCO, 2008)

This summary of the main pressures and challenges journalists experience is closely based upon some of the key indicators that academics, NGOs and international organizations have used when comparing media systems and journalistic practices (Table 2.1). Based on the criteria above, analysts suggested a few typologies. Thus, Freedom House annually categorizes 199 countries in three groups: free, partly free and not free. The Worlds of Journalism (WoJ) study that compared journalistic cultures in 67 countries in its 2012–2016 representative survey of more than 27,500 journalists identified four main types of journalism culture in its 2007–2011 pilot study of 21 countries: opportunist facilitator, critical change agent, populist disseminator and detached watchdog. Opportunist facilitators were seen as tending 'to support official policies and convey a positive image of political and business leadership'. Critical change agents were said to advocate social change, and encourage audiences 'to participate in civic activity and political discussion'. Populist disseminators were viewed as market-driven – their aim being to attract 'the widest possible audience' (Hanitzsch, 2011, p. 486). Detached watchdogs saw themselves as watchdogs of government and business elites. The pilot study concluded that

Table 2.1 Indicators measuring freedom of expression and journalism cultures

Author/ Organization	Focus of interest	Comparative criteria/indicators
UNESCO	National media development	1. Regulation – legal and policy framework; regulatory system for broadcasting; defamation laws and other legal restrictions on journalists; censorship.
		2. Plurality and diversity, a level economic playing field and transparency of ownership – media concentration; range of media; licensing and spectrum allocation; taxation and business regulation; advertising.
		3. Media as a platform for democratic discourse – diversity, public service broadcasting; self-regulation; fairness and impartiality; public trust and confidence in the media; safety of journalists.
		4. Professional capacity building – training; academic courses; trade unions and professional organizations; civil society.
		5. Infrastructure – availability and use of technical resources; press, broadcasting and ICT penetration.
Freedom House	Freedom of expression in 199 countries and territories	1. Legal environment – laws and regulations that could influence media content, and their application.
		2. Political environment – the degree of political control over news media content.
		3. Economic environment – media ownership; the costs of establishing media; advertising; corruption and bribery; the impact of the country's economic situation on the media.
RWB	Journalistic freedom in 180 countries	1. Pluralism – the degree to which opinions are represented in the media.
		2. Media independence – from interference by political, governmental, business and religious sources.
		3. Environment and self-censorship.
		4. Legislative framework.
		5. Transparency.
		6. Infrastructure.
		7. Abuses – level of abuses and violence.

Table 2.1 (continued)

Author/ Organization	Focus of interest	Comparative criteria/indicators
Hallin & Mancini, 2004	National media systems in Western Europe and North America	1. The structure of media markets – the development of mass press, national and local press, tabloids and quality papers. 2. Political parallelism – links between political parties and the media; partisanship of media audiences; journalistic role orientations and practices; pluralism; broadcast regulation. 3. Journalistic professionalism – autonomy; distinct professional norms; public service orientation. 4. The role of the state – degree and nature of state intervention; public service broadcasting; laws.

WoJ, 2007–11	Journalism cultures	1. Role perceptions:
		  a. Interventionism – 'the extent to which journalists pursue a particular mission and promote certain values'.
		  b. Power distance – 'journalist's position toward loci of power in society'.
		  c. Market orientation – 'journalists' perspectives on the audience as either citizens or consumers'.
		2. Epistemologies:
		  a. Objectivism – the distinction between two beliefs: the belief that there is 'an objective truth "out there" that can be reported "as it is"' and the belief that news is 'a subjective representation of the world'.
		  b. Empiricism – the emphasis on an empirical and analytical justification of truth via observation, evidence, experience, reason, opinions, values, etc.
		3. Ethical ideologies:
		  a. Relativism – the extent to which journalists base their personal moral philoso-phies on universal ethical rules.
		  b. Idealism – 'the importance of consequences in journalists' reasoning about ethical dilemmas'. (Worlds of Journalism, 2011)

'the detached watchdog milieu clearly dominates the journalistic field in most Western countries, while the milieu of the opportunist facilitator reigns supreme in several developing, transitional and authoritarian contexts' (Worlds of Journalism, 2011). Weaver and Willnat's (2012, p. 537) edited collection of 33 nationally representative surveys of journalists focused on six professional roles: 'report news quickly', 'provide analysis of events', 'be watchdog of government', 'provide access for public', 'provide entertainment' and 'report objectively'. Hallin and Mancini (2004), on the other hand, described three main types of media systems in Western Europe and North America: the Mediterranean/ polarized pluralist model (France, Greece, Italy, Portugal and Spain), the Northern European/democratic corporatist model (Austria, Belgium, Denmark, Finland, Germany, Netherlands, Norway, Sweden and Switzerland) and the North Atlantic/liberal model (UK, US, Canada, Ireland). Attempts have been made to extend this schema to other countries outside the West (for example, Brazil, China, Lebanon, Poland, Russia, Saudi Arabia and Thailand) where it has proved to be less useful (Hallin & Mancini, 2012). We use these typologies and the indicators they are based upon when drawing comparisons.

Journalism in the Global South

Africa

Africa includes 58 countries and territories (UN, 2013). In the classification of countries, the UN divided the continent into five regions: Eastern Africa, Middle Africa, Northern Africa, Southern Africa and Western Africa. The UN classified 34 countries and territories as 'least developed' and 24 as 'developing'. Fifty-four were included in at least one of the two annual press freedom indexes by the leading NGOs in the field. Only three countries were classified as free in terms of media freedom (5.6 per cent), 27 as partly free (50 per cent) and 24 as not free (44.4 per cent) (Freedom House, 2017a). The three free countries were Mauritius, São Tomé and Principe, and Cabo Verde. Their combined population is very small, which meant that fewer than 0.2 per cent of African people were living at that time in a country with free media. Eritrea had the lowest ranking in the region both according to Freedom House and RWB. In fact, RWB ranked Eritrea as 179th out of 180 countries in terms of press freedom in the whole world (see Case Study 2.1). Equatorial Guinea was also among the ten 'worst of the worst' countries (Freedom House, 2017a). Sudan, Djibouti, Somalia, Libya, Gambia, Swaziland, Ethiopia, Burundi and Rwanda had very bad press freedom rankings as well. On the whole, despite being home to several of the world's worst performing countries in terms of respect for human rights, the region saw overall uneven progress toward democratization during the 1990s and the early 2000s. However, recent years had seen backsliding among both the top performers such as South Africa, and the more repressive countries, such as The Gambia and Ethiopia. (Dunham et al., 2015)

UNESCO (2014d) reported that the processes of democratization and promotion of freedom of expression had slowed down since the turn of the century.

In terms of journalistic practices and cultures, no African countries were included in Weaver and Willnat's (2012) book; nine were included in the WoJ 2012–16 study (Table 2.2). A very high percentage of journalists said that supporting national development was extremely or very important for them. Similarly, advocating for social change was also a very important role for the majority of journalists surveyed. These percentages generally confirmed a wider trend observed in Africa – the dominance of the so-called 'development journalism'. Development journalism is 'the brand of journalism that promotes "positive news"' and advocates collaboration between the state and the media (Obijiofor & Hanusch, 2011, p. 24). Historically, African newspapers and journalists were at the forefront of the battle for liberation of their countries from colonial powers. Freed slaves embarked on journalism 'as a business and as a means of advocacy' (Ibelema & Bosch, 2009), and several nationalists began their careers as journalists and publishers, including the first presidents of both Ghana and Nigeria. In the post-colonial era, 'African leaders advocated a new role for the press' – as a '"servant of the state"' mobilizing 'the population for socio-economic development' (Obijiofor & Hanusch, 2011, p. 24). As Domatob and Hall (1983, p. 9) explained, African leaders such as Ghana's first President Kwame Nkrumah 'saw the media as a revolutionary tool of African liberation from the fetters of colonialism and imperialism' and 'an extension – a significant extension – of the government and its policies of social, economic, and cultural development'.

Africa is the poorest continent in the world and most of its countries are developing, and grappling with a range of issues – from climate change, HIV/AIDS and the Ebola outbreak in West Africa to infrastructure problems, low literacy rates, power cuts and endemic corruption. These issues inevitably affect the work of journalists, and it is not surprising that leaders of developing countries advocate a different role for journalists – 'as instruments for nation building and as facilitators of national socio-economic development through provision of information that contributes to a reduction in hunger, illiteracy and poverty' (Obijiofor & Hanusch, 2011, p. 25). These role perceptions were

Table 2.2 Journalists' role perceptions: Africa

Journalistic roles: Africa	Please tell me how important each of these things is in your work. Percentage saying 'extremely important' and 'very important'									
	Botswana	Egypt	Ethiopia	Kenya	Malawi	Sierra Leone	South Africa	Sudan	Tanzania
Be a detached observer	68.5	92.2	58	61	70.9	68.5	62.5	94.5	26.5
Report things as they are	96.2	85.4	66.4	92.9	96.6	94.9	92.5	90.4	87.9
Monitor and scrutinize political leaders	75.7	74.6	47.5	55.9	74.7	79.8	63.4	83.7	90.8
Monitor and scrutinize business	75	53.8	58.4	54.1	75.7	55.5	61.3	81.7	6.3
Set the political agenda	41.6	56	45.7	48.2	65.6	55.5	17.4	53.5	90.1
Advocate for social change	**73.4**	**76.3**	**79.8**	**78.8**	**82.8**	**90.3**	**55.9**	**93.1**	**93.4**
Be an adversary of the government	28.2	52.3	20.2	36.1	47.1	32.5	13.3	43.2	0
Support national development	**86.8**	**69.6**	**86.7**	**69.2**	**84.6**	**91.3**	**52.2**	**95.6**	**94.5**
Convey a positive image of political leadership	21.9	21.4	49	31.8	40.6	35.4	9	34.2	0
Support government policy	39.3	22.1	56.5	45.9	53	46.2	9.6	34.6	0
Provide the kind of news that attracts the largest audience	**71.7**	**62.7**	**80.8**	**68.1**	**83.5**	**72.4**	**58.8**	**89.1**	**97.8**

Source: Worlds of Journalism 2012–2016 study (2017)

in sharp contrast with the dominant Western view of journalists as detached watchdogs of government, political and business elites. Critics of development journalism argued that the practice restricted freedom of expression and justified repressive practices such as government editorial interference, and even censorship and suppression (Zelizer & Allan, 2010). Proponents of the development journalism approach, on the other hand, claimed that African societies had different cultural traditions, including an oral tradition of storytelling, and Western values of detachment and objectivity did not reflect these traditions (Bourgault, 1995; Shaw, 2009). Both Bourgault (1995) and Shaw (2009) pointed out that pre-colonial African journalism took the form of oral discourse, influenced by oral tradition, folk culture and a general trend towards group solidarity. An exploration into the specific challenges African journalists have faced will show us the extent to which critics of development journalism were right in condemning the practice.

1. Safety Threats, Including Violence Against Journalists

The CPJ (2017) placed Somalia (fourth), Algeria (sixth), Rwanda (17th) and Sierra Leone (19th) on its list of top 20 deadliest countries for journalists, based on the number of journalists killed since 1992. Sixty-two journalists had lost their lives in Somalia, 60 in Algeria, 17 in Rwanda and 16 in Sierra Leone. In addition to that, Somalia topped the list of countries with the worst impunity index. South Sudan was ranked fourth on that list and Nigeria 11th. The impunity index calculated the number of unsolved journalist murders as a percentage of a country's population for countries in which five or more murders of journalists had been committed between September 2007and September 2017 (Witchel, 2017). All murders in Sierra Leone and South Sudan had been unsolved, and the figures were quite high for most African countries (98 per cent for Algeria, 88 per cent for Nigeria and Rwanda, 84 per cent for Somalia). The most common suspected 'sources of fire' were: political groups (100 per cent in South Sudan, 52 per cent in Somalia, 50 per cent in Sierra Leone, and 30 per cent in Algeria and Nigeria), military officials (31 per cent in Sierra Leone, 29 per cent in Rwanda and 20 per cent in Nigeria), and paramilitary groups (71 per cent in Rwanda and 13 per cent in Sierra Leone) (Committee to Protect Journalists, 2017). In 2011 the African Commission on Human and Peoples' Rights adopted a Resolution on the Safety of Journalists and Media Practitioners in Africa, which urged governments to investigate all crimes committed against journalists and to take preventive measures. In addition to the murders, cases of

---

Case Study 2.1: Eritrea

Eritrea has been consistently ranked last out of 180 countries in terms of press freedom by RWB although it was placed 179th out of 180 countries in the most recent index. Abraham T. Zere was a state journalist who got into trouble after publishing a column in the ruling party's *Hidri* magazine in which he claimed that Eritrean youth were disempowered. The article angered the then information minister Ali Abdu (later an asylum seeker himself) who claimed Zere was 'a national security threat'. In an interview (Sutterer, 2017) Zere said: 'I was living in a stifling atmosphere characterized by fear and uncertainty. When prison became a synonym [for] Eritrea; when citizens were left to languish in harsh dungeons merely by association, friendship or suspicion; when you vividly see your bleak future projected, what other options do you have? You can only flee.' This is precisely what he did – he fled to South Africa, and then to the US where he co-founded PEN Eritrea – a centre providing a platform for Eritrean writers and journalists targeted by the government. Zere hoped to 'relieve a fraction of my guilty conscience for staying behind my colleagues who are languishing in Eritrean detention centers'. This was how he described himself on his personal website (abrahamzere.com): 'Do I need to mention how vehemently I hate anything and everything to do with military, centralization, and censorship? ... Let's put it this way: "Suspended in perpetual limbo and in search of home; coincidentally PEN Eritrea's Executive Director and Chief-editor who writes as he drinks mainly about Eritrea's freedom of expression."'

---

attacks, threats and harassment were reported in more than half of the countries in the region. The situation was particularly precarious in Somalia, South Sudan, the Central African Republic, Libya and Mali. Elections were a dangerous time for journalists (UNESCO, 2014d). At least 230 journalists had reportedly fled from their countries since 2005 and lived in exile (Case Study 2.1) due to the threats to their lives (UNESCO, 2014d).

2. Legal Restrictions

The right to freedom of expression is enshrined in the African Charter on Human and Peoples' Rights, which came into force in 1986, and is ratified by all countries with the exception of South Sudan. Freedom of expression was legally guaranteed in the constitutions of all countries, including South Sudan, as they were codified between the 1960s and 2016. However, over time it has not been observed in practice in most countries and various legal restrictions limited the work of journalists. The most extreme examples in this period were countries such as Eritrea, Ethiopia and Equatorial Guinea where prepublication censorship was a legal requirement. A 2014 UNESCO report argued that African journalists faced various content restrictions on different grounds – national security, public order, public morality and public health. Most countries, it was reported, had sedition or national security laws (e.g. Uganda, Tanzania, Zambia, Zimbabwe, Angola, Sudan, Botswana, Swaziland, Gambia, Mali and Lesotho) that limited free speech on national security or public order grounds. The banning of publications on national security grounds was allowed in Seychelles, Tanzania and Cameroon. Ethiopia, Kenya, Cameroon, South Africa, Swaziland and Nigeria also had anti-terrorism laws that inhibited free speech. A journalist in Ethiopia, for instance, was sentenced to 27 years in prison in 2014 on terrorism charges. Journalists in Cameroon could also end up with prison sentences of up to 20 years for 'defending terrorism' (Freedom House, 2017a). Kenyan journalists were not allowed to publish any photographs of victims of terrorist attacks.

In 2017 it was reported that cybercrime laws in Algeria, Cameroon, Mauritania and Nigeria further restricted free speech. Thus, the Algerian cybercrime law allowed the blocking of websites 'contrary to the public order or decency', while the Mauritanian bill prescribed prison sentences for the online dissemination of politically sensitive content (Freedom House, 2016). At this time there were other content restrictions, including: obscene communication was forbidden in Ethiopia and Zambia; the penal code in Ethiopia prohibited criticism of public officials; hate speech and anti-government propaganda in times of war were forbidden in Kenya where journalists also had to seek permission to cover parliamentary proceedings; genocide ideology was a crime in Rwanda; incitement of ethnic and religious hatred was criminalized in the Central African Republic, Chad, Congo, Sudan and Côte d'Ivoire; the publication of false information that could 'disturb the peace' (Freedom House, 2016) was a crime in the Central African Republic, while apartheid-era laws posed limitations for journalists in South Africa. The king in Swaziland had the power to 'suspend' freedom of expression at his discretion (Freedom House, 2016). Media censorship was also permissible in Egypt and Libya. In Sudan editors-in-chief were criminally liable for all content published in their newspapers (Freedom House, 2016).

Defamation has been criminalized in over three-quarters of the countries. Laws against 'defamation of religion' have remained on the books in 13 countries, four countries penalized apostasy and two had anti-blasphemy laws (UNESCO, 2014d). Blasphemy was a crime in Egypt. Criticism of Islam and the monarchy were also prohibited in Morocco. Insulting the head of state was a criminal offence in Guinea, Mali, Malawi, Algeria and Morocco. The 1967 Protected Flag, Emblems and Names Act in Malawi prescribed prison sentences of up to two years for insulting the president and national symbols. In 2007 the World Association of Newspapers and News Publishers

(WAN-IFRA) adopted the Declaration of Table Mountain, which called for the repeal of criminal defamation and 'insult' laws across the African continent. The declaration included an annex listing numerous recent defamation cases that had ended with criminal sentences, including prison terms. However, not much progress has been achieved since in the decriminalization of defamation. Only two presidents (of Liberia and Niger) have signed the declaration. Another major concern that NGOs such as Article 19 have expressed was about the proliferation of laws that criminalized the dissemination of 'false information' (Cameroon, Djibouti, Central African Republic, Gambia, Ghana, Nigeria and Togo). According to Article 19, these legal provisions had a chilling effect on journalists and infringed on the right to freedom of expression. They quoted the UN special rapporteur who argued against false news provisions in 2000:

> In the case of offences such as … publishing or broadcasting 'false' or 'alarmist' information, prison terms are both reprehensible and out of proportion to the harm suffered by the victim. In all such cases, imprisonment as punishment for the peaceful expression of an opinion constitutes a serious violation of human rights. (Anon, 2016a, 2017a)

On the other hand, in 2017 the African Freedom of Expression Exchange listed 22 countries in Africa which had access to information laws (www.africafex.org). Starting with South Africa in 2002, a further 15 had passed freedom of information (FoI) legislation 15 years later (Ethiopia, Mozambique, Rwanda, South Sudan, Uganda, Angola, Burkina Faso, Côte d'Ivoire, Guinea, Liberia, Niger, Nigeria, Sierra Leone, Tunisia and Zimbabwe) and in the others the right to access to information has been constitutionally guaranteed (see also Asogwa & Ezema, 2017). However, in reality journalists faced practical obstacles in most of these countries and governments violated citizens' rights to access information by refusing to provide 'even the most basic information, seemingly due to a combination of impunity and lack of political will, or a lack of systems enabling the state to promptly provide the requested information' (Mohan, 2014). Moreover, most government websites did not contain essential information, and lots of FoI requests either received no reply or asked journalists to specify why they needed the information.

Protection of sources is another issue. Some provisions for the protection of sources were included in the legal frameworks of ten countries but, according to UNESCO (2014d), the implementation of these laws had been problematic in all but three countries. This has inhibited investigative reporting, although other factors (most notably financial and political ones) have also posed challenges (UNESCO, 2014d).

3. State and Political Pressures

Democratic development has been uneven on the African continent. Cheeseman (2015) argued that there were three Africas: the first Africa included established democracies such as Botswana, Benin, Ghana, Mauritius, Senegal and South Africa; the second Africa comprised countries such as Burundi, the Democratic Republic of Congo, Kenya, Uganda and Zimbabwe 'in which leaders with authoritarian inclinations are still attempting to hold out against increasingly confident and popular opposition parties', and the third Africa included firmly established authoritarian regimes such as Cameroon, Chad and Rwanda. The state of political development of each country was closely linked to the degree of media freedom that journalists enjoyed there. Thus, as already indicated, prepublication censorship was a must in the restrictive and secretive countries of Eritrea, Ethiopia, Equatorial Guinea and Sudan. All private media were banned in Eritrea in 2001. Moreover, according to CPJ's prison census at least 15 journalists were imprisoned in Eritrea and some of them had been kept in prison with no charge since 2001. Similarly, the political crisis in Burundi in 2015 led to the closure of all independent media in the country. The situation in Equatorial Guinea, as reported by Freedom House (2015a), was that only journalists from state-owned media had access to public information, and 'they are subject to dismissal if their reporting runs afoul of state censors'. The civil war in South Sudan led to a deterioration in the working conditions for journalists as well as a generally polarized environment where most journalists supported one side in the conflict. Various forms of censorship and/or political harassment of journalists were also reportedly practised in Djibouti, Eritrea, Ethiopia, Mozambique, Somalia, South Sudan, Zambia, Zimbabwe, the Democratic Republic of Congo, Equatorial Guinea, Libya, Sudan, Swaziland, Guinea, Guinea-Bissau, Liberia and Sierra Leone. Self-censorship was widespread on the continent; for instance, 17 newspaper editors in Egypt 'pledged to refrain from criticizing the government, the army, or other national institutions' (Freedom House, 2015a). Freedom House (2016; 2017a) reports showed that the media environment was highly polarized in Madagascar, Somalia, Tunisia, Lesotho, Benin and Togo. Political pressure was exercised on journalists in Uganda, Tanzania, Angola, Cameroon, the Central African Republic, Chad, Gabon, Algeria, Morocco, Namibia, South Africa, Burkina Faso and Nigeria. In Egypt, between the first and second inaugurations in 2013 and 2018 of Abdel Fatah al-Sisi as president, journalists were targeted in a systematic suppression of dissent with several being banned, detained or jailed (Committee to Protect Journalists, 2018b; Guerlin, 2018; Michaelson, 2018).

4. Economic Pressures

In most African countries, although the media were owned both by the state and by private companies, the state remained a powerful actor in the market, particularly in broadcasting, into the second decade of the twenty-first century (Cagé, 2014, p. 3). In 2017 Eritrea was the only country still to forbid private ownership of the news media (www.bbc.co.uk). UNESCO (2014d) reported 'significantly uneven levels of private media development in different regions of the continent' with Anglophone countries experiencing stronger growth than other parts of the region. Radio was the dominant mass medium due to the high level of poverty, high illiteracy levels, power cuts in some countries, high printing costs and the poor infrastructure (UNESCO, 2014d; Dunham et al., 2015). UNESCO (2014d) reported 'an observable growth in private radio and TV ownership across the board; newspaper circulation and readership, however, do not appear to have followed the same trends'. In 28 sub-Saharan countries as recently as 2012 circulations of the most popular newspapers remained small – routinely only 2,000–3,000 copies per issue (Cagé, 2014, pp. 9–10). In 1989, at least seven countries had no daily newspapers at all (Zaffiro, 1997, p. 214). A worrying tendency towards concentration and monopolization was observed in a number of countries (Bussiek, n.d., p. 51).

The biggest challenge for African media and a serious obstacle in the way of plurality has been the lack of sustainable funding. The advertising market has been rather weak and insufficient, and UNESCO's (2014d) report showed that the situation was unlikely to change in the near future. As a result, lots of media outlets relied on government or state-related advertising or funding, which in turn led to widespread self-censorship. In some countries private media were in the hands of politicians or their families (Madagascar, Equatorial Guinea, Algeria). UNESCO (2014d) reported that in at least 18 countries state/government advertising was used as a way of obtaining political support, and the threat of withdrawal of advertising had been used to pressure media outlets. In the French colonies the state had also pro-vided direct financial support for private media but this support had been largely 'allocated on a partisan basis' (UNESCO, 2014d). Cases of denial of advertising as a means of political pressure had been reported in Tanzania, Zambia, Angola, Algeria, Morocco, Botswana, South Africa, Swaziland and Gambia (Freedom House, 2015a, 2016). Even in the 2010s the majority of African journalists received very low pay, which led to corruption, bribes and a culture of 'brown envelope' journalism (most notably in Nigeria) – the practice of sources giving cash to journalists in brown envelopes to ensure (usually favourable) coverage even of the most routine events (Burbidge, 2012; Nwaubani, 2015). Eke (2014) argued that the practice was widespread and it posed serious ethical concerns. UNESCO (2014d) reported that 'the persistent trend of poor remuneration of journalists has continued to be the dominant situation in the vast majority of countries in the region, making it difficult to make a living from the profession'. In the 1990s one of the authors met journalists from Africa whose monthly salaries were $US5 less than the monthly cost of sending a child to primary school in their country.

Finally, as of 31 December 2017, Africa was the continent with the lowest internet penetration in the world: only 35.2 per cent of the African population had internet access (Internet World Stats, 2017) compared to a worldwide average of 50.7 per cent. In December 2017, the countries with the lowest internet penetration rates were: Eritrea (1.4 per cent), Niger (4.3 per cent), Chad (5 per cent), Western Sahara (5 per cent), and the Central African Republic (5.4 per cent). The African countries with the highest internet penetration rates were: Kenya (85 per cent), Seychelles (70.5 per cent), Tunisia (67.7 per cent), Mali (65.3 per cent), Mauritius (63.4 per cent), and Morocco (62.4 per cent).

Asia

Asia includes 50 countries and territories (UN, 2013). The UN divided the continent into five sub-regions: Central Asia, Eastern Asia, Southern Asia, South-Eastern Asia and Western Asia. The UN classified most of the countries as developing. The only exception was Japan, which was classified as a developed country. Afghanistan, Bhutan, Cambodia, Lao People's Democratic Republic, Myanmar, Nepal, Timor-Leste and Yemen were classified as 'least developed'. Forty-nine of these countries and territories were included in at least one of the press freedom indexes. Only three countries were classified as free in terms of media freedom (6.1 per cent) – Taiwan, Japan and Cyprus, 14 as partly free (28.6 per cent) and 32 as not free (65.3 per cent). This made Asia the continent with the worst press freedom ranking (Dunham, 2016). Moreover, six Asian countries were among the ten worst of the worst countries in terms of press freedom according to RWB (Laos, Vietnam, China, Syria, Turkmenistan and North Korea). Similarly, the worst three countries in the world according to Freedom House (2017a) were Uzbekistan, Turkmenistan and North Korea. The CPJ's list of the ten most censored countries included seven Asian countries – North Korea (second), Saudi Arabia (third), Azerbaijan (fifth), Vietnam (sixth), Iran (seventh),

China (eighth) and Myanmar (ninth). Overall, it is difficult to summarize the main trends in the region because of its recent turbulent history and the diverse trends observed. On the one hand, Asia has been recorded as having some of the world's most restrictive authoritarian regimes, such as North Korea, Turkmenistan, Iran and China, where media freedom was severely curtailed, and journalists were predominantly servants of the state with little, if any, scope for investigative and/or critical reporting. However, some differences were noted even between countries such as North Korea and China. Asia also includes Iraq and Syria – two of the countries with the highest death toll of journalists as a result of ongoing war or military conflicts dating back to at least 2003. Journalists continued to experience significant security challenges but censorship was also an issue, especially in the IS-controlled territories where media workers had to abide by IS's 11 rules for journalists between 2014 and November 2017. Finally, the region is the location of some of the world's biggest economies with rapidly developing media markets, such as China, Japan and India.

In terms of journalistic practices and cultures, Weaver and Willnat (2012) had ten chapters on Asian countries but not all surveys presented included measures of professional roles. The ones which did were from Hong Kong, Indonesia, Japan, Korea, Malaysia, Singapore, Taiwan, Israel and the United Arab Emirates (UAE). 'To be a watchdog of government' was extremely important for 61.9 per cent of journalists in UAE, 40 per cent in Korea, 39 per cent in Indonesia, 35.6 per cent in Singapore, 32.9 per cent in Taiwan, 23.3 per cent in Hong Kong, 21 per cent in Malaysia and 2.5 per cent in Japan. 'Provide entertainment', on the other hand, was extremely important for 35 per cent of journalists in UAE, 27.2 per cent in Malaysia, 25.5 per cent in Taiwan, 23.8 per cent in Singapore, 16.1 per cent in Hong Kong, 13.6 per cent in Korea and 9.6 per cent in Japan. Eighteen Asian countries were included in the WoJ study (Tables 2.3 and 2.4). The study found significant variations in the role perceptions of journalists. In some countries supporting national development and advocating for social change were the dominant role perceptions, while in others journalists considered it important to be detached watchdogs or be opportunist facilitators.

The findings reflect some of the notable differences between the more advanced democratic countries and the dictatorial regimes but they also allude to an important debate that Asian journalists have grappled with – whether to endorse Asian values as opposed to Western models of journalism (Xu, 2005).

Asian values that were deemed applicable to journalists and their development role were respect for elders and leaders, concern for upholding harmony, respect for the importance of 'saving face', and a preference for communicating criticism in a mild and courteous rather than a brusque fashion. (Romano, 2005, pp. 6–7)

Most Western scholars have dismissed the 'Asian values' approach as 'authoritarian' and 'paternalistic' (Zelizer, 2004, p. 154). At its heart is the belief that journalists should uphold 'a deference to order and authority', and it involves 'the twinning of press freedom and responsibility, and the privileging of national interests over individual ones, in which journalism was harnessed to aims of national betterment' (Zelizer, 2004, p. 155). Proponents of this approach, on the other hand, have praised its non-adversarial nature and have claimed that it reflects some of the religious beliefs held in the region such as Buddhism and Confucianism (Seneviratne, 2015).

Romano (2005) argued that Asian values journalism was a type of development journalism. In fact, she claimed that the concept 'development journalism' was first coined in Asia in 1968 at a training course for economic

Case Study 2.2: China

China is one of the most censored countries in the world. The International Federation of Journalists (IFJ) reported that since 2014 the main ideological principle affecting the work of journalists has been: 'Strictly follow party political discipline' (Woo, 2015). A number of state agencies/regulators, led by the Central Propaganda Department, police the work of journalists. Immediately after becoming President in 2012, Xi Jinping set up and chaired China's National Security Commission and Central Internet Security and Informatization Leading Group because 'without cyber security, there is no national security'. On Journalists' Day 2014 President Xi listed ten qualities a good journalist should have, such as reporters being accountable to the people, and to the ruling party, and guiding 'the world to have an "objective" view of China, i.e. they should tell a good China story' (Choi, 2014). Also, after 2014 journalists were required to pass a national accreditation exam to practise their profession. According to the IFJ, 'the training materials for the examination contain a great deal of Socialist ideology and clearly demand that journalists act as mouthpieces for the Communist Party and the government'. The Propaganda Department of the Communist Party also appointed Communist Party members to the journalism faculties of China's top ten universities 'in an attempt to ensure their teaching is in line with the directives of the authorities'. China's stringent media regulator issued a notice in 2014 banning the publication of 'critical reports' and barring journalists from doing work 'outside their assigned area of coverage'. In 2017 The Committee to Protect Journalists categorized China as the world's second 'worst jailer of journalists'.

Table 2.3 Journalists' role perceptions: Southern and South-Eastern Asia

Journalistic roles: Southern and South-Eastern Asia	Please tell me how important each of these things is in your work. Percentage saying 'extremely important' and 'very important'							
	Bangladesh	Bhutan	India	Indonesia	Malaysia	Philippines	Singapore	Thailand
Be a detached observer	**47.9**	**73.3**	**76**	**64**	**71.5**	**70.8**	**42.6**	**82.1**
Report things as they are	**76.8**	**79.8**	**88.4**	**94.1**	**79.3**	**63.4**	**49.5**	**88.7**
Monitor and scrutinize political leaders	63.2	66.3	62.8	56	50.3	80.7	50.6	73
Monitor and scrutinize business	51.3	58.9	50.7	44.3	48.7	72.8	35.5	67.8
Set the political agenda	40.2	49.4	38.4	28.3	33.2	44.3	44.8	65
Advocate for social change	79.6	53.3	74.5	81	61.7	85.3	41.9	75.2
Be an adversary of the government	28.9	34.4	34	10.5	45.6	26.1	39.1	61.2
Support national development	**76.3**	**47.2**	**81.7**	**75.1**	**66.8**	**73.5**	**41.5**	**77.4**
Convey a positive image of political leadership	37.3	33	32.5	36.3	44.3	15.6	40.2	55.8
Support government policy	28.7	34.4	35.1	30.4	51.7	24.9	36.7	57.1
Provide the kind of news that attracts the largest audience	75.9	58.9	69.7	76.2	67.6	52.3	38.9	73.8

Source: Worlds of Journalism 2012–2016 study (2017)

Table 2.4 Journalists' role perceptions: Eastern and Western Asia

Journalistic roles: Eastern and Western Asia	Please tell me how important each of these things is in your work. Percentage saying 'extremely important' and 'very important'									
	China	Cyprus	Hong Kong	Israel	Japan	Oman	Qatar	South Korea	Turkey	UAE
Be a detached observer	64.4	72.7	58.7	50.9	44.1	89.5	53.2	69.3	91.5	49.3
Report things as they are	83.8	97.1	79.8	92.9	65.1	63.4	54.5	92.9	97.9	71.2
Monitor and scrutinize political leaders	40.7	64	80	62.9	90.8	33.5	29.7	86	86	49.3
Monitor and scrutinize business	40.5	48.3	75.4	57.3	62.9	54.5	29	88.3	63.4	30.5
Set the political agenda	29	29.5	30.2	50.9	60.5	44.4	36.4	66	69.6	29.1
Advocate for social change	**45.2**	**70.6**	**38.3**	**80.2**	**31.6**	**76.7**	**57.1**	**59**	**81.7**	**47.6**
Be an adversary of the government	25	23.6	14.4	42.9	10.4	20.2	16.5	17.9	35.9	15.6
Support national development	**68.7**	**75.9**	**14.2**	**54.9**	**45.6**	**76.7**	**56.6**	**45.6**	**56.7**	**76.4**
Convey a positive image of political leadership	48.8	18.2	8.1	7.2	1.1	40.1	48.8	3.7	11.8	75.4

Source: Worlds of Journalism 2012–2016 study (2017)

writers. Romano (2005) identified four models of development journalism in Asia: journalists as nation builders (very similar to the development journalism approach adopted in most African countries); the 'Asian values' approach; journalists as agents of empowerment; and journalists as watchdogs. The empowerment model was based on the belief that journalists should be advocates in the process of empowerment of the masses. Another term used for this type of journalism was 'emancipatory journalism', where media were seen as 'participants in a process of progressive social change' (Shah, 1996 as quoted in Romano, 2005, pp. 7–8). Both the empowerment and the watchdog models of development journalism encourage investigative reporting, and are more adversarial than the nation builders and Asian values approaches. Moreover, as UNESCO (2014b) reported, 'in several countries in South-East Asia, reporters' low salaries had continued to sustain a culture of [brown] "envelope" journalism, in which cash had been accepted as an inducement for attending press conferences and conducting interviews'. Another ethically questionable practice was of 'paid news' in which newspapers sold editorial space without clearly identifying it as advertising (UNESCO, 2014b). The four different models highlight the big variations in journalistic practices and cultures in Asian countries due to the differences in political, cultural and economic contexts, which are further explored in the next sections.

1. Safety Threats, Including Violence Against Journalists

UNESCO (2014b, p. 24) warned that the safety of journalists in Asia had become 'more precarious over the last six years amid an increase in the number of killings of journalists and media workers. Countries that were already unsafe for journalists had generally become even less safe'. The most dangerous sub-regions were South and South-East Asia. The CPJ included 11 Asian countries in its list of the top 20 deadliest countries for journalists. Iraq was the deadliest country for journalists in the world: 186 journalists have been killed there since 1992. Syria was second in that list with 119 murdered journalists and the Philippines was third with 79 killed. The other countries were: Pakistan (60 killed journalists); India (48); Afghanistan (45); Turkey (25); Bangladesh (21); Sri Lanka (19); Israel and the Occupied Palestinian Territory (18); and Tajikistan (17). In addition to that, the majority of countries with the worst impunity records were from Asia. Syria was ranked second on the Global Impunity Index compiled by the CPJ; Iraq third; the Philippines fifth; Pakistan seventh; Bangladesh 10th and India 12th (Witchel, 2017).

All murders in Syria were unsolved, and the figures were also very high for most Asian countries (99 per cent for Iraq, 96 per cent for India, 91 per cent for Pakistan and Philippines, 84 per cent for Bangladesh, and 67 per cent for Afghanistan). The high death tolls in Iraq and Syria were due to the military conflicts within the territories of these countries. It was estimated that 95 per cent of the journalists killed in Syria and 71 per cent in Iraq were war reporters. Ninety-three Syrian and 55 Iraqi journalists were killed in crossfire/combat. The number of deaths in Syria since 2012 outnumbered the number of deaths in the rest of the world. Terrorist organizations such as al-Qaeda and IS were responsible for 40 per cent of the murders of journalists in the world in 2015 and this applied to most of the murders in Syria. The main 'suspected sources of fire' in the most dangerous Asian countries were: political groups (24 per cent of the Syrian cases, 45 per cent in Afghanistan, 42 per cent in Sri Lanka, 48 per cent in India, 58 per cent in Pakistan, 57 per cent in Bangladesh and 71 per cent in Iraq); military officials (10 per cent in Pakistan, 15 per cent in Iraq, 16 per cent in Afghanistan, 26 per cent in Sri Lanka, and 53 per cent in Syria); government officials (26 per cent in Sri Lanka and 65 per cent in Philippines) and criminal groups (20 per cent in India and 19 per cent in Bangladesh) (Committee to Protect Journalists, 2017).

In addition to the high number of murders, journalists in Tajikistan, Turkmenistan, Uzbekistan, Hong Kong, Mongolia, Afghanistan, Bangladesh, India, Maldives, Nepal, Pakistan, Sri Lanka, Cambodia, Indonesia, Myanmar, Philippines, Thailand, Vietnam, Armenia, Azerbaijan, Iraq, Lebanon, Palestine, Syria, Turkey and Yemen have also been subjected to physical attacks, aggression and verbal threats (UNESCO, 2014b; Freedom House, 2015a, 2016). The situation in Turkey worsened markedly after a supposed failed military coup in 2016: journalists were particularly targeted by the government of Tayyip Erdoğan. In the spring of 2018 the Stockholm Freedom Center listed 61 journalists convicted of crimes; 192 arrested; and 142 on a 'wanted' list in Turkey (https://stockholmcf.org).

2. Legal Restrictions

As of July 2018, freedom of expression was guaranteed in the constitutions or basic laws of 47 of the 50 countries and territories in Asia. Only Thailand, Israel and Saudi Arabia did not guarantee this right. Israel did not have a written constitution. Thailand's constitution was suspended in 2014 by the military coup leaders. There was no freedom of expression guarantee in Saudi Arabia's Basic Law of Governance. In spite of the constitutional guarantees in the majority of countries, the right to freedom of expression has not been upheld in most of them. Journalists faced a range of legal restrictions. Similar to some African states, prepublication censorship was practised in China, Kazakhstan (only in a state of emergency), Jordan (reports about the armed forces), Lebanon (foreign publications), Qatar, UAE and North Korea (Freedom House, 2016). In Vietnam, all foreign news, education and information content on television had to be translated into Vietnamese and censored before airing (Freedom House, 2016).

The most common restrictions were imposed on the grounds of national security, terrorism, blasphemy, incitement of ethnic hatred or preserving public order (UNESCO, 2014b). Journalists in Israel, Sri Lanka, Indonesia, Bahrain and Turkey faced prison sentences (up to 14 years in Sri Lanka) if they published leaked 'state secrets' or classified information. The Press Council Act of Sri Lanka also prohibited disclosure of fiscal, defence and security information (Freedom House, 2016). Sedition laws were particularly problematic because of the vague definitions of sedition and the harsh sentences. The 1948 Sedition Act in Malaysia defined sedition as any act that might 'excite disaffection' or 'bring into hatred or contempt' the rule of government (Freedom House, 2015a). Similarly, India's sedition law banned any speech that could cause 'hatred or contempt, or excites or attempts to excite disaffection' toward the government (Freedom House, 2016). Bangladesh's sedition laws were even more restrictive because 'offenders' faced fines, life imprisonment or even the death penalty. Despite being one of the freest countries in the region, Israel also had very tight security rules. Any expressions of support for terrorist organizations or groups that called for the destruction of Israel were forbidden, and according to the Censorship Agreement between the media and the Israel Defence Forces, the military censor had 'the power to penalize, shut down, or halt the printing of a newspaper for national security reasons' (Freedom House, 2016). Iraqi journalists also faced severe restrictions because of the 'war on terror'. The media had to 'hold on to the patriotic sense' and 'focus on the security achievements of the armed forces' (Freedom House, 2015a, 2016). Prison sentences of up to two years were also prescribed by the penal code of Turkey for 'denigration of the Turkish nation'; for example discussing the division of Cyprus or claims about the Armenian genocide (Freedom House, 2016). Other countries in Asia (Oman, Qatar, Turkmenistan, Uzbekistan, Myanmar, Philippines, Saudi Arabia, Kyrgyzstan, Palestine) had restrictions related to moral values or taste. Pornography and sites that 'reject family values' were forbidden in Turkmenistan, while articles that incited religious confrontation, separatism and ethnic discord were banned in Uzbekistan. Publications that 'affect the morality or conduct of the public or a group of people that would undermine the security of the Union or the restoration of law and order' were also banned in Myanmar. Materials that 'detract from a man's dignity' were prohibited in Saudi Arabia. Obscenity laws still existed in Philippines. A journalist in Kyrgyzstan was serving a life sentence for inciting ethnic hatred and complicity in the murder of a police officer during ethnic unrest in 2010 (Freedom House, 2015a).

Defamation has been decriminalized in only eight of the 50 countries and territories in Asia – Kyrgyzstan, Tajikistan, Maldives, Sri Lanka, Timor-Leste, Armenia, Cyprus and Georgia. Thirty-one countries in Asia and the Pacific and the Arab world regions had blasphemy and/or 'defamation of religion' laws (UNESCO, 2014b). Islam-related offences were criminalized in Afghanistan, Iran, Maldives, Bahrain, Jordan, Kuwait, Oman, Saudi Arabia and Yemen. Any insults to religion were punishable by death or prison of up to five years in Iran where 'enmity against God' was a crime. Apostasy and insults of Islam were potentially punishable by death in Saudi Arabia. The Press and Publications Law prohibited the publication of material that insulted God, the prophets, or Islam. Online blasphemy was a crime in Bangladesh. In 2017 a Christian man was sentenced to death in Pakistan for sharing material ridiculing the Prophet Mohammed on WhatsApp. The country's constitution restricts freedom of expression 'in the interest of the glory of Islam' or on morality grounds. Two journalists in Afghanistan were sentenced to execution in 2009 for publishing a cartoon depicting a monkey evolving into a man with the words, 'Government plus religion equals cruelty.'

Defamation of public officials, the royal family or politicians was a criminal offence in a few countries. Criticism of the monarch and/or the royal family were prohibited in Bhutan, Bahrain, Kuwait, Oman, Thailand and UAE. Criticisms of the emir in Kuwait were penalized with prison sentences of up to five years. Similarly, insulting the royal family was criminalized in Jordan. Thailand had the so-called lese-majesty laws that prescribed up to 15 years in prison for anyone who 'defames, insults, or threatens the King, Queen, the Heir-apparent, or the Regent' (Freedom House, 2016). Complaints could be brought by citizens, and Freedom House (2016) claimed that defendants were almost always denied bail. Moreover, the media regulator has instructed internet service providers to monitor and shut down any websites that carry lese-majesty content. Thai media were also prohibited from criticizing the coup regime. Freedom House (2016; 2017a) reported that criticisms of the government were prohibited, too, in Vietnam and UAE. Criticism of the king and statements calling for the overthrow of the regime were forbidden in Jordan. Iraqi journalists could receive up to seven years in prison for insulting the government. Journalists faced prison sentences of up to one year in

Yemen, two years in Azerbaijan and four years in Turkey for defaming the president. A Turkish writer and columnist was awaiting trial in 2017 after calling the president 'a wild tiger'. Iranian journalists were frequently prosecuted and faced prison sentences of up to two years and 74 lashes for creating 'anxiety and unease in the public's mind', spreading 'false rumours', writing about 'acts that are not true' or criticizing public officials (Freedom House, 2015a). In 2014 a journalist in Tajikistan was found guilty of causing 'physical and mental suffering' to the country's intelligentsia (Freedom House, 2015a). An online editor was arrested in Bangladesh in 2015 for 'tarnishing the image' of a cabinet minister. Any form of propaganda against the state was penalized by the penal code in Iran with a prison sentence of up to a year. Similarly, insulting the head of state or foreign leaders was a crime in Lebanon. Incitement and the dissemination of disinformation could result in prison sentences of up to three years in Cambodia. Dissemination of false information also led to long prison sentences in Kazakhstan. Website owners and editors were criminally liable for any content that the government found objectionable in Singapore (Freedom House, 2016).

Twenty-nine countries and territories had legal provisions for access to information in 2017 – in most cases dedicated FoI Acts. The situation in Asia was not much different from Africa. While the legislation was effective in some countries, these laws were not observed in all countries. China was the prime example of that but the relevant FoI Acts were also not fully implemented in other countries such as Azerbaijan, Georgia, Jordan and Yemen.

3. State and Political Pressures

The press freedom rankings and the outline of legal restrictions already showed that the majority of Asian journalists faced significant political pressures. At least 140 journalists in the region had reportedly gone into exile between 2007 and 2014 (UNESCO, 2014b). According to the CPJ prison census (2016b), 185 of the 256 imprisoned journalists around the world were from Asia. The number of imprisoned journalists rose to 262 in 2017 with Turkey the biggest jail for journalists (73), followed by China (41). The situation in Turkey has been particularly precarious since 2016. According to RWB, by 2017 149 media outlets and 29 publishing houses were closed arbitrarily, and at least 775 press cards were rescinded. Internet censorship reached 'unparalleled levels' (Reporters Without Borders, 2017a). Journalists in North Korea and Uzbekistan faced the threat of political prison camps or 'penal colonies'. Propaganda was prevalent in a few countries, most notably in North Korea and China. Media professionals operated in an atmosphere of fear in Turkmenistan and Azerbaijan as well, where censorship was 'extensive' (Freedom House, 2016).

The media landscape was politicized and journalists faced various political pressures in Mongolia, India, Nepal, Sri Lanka, Cambodia, Indonesia, Laos, Malaysia, Singapore, Vietnam, Armenia, Georgia, Iraq, Jordan, Lebanon, Palestine and Turkey. In Cambodia, the country's first English language newspaper, the *Cambodia Daily*, founded in 1993, was forced to close in 2017 after the government demanded payment of a $6.3m tax bill in what was described as a politically motivated move. Less than a year later, most of the staff of the *Phnom Pen Post* resigned after its new owner wanted to remove an article. One of its former journalists described the state of press freedom in Cambodia as 'dire' (Forsdick, 2018; Ponsford, 2017). Up to 2018, foreign media remained banned in North Korea and Turkmenistan. Internet censorship was practised in Kazakhstan, Kyrgyzstan, Tajikistan, Uzbekistan, China, Iran, Maldives, Pakistan, Sri Lanka, Cambodia, Indonesia, Vietnam, Azerbaijan, Bahrain, Oman, Qatar, Saudi Arabia, UAE and Turkey. The relationship between politicians and journalists was ethically questionable even in the freest country in Asia – Japan. A system of exclusive press clubs (kisha clubs) operated there. Separate clubs covered the prime minister, the foreign ministry, the Diet (Japanese Parliament), the Imperial Household, and the Tokyo Stock Exchange. Membership was required for journalists to gain access to press conferences and briefings. 'A primary condition of membership in a press club is that no journalist will report any information that is not freely available to every other member, which discourages investigative reporting' (Brislin, 1997). A similar system existed in South Korea. Self-censorship was generally prevalent in most Asian countries.

4. Economic Pressures

A diversity of economic models characterized the Asian media landscape (UNESCO, 2014b). As a whole, UNESCO described a trend towards rapid liberalization, deregulation and privatization. State broadcasters still dominated the market but private media have also evolved. Another key trend was the growth of the internet and related digital technologies, which according to UNESCO (2014b) had 'transformed the business of journalism in the region, particularly with migration to online news, increasingly via mobile digital devices'. Contrary to the trends observed in the West, print media were growing rapidly in some of the biggest Asian economies – most notably, India and China (Hooke, 2012). However, there were still a significant number of countries with tightly controlled and highly regulated media regimes. There were no private media in North Korea. The state dominated the market in Kazakhstan, Uzbekistan, China, Myanmar, Singapore, Vietnam, Azerbaijan, Qatar, Iraq, Yemen and UAE. Direct state subsidies were available in Kazakhstan, Kyrgyzstan, China, Mongolia, Timor-Leste and Armenia (Freedom House, 2015a).

In some countries private media were in the hands of politicians, their families or the royal family (e.g. Kazakhstan, Mongolia, Qatar, Saudi Arabia). Freedom House (2016) reported cases in which advertising had been used as a way of obtaining political support. Journalists in some countries (India, Uzbekistan, Bangladesh, Pakistan, Sri Lanka, Cambodia, Indonesia, Philippines, Kuwait) received very low pay and bribery was an issue (Freedom House, 2016, 2017a). Another trend was the prevalence of 'envelope journalism' (not brown as in Africa, but white envelopes in South Korea and red in Japan, for example) (Brislin, 1997).

Finally, as of 31 December 2017, Asia was the continent with the second lowest percentage of internet penetration. Just 48.1 per cent of the Asian population had internet access (Internet World Stats, 2017) as compared to the worldwide average of 50.7 per cent. As of 31 December 2017, the countries with the lowest internet penetration rates were: North Korea (0 per cent), Afghanistan (15.7 per cent) and Turkmenistan (17.9 per cent). Only 20,000 people out of a population of 25,610,672 people in North Korea had internet access (Internet World Stats, 2017). Only the political elite had access to the global version of the internet. Everyone else could only access the intranet, North Korea's own version of the virtual space. The countries with the highest internet penetration rates were: Brunei Darussalam (94.6 per cent), Japan (93.3 per cent), South Korea (92.6 per cent) and Taiwan (87.9 per cent) (Internet World Stats, 2017).

Latin America and the Caribbean

The Latin America and Caribbean region includes 52 countries and territories (UN, 2013). They are all classified as developing with the exception of Haiti, which was classified as 'least developed' (UN, 2013). Thirty-three of these countries and territories were included in at least one press freedom index. Fourteen countries were classified as free in terms of media freedom (42.4 per cent), 14 as partly free (42.4 per cent) and five as not free (15.2 per cent) (Freedom House, 2017a). There was a noticeable difference between the Latin American and the Caribbean countries. Only five of the Latin American countries were rated as free, which meant that 4.5 per cent of the population lived in free media environments. By contrast, all the other free countries and territories were in the Caribbean but they did not have such large populations. Cuba had the lowest ranking. Overall, 'after three decades of democratization, the current state of freedom of expression in Latin America is undoubtedly more open than in the period of military rule' (Debevoise & Plimpton LLP, 2016), but Freedom House reported a steady deterioration over the past few years. The regional score was at its lowest level for the past five years. The declines observed were in all categories: legal, political and economic, and there has been a notable increase in the number of cases involving violence and intimidation from criminals and from government authorities (Dunham et al., 2015; Freedom House, 2017a).

In terms of journalistic practices and cultures, only three countries were included in Weaver and Willnat's (2012) edited volume – Brazil, Chile and Colombia, and results on professional roles were not presented for Colombia. 'Being a watchdog of government' was 'extremely important' for 38.9 per cent of Chilean journalists and 14.6 per cent of Brazilian journalists. Providing entertainment was 'extremely important' for 19.9 per cent of journalists in Brazil and 11.2 per cent of journalists in Chile. Seven countries were included in the WoJ study (Table 2.5). The study found that while for the majority of journalists reporting things 'as they are' was extremely or very important, advocating for social change was also considered a very important role for more than two-thirds of the journalists in most of the countries. Similarly, supporting national development was more important for journalists from Mexico, El Salvador, Ecuador and Colombia than for journalists from Brazil, Argentina and Chile. In general, Latin American journalists had a reputation of being 'very political' (Salwen & Garrison, 1991, p. 34). The processes of democratization in the past three decades contributed to the abandonment of the military dictatorships and to a range of political and economic changes (Obijiofor & Hanusch, 2011). These changes have inevitably affected the work of journalists and there was a trend towards encouraging more investigative reporting and Western values of journalism. However, these positive trends have also been coupled with a worrying development – as Lugo-Ocando (2008, p. 2) argued, 'many repressive elements of the dictatorship period remain in place or have mutated into more subtle means of censorship and control'. Political and business elites have attempted to use 'the media's increasingly prominent role in politics to pursue their own agendas and interests', resulting either in 'an inappropriate degree of collaboration between politicians and the media', reducing journalism to 'a decorative role' and leading to a preoccupation with scandals, or to open confrontation which involved journalists playing 'a subversive role' and being 'pro-active in conspiracies to overthrow governments'

Table 2.5 Journalists' role perceptions: Latin America

Journalistic roles: Latin America	Please tell me how important each of these things is in your work. Percentage saying 'extremely important' and 'very important'						
	Argentina	Brazil	Chile	Colombia	Ecuador	El Salvador	Mexico
Be a detached observer	52.1	73.1	54.4	43.1	49.4	52.1	58.4
Report things as they are	**91.1**	**89.4**	**88.2**	**92.5**	**88.8**	**93.2**	**95.5**
Monitor and scrutinize political leaders	71.7	52.1	66.4	78.9	73.7	86.4	86.9
Monitor and scrutinize business	59.4	35.2	61.1	67.8	52.5	64.1	60.2
Set the political agenda	48	20.5	50.5	65.3	59.4	68.8	70.7
Advocate for social change	**69.7**	**64.1**	**61.1**	**84.7**	**76.3**	**78.4**	**89.7**
Be an adversary of the government	11.7	7.2	13.5	19.8	22.3	18.1	21.1
Support national development	**53.8**	**51.6**	**60**	**76.3**	**81**	**80.8**	**82.7**
Convey a positive image of political leadership	7.4	5.6	12.3	18.7	34.7	22	14.8
Support government policy	20.1	7.4	24.7	32.2	46.3	35.9	35.8
Provide the kind of news that attracts the largest audience	40.9	43.9	57.7	65.4	70.8	62.9	74.2

Source: Worlds of Journalism 2012–2016 study (2017)

Case Study 2.3: Mexico

RWB (2017b) labelled Mexico as 'the land of the drug cartels' and therefore 'the western hemisphere's deadliest country for the media'. The organization claimed that 'murders of journalists are typically carried out in cold blood, like executions, and almost always go unpunished'. More journalists were killed in Mexico in the twenty-first century than in any country not formally at war. The killings accelerated following the government's offensive against organized crime which began in December 2006. Between then and May 2018, at least 30 journalists had been murdered: 12 reportedly died in 2017 alone (Committee to Protect Journalists, 2018a). The daily *El Norte* newspaper was closed down in 2017 out of fear for journalists' safety. However, the number of victims may have been even higher with estimates varying from 52 to 80 between 2006 and 2016, and 104 between 2000 and 2017 (Agren, 2018; Ahmed, 2017; Dearman, 2016). Marcos Hernández Bautista, a reporter for the daily newspaper *Noticias, Voz e Imagen de Oaxaca*, was shot in the head with a 9mm pistol on 21 January 2016 in Oaxaca, Mexico (Committee to Protect Journalists, 2017). According to his editorial director, Hernández wrote about cacicazgos – 'strongmen' who rule parts of the region. 'He was often in fear', his editorial editor told the CPJ. News reports claimed that a local police commander was charged with the journalist's murder but it was not clear how far the case had proceeded. A column published in his newspaper described Hernández 'as a brave reporter covering a region beset by political violence and, increasingly, drug cartels'. The columnist also claimed 'corrupt public functionaries' were suspected of 'being linked with narcotics trafficking activities' (Committee to Protect Journalists, 2017).

(Lugo-Ocando, 2008, pp. 2–3). 'The legislative and judicial reforms necessary to institutionalize freedom of expression are still widely lacking' (Debevouse & Plimpton LLP, 2016).

1. Safety Threats, Including Violence Against Journalists

The Committee to Protect Journalists (2017) placed Colombia, Brazil and Mexico on its list of top 20 deadliest countries for journalists, based on the number of murdered journalists since 1992. Fifty-one journalists had lost their lives in Colombia, 45 in Mexico and 41 in Brazil. Hundreds of journalists had also been attacked or threatened annually (UNESCO, 2014c). The high level of impunity was particularly notable – complete impunity was reported in 90 per cent of the Colombian cases, 93 per cent of the Mexican cases and 95 per cent of the Brazilian cases. These figures placed Mexico and Brazil in the list of top ten countries in the world with the worst impunity index where 'journalists are slain and the killers go free' (Witchel, 2017). The two most common suspected 'sources of fire' were: criminal groups (57 per cent in Mexico, 36 per cent in Brazil and 11 per cent in Colombia) and government officials (44 per cent in Brazil, 17 per cent in Colombia and 6.7 per cent in Mexico) (Committee to Protect Journalists, 2017). Journalists in Mexico, for example, experienced 'multiple attacks', especially in areas 'heavily affected by drug-related violence'. Threats were prevalent and some of the attacks by gunmen took place in the editorial offices. Human Rights Watch (2018) reported that the protection programme for journalists and human rights defenders had been undermined by a lack of funding and political support. Detentions and arbitrary inspections of journalists' offices as well as police brutality, harassment and threats were reported in other countries with a strong drug-trafficking trade such as Argentina, Colombia, the Dominican Republic and Honduras. UNESCO (2014c) monitored the situation in 11 countries where 'gangs and drug cartels have killed journalists with the intention of sending a message to media outlets that some topics are off limits'. In general, the highest number of cases of aggression and murders of journalists were in the countries with high rates of violence, drug trafficking and corruption (UNESCO, 2014c). Journalists exposing corruption or links between the authorities and the criminal gangs were at a particular risk (see Case Study 2.3).

2. Legal Restrictions

While freedom of expression was constitutionally guaranteed in most countries, it was not respected in practice in some of them. Cuba was the most extreme example of that – it had 'the most restrictive laws on freedom of expression and the press in the Americas' (Freedom House, 2016). Article 53 of the Cuban constitution (1976) stated:

> citizens have freedom of speech and of the press in keeping with the objectives of socialist society. Material conditions for the exercise of that right are provided by the fact that the press, radio, television, movies and other organs of the mass media are State or social property and can never be private property. This assures their use at the exclusive service of the working people and in the interest of society.

Other content restrictions journalists in the region faced included: broadcast and electronic media in Venezuela were banned from broadcasting content that 'could incite or promote hatred', 'foment citizens' anxiety or alter public order', 'disrespect authorities', 'encourage assassinations' or 'constitute war propaganda'; in Guatemala radio transmissions 'offensive to civil values and the national symbols … and contrary to morals and good etiquette' were prohibited; and Argentinian journalists 'could be held accountable … if they published material that "terrorizes" the public' (Freedom House, 2015a).

A 2016 report into criminal defamation laws in the Americas showed that all countries with the exception of Jamaica 'penalize defamation with criminal laws that are often invoked to punish critical journalists and create a chilling effect for the press' (Committee to Protect Journalists, 2016a). Criminal defamation laws have resulted in imprisonment in as many as 22 countries. The report recognized that few cases ended up with imprisonment but it remained the case that 'these laws are frequently used as a way to intimidate journalists and to limit the debate on issues of national concern'. Lawsuits were frequently brought against journalists in Costa Rica, Guatemala, Honduras, Nicaragua, Panama, Cuba, Dominican Republic and Haiti as well as most South American countries. High-profile politicians or other authority figures often initiated lawsuits (e.g. Ecuador, Guatemala, Honduras, Peru, Trinidad and Tobago, Suriname, Venezuela). The special rapporteur for freedom of expression of the Inter-American Commission on Human Rights (IACHR) of the Organization of American States (OAS) recommended repealing or amending laws that criminalized 'desacato' (expressions deemed offensive that are directed at public officials), and had also expressed concern over the use of terrorism or treason offences against journalists who were critical of their governments (UNESCO, 2014c). Suriname had 'some of the most severe criminal defamation laws in the Caribbean'. 'Public expression of enmity, hatred, or contempt' toward the government was penalized with up to seven years in prison, and insulting the head of state could lead to five years in prison (Freedom House, 2015a) as well as a loss of the right to vote (Freedom House, 2016). Some improvements have been noted. For example, defamation on matters of public interest was decriminalized in Argentina in 2009, and 13 countries in total had made amendments to their criminal defamation laws. Overall, there was no trend to decriminalizing these laws in the region.

UNESCO (2014c) also reported a trend towards increased transparency – at least 18 countries had FoI laws but journalists often faced bureaucratic obstacles or restrictions (e.g. El Salvador, Guyana, Jamaica, Mexico, Nicaragua, Panama). Protection of sources was legally guaranteed in most Latin American countries, including as a constitutional right in at least six countries (UNESCO, 2014c).

3. State and Political Pressures

While there were no reported instances of prepublication censorship, a range of state and political pressures were exercised upon journalists especially in the 'not free' countries. Cuba and Venezuela were prime examples. As already indicated, by constitution all Cuban media were state-owned and 'all content is determined by the government' (Freedom House, 2016). In addition to the legal restrictions constraining the work of journalists (laws criminalizing 'enemy propaganda' and 'unauthorized news'), numerous cases of harassment, detentions, beatings, threats, demotions and internal deportations of dissidents and critical journalists were reported. There has been a recent trend towards modernization of the press and reduction in the levels of censorship and secrecy but despite the increase in critical reporting, 'outright criticism of the government or political system does not occur' (Freedom House, 2016). Nicaragua also has a strong culture of secrecy – the president has not given a single press conference in nine years (Freedom House, 2017a). While most media markets were reasonably diverse in terms of political partisanship, a few countries were severely polarized, and as a result the media were frequently accused of bias (UNESCO, 2014c). Cases of political interference, partisan media and/or practices of self-censorship were reported in Antigua and Barbuda, the Dominican Republic, Haiti, Costa Rica, El Salvador, Guatemala, Honduras, Mexico, Nicaragua, Argentina, Panama, Brazil, Colombia, Ecuador, Guyana, Peru and Venezuela.

4. Economic Pressures

Significant variations are evident in the region. Private ownership was booming in most Caribbean and Latin American countries but one notable exception was Cuba where private ownership of media outlets was prohibited. In general, the region was characterized by a high concentration of media ownership. A 2014 UNESCO report claimed that 'in much of the region, on average, almost half of the products and services of the information and communications markets of each country were controlled by one provider'. Some of these owners had strong political interests (e.g. in Brazil, Honduras and Nicaragua). In fact, the president's family in Nicaragua owned three channels and controlled a public channel. In addition to pressures towards commercially driven journalism, editorial independence have also been challenged as a result of the prevalence of state advertising and pressures from commercial advertisers (UNESCO, 2014c). Some practices included: discriminatory allocation of state advertising (Panama, Argentina, Ecuador, Suriname); 'strategic taxation and buyouts' (Bolivia); and statutory obligation on private media to broadcast/disseminate the so-called cadenas – official statements and programmes (Ecuador).

Finally, as of 30 June 2017, the countries in South America had an internet penetration rate of 71.5 per cent; in Central America it was 59.7 per cent (as of 30 June 2017) and in the Caribbean 43.7 per cent (as of 30 June 2016). The countries with the lowest internet penetration rates were: Haiti

(12.8 per cent), Nicaragua (30.6 per cent), Honduras (32.5 per cent) and Cuba (33.6 per cent). The countries and territories with the highest internet penetration rates were: Uruguay (88.2 per cent), Paraguay (89.6 per cent), Curaçao (93.1 per cent), and Falkland Islands (99.2 per cent) (Internet World Stats, 2017).

Journalism in the Global North

Europe

Europe includes 52 countries and territories (UN, 2013). The UN divided the continent into four sub-regions: Eastern Europe, Northern Europe, Southern Europe and Western Europe. All European countries were classified as developed with the exception of Moldova and the Former Yugoslav Republic of Macedonia, which were classified as developing. Forty-three of these countries and territories were included in at least one press freedom index. The majority of countries (27 or 62.8 per cent) were classified as free in terms of media freedom, 30.2 per cent were partly free (13) and three countries (7 per cent) were not free – Belarus, Russia and the Former Yugoslav Republic of Macedonia (Freedom House, 2017a). This made Europe one of the freest regions in the world with no countries in the 'worst of the worst' list. Moreover, the top ten countries in Freedom House's ranking were all European states – Norway, Sweden, Finland, Netherlands, Belgium, Denmark, Luxembourg, Andorra, Switzerland and Liechtenstein. Similarly, seven of the top ten countries according to RWB were European countries – Norway, Sweden, Netherlands, Finland, Switzerland, Belgium and Denmark. However, despite the fact that the region was a leader in terms of press freedom, especially Northern and Western Europe (most notably the Scandinavian and the Benelux countries), Dunham (2016) reported a worrying recent trend. The report claimed that 'over the past 10 years, Europe as a whole has suffered the largest drop in press freedom of any region … driven in part by weakened European economies and shrinking advertising revenues, which have led to layoffs, closure of outlets, and further concentration of media ownership'. In addition to that, there has been an increase in the number of laws restricting journalistic activity – in particular, surveillance legislation. Moreover, a 2016 study of media freedom and pluralism in seven EU member-states commissioned by the European Parliament showed:

> [D]emocratic processes in several EU countries are suffering from systemic failure, with the result that the basic conditions of media pluralism are not present, and, at the same time, that the distortion in media pluralism is hampering the proper functioning of democracy.

The report was prompted by a general concern that in all member states 'business powers have allied with political powers to exert pressure on the media, which are experiencing financial and cultural difficulties to fulfil their watchdog function' (Bárd & Bayer, 2016, p. 11).

In terms of journalistic practices and cultures, 29 European countries were included in the WoJ 2012–2016 study (Tables 2.6–2.9). The results showed notable differences between Eastern and Southern European countries, on the one hand, and Western and Northern European countries, on the other hand. In all countries 'report things as they are' was the role chosen by the highest proportion of journalists. Being detached watchdogs, while picked by the majority of European journalists, was not that important for Danish, Russian, Dutch, Serbian, Greek and Spanish journalists. Two roles that were much more important for Eastern and Southern European journalists were: 'advocate for social change' and 'support national development'. In all countries journalists strongly rejected the opportunist facilitator role. However, there were interesting cross-national differences in the endorsement of the populist disseminator role – rejected in countries with strong interventionist policies such as the Scandinavian countries and France but endorsed by the majority of journalists in Germany, Estonia and Albania. It was also interesting to note that while 'monitor and scrutinize political leaders' was the norm for Scandinavian, Spanish, Portuguese and Croatian journalists, it was not universally accepted as an important role by their colleagues from other European countries, with the lowest percentage of support from Russian journalists. Weaver and Willnat's (2012) book included 14 chapters on European countries but data on professional roles were available for only nine of them: Belgium, Denmark, Germany, Netherlands, Slovenia, Poland, Sweden, Switzerland and Russia. Being a watchdog of government was extremely important for 69 per cent of journalists in Belgium, 53 per cent in Russia, 51 per cent in Slovenia, 42.6 per cent in Poland, 26.9 per cent in Switzerland, 22 per cent in Sweden, 18 per cent in Netherlands and 7 per cent in Germany (Weaver & Willnat, 2012, p. 537).

Case Study 2.4: Scandinavian countries

The Scandinavian countries – here, encompassing Sweden, Finland, Norway and Denmark – have invariably topped the press freedom rankings. As Kircher (2012) pointed out, they 'are consistently ranked highest in the world for both freedom of the press and participatory democracy. The Scandinavian population has among the highest news readership in the world, and can choose among the world's greatest number, per capita, of local and national newspapers'. Kircher (2012) came up with a list of seven lessons Scandinavian media can teach American media. (1) Public service broadcasting should 'go big or go home'; (2) Teletext services had been very successful because they had been updated for younger audiences and newer devices so while 'media continue to experiment with new online technology and app platforms, they don't have to start from scratch'; (3) Self-regulation worked well. Scandinavia's press councils were powerful independent organizations; (4). Public broadcasters were strong and non-biased. They were 'the fairest and most trusted sources of news'; (5) Governments experimented with new business models. One example was a PBS radio auctioned in Denmark and sold to private owners who still received public funding and had public service duties; (6) Protection of whistleblowers – transparency was a key feature and 'the idea of the publicity of official documents is holy' and 'government employees were encouraged to provide information to journalists and punishing them for doing so is prohibited'. Moreover, they had strong shield laws – if a journalist published information from an anonymous source, it was against the law to 'even ask the journalist to reveal the source', and (7) Accessible journalism training with a long paid internship in the middle of the programme.

Case Study 2.5: Bulgaria

Bulgaria is a former communist country situated in Eastern Europe, a member of both the EU and NATO. Bulgaria's rapid transformation from a communist country with a planned economy to a capitalist democratic country with a liberal economy is not unusual for the region because a number of Central and Eastern European countries went through a similar process after the fall of the Berlin Wall in 1989. Bulgaria, is, however, the poorest EU member state, with the lowest press freedom ranking in the EU. RWB placed Bulgaria as 38th out of 139 when it published its first press freedom index in 2002 but from 2007 Bulgaria's ranking has significantly deteriorated – from 51st out of 169 countries in 2007 to 111th out of 180 countries in 2018. These negative trends are a result of a number of factors: increased editorial interference by the authorities; the economic recession and the withdrawal from the Bulgarian media market of foreign investors, resulting in job losses, mergers and shutting down of publications, and the advent of mini-Murdochs – local owners with strong political agendas (Štětka, 2012a). What is particularly noticeable in the Bulgarian case is the complicated web of relationships between politicians, business people and the media, the lack of transparency of media ownership, the financial struggles of the main media outlets in the country and low morale among journalists. The majority of Bulgarian journalists who took part in the Worlds of Journalism study reported largely negative trends over the past five years, indicating 'a substantive deterioration of working conditions in the profession and a declining credibility of journalism' and its relevance in society (Slavtcheva-Petkova, 2017). The levels of trust in public institutions (especially in the judiciary and the government) and the news media were among the lowest in the world (Slavtcheva-Petkova, 2017).

Table 2.6 Journalists' role perceptions: Eastern Europe

Journalistic roles: Eastern Europe	Please tell me how important each of these things is in your work. Percentage saying 'extremely important' and 'very important'						
	Bulgaria	Czech Republic	Hungary	Moldova	Romania	Russia
Be a detached observer	89	91	86.5	82.7	85.6	61.3
Report things as they are	**98.8**	**98.3**	**91**	**97.3**	**95**	**78.7**
Monitor and scrutinize political leaders	56.3	51.9	43.7	57.5	51.2	28.5
Monitor and scrutinize business	47.3	39.1	38.9	38	38.1	23.8
Set the political agenda	24.3	31.6	25.1	34.1	30.5	18.2
Advocate for social change	**69.6**	**25.4**	**50**	**72.9**	**70.9**	**66.2**
Be an adversary of the government	35.2	1.8	23.5	32.2	14.4	17.2
Support national development	**80.9**	**26.1**	**52.9**	**68.2**	**71.7**	**51.9**
Convey a positive image of political leadership	2.7	4.3	16.4	4.7	3.8	10.3
Support government policy	3.5	1.4	18.3	8.9	5.3	11.3
Provide the kind of news that attracts the largest audience	54	38.9	61.9	60.1	62.4	66.2

Source: Worlds of Journalism 2012–2016 study (2017)

Table 2.7 Journalists' role perceptions: Northern Europe

Journalistic roles		Please tell me how important each of these things is in your work. Percentage saying 'extremely important' and 'very important'							
	Denmark	Estonia	Finland	Iceland	Ireland	Latvia	Norway	Sweden	UK
Be a detached observer	63.2	91.2	91.5	76.7	75.2	96.4	62.7	90.4	76.8
Report things as they are	**90.9**	**94.9**	**91.5**	**97.3**	**94.4**	**99.4**	**87.8**	**96.4**	**93**
Monitor and scrutinize political leaders	80.4	53.3	63.8	42.6	61.5	51.9	38.6	87.1	48.1
Monitor and scrutinize business	74.2	47.8	55.8	48.4	50.7	36	34.2	82.5	58.6
Set the political agenda	30	43.6	15	2.9	20.5	27.8	36.9	18.4	15.1
Advocate for social change	26	54.9	30.9	12	36.8	68.2	32.9	38.5	28.8
Be an adversary of the government	43.7	15.5	11	5.5	16.8	7.1	23.4	36	9.4
Support national development	27	51.8	27.6	22.9	24.5	61.9	24.1	14.4	20.2
Convey a positive image of political leadership	0.5	2.2	1.1	0	3	4.5	2.4	1.4	2.1
Support government policy	0.2	3.3	0	0.6	1.7	6.9	0.3	0	1.2
Provide the kind of news that attracts the largest audience	7.4	80.6	42.6	34.8	42.9	57.8	30.2	5.4	45.4

Source: Worlds of Journalism 2012–2016 study (2017)

Table 2.8 Journalists' role perceptions: Western Europe

Journalistic roles	Please tell me how important each of these things is in your work. Percentage saying 'extremely important' and 'very important'						
	Austria	Belgium	France	Germany	Netherlands	Switzerland
Be a detached observer	88.3	85.3	77.6	82.5	64.9	82.8
Report things as they are	**95.5**	**94.2**	**96.5**	**90.7**	**92.9**	**94.4**
Monitor and scrutinize political leaders	45.4	55	56.1	36.3	28.1	46.6
Monitor and scrutinize business	39.8	46.2	45	34.2	30	38.1
Set the political agenda	9.8	26.7	15	9.8	16.9	19.9
Advocate for social change	32.4	21.6	21.4	29.5	23.1	21.5
Be an adversary of the government	20.3	2.2	0.5	19.9	46.2	22.2
Support national development	13.4	16.9	18.1	13.3	10.6	11.9
Convey a positive image of political leadership	0.7	1.1	1	0.7	1	0.4
Support government policy	0.9	1.1	1.5	0.4	2	0.9
Provide the kind of news that attracts the largest audience	60.7	32	21.1	73.5	29.3	46.5

Source: Worlds of Journalism 2012–2016 study (2017)

Table 2.9 Journalists' role perceptions: Southern Europe

Journalistic roles: Southern Europe	Please tell me how important each of these things is in your work. Percentage saying 'extremely important' and 'very important'								
	Albania	Croatia	Greece	Italy	Kosovo	Portugal	Serbia	Spain
Be a detached observer	90.8	83.1	70.4	86.6	94.9	85.9	65.7	70.3
Report things as they are	**98**	**96**	**96.8**	**90.4**	**98.5**	**94.8**	**97**	**96.9**
Monitor and scrutinize political leaders	36.5	88.4	65.3	44	63.5	78.4	69.9	79.2
Monitor and scrutinize business	27.9	87.5	57.2	44.2	46.4	75.1	69.3	77.7
Set the political agenda	19.7	51.5	16	22.3	38.2	29.1	43.1	37
Advocate for social change	**72.3**	**75.6**	**68.4**	**46.9**	**72.3**	**47.9**	**76.9**	**69.5**
Be an adversary of the government	64.9	18.4	18.9	4.2	74.5	–	32.7	18.1
Support national development	**73.4**	**71.9**	**54.8**	**1.6**	**70.4**	**54.8**	**75.4**	**56.1**
Convey a positive image of political leadership	18.6	13.2	6.3	2.3	25.3	4.7	12.6	3.4
Support government policy	9.7	12	2.8	1	13	1.7	8.9	9.4
Provide the kind of news that attracts the largest audience	81.6	38.5	30.6	38.5	62.1	24.6	49.1	33.4

Source: Worlds of Journalism 2012–2016 study (2017)

Hallin and Mancini's (2004) typology of the media systems in Western Europe and North America offered a useful conceptualization of some of the common trends. They identified three main models of media systems. Their framework (Hallin & Mancini, 2004, p. 21) was based on four dimensions: the development of media markets; political parallelism – 'the degree and nature of the links between the media and political parties or, more broadly, the extent to which the media system reflects the major political divisions in society'; the development of journalistic professionalism; and state intervention in the media system. While all these factors influenced the work of journalists and some of them are explored in the next few sections, for now it is worth focusing on journalistic role perceptions and practices. Hallin and Mancini (2004, p. 73) argued that journalists in the Mediterranean countries favoured 'commentary-oriented or advocacy journalism', and journalism was 'not as strongly differentiated from political activism'. The North/Central European countries, on the other hand, combined features of commentary-oriented journalism and 'a growing emphasis on neutral professionalism and information-oriented journalism' (Hallin & Mancini, 2004, p. 74). Finally, information-oriented journalism was the norm in the liberal countries but the British press was 'highly partisan' (Hallin & Mancini, 2004, p. 75). Britain has a history of strong and impartial public broadcasting, and the role of the state has been considerably more limited than in the other Western European countries.

Dobek-Ostrowska (2015), on the other hand, identified four main types of media systems in Central and Eastern Europe. The first one was the hybrid liberal model, which included the West Slavonic (Czech Republic, Poland and Slovakia) and the Baltic states (Estonia, Latvia and Lithuania). These countries were the richest and the freest in terms of press freedom. In terms of journalistic practices, they were characterized by weaker politicization, and domination in the market of foreign companies, which in turn led to 'strong commercialization and tabloidization' (Dobek-Ostrowska, 2015, p. 28). The second model was the polarized media model, and it included Bulgaria (Case Study 2.5), Croatia, Hungary, Romania and Serbia. They were poorer and they were classified as 'partly free' by Freedom House. The situation was much more dynamic in these countries. Journalism was strongly politicized, including public service broadcasting. Some owners and journalists had very strong political interests and showed bias. A distinctive feature was the 'lack of clear separation between the world of politics, business and media' (Dobek-Ostrowska, 2015, p. 29). The third model was the media in transition model, and it included Moldova, Macedonia, Montenegro, Albania, Bosnia and Herzegovina, and Ukraine. Common characteristics were poverty, small size of the market, strong politicization and control of the media, and low professionalism. Finally, the authoritarian model included Russia and Belarus. The two countries were not free, their mass media were 'extremely highly politicized' and 'were used by political authorities as an instrument of strong political propaganda' (Dobek-Ostrowska, 2015, p. 35).

1. Safety Threats, Including Violence Against Journalists

Europe as a whole is one of the safest regions for journalists. Journalists in Western Europe in particular 'have enjoyed a high degree of safety and low risk of being targeted for exposing cases of corruption or for criticizing governments' (UNESCO, 2014a). However, the Charlie Hebdo terror attack in Paris in 2015 when 12 people were killed, eight of whom were journalists, tarnished Western Europe's image as a safe region. The mass shooting placed France among the top three deadliest countries for journalists in 2015 (Committee to Protect Journalists, 2017). The Committee to Protect Journalists (2017) also ranked Russia and Bosnia as being among the 20 deadliest countries based on the number of journalists killed since 1992. Russia was seventh with 58 murdered journalists and Bosnia was 16th with 19 journalists. The journalists who lost their lives in Bosnia were war reporters during the 1992–95 war. Safety for journalists there has significantly improved since, with the last recorded murder in 1994. The situation in Russia was different because even though there has been no military conflict on Russian territory, Russia was still considered to be one of the most dangerous countries. There were two recorded murders in 2017. The suspected sources of fire were: military officials (36.2 per cent), government officials (21 per cent), criminal groups (17.2 per cent) and political groups (8.6 per cent). Impunity was a big issue because there had been complete impunity for 65.5 per cent of the killers. In terms of beats covered, 21.9 per cent of the killed journalists before July 2018 worked on corruption cases, 20.8 per cent were war reporters, 22.9 per cent were political reporters and 13.5 per cent crime reporters (Committee to Protect Journalists, 2017c, personal communication). A UN report (2014, p. 25) claimed that 'the Council of Europe found that in many cases, attacks against journalists have been followed by inadequate investigations or none at all and that this created a cycle leading to further attacks'. As a whole, the number of physical attacks and death threats against journalists has increased in South-East Europe, while Baltic States and Central European countries 'can generally be considered as having been less dangerous for journalists'. Moreover, 'cases of assaults against journalists from criminal and mafia groups have become increasingly frequent' especially against investigative journalists in South-East Europe.

2. Legal Restrictions

Freedom of expression is constitutionally guaranteed in all European countries. All countries with the exception of Belarus signed and ratified the Council of Europe's Convention for the Protection of Human Rights and Fundamental Freedoms. Freedom of expression is protected under Article 10 of the convention but it is not an absolute right. It is balanced against other rights such as privacy, the right to protection of the reputation and rights of other people as well as the interests of national security and public safety, with the aim of maintaining the impartiality of the judiciary or for the protection of public health or morals. The work of journalists has been constrained by a range of laws that balance the right to freedom of expression against these other rights. Hate speech was banned in most countries in 2018. Nazi propaganda was prohibited in Germany and Austria. Denial of the Holocaust or the Armenian genocide was criminalized in Slovakia. Denial of Soviet or Nazi crimes was prohibited in Lithuania. At least 22 countries in Western Europe and North America had privacy laws. There has been a trend towards introducing more anti-terrorism and cyber security legislation as a result of the terror attacks over the past decade and a half and the increasing role digital communications played. France tightened up its legal framework after the Charlie Hebdo attacks by allowing surveillance of electronic communications and the blocking of websites with little judicial oversight (Freedom House, 2016). The British 2006 Terrorism Act criminalized speech that encouraged terrorism. A TV station in Denmark had to file for bankruptcy after a court imposed a hefty fine on it for 'promoting terrorism' (Freedom House, 2015a). Spanish journalists could not disseminate pictures and videos 'damaging' to Spain's police and security forces, especially during protests and demonstrations. Internet filtering and the blocking of websites on security or copyright grounds or to counter pornography and extremism were becoming prevalent (Dutton et al., 2011).

Although there has been a slow trend towards decriminalization of defamation, it remained a criminal offence in most countries. Defamation has been decriminalized in Moldova, Ukraine, Denmark, Estonia, Ireland, the UK, Bosnia and Herzegovina, Montenegro, Serbia and Macedonia. Libel convictions could result in prison sentences in Belarus, the Czech Republic, Hungary, Slovakia, Russia, Iceland, Lithuania, Norway, Sweden, Greece, Italy, Belgium and the Netherlands. Spampinato (2016) argued that in Italy alone in five years at least 18 journalists had faced custodial sentences for a total of 30 years. In some countries, defaming the head of state or public officials was still a crime in 2018. Thus, insulting the monarchy was a criminal offence in the Netherlands. Defamation of the state, the nation and its institutions was criminalized in Poland. Similarly, insulting the 'Republic of Croatia, its coat of arms, national anthem, or flag' was a crime penalized with prison sentences. Penalties for defaming public officials were increased by half in Portugal. Religious defamation/blasphemy laws were still on the books in Poland, Ireland, Greece and Malta in 2018. Common defences against defamation were truth and the public interest but while they 'have served to protect journalism in many cases', defamation laws have definitely had 'a chilling effect on media freedom' due to the high number of cases and the significant costs (UN, 2014). England was a prime example of that since London had indeed turned into 'the libel capital of the world', prompting the passing of the 2013 Defamation Act that formally introduced the 'serious harm' threshold for claimants in part to deter 'libel tourism' in which foreign nationals brought cases in the English courts which were unrelated to publication in the UK.

Russia and Belarus had the most restrictive legal frameworks in the region. Criticism of the government and the president was a criminal offence in Belarus. Russia had a range of laws that significantly restricted the work of journalists. A law signed in May 2015 allowed the prosecutor general's office to designate organizations as 'undesirable', and anyone who worked with them could face prison sentences of up to seven years (Freedom House, 2016). Another law restricted foreign ownership in media companies to 20 per cent. In 2017 Putin also signed a law that allowed the government the power to designate media companies as foreign agents. Almost immediately after the law came into force, the Justice Ministry designated Radio Free Europe/Radio Liberty (RFE/RL), Voice of America (VOA), and several affiliated news services as 'foreign agents'. The law was passed in retaliation to the US authorities' requirement for RT to register under the US Foreign Agents Registration Act.

On a more positive note, some European countries, especially in Scandinavia, have very strong legal protections for journalists, including dedicated press laws. All countries have FoI Acts or the right was enshrined in their constitutions. The Scandinavian countries were exemplars in that respect (see Case Study 2.4). Sweden's Freedom of the Press Act 1766 (Act) is considered the oldest piece of FoI legislation in the world. It allows everyone to request information without revealing their name, address or the reason for their request. Even the most transparent and open countries, however, impose some restrictions, mainly on national security or data protection grounds. Moreover, while there is a strong tradition of implementation of these pieces of legislation, journalists face a range of practical difficulties, even in the most established democracies. Similarly, protection of sources was legally guaranteed in more than two-thirds of the Western European countries (UN, 2014), but there were still cases when journalists came under pressure to reveal their sources during criminal investigations. Estonian journalists, for example, faced prison sentences for refusing to disclose their sources in cases involving major crimes. An Irish Act limited journalists' contact with police officers by prescribing fines, imprisonment or loss of jobs for police officers who spoke with the media without prior authorization (Freedom House, 2015a).

3. State and Political Pressures

Most European countries are democracies and 28 of them are also members of the EU although the UK was in the process of leaving the organization after the referendum on EU membership in June 2016. The EU does not have any explicit competences to regulate media pluralism but the right to freedom of expression and information, including the freedom and pluralism of the media, is enshrined in Article 11 of the EU Charter of Fundamental Rights. Bárd and Bayer (2016) argued that the EU could take action against member states that do not observe these rights because they were legally enshrined in EU law and so ultimately the functioning of democracy and the rule of law were jeopardized. However, they recognized it was unlikely for member-states to reach consensus on such measures because they might require a common regulatory framework and harmonization of ownership concentration rules.

Hallin and Mancini's (2004) and Dobek-Ostrowska's (2015) models highlighted the different role the state played in European countries and the degree of political polarization. The state played a very strong role in Russia and Belarus as well as in the Mediterranean countries, France, and the North/Central European countries. Russian and Belarusian media were under the tight grip of their authorities, which used a range of legal and para-legal measures to turn the media into propaganda machines. However, Belarusian media were considerably more restricted than Russian media. Strong state intervention and press subsidies were also a typical feature of the Mediterranean media but these countries had left behind their history of dictatorships, and the role of the state was not as controversial as it was a few decades ago. Finally, the state played a strong positive role in the Scandinavian countries by legally protecting press freedom and subsidizing media outlets to foster pluralism as well as allowing for strong public service broadcasting. The role of the state was the weakest in the liberal countries of Britain and Ireland (Hallin & Mancini, 2004).

In terms of political polarization, there has been a trend towards Berlusconization, Italianization or Mediterraneanization in the post-communist countries of Central and Eastern Europe (Dobek-Ostrowska, 2012; Jakubowicz &

Sükösd, 2008). These terms referred to 'a lack of clear separation between the world of politics, business and media' (Dobek-Ostrowska, 2015, p. 29) similar to the situation in Italy when Silvio Berlusconi was prime minister while owning the largest commercial broadcasting company. These trends were exacerbated by the global financial crisis, which led to the withdrawal of some foreign investors and the appropriation of media companies by politicians or local businessmen with very strong political interests. Štětka (2012a, p. 441) argued that investors also withdrew due to 'the increasing inability to compete in an environment ruled by other-than-market rules'. As a result, the region was 'plagued by their own mini-Murdochs' (Štětka, 2012b). According to Bodo Hombach, a German politician and former Managing Director of WAZ, oligarchs were buying local media 'not in order to win money' but 'in order to exert political influence' to 'promote business or political interests' (Štětka, 2012a, p. 441). The Czech finance minister Andrej Babiš, for example, bought himself a media empire four months before the elections and was labelled 'Babisconi' in reference to Berlusconi (Foy, 2016). Similarly, a very controversial long-serving MP and former deputy minister in Bulgaria, Delyan Peevski, appropriated one of the biggest media companies in the country.

The situation in Hungary and Poland is particularly precarious in 2018. Chapman (2018) described Poland as 'a crucial battleground in the drive by authoritarian-minded leaders to gain control over political discourse and limit media pluralism', and depicted the situation in the country as an 'assault on press freedom'. Similarly, as a result of Hungarian Prime Minister's policy of 'illiberal democracy' (the term Viktor Orbán himself used), namely the systematic erosion of democracy and its institutions, pro-government media outlets 'have come to dominate the media market to an overwhelming degree, unimaginable even a year earlier' (Hegedüs, 2018). Freedom House's Nations in Transit 2018 report claimed that Orbán's:

> government and its associated oligarchs consolidated their dominant position in the Hungarian media market and, with few exceptions, acquired the last bastions of independent print media in the country. The content and messages published in government-friendly outlets seem to be directly coordinated by the prime minister's cabinet office led by Cabinet Chief Antal Rogán, often labeled by investigative media as the 'propaganda ministry'. (Hegedüs, 2018)

Polarization and partisanship were also evident in other countries. The British print media landscape was dominated by conservative newspapers with very strong political agendas. Rupert Murdoch's newspaper *The Sun*, for example, has always supported a particular political party and prided itself on influencing the outcomes of democratic elections. The relationship between politicians and the press was investigated during the Leveson Inquiry into the culture, practices and ethics of the British press as a result of the phone hacking scandal. It concluded that politicians had developed 'too close a relationship with the press in a way which has not been in the public interest' (Leveson, 2012).

Finally, the conflict between Russia and Ukraine also transcended into the media space. The retransmission of Russian programmes was blocked in Ukraine, Lithuania and Latvia because the Russian channels allegedly carried 'aggressively propagandistic content that was apparently designed to support the Russian occupation of Crimea, encourage pro-Russian separatism … and discredit the new government in Kyiv' (Freedom House, 2016).

4. Economic Pressures

All countries in Europe have both private and state media or public service broadcasters. The developed democracies of Western and Northern Europe have a strong tradition of public service broadcasting, whereas some Central and Eastern European countries still have state-owned media. Press markets have been relatively concentrated in Central and Eastern Europe, and there has been a trend towards greater concentration of media ownership through-out Europe (UN, 2014). In some countries this was coupled with a lack of transparency. In addition to that, the global recession and the advent of the internet and digital technologies led to a reshaping of the traditional busi-ness models. Newspapers experienced lots of financial challenges. Publications throughout Europe had to lay off journalists or close down. The local press was strongly affected. The situation was particularly dire in Greece and Spain. Job insecurity and low pay were still major issues for local and national press journalists throughout Europe in 2018. The withdrawal of foreign invest-ment in Central and Eastern Europe had 'increased the role of state financial support' in the region, and lots of media were strongly dependent on state advertising or subsidies (UN, 2014, p. 16). As a whole, advertising income, 'which was already declining for traditional media prior to the 2008 financial crisis, has shrunk significantly' and recovery had been slow, especially in terms of print advertising (UN, 2014). One consequence of that was the increased blurring between editorial and advertising content, and the relative decline of investigative journalism (UN, 2014). There has also been a general trend towards commercialization and fragmentation. While television remained the most widely consumed media, internet penetration rates have been growing at a fast pace (UN, 2014). Most journalists worked in a converged environment and prepared 'packages' for a range of audiences. Revenues from online advertising for news media were generally lower than revenues from print advertising, which had been a major source of income. As of 31 December 2017, the average internet penetration rate for Europe was 85.2 per cent, which was considerably higher than the worldwide average of 50.7 per cent (Internet World Stats, 2017). The countries and territories with the lowest internet penetration rates were: San Marino (52.7 per cent), Vatican City State (60.6 per cent), the Isle of Man (61.3 per cent) and Albania (65.8 per cent). The countries with the highest internet penetration rates were: Norway (99.2 per cent), Iceland (99 per cent), Estonia (97.7 per cent) and Liechtenstein (98.4 per cent).

North America

The North America region includes Bermuda, Canada, Greenland, Saint Pierre and Miquelon, and the United States of America (UN, 2013). Only the US and Canada were included in the press freedom indices, and both countries were classified as free. Canada was ranked 20th by Freedom House and 18th by RWB, and the US 33rd by Freedom House and 45th by RWB. The US has a reputation for being a champion for media freedom across the world. As Daly (2012, p. 3) argued, 'journalism is central to the very idea of America', and it had been instrumental in the creation of the American nation. In terms of journalistic practices, the US has had a strong influence over the rest of the world – instilling journalistic values of objectivity and balance, promoting the media's role as a 'watchdog' of society or as the 'fourth estate'. The US also led the way in the trend towards the professionalization of journalism. The very core of what has been recognized, if not always accepted, globally as journalism practice – the event; the interview; the inverted pyramid; news values; and objectivity – it has been argued, diffused from the US to Europe and other parts of the world (Høyer, 2005, pp. 11ff). Willnat and Weaver's (2014) representative survey showed that being detached watchdogs of government was the most important function for US journalists (78.2 per cent). The latest percentage was the highest recorded since 1971. This percentage was slightly lower in the WoJ 2012–2016 study (Table 2.10). Another important function was 'analysing complex problems' (68.8 per cent). Reaching 'widest possible audience' was important for only 12 per cent – a considerable drop in comparison with previous surveys (Willnat & Weaver, 2014). However, according to the WoJ survey more than half of American journalists considered it extremely or very important to 'provide the kind of news that attracts the largest audience' whereas this was important for only a quarter of Canadian journalists.

1. Safety Threats, Including Violence Against Journalists

Both Canada and the US are generally very safe countries. Attacks on journalists are very rare. Only two Canadian journalists have been killed since 1992. Sports broadcaster Brian Smith was shot by an angry viewer. Tara Singh Hayer, the publisher of *Indo-Canadian Times*, was shot dead in 1998. Although no one was charged, his murder had been linked to his criticisms of Sikh fundamentalist violence. He had also allegedly agreed to be a witness in a case about the Air India bombings that caused 331 deaths in 1985. Seven journalists were killed in the US between 1992 and 2018 (Committee to Protect Journalists, 2018a). Two of the murders were from 2015, when a cameraman and a female reporter were shot dead by a former colleague during a live transmission from Virginia.

2. Legal Restrictions

As of July 2018, freedom of expression was constitutionally guaranteed both in the US and Canada. The US has one of 'the world's strongest systems of legal protection for media independence' (Freedom House, 2016). The First Amendment of the US constitution guarantees freedom of expression. Hallin and Mancini (2004, p. 229) argued:

> [B]oth legal doctrine and political culture in the United States tend to treat the First Amendment in a more absolutist way, and this means that many kinds of media regulation that are common in Europe – privacy rules, regulations on political advertising, free time requirements for political communication, and right-of-reply laws … – are politically and legally untenable in the United States.

Journalists also generally enjoyed protection from defamation suits by public figures because there was a clear differentiation in the treatment of public figures and everyone else. In 2018 defamation was a criminal offence in Canada and in some US states. Both in Canada and in the US there has been a trend towards restricting freedom of expression on national security and terrorism grounds. Protection of sources was also an issue. The Edward Snowden revelations showed that the National Security Agency had carried out mass surveillance of electronic communications. Freedom House (2015a) claimed that the Obama administration 'has brought more criminal cases against alleged leakers than were brought by all previous administrations combined'. Canada also passed new anti-terror legislation after the deadly terrorist attack on Parliament in 2014. Particularly controversial was Bill C-51, which criminalized 'the promotion of "terrorism offences in general", potentially subjecting reporters to prosecution for covering or quoting alleged terrorists and their activities' (Barber, 2015).

3. State and Political Pressures

US and Canadian media are among the freest in the world, and both countries were classified by Hallin and Mancini (2004) as liberal. The role of the state was 'relatively limited and the role of the market and private sector relatively large' (Hallin & Mancini, 2004, p. 228). Commercial broadcasting dominated the US market but less so in Canada where there was also a tradition of public service broadcasting, which was very weak in the US. Both American and Canadian journalists had an adversarial attitude towards state officials, and some landmark investigations such as the Watergate affair in the US best illustrated the role that journalists in these countries aspired to play. Political parallelism in the press sector was 'unusually low' (Hallin & Mancini, 2004, p. 213). The principles of neutrality and objectivity were very strong as well. US newspapers were considerably more objective and non-partisan than UK newspapers but impartiality was not a legal requirement for US broadcasters, and some TV stations such as Fox News showed a very clear political bias. Moreover, Donald Trump's election and his negative attitude towards liberal media have proved to be a major challenge (Case Study 2.6).

4. Economic Pressures

The economic developments in North America were very similar to the ones European journalists have experienced as a result of the global recession and the advent of the internet and digital communications. Willnat and Weaver's (2014) survey confirmed these trends. The majority of US journalists reported that their workforces had shrunk in the past year as a result of 'the economic downsizing during the great Recession of 2007–09 as well as the tremendous loss of advertising revenue to the internet' (p. 4). Willnat and Weaver's estimates showed that the US news media had shrunk by 32 per cent since 1992. Only 13.2 per cent of journalists reported that the size of their workforces had grown, which was probably a result of the fact that 'skilled journalists adept at working in the new media environment are currently in high demand … among a small number of U.S. news organizations' (p. 4). As of 30 June 2017, the internet penetration rate was the highest in the world – 88.1 per cent (Internet World Stats, 2017). It was the highest in Bermuda (98 per cent), followed by Greenland (92.5 per cent), Canada (90.1 per cent), the US (87.9 per cent), and Saint Pierre and Miquelon (71.2 per cent).

Table 2.10 Journalists' role perceptions: Northern America and Oceania

| Journalistic roles: Northern America and Oceania | Please tell me how important each of these things is in your work. Percentage saying 'extremely important' and 'very important' | | | |
	Australia	Canada	New Zealand	US
Be a detached observer	76.9	78.4	71.5	75.5
Report things as they are	**94.7**	**96.9**	**94**	**98.3**
Monitor and scrutinize political leaders	60.4	67.8	61.6	86.1
Monitor and scrutinize business	54	62.6	57.6	69.3
Set the political agenda	18.9	23.4	18.2	11.3
Advocate for social change	37.8	35.7	39	29.6
Be an adversary of the government	11.7	13.9	11.9	18.2
Support national development	26.5	18	24.5	13.7
Convey a positive image of political leadership	3.8	.3	3.5	3.9
Support government policy	1.3	.9	1.4	3.6
Provide the kind of news that attracts the largest audience	61.4	24.7	43.5	53.2

Source: Worlds of Journalism 2012–2016 study (2017)

Case Study 2.6: Donald Trump and the American media

The election of Donald Trump as president of the US not only took the world by surprise but put American media in the spotlight. During the presidential campaign Trump accused mainstream media of supporting his opponent Hillary Clinton. Once he took power the war between Trump and US media reached new heights. President Trump's former chief strategist Stephen Bannon described US mainstream media as 'the opposition party', saying it should 'keep its mouth shut'. Trump himself claimed the media were 'the enemy of the American people'. In an angry tweet on 17 February 2017 Trump said: 'The FAKE NEWS media (failing @nytimes, @NBCNews, @ABC, @CBS, @CNN) is not my enemy, it is the enemy of the American People!' The following day he added: 'Don't believe the main stream (fake news) media. The White House is running VERY WELL. I inherited a MESS and am in the process of fixing it.' Trump's verbal attacks during the election rallies and subsequently during his White House press conferences and on Twitter were widely condemned by journalists, celebrities, NGOs and politicians from other countries who expressed concerns about the future of American journalism and democracy, and the extent to which freedom of expression was likely to be upheld as a fundamental human right. The US has been a 'champion' of media freedom with a very strong influence over the rest of the world – instilling journalistic values of objectivity and balance, promoting the media's role as a 'watchdog' of society or the 'fourth estate'. Cockburn (2017), however, argued that 'this is a golden era in American journalism, because established media outlets such as CNN, *The New York Times* and *The Washington Post* find themselves under unprecedented and open attacks from the powers that be'.

Oceania

Oceania includes 29 countries and territories (UN, 2013). Australia and New Zealand were classified as 'developed' countries, and all other countries and territories were classified as 'developing'. Fourteen were included in at least one press freedom index by the leading NGOs. The majority of countries (12 or 86 per cent) were classified as free in terms of media freedom, and only Nauru and Fiji were partly free (Freedom House, 2017a). In terms of journalistic practices, Australia and New Zealand were included in the WoJ 2012–2016 study (Table 2.10). The two main roles endorsed by journalists were: 'report things as they are' and 'be a detached observer'. Another role selected by 60.4 per cent and 61.6 per cent of journalists from Australia and New Zealand, respectively, was to 'monitor and scrutinize political leaders'. These results partially confirmed Josephi and Richards's (2012, p. 121) survey findings in which 90 per cent said it was extremely important for them to 'investigate government claims'. Surprisingly, in the same survey only

35 per cent of Australian journalists said it was extremely important for them to 'serve as adversary of government', and that percentage was considerably lower in the WoJ study. Hanusch and Upal's (2015) survey of journalists in Fiji showed that they 'lean most strongly towards a watchdog role of the media, but there is also evidence to support the existence of a development journalism orientation'. About a quarter of journalists also appeared to lean towards this development journalism orientation according to the WoJ study (Table 2.10).

1. Safety Threats, Including Violence Against Journalists

Oceania was the safest region in the world based on the number of killed journalists. Only one journalist has been killed since 1992. A Swedish journalist lost his life in Papua New Guinea in 1992 but it was not entirely clear whether he took his own life or whether he was killed because of an investigation he was working on about the guerrilla organization Free Papua Movement (Committee to Protect Journalists, 2017). Journalists in Papua New Guinea experienced threats and harassment, particularly in reprisal for investigative reporting (Freedom House, 2015a).

2. Legal Measures

As of July 2018, freedom of expression was not constitutionally guaranteed in Australia and New Zealand but it was guaranteed by convention and statute in New Zealand, and has been respected in practice in both countries. The right was constitutionally guaranteed in Fiji and Papua New Guinea but in Fiji it could be curtailed on national security, public health, safety and morality grounds. Journalists' work in all countries has been restricted by defamation laws and security legislation. In 2018 defamation was a criminal offence only in Australia but it was rarely invoked. However, under the National Security Legislation Amendment Act in Australia journalists could end up with prison sentences of up to five years for disclosing information relating to a 'special intelligence operation', or an even higher sentence of up to ten years for endangering 'the health or safety of any person or prejudice the effective conduct of a special intelligence operation' (Freedom House, 2016). Coverage of immigration detention centres was also severely restricted in Australia and Papua New Guinea. Fiji and Papua New Guinea did not have FoI laws, and access to public information was difficult. Protection of sources was also an issue.

3. State and Political Pressures

Australia and New Zealand are free, generally liberal countries, showing similar traits to the countries in Hallin and Mancini's (2004) liberal model. Fiji's recent history has been rather turbulent. Fijian journalists worked in an atmosphere of censorship and self-censorship after the 2006 coup. However, official censorship ended in 2012 and 'observers noted a slight opening of the media environment for discussion of political issues' in the lead-up to the 2014 elections.

4. Economic Pressures

Most media were privately owned in the developed countries, and Australian-owned companies dominated the market (Freedom House, 2016, 2017a). Concentration of ownership was an issue. Australia also had a history of strong public service broadcasting. The region was also affected by the global recession and the advent of digital technologies. As of 30 June 2017, the average internet penetration rate was 69.6 per cent but there were significant differences between countries. Antarctica (100 per cent), New Caledonia (89 per cent), New Zealand (88.7 per cent) and Australia (88.2 per cent) had the highest internet penetration rates, while Solomon Islands (11 per cent), Papua New Guinea (11.4 per cent) and Kiribati (13.7 per cent) had the lowest rates (Internet World Stats, 2017). The developing countries experienced a range of economic issues that hindered the development of mass media.

Case Study 2.7: Pacific journalism

The term 'the Pacific way' has been used both in academic and policy discourse to describe not just the arguably different way in which journalism is practised in this region but also the overall pattern of communication and interactions (Papoutsaki & Harris, 2008). Papoutsaki and Harris (2008, p. 1) also used the term 'Pacific "Islandness"' because in their view these communities are both 'isolated and connected'. Russell (1996, p. 57 as quoted in Robie (2013, p. 92) even referred to them as 'Fourth World nations' – 'indigenous people, residing in developed nations, but living in Third World conditions'. A key issue is that they 'cannot separate from imperial power because of their location within the boundaries of the imperialist nation' (Russell, 1996, p. 57 as quoted in Robie, 2013, p. 94). The Cook Islands, for example, is a self-governing South Pacific country consisting of 15 islands, which is in free association with New Zealand. The free association agreement means that Cook Islanders keep New Zealand citizenship and 'the country remains part of the Realm of New Zealand' with

Queen Elizabeth II as the Head of State but 'the Cook Islands Government has full executive powers' (Cook Islands Government portal, 2017). Robie (2005, p. 87) argued that the media in the Pacific countries played a key role in this battle for either political autonomy or 'equal access to the political and economic opportunities of the democratic society'. As a result, the 'news values exhibited by indigenous media are often at variance with those of the West (First World), East (Second World remnants) and developing nations (Third World)'. Robie claimed that the news values typical for those indigenous media were an '"independent [political] voice", "language", "culture", "education" and "solidarity"' (Robie, 2001, p. 13 as quoted in Robie, 2005, p. 87). These values were informed by the overriding principle of 'self-determination' – 'challenging mainstream media perspective', 'reaffirming a distinct cultural identity' and 'teaching in own language "nests"' (Robie, 2005, p. 88). Robie (2008) acknowledged there were different views on the journalistic values and practices in the Pacific Islands. On the one hand, some academics argued that Pacific media and journalists had largely embraced Western ideals and standards such as objectivity and facticity but on the other hand others claimed that the journalism practised was similar to the journalism practised in other developing nations. The third view, as already indicated, was that Pacific journalists had indeed adopted a distinctive style of journalism known as 'Pacific journalism', which had largely been conceptualized as a form of development journalism (Robie, 2008).

Summary

The comparison between journalistic practices and contributing factors in the global South and the global North shows that, in general, journalists in the South have experienced most, if not all, of the pressures and challenges described so far, while journalists in the North have faced predominantly legal restrictions, and some economic and political pressures. These trends do not apply to every single country and there are significant regional variations. In terms of journalistic practices, while the detached watchdog role has been endorsed by North American and Western European journalists, and promoted around the world, other traditions still play an important role in the global South. Development journalism is prevalent in Africa and among some journalists in Asia and Latin America. Advocacy journalism is popular among Asian journalists as well as among journalists in the Mediterranean countries, and in some Central and Eastern European countries. Most importantly, context matters and while there are common trends between and within regions, there are huge sub-regional differences particularly in Africa and Asia. This is all set against the underlying conditions of media freedom which differ not only in nuanced ways from place to place but globally between the minority of countries with media which were designated as being 'free' and the majority where that was not the case. Importing values, experiences and practices from the former into the latter is fraught with problems. Finally, while the right to freedom of expression is enshrined in the constitutions and legal frameworks of most countries, these provisions were compromised on a daily basis by the increasing number of legal and para-legal restrictions, the complicated web of relationships between political and business elites and the media, and the resulting journalistic practices. 'Real journalism' often differs from 'ideal journalism' – the ideals cherished by journalists themselves and the expectations of their audiences (Slavtcheva-Petkova, 2016a). Furthermore, being a journalist remains a dangerous job for many in the global South. The role of activists and NGOs such as Freedom House, the CPJ, RWB, Article 19 and others as well as the UN and UNESCO in highlighting these cases and demanding justice is undeniable but national and local authorities still all too often pay lip service to these issues without taking any real measures to eradicate them. It remains to be seen whether the 2012 UN Plan of Action on the Safety of Journalists and the Issue of Impunity will bring about any tangible changes.

Further Reading

1. Bárd, P. & Bayer, J. (2016) 'A comparative analysis of media freedom and pluralism in the EU member states', *European Parliament*, www.europarl.europa. eu, accessed 12 September 2017.
2. Committee to Protect Journalists (2018a) '1310 journalists killed since 1992', www.cpj.org, accessed 10 July 2018.
3. Dobek-Ostrowska, B. (2015) '25 years after communism: four models of media and politics in Central and Eastern Europe' in D. Ostrowka & M. Glowacki (eds), *Democracy and Media in Central and Eastern Europe 25 years on* (New York: Peter Lang), pp. 11–46.
4. Freedom House. (2017a) 'Freedom of the press 2017: Press freedom's dark horizon report and country reports', https://freedomhouse.org, accessed 14 May 2018.
5. Hallin, D.C. and Mancini, P. (2004) *Comparing Media Systems: Three Models of Media and Politics* (Cambridge, UK: Cambridge University Press).
6. Obijiofor, L. & Hanusch, F. (2011) *Journalism Across Cultures: An Introduction* (Basingstoke: Palgrave Macmillan).
7. UNESCO. (2014c) 'World trends in freedom of expression and media development: regional overview of Latin America and the Caribbean', www.unesco.org, accessed 17 February 2017.
8. Worlds of Journalism 2012–2016 study. (2017) 'Data and key tables 2012–2016: Aggregated data on key variables', www.worldsofjournalism.org, accessed 26 April 2018.

3

From the Ground Up: Theories of Global Journalism

Chapter overview

This chapter explores a range of theoretical approaches to global journalism. Theory is defined as a set of principles through which to understand global journalism critically, systematically and independently. Normative theories – and in particular that of liberal democracy – which tend to dominate are explored. The conflict between these theories, which largely reflect practical concerns, and other theories, which draw on more abstract thinking, is examined. The chapter also reviews non-normative grounded theories – namely theories based in data ('the facts'). We argue that it is most useful to avoid any theory–practice divide, and that accounting for both practical experience and interests and abstract ideas is beneficial. As theories are derived from, and reflect, ideology (a set of beliefs) and their biases, we urge that they should be approached critically through an understanding of their origins, histories and manifestations.

Learning outcomes

After having read this chapter you will be able to:

1. Understand the link between contexts, practices and theories
2. Evaluate normative and other theories applicable to global journalism
3. Compare and contrast normative and other theories applicable to global journalism
4. Explore how theories can explain how 'the news' is produced, disseminated and received in different contexts.

In English, the word *journalism* has been used almost exclusively in the singular. The global variations in the conditions of journalism, scoped in the previous chapter, raise the question of whether journalism is one occupation – one set of practices – negotiating different contexts, or, alternatively, a multiplicity of activities lodged in specific cultures with only superficial similarities. In other words, should we use the plural of the word – *journalisms* – to better capture its global nature? Of course, there was an inescapable reality to the material conditions of journalism; for example, that between 1992 and 2018 844 journalists were murdered, of whom more than two-fifths died in five countries (Iraq, Philippines, Algeria, Colombia and Somalia) (https://cpj.org). However, what is the link between contexts, the relevant journalistic practices and the broader role that journalists play in their respective countries? As Chapter 2 demonstrated, while there was a degree of similarity of journalistic values and ethical principles that journalists around the world share, it would be an overstatement to claim that the role of the media as the Fourth Estate – or the fourth branch of government – has been universally accepted. This role appeared to be endorsed predominantly in the Global North. Was there a shared commonality across journalism; a universality of ethos characterized by what journalists did (and put them occasionally at odds with other institutions of power)? Operating outside government, journalism appeared to empower citizens directly to access 'truth' in order to be self-determining; but this idea was met with different degrees of receptiveness and hostility. This journalism seemed to be more effectively practised in situations where liberal and democratic values, such as popular or parliamentary sovereignty, prevailed, and less so in dictatorships and under authoritarianism. We explore this relationship between journalism practices, theories and contexts by focusing on a few key theories as well as their historical development.

Journalism and its Role in Society: Practice vs Theory

Practical concerns do not always provide us with a set of principles through which to understand critically, systematically and independently what it is we are interested in. They may be too random, too transitory, too particular or atypical. On the other hand, journalists often explore their occupation through insider discussions, or 'shop talk'. This can provide us with insights into journalism which are not apparent to outsiders. In October 2015 we asked a random sample of journalists and former journalists from outside the global West what issues they believed journalism was confronting. Their list, in no priority order, was:

* Such fundamental changes in context (for example, the ending of apartheid in South Africa in 1994 and the collapse of the Soviet Union in central and eastern Europe from the 1980s) that journalism had effectively to be re-invented
* The precariousness of journalism in many places – from exposure to extreme physical danger to low pay and low status
* The (obvious) lack of relative freedom of expression in authoritarian states, and the normalization of this condition
* The struggle for indigenous voice and style
* Almost perpetual crises
* Trying to escape the 'coups and earthquakes' syndrome (an unwarranted focus on political violence and natural disasters) (see Chapter 4)
* Whether (mobile) digital technologies were liberating or disabling.

These apprehensions chimed with many of the issues preoccupying journalists in the global North – that the so-called 'business model' which has supported journalism through the mechanism of the modern mass media (both statal and commercial) was disintegrating; that substitutes provided insufficient resources, and that, as a consequence, journalism was increasingly a precarious occupation; that states with relatively positive records on freedom of expression were reversing their positions on this; that a curtailed journalism was focused on a narrowing agenda which excluded many voices; that digital technologies were severely disruptive of established practices. The difference appeared to lie in the extent and intensity of the difficulties journalists had, or perceived themselves to be facing, in pursuing the tenets of their occupation (see Davies, 2008; Henry, 2007; Jones, 2009).

This presumed, too, that what journalists did – which might be labelled as producing news – was more rather than less common across the world, and that what constituted *news* was also pretty much the same everywhere; that inherent in the idea of journalism was journalists' subscription globally to a collective sense of news values and newsworthiness, and that everyone else recognized news as broadly the same thing when they saw, heard or read it. Yet in many instances key media characteristics – whether newspapers, television, radio or the internet were the most important news media, and whether they were state or privately owned – varied. In circumstances where the material availability and apparent use of the media were different, was it possible to have a shared understanding of the role of journalism and journalists, and the concept of 'news'?

What supposedly provided commonality was an ideological commitment to (a belief in) a 'free press' – that the flow of news should be unhindered, and 'that our social, cultural and political life needs media communication that is not only accessible and intelligible but can be assessed for its reliability and provenance' which O'Neill (2012b) equated to 'good journalism'. Journalism, then, contributed towards the individual 'right of freedom of expression, thought and conscience' and the social 'responsiveness and accountability of governments to all citizens ... [by] providing a pluralist platform and channel of political expression for a multiplicity of groups and interests' (Norris, 2006, p. 2). The twentieth-century British editor C.P. Scott (1921, 1997) argued that journalism should be honest, untainted, courageous, dutiful and based in 'facts' which, he wrote, were 'sacred', providing citizens with objective and impartial news (Allan, 1997). In this way, journalism could contribute to the formation and maintenance of civil society and what Habermas (1989) called the 'public sphere' – an idealized space where private citizens could deliberate rationally, and independently of interest, on public matters. Perhaps the most succinct recent expression of this came from Kovach and Rosenstiel (2001, pp. 12–13):

- journalism's first obligation is to tell the truth
- journalism's first loyalty is to citizens
- the essence of journalism is a discipline of verification
- journalists must maintain an independence from those they cover
- journalists must serve as an independent monitor of power
- journalism must provide a forum for public criticism
- journalists must make the significant interesting and relevant
- journalists should keep the news in proportion and make it comprehensive
- journalists have an obligation to personal conscience

Theirs was a response to their understanding of the contemporary condition of journalism in the US – the challenging expansion of public relations; the accelerated pace of news production and consumption; the growth in media capacity which demanded more content and provided enhanced opportunities for imitation journalism; greater sensationalism; dumbing-down; a loss of journalism's mission, and a general decline in what they considered to be journalism's standards. Their agenda was a return to 'the old brands of journalism and the old journalistic norms' (Kovach & Rosenstiel, 1999, pp. 6–8, 2010, pp. 6–7). Many journalists themselves believed it was more difficult to practise 'quality journalism' (Cozma, 2012, p. 41).

Much of the way of thinking about journalism drew on practical experience – not just, as in this case, of journalists, who review and reflect on what they do, most usually among themselves in a form of 'shop talk', but also more widely of people in general on an everyday basis who have an interest in journalism and the news, and how these contribute to their lives. These are commonly more informal modes of analysis. From the 1960s in particular, more formal ways of analysing journalism developed in occupational review journals (*American Journalism Review, Australian Journalism Review, British Journalism Review, Columbia Journalism Review, Online Journalism Review, Pacific Journalism Review, Rhodes Journalism Review* and others), and reporting and commentary on journalism in the mainstream media.

There was often conflict between this way of analysing journalism and the more scholarly approaches of media, communication and cultural studies, resulting in extreme cases in 'media wars' (Turner, 2001). This was especially evident in what Hallin and Mancini identified as liberal countries, such as Australia and the UK. Elsewhere, this was much less the case (see Chapter 8). An alternative lay in 'integrating professional and academic knowledge … to bridge the gap between journalistic practice and theory' (Silverman, 2013). As more journalism programmes were introduced in higher education, employing more journalists with academic qualifications and producing more journalists who were graduates, so that more people had training and practice in both scholarship and journalism, the theory–practice divide appeared to be less stark (Bromley, 2013).

Liberal Theory – The Dominant Paradigm?

The liberal norm reflected a wider liberal theory, more specifically process-oriented democracy which was based in part on 'enlightened understanding' facilitated by freedom of expression and plural sources of information (Bühlmann & Kriesi, 2013, pp. 44–45). This form of democracy ideally guaranteed the right to ongoing public debate, transparency and accountability in which governance (historically, by the feudal estates of the monarchy/aristocracy, established religion and restricted commons) was held in check by the Fourth Estate to deliver on recognized (often 'natural') rights and liberties (see the following section). It could be seen in contrast to procedural democracy in which elections (the democratic procedure) led to majority rule with fewer checks and balances: once elected, a government could enact any laws it saw fit without having to abide by established rights and liberties, including denying free speech (Rawls, 2001). (The distinctions were not always that clear-cut, however.) What was expressed above, then, was a normative liberal theory of journalism (Craft & Davis, 2016), and liberal norms were increasingly presented as objects of global aspiration. This was the dominant global theory of journalism, explaining the way journalism ought to be everywhere. The promulgation of this view of journalism has been intimately tied to a global liberal democratization project as an indicator of a healthy democracy alongside such things as the rule of law, political equality, the operation of human rights and the establishment of NGOs, as well as free and fair elections. The World Trade Organization's (WTO) worldwide governance indicators included 'free media' (Greenidge et al., 2016, p. 21). The African Union was among the organizations which had adopted this objective of instituting these 'free media' (Kendo, 2010, p. 94). Hallin and Mancini (2004, p. 251) noted that the liberal norm had 'clearly become dominant … across much of the world'.

The Free Speech Debate, a research project of the Dahrendorf Programme for the Study of Freedom at St Antony's College, University of Oxford, UK, produced in 13 languages, claimed to reach out to dozens of countries across the world. Among its ten principles was journalism in a context of free expression (http://freespeechdebate.com/en – emphasis added):

- Lifeblood – We – all human beings – must be free and able to express ourselves, and to seek, receive and impart information and ideas, regardless of frontiers.
- Knowledge – We allow no taboos against and seize every chance for the spread of knowledge.
- *Journalism – We require uncensored, diverse, trustworthy media so we can make well-informed decisions and participate fully in political life.*
- Diversity – We express ourselves openly and with robust civility about all kinds of human difference.
- Privacy – We must be able to protect our privacy and to counter slurs on our reputations, but not prevent scrutiny that is in the public interest.
- Secrecy – We must be empowered to challenge all limits to freedom of information justified on such grounds as national security.
- Icebergs – We defend the internet and other systems of communication against illegitimate encroachments by both public and private powers.

Its leader, a historian who wrote a column for the London *Guardian* newspaper, argued:

> [T]here is a crying need for a global conversation engaging people, and not just governments, from east and west, north and south. Only by having this conversation, in a frank, open, well-informed way, can we discover what is – or could become – genuinely universal and what remains stubbornly local. ... The fact that freedom of expression first became effectively institutionalised, and protected by the rule of law, in the modern west, does not mean that it is a value alien to or incompatible with other cultures.
>
> ... the time has come to work towards a more genuinely universal universalism. One way to do that is to advance principles that we believe both should and can apply for all women and men everywhere, whatever their nationality, religion or cultural heritage – and then be open to revisions, challenges and alternatives. (Ash, n.d. b)

The Origins of Normative Liberal Theory

The notion of 'global journalism' was itself a product of theorization, and the most common way we have come to express the object of our interest in the early twenty-first century. It drew on the idea of globalization which suggested the integration of activities – including journalism – on a worldwide basis rather than in any nation-state or group of nation-states. A previous descriptor was 'international journalism' which captured a process of producing 'foreign news' (Williams, 2011, p. 1); that is, information originating somewhere other than the nation-state in which it was being disseminated (see Chapter 5). In turn, this distinction indicated multilateral relationships between nations. Many nation-states, especially in Western Europe, established or aspired to establish national broadcasting organizations, such as the BBC (Roosvall & Salovaara-Moring, 2010) and in some cases national news wire agencies (the Russian TASS and the Chinese Xinua agencies were examples), wholly or partially under public control, essentially to curate the national culture at an accessible and popular level. This applied both to making sense domestically of 'foreign' events and to communicating domestic events internally and to other nations. Based originally on short-wave transmissions, and established, maintained and (part-) funded by governments, external radio services had main carriage of parallel broadcasting of 'the nation' and national interpretations outside national boundaries (Price, 2001).

Newspapers played a slightly different, commonly more commercially driven, role (although some, mostly outside the global West, were formally sponsored by governments). Their characteristics were determined sometimes by their national geographical reach (the most well-known example of such national newspapers being those of the UK). However, some were identified more qualitatively as the carriers of legal, court and government notices, and thus newspapers of official (national) record. Others gained reputations (not always unchallenged) for publishing the most comprehensive and authoritative accounts of events – sometimes called 'newspapers of record' – thereby standing as a proxy for purveyors of this level of national culture (Martin & Hansen, 1998, pp. 7–8). Some published editions outside their domestic territories; the *Paris Herald*, an edition of the *New York Herald*, first appeared in 1887. Prior to the introduction of the international telegraphic cable in 1850, which carried news produced by the wire services chiefly for newspapers, not citizens directly, newspapers were physically shipped around the world both to be read and their items to be reproduced locally (Schwarzlose, 1973). Correspondents' letters from overseas were also carried by ship, and sometimes pigeon post (see Chapter 5). The introduction of the cable, followed by radio, facilitated the systemic internationalization of journalism, signified by the establishment of permanent foreign reporting services, and fuelled to a large extent by imperial and colonial communication imperatives – primarily those of the UK and the US which intersected (Bromley & Clarke, 2012; Bromley et al., 2015; Hamilton, 2012). Foreign correspondence contributed, therefore, to what has been described as 'the diffusion of the news paradigm' from initially the US to, first, the UK, then much of the rest of Europe, and eventually elsewhere, helping to establish 'professionalism' in journalism, centrally including the precept of objectivity, which was inherent in the liberal model (Schudson, 2013, p. 191).

This derived from the emergence of liberal democracies in Europe and North America in the early modern period. Freedom of speech and the freedom to petition were included in the English Bill of Rights of 1688. These were promoted as 'natural' rights arising out of the human condition, and not rights granted by states. The English poet John Milton (1644) identified 'the liberty to know, to utter and to argue freely' as the primary individual freedom of liberalism. Two centuries later the American journalist Frederick Douglass (1860) reinforced a key element of Milton's argument, that freedom of expression belonged both to the 'speaker' and the 'hearer'. At the same time, the English philosopher John Stuart Mill (1859, 1997) emphasized 'the liberty of thought and discussion'. Possibly, the best known expression of these liberties is the First Amendment to the US Constitution (1791): 'Congress shall make no law ... abridging the freedom of speech, or of the press; or the right of the people peaceably to assemble, and to petition the Government for a redress of grievances.' Subsequently, 'freedom of the press' has been widely interpreted as 'the right of newspapers, magazines, etc., to report news without being controlled by the government' (a definition taken from the online Merriam-Webster dictionary). However, the American journalist A.J. Liebling (1960) famously remarked: 'Freedom of the press is guaranteed only to those who own one.' It may be argued that the First Amendment, Milton, Mill and Douglass all referred rather to the means and acts of communication more widely; to journalism being less a one-way, one-to-many 'lecture', and 'more of a conversation or a seminar' with citizen participation (Gillmor, 2004, p. xxiv). The essential quality of journalism to liberal democracy was expressed by Thomas Jefferson (1787, 1903):

> The basis of our governments being the opinion of the people, the very first object should be to keep that right; and were it left to me to decide whether we should have a government without newspapers or newspapers without a government, I should not hesitate a moment to prefer the latter. But I should mean that every man should receive those papers and be capable of reading them.

The Liberal Model and its Discontents

At the extreme, accepting this normative theory, it would be wrong to describe as journalism mediated forms of news communication in countries such as China, Qatar or Singapore (the selection was made by Josephi (2005)) since the precondition of liberal democracy was not met in these places. It took 'media liberalization', replacing state control with private ownership, increasing popular access, reducing censorship, introducing pluralism and providing more platforms, to stimulate democratization and to be more democratic (Norris, 2006, p. 2). Allied to notions of 'the global village', first proposed by McLuhan (1962), it seemed that this project of seeding journalism across the world could lead to a universal democratic state. Moreover, the material bases of journalism (from the telegraph to the internet) connected the world physically. The conditions appeared to be present, then, for 'communication media ... [to] be used as a tool to transfer the political-economic model of the West to the growing independent societies of the South' (Matos, 2012, p. 1330). Democratization was to be accompanied by development. The Nobel Prize winning economist Amartya Sen (1999, pp. 7–8), linking 'political rights and economic performance', argued that 'no substantial famine has even occurred in any independent and democratic country with a relatively free press'.

This project faltered in a number of significant ways, however. First of all, communication power (along with other forms of power) lay with the West (and the industrialized North), resulting in severe imbalances of news flows (from the West/North to the rest), giving rise in the 1970s to the demand for a New World Information and Communication Order (NWICO) which would redress this; tackle media monopolies; develop journalistic capacity outside the West; transfer resources to 'developing countries'; and facilitate participation on the basis of cultural equality (UNESCO, 1980) (see Chapter 4). Second, the capacity of journalism to promote democracy could be captured by autocracies to 'reinforce crony capitalism' and consolidate inequitable political and economic power (Norris, 2006, p. 4). In poorly resourced countries dictators might encourage 'free media' as a way of hanging on to power by pressuring bureaucratic systems into improvements which artificially boosted their acceptability (Egorov et al., 2009). Finally, there was a growing discontent with the performance of journalism in its supposed heartland, the liberal democratic West and industrialized North, and the perceived failure to maintain 'an independent press system that monitors those in power and provides the necessary information to those without property … a commitment to the establishment of an independent largely non-commercial media sector' (McChesney, 2014).

During the 1980s many state-sponsored public service broadcasting (PSB) corporations were further liberalized, chiefly through the mechanism of deregulation and the ending of PSB monopolies, privileging instead 'market forces' in determining whether alternative, privately owned stations replaced them wholly or in part (O'Malley, 2001; Turner, 2001; Williams, 2001). What resulted was a struggle between differing liberal views – on the one hand, a commitment to what the BBC called 'journalism of impartiality and authority' and, on the other hand, the media as enterprises which had to produce popular journalism to remain in business. This led to a renewal of a debate which had begun at least 90 years earlier about whether the role of journalism was to attract as large an audience as possible by providing what was in demand to ensure the widest dissemination, or to 'tell it like it is' irrespective of how it might be received; and could the two approaches be reconciled? (Holland, 2001, pp. 81–82).

By the second decade of the twenty-first century there was a strongly held view that commercialism, driven by the industrialized North, had triumphed. In 2015, *Forbes* listed eight US and two UK companies as the world's largest media organizations: between them they owned many of the major news providers. The five largest newspaper companies were also exclusively American and British, controlling broadcasting as well as print outlets. However, this concentration of ownership was felt most acutely within Western and Northern countries. It was estimated that 90 per cent of US media were controlled by the 'big six' corporations (see www.frugaldad.com). Australia was calculated to have 'one of the most concentrated media environments in the western world' (Phillips, 2015b). Concentration in the UK was tracked by a Media Reform Coalition (2014). There were also concerns in Sweden, Germany and Canada. One of the harshest critics, the Australian-British journalist John Pilger (2007), argued: 'Liberal democracy is moving toward a form of corporate dictatorship.'

Arguably the two most egregious examples of the failure of the Western democratic model were the merging of media ownership and control and politics in Italy by Silvio Berlusconi which resulted in 2001 in his government overseeing both the PSB Rai and his own Mediaset corporation which together accounted for 90 per cent of television viewing in the country (Dohnanyi, 2003, pp. 187–88; Pavli, 2010), and the so-called hackgate scandal in the UK, in which journalists working for Rupert Murdoch's *News of the World* newspaper were able systematically and illegally to tap into people's telephone voicemails while the authorities failed to intervene, largely, it was said, because politicians, the police, regulators and others feared Murdoch's power and cosied up to him (Davies, 2014). One of the most notable critiques of the liberal model has been the alternative 'propaganda model' proposed by Herman and Chomsky (1988) which suggested that the media in the global West and North, partially through ownership and the drive to be profitable, promoted the interests of the powerful, marginalizing opposing views.

Pluralism

The Council of Europe adopted 'a string of resolutions' addressing the control of media concentration, and has a working definition of the condition which it has positioned in opposition to ideals of pluralism (defined as 'the scope for a wide range of social, political and cultural values, opinions, information and interests to find expression through the media' (Dohnanyi, 2003, p. 27)). The European (Union) Commission has supported an ongoing media pluralism monitoring project since 2009. It based its assessment of pluralism within Europe's media on four criteria – basic conditions, such as freedom of speech, independent regulation and media literacy levels; concentration of ownership and control; media types and genres; political, cultural and geographical bias (http://cmpf.eui.eu/media-pluralism-monitor).

Nevertheless, at the same time, the dismantling of the previous dominant and protected state-sponsored public service (broadcast) media has been far from complete or uniform (Williams, 2001). In the UK, notwithstanding a concerted onslaught originating in the governments of Margaret Thatcher, the BBC remained into the second decade of the twenty-first century the largest single media 'voice' in the country with what many claimed was 'an unfair advantage' and a distorting 'effect on audience share in a way that undermines commercial business models'; creating damage to 'a wide range of players'; 'crowding out commercial competition' and reducing user choice at a time when more than 200 newspapers closed at the cost of up to 60 per cent of jobs in local journalism (Bromley, 2003; News Media Association, 2015). In Australia, too, the presence of the publicly funded Australian Broadcasting Corporation (ABC(Aus)) drew criticism for supposed incursions into the commercial market (Meade, 2016). On the other hand, elsewhere, to protect and promote pluralism, states, including Austria, Finland, France, Italy, Luxembourg, Netherlands, Norway, Portugal, Spain and Sweden, provided direct subsidies to the press as a counter to the vagaries of market forces, and many others supported commercial media with indirect financial support (Schweizer et al., 2014). As already indicated in Chapter 2, Hallin and Mancini (2004) proposed that the Western liberal democratic model had at least three variants, each with permeable boundaries – the north Atlantic which was perhaps closest to the liberal norm and found in so-called Anglo-Saxon countries, such as the US, the UK, Ireland, Australia, Canada and New Zealand; the polarized pluralist, characterized by partisan journalism and low levels of regulation, evident in southern Europe; and, somewhere between the two, the democratic corporatist, more common in social democratic northern and central Europe with partisanship moderated by journalism 'professionalism' and by state intervention. They also allowed for 'mixed' models (Hallin & Mancini, 2012, p. 4).

Cutting across these variables were theories concerned with the efficacy of democratic institutions: was democracy best assured through representation or participation? This had implications for journalism and, roughly speaking, mapped on to the 'quality'/tabloid news divide. On the one hand, it was argued that the overwhelming majority of citizens did not have the capacity to make informed decisions on the complex and difficult task of attending to matters of governance; even if they did, it would distract them from making other essential social contributions, and involving so many people would render decision-making too cumbersome and the outcomes too unpredictable. Therefore, democracies were best run by responsible, technically capable, expert elites who competed for popular support through proposals for policy. Journalists could play two roles – as publicists and amplifiers of competing ideas, and as specialists themselves, holding elites to account through quality, watchdog journalism. On the other hand, citizen participation was seen as a guarantee against elite domination, and the role of journalists was to engage publics directly and as widely as possible with popular forms of journalism which could stimulate interest in and understanding of complex issues. This would also overcome tendencies to exclude sections of the public, such as women, ethnic and other minorities, and disabled and young people. From the 1970s neo-liberals contended that popularity was most effectively measured by market success; the larger the readership, viewership or listenership, the more participation-oriented the journalism (Benson, 2008; Christiano, 2015). This division over the primacy of quality or quantity lay behind what has become known as the Lippmann-Dewey debate in the US in the 1920s, and has been influential in theorizing journalism (Schudson, 2008; Whipple, 2005).

It appeared clear, then, that this Western norm was neither monolithic nor wholly successful. Journalism practice did not always – indeed, perhaps only infrequently – align with theory.

> In practice, most people on this planet are still informed and influenced by a limited range of media … Both private and public powers shape and limit what we receive and impart: be they the state, telecommunications companies, Ayatollahs in Iran, Silvio Berlusconi in Italy or Rupert Murdoch in Britain. (Ash, n.d. a)

Other Norms

Benson (2008, p. 2592) noted: 'In principle, there are as many normative theories of journalism as there are political systems.' To that we should perhaps add social, economic and cultural contexts and history, giving rise to theorizations of journalism drawing on geo-cultural, historical and social contingencies, as well as political and economic systems (Blum, 2005; Hardy, 2014; Mellado & Lagos, 2013). Given the amount of attention paid to the democratic norm, it has been tempting to set all other norms in opposition (and to imply, if not make manifest, their inferiority). In an early work two democratic variants (libertarian and social responsibility) were set straightforwardly against two undemocratic ones (authoritarian and Soviet Communist) (Siebert et al., 1956). Voltmer (2008), however, called for a more differentiated understanding of variations across non-democratic systems which influenced the democratization project. Blum (2005) added three further categories to the tripartite analysis of Hallin and Mancini based on geo-cultural contexts – eastern Europe, the Arab region and Asia/Caribbean. Others have proposed normative theories arising out of post-totalitarianism, sultanism, post-colonialism, post-communism, development, and transitioning, emerging and new democracies, as well as mixed (hybrid) situations (Hardy, 2010; Mellado & Lagos, 2013; Voltmer, 2013). Voltmer (2013) sub-divided dictatorships and one-party states alone into four distinct categories – military dictatorships/juntas (these have existed in the past and up to the present in Fiji, Pakistan and Mauritania); communism (People's Republic of China, North Korea); one-party domination (Syria); and personality dictators (Robert Mugabe in Zimbabwe). Furthermore, it may be more pertinent in some conditions to consider traditional, customary and informal practices and contexts (Scott & Mcloughlin, 2014). Finally, such nation-state situations have themselves been impacted by 'the breaking down of borders, both geographical and industrial … global and converging changes' (Mastrini & Becerra, 2011, p. 59).

Given the wide range of operative political systems and potential theoretical norms, there may be an argument for abandoning normative theory altogether as practically meaningless. However, Benson (2008) has argued that all such theories help identify the complexities of journalism as it is conceived and practised in an almost endless diversity of contexts. These contexts have been most commonly presented under broad headings, each suggesting a degree of state monopoly on news:

- *Authoritarian* – journalism is supervised by the state and its agencies, including prohibitions on news which is believed to counter the state's position. No criticism of government is allowed. Journalism is required to support the status quo and government policies. This does not necessarily involve prior censorship but *post facto* punishment which tends to encourage self-censorship.
- *Development* – journalistic freedom is subordinated to development and nation building. It was originally envisaged that journalism would help populations understand processes of development by presenting them in accessible ways and aiding empowerment (a more participatory model). Subsequently, the idea became more associated with nation building and journalists as 'government partners' (Romano, 2005, pp. 1–10).

* *Totalitarian* – in communist, fascist, and Islamist and other theocratic states journalists are regarded as servants of 'the people' (that is, the state which represents 'the people'). Journalism is seen as a tool for eliminating 'wrong' thinking and facilitating emancipation. Nevertheless, this most often includes 'fierce state censorship' (Mellor, 2011, p. 3).

What linked these models was a shared set of objectives – among them, 'forging national unity and national identity; development, however it was defined; and additionally for the more radical … states, supporting the anti-colonial struggles elsewhere' (Karikari, 2007, pp. 13–15). Media systems (especially broadcasting monopolies) were commonly inherited from the colonial and imperial powers and their control passed more or less seamlessly to the new states, or were taken over and often nationalized (Karikari, 2007).

Many of the contextual (political) concepts which supposedly gave rise to journalism models are both 'semantically vague and ideologically contested' (Postoutenko, 2010, p. 11). Similarly, those models are not 'neatly definable, uniform and uncontested' (Romano, 2005, p. 9). Moreover, many places straddle more than one 'system'. Journalists in Asia have had to negotiate global and transnational impulses and 'current Asian experiences' (Romano & Bromley, 2005, p. xi). Arab journalists have served as a '"bridge" between their native culture and Western culture' (Mellor, 2011, p. 45). In the South Pacific, journalism 'struggles to find new connections and relational possibilities on a more equal footing' (Papoutsaki & Harris, 2008, p. 1). Consequently, much journalism is a hybrid of multiple norms (Masterton, 1996), albeit often under the burden of a 'deep-rooted culture of dependency on neo-colonial relationships' (Papoutsaki & Harris 2008, p. 1).

Norms vs Contexts and Traditions

Political, social, economic, cultural and historical realities on the ground shape journalism practices and often render the normative Western liberal 'watchdog' model inappropriate (Romano, 2005, p. 14). Robie (2005, p. 102) has written of 'a collision of media models, culture and values' which manifests itself differently in geographical and cultural neighbours. In much of the post-imperial and post-colonial world – Asia, Africa, Latin America – modern states were constructed by imperial and colonial powers out of sometimes quite arbitrary multiple cultures. In such circumstances, journalism's primary aim was not to act as the Fourth Estate: in Asia one noted editor argued that journalists are still voluntary members of what might be called the national system. If they repudiate the government's concerns – as some do – it is only because they align themselves with the opposition. Not because they have taken up a position outside the political process. No Asian media can afford to ignore the consequences of thoughtless reporting on religious or ethnic harmony, necessary economy plans, fragile institutions of state, or political stability. (cited Menon, 1996)

Case Study 3.1: 'Good news' in Grenada

In 1979 the Marxist New Jewel Movement (NJM) assumed power in a coup in Grenada, a former British possession in the Caribbean, and established the People's Revolutionary Government (PRG) (Williams, 2007). The Cuban leader Fidel Castro called this 'a big revolution in a small country' (Puri, 2014). Under the previous Grenadian 'authoritarian and dictatorial' prime minister Eric Gairy, Grenadians had 'developed an instinct not to talk to the press'. Gairy 'threatened media right and left', and journalists were publicly disparaged. In the 1970s legislation was used to curtail press freedom. The Gairy government effectively banned the *Torchlight* newspaper, and people who bought *Vanguard* felt compelled to hide their purchases. Vendors selling *New Jewel* were arrested and it was an offence to buy or read the paper. The Grenadian arm of the Windward Islands Broadcasting Service (WIBS) was under government control. Even so, prior to 1979 newspapers, newsletters and journals circulated freely; radio and television broadcasts were received, although the introduction of a Newspaper (Amendment) Act in 1975 reduced the number of newspapers in circulation from 17 to six. These were produced both within Grenada and outside, in other Caribbean countries, the UK and the US (Hopkin, 2014; Wilder, 2016).

The PRG produced a ten-point platform for government. Item 5 included government accountability and 'free speech'. In 'a people's revolution', it was asserted, there was 'the right to democratic participation' (cited Hopkin, 2014). Initially, the PRG allowed the continued importation of newspapers and magazines from the US (*Time, Newsweek, US News and World Report*) and other Caribbean countries (*Trinidad Express, Jamaica Gleaner, Barbados Advocate*). The Associated Press stationed a correspondent on the main island. More than 50 per cent of Grenadians got their news from radio through Radio Guardian of Trinidad and the WIBS. By the middle of 1981, however, the PRG had 'established media control'. It owned the major newspaper, the *Free West Indian*, the sole local television and radio stations, Television Free Grenada and Radio Free Grenada, as well as a publishing house. The media were 'firmly government controlled' with the Government Information Service dictating what was news (Williams, 2007, p. 64). The PRG followed Gairy in not just banning but formally closing down *Torchlight* in 1979 (Williams, 2007). Journalists and others associated with the media were detained, often without charge or proper trial (Wilder, 2016). At the core of this effort was an attempt to disseminate 'good news' about Grenada and its government. The PRG was concerned to redress what it saw and the effects of colonialism and incursions of external media (regional, colonial and global), particularly the BBC. Maurice Bishop, the PRG leader, said in 1981:

> We find that the national information and communications system that we have is only slightly developed, or just beginning to develop. That is true of most of our country. We find, secondly, that we have to depend almost completely on the imperialist trans-national information monopolies and communication companies which operate on a large scale and control the flow of information ... We find that the contents of the information circulated by the western mass media in developing countries is one-sided – they distort realities and they neglect our national interest. (cited Wilder, 2016)

Wilder's (2016) analysis was:

> To the fledgling People's Revolutionary Government (PRG) it looked as if they were only trying to do good for the country, hoe a new path, and lead Grenada on the road forward. Raising people's consciousness and knowledge, and how to bring about change in a revolutionary way, was one top priority.

In this instance, there was, using Robie's term, a 'collision' of normative theories about the role of journalism – Western (liberal); authoritarian; development; post-colonial and Marxist-Leninist – and what role journalists ought to play in a national context embedded in impinging wider regional and global environments. One aspect, however, is clearly missing: the view of the users of the media. In the end, Wilder (2016) argues, a continual steam of government 'good news' lost any attraction it may have had and became 'boring and irrelevant'. The theorist C.B. Macpherson (1977) has argued that, even within societies which value equality, inequalities will continue to exist if they command popular support.

Normative theories of journalism, therefore, may be most useful as heuristic tools providing a basic outline of practical societal expectations rather than as abstract prescriptions for journalism's role.

Taking up the suggestion made by Scott and Mcloughlin (2014), noted before, it is as well to remember that models of journalism can also be determined by tradition. Robie (2005, pp. 104–06) proposed a 'four worlds' schema which accounted for the (Western) first world with its liberal norm; the communist second world with a 'collective agitator' model; a third world with a national building norm, and a fourth world, comprised of first nations, in which the model for journalism is in support of language, education, culture, 'solidarity' and 'voice'. Here, too, 'there can be a constant tension between traditional processes of discussion and decision-making and ...

"modernising" constraints' (Molnar & Meadows, 2001, p. xii). In Canada, native journalists have been criticized for trying to imitate 'white' practices (Molnar & Meadows, 2001, pp. 156–57). The kind of news communication associated with modern journalism was often undertaken, at least in part, by 'traditional storytellers, orators and messengers', but often acting on behalf of a traditional leader (Hayes, 2005, p. 261). The concept of 'news' did not always translate (Molnar & Meadows, 2001, p. 176). Contemporary journalists in the Pacific state of Tuvalu are called *Tino Tusitala* ('person who writes stories or tales') (Hayes, 2005, pp. 260–61). Rather than simply importing Western journalism norms to Tuvalu, they are 'central and essential parts of their respective cultures and societies' (Hayes, 2005, p. 270). In China the supplanting of 'propaganda and class-oriented' Communist Party journalism theory with Western (liberal) theory, drawing mainly on norms, tended towards the supposition of a 'one-way process of modernization' which elided China's specific historical and cultural experiences, notwithstanding its formal adoption of neo-liberalism (Hu & Ji, 2013, pp. 6, 10).

Beyond Norms – Towards Understanding Journalism as it is, Not as it Should Be

The limitations of normative theories open the possibility of alternative theoretical explanations. McQuail (2010), Steensen and Ahva (2014) and Zelizer (2004) noted that scholarship had addressed journalism through the prisms of a wide range of academic fields and disciplines – history, political science, psychology, cultural studies, economics, sociology, linguistics, ethnography, law, technology, philosophy. In doing so, scholars have engaged with a range of theoretical approaches such as political economy, Marxism, technological determinism, feminism, structural functionalism, post-structuralism, postmodernism. These lead analyses away from a simple examination of what journalists do, or ought to do, towards a critical, analytical understanding of journalism as it is (Smythe & Van Dinh, 1983, p. 123). Theories have been applied to who journalists are; how journalism identities are formed; how journalists work; how they determine what 'news' is; how they construct news (stories and reports); and how news is received and used (Neff, 2015, p. 75). Most of these studies have been confined to individual journalists, news settings and national domains, particularly in the global West, although Josephi (2005) recognized studies undertaken in Nepal, China, Tanzania and Uganda. Mellor (2010) noted the restricted socio-economic theoretical repertoire of Arab researchers. Papoutsaki and Harris (2005, p. 3) also regretted the absence of 'a sustainable internal research culture from within that reflects local epistemological frameworks'. The WoJ study tracked journalism cultures, influences and trust in 67 countries although its organizing orientation is methodological rather than theoretical (www.worldsofjournalism.org). Singer (2004) found that few, if any, new theories about journalism had been produced over a period of two decades. Moreover, the nature of the field of journalism studies is that it has embraced 'a multitude of theoretical perspectives' (Steensen & Ahva, 2014, p. 3).

McQuail (2010) suggested broad non-normative categories of theorization of journalism – the structural, the behavioural and the cultural:

* *Structural* theory tended to be socio-centric, examining journalism in wider society, 'the exercise of power', the economy and the social, and the formation of policy; for example, how the ownership and control of media shaped journalism performance.
* *Behavioural* theory addressed individual and collective decision-making, choosing and processing; for example, how journalists decided what was news.
* *Cultural* theory explored meaning and the making of meaning; for example, whether journalists' understandings of news align with those of other groups.

International to Transnational Journalism

International news was a product of journalism located in nation-states even if it addressed extra-territorial populations. Transnational journalism became noticeable in the 1980s with journalists producing news in more than one country; that news being disseminated in more than one country; and news organizations being based in more than one country. This development was particularly associated with the introduction of cable and satellite broadcasting. However, print media also had transnational characteristics; for example, while Rupert Murdoch's newspapers (the London *Times, New York Post, The Australian*) were produced and circulated in hard copies in their respective locations, exchanges of content occurred among them with the work of journalists in Australia, the US and the UK appearing in print in other countries. Thus journalism in the precursors of what in 2016 was News Corp operated at a national level but also across national boundaries. Similarly, newspapers began publishing editions and operating editorial offices outside the nation-state: the *Wall Street Journal Asia*, founded in 1976, was eventually printed in nine Asian cities with a regional office in Hong Kong. The London *Financial Times Deutschland*, launched in 2000, had an editorial office in Hamburg. Cable and satellite broadcasting allowed transnational journalism to occur more immediately. CNN, the first 24/7 news channel, broadcast to the US and Canada and, through its associated network, CNN International, to most countries using studios in London, Mumbai, Hong Kong and Abu Dhabi. The Al Jazeera channels operated at various times from bases in Doha, London, Sarajevo, Washington and Kuala Lumpur broadcasting in Arabic, English, Bosnian, Serbian, Croatian and Turkish.

Two examples of transnational journalism stood out. In the Arab region, media (especially satellite television) were seen as mechanisms for asserting 'cultural and intellectual' influence, promoting image and establishing regional primacy. Apparently free from state control, whether based in Lebanon, Dubai, Egypt, Saudi Arabia or Qatar, they aimed to attract viewers from across the region. Kraidy (2000, pp. 1–2) argued that 'transnational Arab broadcasting holds the promise of integrating Arab nations in a cultural regionalism'. Adopting the theory of 'asymmetrical interdependence', transnational journalism provided a way for smaller nations to avoid the domination of larger ones. The European Journalism Centre has focused on bringing European journalists together and addressing pan-European issues (http://ejc.net/about/mission_statement). The European Journalism Training Association primarily works to the 1999 pan-European Bologna Declaration creating a European higher education area (www.ejta.eu/introduction). However, whether the concept of asymmetrical interdependence could be applied to these European activities remained moot. They tended to be dominated by Western EU member states such as Belgium, Germany, Netherlands and the UK with smaller nations on the periphery. It was possible for news from more dominant nation-states to reinforce its traditional role as news for the whole world (a theme taken up in the next chapter). Nevertheless, journalists could act as 'bridges' between their national culture and other cultures (Mellor, 2011, p. 45). What Billig (1995) called 'banal nationalism' – that is, the everyday reference to symbols and tropes of nation-state identities – was perhaps being replaced by 'banal cosmopolitanism' in which those references were global rather than national (Beck et al., 2003, pp. 21–22; Mellor, 2011, p. 147). In such conditions, 'the terms "foreign" and "domestic" journalism are rapidly becoming obsolete' (Volkmer, 2002, p. 242).

Globalization and Digitization

Beck et al. (2003, p. 21) described cosmopolitanism as 'inner globalization'. Theories of the process of globalization suggested, on the one hand, that journalism and news were becoming more homogenized across the world particularly under the Western model, as referred to above; while, on the other hand, the importance of localized cultures, social norms, political structures and economic circumstances in shaping distinctive forms of journalism (many journalisms) was reinforced by their affordances. It was difficult to reconcile the two (Hu & Ji, 2013). One way in which the relationship of the global and the local has been theorized is through the concept of *glocalism*. 'Globalization does not mean that Western … ideas and values merely sweep over the rest of the world' (Wasserman, 2006). Global forces and trends may be adopted and adapted (not necessarily rejected) in response to local conditions to take on new hybrid forms. Taking journalism ethics as an example, Wasserman (2006) noted that African journalists recast Western ideals such as objectivity and neutrality into a more communitarian Africanist approach.

In practice, it became more problematical to determine who was a journalist – the Western 'professional' or just anyone? After all, the right to free speech, as noted above, belonged to everyone. Or should the focus be not on journalists but on the processes of journalism – how journalism, the artefact, was made accounting for all the contributions, human, technological, organizational, using actor-network theory (Primo & Zago, 2015)? Technologies, also mentioned above, which facilitated the internationalization of journalism have promoted its globalization through the 'global connectivity' of digitization. Journalism may be seen as less the production of content for various media, and more as the workings of nodes in networks of actors, citizens as well as professionals; social media as well as legacy media; YouTube as well as CNN (Reese, 2016). Consequently, Reese (2016) argued that past theoretical approaches were no longer as applicable.

Social network theory explored the connections and relationships between people and organizations (nodes). These may be ego-centric (arrayed around one person or organization (node), such as a journalist networking with her/his contacts; socio-centric (within a bounded environment such as journalists (nodes) in a newsroom), or open (outside a bounded environment; for example, the ways in which journalists (nodes) interacted with citizens producing so-called user-generated content (nodes)). Open connections and relationships might transcend or supplant ego- and socio-centric networks, leading to new spatial arrangements; for example, journalists networking with citizens rather than within news organizations. This may be seen as a manifestation of a 'global cultural economy' in which *scapes* (fluid, unstable, multi-directional networks without centres or peripheries) (Appadurai, 1990) captured the ways in which culture flowed and contra-flowed almost anarchically. The suggestion was that journalism, the structured profession, may be morphing into a journoscape.

Conversely, Sassen (1991) proposed that an escalating complexity in networks demanded controlling nodes where the simultaneous dispersal and integration of activities could be coordinated. In defining 'the network society' (social networks using digital technologies) Castells (2004, p. 3) raised the possibility of the role of journalists being either more exclusive or more inclusive. One unresolved question, therefore, was whether global journalism represented the corporate dominance of global media and the presentation of the neo-liberal agenda, based on consumerism rather than citizenship, or contributed to an expanded global public sphere, even if inadvertently; for example, by bringing a 'watchdog' approach which exposed human rights violations (Murphy, 2003, pp. 62–63).

Finally, the very ideas of the global and of global journalism were shaped and framed by journalism itself through the selection, prioritization and presentation of certain topics; for example, climate change, or Islamism, or war. Fishman (1980, p. 51) noted how 'the world is bureaucratically organized for journalists' by which those seeking positive interaction with journalists structured their activities to suit the journalists, the most obvious examples being collaborating with deadlines and providing broadcastable sound bites. On a larger scale, 'mediatization' has been used to describe

> the process whereby society to an increasing degree is submitted to, or becomes dependent on, the media and their logic. This process is characterized by a duality in that the media have become integrated into the operations of other social institutions, while they also have acquired the status of social institutions in their own right. As a consequence, social interaction – within the respective institutions, between institutions, and in society at large – take place via the media. (Hjarvard, 2008, p. 113)

Within processes of mediatization (which address all media) has the role of journalists in 'intervening into ... social interaction' given rise to a parallel *journalization* specific to news media (Hjarvard, 2008, p. 120)? Insofar as journalism constructs shared experiences, has global journalism contributed to a more global sense of identity and community (Hjarvard, 2008, p. 126)? Benedict Anderson (2006, p. 36) argued that the newspaper (medium) reassured its reader (audience member) of the everyday anchorage of the imagined national community in that the act of accessing the artefact itself could be imagined as a shared activity which connected people otherwise unknown to each other. Such imaginings, however, may not be constructed around the physical nation-state alone but around interests with little or no territorial reference; for example, the presentation of sport (broadcasts of English Premier League games around the world, some of which are not shown 'live' in the UK) may create similar feelings of sharing a global journalized experience (Blackshaw, 2013, pp. 29–30).

Summary

Auditing scholarly output on journalism in English language journals in the twenty-first century, Steensen and Ahva (2016) noted a shift in theorization from political science (using terms such as 'democracy') to sociology, and a greater acknowledgement of theorization. This perhaps reflected the declining salience of especially Western liberal normative theories to critically understanding journalism. What was once an apparently relatively straightforward theoretical project of aligning journalism with democracy was now far more complex. Steensen and Ahva (2016) counted more than a hundred different theories in use. As journalism, as a modern concept, became more global it necessarily interacted with multiple contexts and their social, cultural, economic and historical, as well as political, specificities. These included diasporic and migrant conditions. At one level, it was projected that such disparities would lead to shared mediated experiences which made sense across geo-political boundaries in particular, facilitated by digital communication capacity. Satellite television and the internet especially allowed the flow of the same journalistic content – the same news – globally leading to less direct reference to nation-states. Migration, climate change, terrorism, sport, religion were among the contemporary topics of journalism with inherently global dimensions of interest to 'the global village'. The same global journalism, however, also reinforced local identities by addressing both domestic and diasporic communities on shared levels; for example, Shavit (2009, p. 2) traced the formation of an extra-territorial 'religious-political global Muslim nation' with a large migrant presence. Nevertheless, much journalism remained oriented primarily to the nation-state. Hafez (2009, p. 2) reckoned that 'what we call "global news" is but a tip of the iceberg of all … news produced daily around the world', the vast bulk of which is never seen outside the nation-state in which it is produced. Moreover, 'what is left – the very tiny global news agenda – is regularly framed according to home-grown narratives' (Hafez, 2009, p. 2). Thus it seemed imperative not to confuse global with universal, or to assume that the news was the same everywhere.

A cursory glance at up to 1,000 newspaper front pages from around 80 countries posted online daily by the Newseum in Washington, DC (www.newseum.org) reveals a wide diversity of news values, even on dates deemed to be of 'historical significance'. These provide a litmus test of what constitutes global news in practice and whether the world's press reaches a consensus on the main news of the day. What makes a front page appears still to be more often than not shaped by assumptions of form and content based in the culture of the nation-state (Schudson, 1996).

As journalism has become global, it has had to challenge these assumptions to assert different, less ethnocentric, less Western news values. If that is indeed the project under way, then examining it theoretically can help with assessing its success or failure if only because immediate practical concerns in specific contexts are not necessarily applicable everywhere. Global journalism invites more systematic analysis, independent of, but sympathetic to, particular cultural concerns. At the same time, journalism, as both practice and content, leaves evidential traces (data). People discuss 'the news' and the performance of journalists on an everyday basis. Journalists themselves reflect and comment on their own occupation. More often than not, these activities concern practical matters. Insofar as non-normative theories, clustered around the structural, behavioural and cultural, aim to address similar issues, such as those introduced above, of how the ownership and control of media shape journalism performance; how journalists decide what is news, and whether journalists' understandings of news align with those of others in society, the practical experiences of journalists and users of journalism provide evidence on which to base more abstract analyses, suggesting a stronger connection between practice and theory than is often allowed.

Further Reading

1. Christians, C.G., Glasser, T.L., McQuail, D., Nordenstreng, K. & White, R.A. (2009) *Normative Theories of the Media: Journalism in Democratic Societies* (Champaign, IL: University of Illinois Press).
2. Deuze, M. (2005) 'What is journalism? Professional identity and ideology of journalists reconsidered', *Journalism* 6(4), 442–64.

3. Josephi, B. (2005) 'Journalism in the global age', *Gazette: The International Journal for Communication Studies* 67(6), 575–90.

4. Steensen, S. & Ahva, L. (2015) 'Theories of journalism in a digital age', *Journalism Practice* 9(1), 1–18.

5. Williams, K. (2003) *Understanding Media Theory* (London: Arnold).

6. Zelizer, B. (2004) *Taking Journalism Seriously: News and the Academy* (Thousand Oaks, CA: Sage).

4

Global Journalism Flows and Contra-Flows

Chapter overview

This chapter examines how news flows around the world, and the impact digitized communications have had on disrupting the flow and facilitating contra-flows. The dominant flow of news has been from the global North to the global South. The major Northern media, particularly 'big' global media, such as the BBC and CNN, have the capacity, built on the size of their operations, their wealth and their political connections, to distribute their versions of news to the rest of the world. Contra-flow is used to describe the dissemination of news originating outside these 'big' media, particularly in the global South, which reaches a global audience. For 40 years debate has centred on how to ensure more global plurality, equity and diversity in news without sacrificing freedom of expression, and to strike a balance between the global and the local. The chapter asks whether digitization has aided this process by making it easier to access a diversity of sources of news, or has undermined the reliability of news by allowing anyone to make and distribute it through mechanisms such as social media.

Learning outcomes

After having read this chapter you will be able to:

1. Track news flows and contra-flows globally and locally
2. Determine the role of news in flows and contra-flows of information
3. Evaluate the roles of the printed press, broadcasting and the internet in the flows and contra-flows of news.

In the second decade of the twenty-first century, an apparently increasingly connected world was still divided in many ways. From the 1980s there was a growing concern in particular about the division globally between information wealth and information poverty. The issue became associated with the concept of the digital divide – that some people benefited from the accelerating availability, reach and power of digitally based ICTs, while others were excluded. The foundation for this was existing conditions. Globally, information wealth and poverty were seen chiefly as functions of the divisions between the economically rich (the industrialized global North) and the economically poor (the developing global South); between elites (those with high levels of other forms of capital, too) and the disadvantaged (those with low levels of such capital), and between societies ideologically committed to free flows of information (the global liberal democratic West) and those which were not (chiefly classified as authoritarian). This last relationship reflected prior existing free and constrained flows of information and the parallel patchy development of the 'right to know' as a global project driven primarily by the West. 'Freedom of information is an idea and a global crusade', a former editor of *The Guardian* (London) opined: 'a democratic gift to the world' (Preston, 2015, p. 3). However, at the same time, states transitioning from communism and other forms of autocracy were doing so at different speeds, on different trajectories and with different proposed end-points.

Consequently, while it is more or less commonly assumed that economic, social, cultural and political advantage, based in a vibrant enfranchised civil society and capitalist enterprise albeit with degrees of state intervention, and usually described as 'liberal democracy', indicates freer information flows, not every democratizing state always maintains that objective. The prime exemplar of the liberal free flow of information was the 1791 First Amendment to the US Constitution, although, as already noted, Sweden passed the first FoI law in 1766. In 1951 Finland enacted an access to information law; in 1966 the US Congress passed an FoI Act. In 2014 Paraguay became the hundredth nation to enact FoI (McIntosh, 2014; Mendel, 2008). The free flow of information depended on the three acts of seeking, receiving and imparting information and ideas (Article 19 of the Universal Declaration of Human Rights, cited Felle, 2015). The centrality of the modern mass media to building and maintaining such free flows of information is widely recognized (Carlsson, 2016).

Information provided via these media was shaped in part, and crucially, by journalism in the form of the broad category of news. It was self-evident that the increase in communication capacity offered through the application of digital technologies, especially after the introduction from about 2002 of

Web 2.0 which facilitated user-generated content and social media, could lead to a greater creation and diffusion of journalism, representing a step change in the free flow of information. Passive recipients of news produced by journalists working for media institutions offering top-down, one-to-many transmission of a relatively scarce resource – even using the more static Web 1.0 from the mid-1990s – could be transformed into co-producers of that news in peer-to-peer multi-dimensional digital networks of plenty, thereby enhancing the democracy which valued and relied on the free flow of information. Gillmor (2004) wrote about 'grassroots journalism by the people for the people'. The term *produsage* was devised by Bruns (2007) to describe this new arrangement.

Evidence of the diffusion of information wealth and power resulting in freer flows of news was supposedly seen in the Arab Spring anti-authoritarian protests and demands for reform in 2010–11 during which groups and individuals without access to orthodox national media used both social media and digital links to Western media to 'report' on their countries (Howard et al., 2011, pp. 2–3). Similarly, the pro-democracy Green Movement in Iran in 2009 used social media to circumvent censorship and government restrictions on the free flow of information and to bring their protests to global attention (Lanzillo, 2011). In South Korea a student movement of the 1980s protesting against restraints on the flow of news by an institutional press supposedly too tied to the country's ruling elite turned to digital ITCs, and from 1999 citizen journalism through the site OhmyNews (Bromley, 2010; see Chapter 6 as well). In these cases web-based communications were utilized to help galvanize and organize the populations, supplementing (perhaps rendering more effective and more accessible) existing traditional communications. Globally, some of the people who historically had been informed but unable to express themselves were gaining voices, while those who had been kept uninformed were becoming informed, sometimes by informing themselves, and digital ICTs were aiding the process.

However, there was also the threat that both the informed and uninformed would be mis-informed, and, at the extreme, dis-informed, as controls over the supply of news weakened. News as a resource produced by journalists within media institutions might be supplanted by gossip, rumour, propaganda, lies and just nonsense posing as news as ICTs provided 'new ways to mislead' (Carlsson, 2016, p. 13; Gillmor, 2004, p. 177). Opinions were divided over whether the new produser arrangement delivered the wisdom of crowds (the efficacy of the average of independent judgements of a collective mass over an individual making a so-called expert decision in isolation) or the mob rule of 'the incompetent multitude' engaged in groupthink which denied inconvenient evidence and expert understanding, or if crowd preferences could aid expert decision-making (Landemore, 2013, p. 27; Mollick & Nanda, 2015; Surowiecki, 2004). Furthermore, a knowledge gap theory suggested that produsage would further increase the flow of news for the already information rich, not only in the global North and West but also in the global South and more authoritarian states where information capital was progressively being built, associated with the spread of the Western democratic ideal, but that others would be left relatively worse off by this (Hwang & Jeong, 2009).

News Flows and Contra-Flows

Schiller (1975, p. 75) argued that the global promotion of free flows of information was intimately tied to 'United States imperial ascendancy' in the period after the Second World War. As a function of its dominant economic power, which allowed the industrialization and commercialization of mass media, the US shaped these media globally, even though such media were published in many other places but commonly for local rather than global reception. Tunstall (1977) went so far as to categorize the media as a global phenomenon *as* American. As an example, and notwithstanding ideological differences, from the 1950s, and intensifying in the 1970s, the communist media in Central and Eastern Europe were not immune to this influence: on the one hand, many of the local media imported Western content, while elsewhere people had direct access to Western television and radio broadcasts. This led to an increasing Westernization of media, including changes in journalism (Mihelj, 2013; Sparks with Reading, 1998; Stokes, 1993).

Categorized as a form of 'media imperialism', this worked both quantitatively (given the sheer volume of media and media content circulating globally) and qualitatively in that these media conveyed very little, including news, that was not Northern and Western in origin or inflected through a North/West prism, reflecting their values, although the effects were commonly less evident than the production and distribution processes (Tomlinson, 1991). In the news sphere, by the close of the twentieth century an overlapping combination of the major wire services (news agencies) (Reuters, AP, AFP), including their video news arms, global broadcasters (CNN, BBC, Sky/Fox/Star), news exchange networks (Eurovision, Asiavision) and online services (Bloomberg, CNBC) had established Western news mediation and values as more or less global norms (see Table 4.1). To do this, they had leveraged their origins in imperial centres and associations with elite nations; the economic wealth of their domestic markets; independence from government; sector competitiveness; and a focus on fact-based 'objective' journalism. A number of studies

Table 4.1 Major global news providers*

Global news agencies/wires	Global television broadcasters**	Global radio broadcasters	Global newspapers§
Xinhua	CNN/CNN-I	BBC	*New York Times*
Thomson Reuters	BBC	Voice of America	*The Guardian*
AP	Al Jazeera	Radio France International	*Daily Mail*
RIA Novosti [Now Sputnik International]	CNBC	Deutsche-Welle	*China Daily*
Al Jazeera	Bloomberg TV	Voice of Russia	*Washington Post*
UPI	Fox News	Voice of the Islamic Republic of Iran	*Daily Telegraph*
AFP		China Radio International	*Wall Street Journal*
TASS			*USA Today*
Bloomberg			*Times of India*
CNBC			*The Independent* (UK)

*There is no single, formal, agreed way of ranking these entities. The listings are indicative.
**Rai & Cottle (2016, p. 145); see Rotheray (2010, pp. 17–18)
§By web access.

Sources: 4 International Media & Newspapers (2016), Rai & Cottle (2016), Rotheray (2010)

demonstrated that up to 87 per cent of non-domestic news published by newspapers in 31 countries in Europe, Asia, Africa, MENA, Latin America and North America was supplied by the major international wire services (Mowlana, 1997/2005). In 2017, AP claimed that 'On any given day, more than half the world's population sees content from AP' (www.aptn.com). Referring to the video (television) arms of these agencies and their primary geographical location, Paterson (2011) said they provided a view of the world specifically 'from London'.

In 2016 of the world's 30 largest media companies, half, including Rupert Murdoch's News Corp, Time Inc., Yomiuru Shimbun, Gannett, Axel Springer, Hearst, Grupo Globo and CBS, were either wholly or significantly producers of news (O'Reilly, 2016). Financial size did not always translate directly into power in the news business, however, where the content media published could 'influence the way the people make sense of the world', and could be exercised at regional, local and geolinguistic levels (Birkinbine et al., 2017, p. 6). In terms of influence, Google calculated that the list of news media most

Table 4.2 Calculations of the world's most influential news media

Influence by Google news and blog citations	Influence by Google+ engagement	Influence by Twitter feeds
AP	*New York Times*	Mashable
New York Times	Mashable	CNN
Reuters	The Next Web	The Big Picture
Wall Street Journal	National Public Radio	*The Onion*
Bloomberg	Breaking News*	*Time*
BBC	*Time*	Breaking News*
AFP	NBC News	BBC
CNN	*The Atlantic*	ESPN
Washington Post	*Wall Street Journal*	*Harvard Business Review*
TMZ	TechCrunch	Gizmodo

*Breaking News ceased operations in 2016

cited in its news and blogs in 2011 was dominated by legacy media. However, when Google calculated the media which stimulated most engagement on its social networking platform Google+ in 2012, the list looked quite different, including the inclusion of a number of new online sites, and a third listing in 2010 of the most influential news media Twitter feeds showed more variations (Bercovici, 2011; Hernandez, 2012; Pompeo, 2010) (see Table 4.2).

The uptake of digital ICTs, not least in the so-called developing world, seemed to signal a major shift in patterns of news media usage. In 2016 about half the world's population had access to the internet (see Chapter 2). There were 3.8bn unique mobile phone users, of whom 2.1bn used smartphones. About 2.3bn people were active on social media.

Those figures compared to the world's stock of 5.84bn television receivers, 2.4bn radios and 2.7bn readers of printed newspapers. As Bromley (2016, p. 137) noted, the news ecology was changing, and with it 'the news habit'. In this new global environment, places such as Brazil, the Philippines, the United Arab Emirates, Bermuda, Nigeria, Taiwan, Qatar, Malaysia, Thailand and Indonesia were utilizing online access, social media and mobile connectivity to formulate new configurations of news production, access and use (Kemp, 2016).

Challenging the Oligopoly

National news agencies in the global South, fostered by UNESCO from the 1980s as a means of promoting diversity in the global provision of news, and many of which were government funded, nevertheless remained subservient to the limited number of dominant international agencies, which carved up the world between them (see Chapter 5), constituting an oligopoly (Boyd-Barrett, 1997). By the turn of the twenty-first century many of these newer agencies were 'in crisis' as they attempted to reconcile the often mutually hostile demands associated with state support, growing commercialization and editorial independence (Shrivastava, 2007, p. 28). However, at the same time, the internet 'opened up new opportunities', particularly for the dissemination of content (for examples, see the Mongolian news agency Mongol tsahilgaan medee (MONTSAME) and the Philippines News Agency (PNA) (Shrivastava, 2007, pp. 218–19, 230–31)). The establishment of regional agencies, again under UNESCO's auspices, was intended to increase the global flow of news directly between member states within the global South, allowing countries to 'express themselves in their own way' rather than via the West/North (Mowlana, 1997/2005, pp. 47–48). The Middle East News Agency was established in 1955, a regional agency for Africa was proposed in 1961 and a number of other regional agencies were set up in the 1970s. Some failed although at least one, the Caribbean News Agency (1976), appeared to be a success into the second decade of the twenty-first century (Shrivastava, 2007). The Pan-African News Agency (PANA) itself endured a troubled existence: formally established in 1977, it was not recognized until 1979; in 1980 it was designated a news pool rather than an agency, and it began operating on an experimental basis only in 1983, finally being closed in 1997 and replaced by a commercial enterprise, Panapress Ltd. (Shrivastava, 2007). The pool, rather than agency, model, in which individual national wire services supplied content to a central regional distribution hub, dated from 1975 with the launch of the Non-Aligned News Agency Pool (NANA). The thinking behind these initiatives, given expression by the Indian prime minister, Indira Ghandi, was to counter the idea that 'Even our image of ourselves, not to speak of the view of other countries, tends to conform to theirs [the view of the former colonial powers]' (Shrivastava, 2007, p. 24). Regional news agencies continued to be established into the twenty-first century; for example, the African News agency (afrol) opened in 2000 and in 2016 it co-operated with a new agency addressing the 15-State Southern African Development Community (SADC), SADC+ (www.afrol.com).

One of the major issues raised by these developments was the perception held in the global West that such agencies had conflicting agendas – promoting state initiatives, development, artificially constructed 'good news', relying on financial aid from governments and UNESCO, all the while professing to produce free-flowing 'neutral' journalism independent of external political, economic and social power. The involvement of politicians and bureaucrats, and in some cases, their cronies in business, it was believed, would stifle the free flow of news and lead even to the licensing of journalists, resulting in the dissemination of no more than sanctioned, perhaps even mandatory, 'official information' (Thussu, 1998, p. 76; van Ginneken, 1998, p. 139). Yet, at the same time, such agencies wished to establish new potentially disruptive conditions – the contra-flow of news (from the rest to the rest and to the West), and a counter to Western news values (van Ginneken, 1998). This appeared invariably to include a counter-ideological position; for example, the Inter Press Service (IPS), with its focus on development in the global South, social change, representing the world's poorest people and providing a Southern perspective, appeared to be a genuine 'alternative' to the dominant mainstream international news agencies (Boyd-Barrett & Rantanen, 1998; Joye, 2009).

The IPS, which was formed in 1964, declared information to be 'an agent of change' and 'a precondition for lifting communities out of poverty and marginalization'. Its mission was to act as a 'communication channel that privileges the voices and concerns of the poorest'. Therefore, as well as operating as a news agency, the IPS was committed to capacity building and working with not only journalists and media but also civil society, international institutions, policy-makers, donors and individual users (Inter Press Service, 2017).

Countering the Hegemony of the Global North – NWICO and Beyond

The potential for a cacophony of news ricocheting around networks of produsers in the limitless, time-distorting, de-territorializing digital domain complicated the idea of news flows and contra-flows. As a category news was both a compilation of content (what was made from interactions with events and discourses) and the dissemination of that content (making it accessible to users). What journalists (or others) produced was not by itself news until it had been at least offered to users as such. This might be thought of as part of the information paradox, whereby information had value only when the person receiving it knew what it was, and how much they were willing to pay for it; yet once it was known, its value had been spent. Therefore, news users took news from journalists on trust without knowing beforehand whether it really was news (Bakker, 2007). Consequently, the processes of not only the collection, creation and distribution of news but also its reception constituted the flow of news. This was analysed chiefly at three levels – journalistic practice (how journalists developed their news values and what they reported and how), how the news media functioned, and how users responded to both. As Hjarvard (1995) has pointed out, these elements involved selection – what journalists chose as material to report; which elements within the material they opted to emphasize or ignore; the organizational choices of the news media in identifying their roles, and thus what to disseminate; and what users read, listened to and viewed. These elements were intimately connected – journalists' practices were influenced or even directed by news media, and the news media established their popular legitimacy by conforming to journalistic practices and definitions of news which met user criteria.

Within the broader category of information, 'news' had specific characteristics. First and foremost it was based in facticity, reporting demonstrably evident events and discourses. It was founded in what was literally new, recent and noteworthy. It presented a journalistic truth, scoping what was going on; giving meaning to events and views; transmitting shared experiences and values; and providing distraction (Perse & Lambe, 2017). As well as relaying so-called facts (who, what, where, when), journalism ideally offered explanations (why) and understandings of process (how). It supplied general, as opposed to specialized, information. People spoke in English about 'keeping up with the news'. The Media Insight Project asked US millennials (adults under the age of 35 years) – a demographic segment supposedly rapidly losing interest in the modern mass news media (Mindich, 2005) – whether they considered this important: 38 per cent said it was extremely or very important and a further 47 per cent said it was somewhat important. The survey also explored their motivations for keeping up with the news. The responses were:

- Civic engagement
- Social networking
- Practical information

The most common response was 'it helps me stay informed to be a better citizen' (57 per cent), followed by 'I like to talk to friends, family and colleagues about the news' and 'it's enjoyable or entertaining' (both 53 per cent) (The Associated Press/NORC 2015, p. 6). Another survey in the US in 2016 found that only 1 per cent of respondents said they never accessed the news. The motivations for accessing news appeared not to have changed much over time, even if the ways in which people accessed news had: although 57 per cent of Americans still often got their news from television, 38 per cent used online sources – and that was around 50 per cent for 18–49 year olds (Mitchell et al., 2016).

Debate over global news flows and contra-flows shifted with the uptake of digital ICTs, therefore. Penetration levels varied considerably and were not directly correlated with indices of press freedom in all cases – and, therefore, news flows (although the data were not always reliable; however, they were indicative) (see Table 4.3). What was suggested by the statistics was that use of the internet and social media was determined by more factors than a desire to access news and journalism, and might be affected by specific material conditions, such as the availability of electricity; affordability of digital devices; language; etc. It may have been the case that in countries with a freer press, social media sites such as Facebook were used less because it was felt there was no need to seek alternative sources of journalism. Finland may have been in this category. Conversely, a country such as Vietnam with an unfree press might have had a relatively high use of social media to bypass restrictions on journalism. This served as a reminder that journalism involved not only technological creation and distribution (by journalists) but also reception and response (by users) and, in a digitally empowered environment, that there was an interaction between the two constituencies (see Table 4.3).

In a report and analysis of global information flows completed in 1985, Mowlana (1985) made the point that it was necessary to study both production and dissemination and the hardware and software deployed; how information was sourced and then turned into content; how that content was absorbed, internalized and utilized; and the various contexts within which these activities occurred. In a subsequent work, he argued that 'the international flow of information, if it is studied comprehensively, must include a careful consideration of four distinct but related stages of the communication process: the source, the process of production, the process of distribution and the process of utilization' (Mowlana, 1997, p. 223). More than 30 years later, with digital ITCs collapsing both time and space differentiations, the exhortation seemed to be particularly appropriate.

Online Flows and Contra-Flows

Many countries sought to limit access and to censor online content (and to track its creators and users) which would fall within the domain of journalism – calling governments to account; exposing corruption; social commentating; airing the views of the political opposition; even just sharing news (Kelly et al., 2016; Schmidt, 2014) – and to re-write the news itself

(Denyer, 2016). From 2006 RWB produced an annual list of 'enemies of the internet': in 2016 it cited Belarus, Burma, China, Cuba, Egypt, Iran, North Korea, Saudi Arabia, Syria, Tunisia, Turkmenistan, Uzbekistan and Vietnam for inter alia preventing independent journalists from accessing the internet; harassing website editors; and punishing people for posting independently sourced news (https://rsf.org). By 2018, the list had expanded to include Bahrain, Ethiopia, India, Pakistan, Russia, Sudan and even the UK and US (largely as a fallout from the Snowden affair), although Burma, Egypt and Tunisia had been removed from the list. (sahrzad.net).

Table 4.3 Press freedom rankings and internet and Facebook users, 2017

Press freedom ranking*		Press freedom status**	Internet users/ population[§]	Facebook users/ population[§]
	1. Norway	Free	99.6%	63.8%
	2. Sweden	Free	92.9%	62.5%
	3. Finland	Free	92.5%	48.7%
	4. Denmark	Free	96.9%	64.8%
	5. Netherlands	Free	94.8%	58.7%
Highest 10	6. Costa Rica	Free	86.9%	59.2%[†]
	7. Switzerland	Free	89.4%	43.8%
	8. Jamaica	Free	53.2%	37%[†]
	9. Belgium	Free	87.9%	56.8%
	10. Iceland	Free	100%	74.4%
	49. Tonga	Free	46.2%	40.8%
	54. Poland	Partly free	72.4%	36.3%
	58. Senegal	Partly free	25.7%	14.3%
Mid-range 10	63. S. Korea	Partly free	75%	33.5%
(selected)	71. Hungary	Partly free	80.5%	54.1%
	94. Liberia	Partly free	8.4%	7%
	95. Kenya	Partly free	89.4%	12.8%
	104. Kuwait	Partly free	78.4%	56.1%
	116. Mali	Partly free	11.8%	7.4%
	133. Morocco	Not free	58.3%	31.4%
	171. E. Guinea	Not free	23.8%	7.5%
	172. Djibouti	Not free	19.8%	19.8%
	173. Cuba	Not free	33.6%	19.95%[†]
Lowest 10	174. Sudan	Not free	28%	7.1%
	175. Vietnam	Not free	67.1%	67.1%
	176. China***	Not free	53.2%	24.1%[§§]
	177. Syria	Not free	31.9%	31.7%
	178. Turk'stan	Not free	18%	0.3%
	179. Eritrea	Not free	1.3%	1.1%
	180. N. Korea	Not free	1%	0.1%

*2017 World Press Freedom Index (RWB, 2017a); ** Freedom of the Press, 2017; *** Excluding Hong Kong and Macau SARs; [§] Internet World Stats, 2017; [§§] Figure is for Weibo and Facebook combined; [†] 2016 figure

On the other hand, some countries with only partly free media (Argentina, Kenya) were reported by Freedom House (2017b) as having high levels of freedom on the internet. In 2016–18 Singapore had one of the highest penetrations of the internet (measured at 82.5 per cent) and social media (75 per cent) but only part freedom on the net, and a low press freedom ranking (151st out of 180) (Freedom House, 2017b; Internet Live Stats, 2016; Tan, 2017; https://rsf.org/en/singapore). In both Singapore and Malaysia (press freedom ranking 146th), governments invested heavily in digital technology as a means of state modernization (primarily to stimulate e-commerce through establishing a wired economy) which relied on relatively free access, providing unintended opportunities for journalists to circumvent the heavily controlled legacy media with the emergence of sites like Malaysiakini which gave rise to Citizen Journalists Malaysia (Balaraman et al., 2015; Bromley, 2010; Shufiyan, 2010). However, the idea that such journalism might bypass traditional news media was challenged (George, 2012).

Nevertheless, the situation was far removed from the 1960s when, crudely speaking, if users in one city in a country in the global South wanted to access news from another city in a neighbouring country, they commonly had to rely on a professional journalist from a third, usually global West/North country, sending information (reporting) to a wire service, publisher or broadcaster in one or other West/North country where it was processed (edited) and then transmitted globally via a wire service, syndication arrangement or exchange system back to the first place in the chain. This was largely a function of the material conditions of news production: the G-7 group of major industrialized countries (Canada, France, Germany, Italy, Japan, the UK and the US), as van Ginneken (1998) noted, dominated, and within those nations the media were controlled by limited oligopolies. Consequently, the relatively expensive business of gathering global news could be afforded by only a restricted number of media organizations – the international news agencies, newspapers such as the *New York Times, Washington Post,* (London) *The Times, Le Monde,* and major broadcasters (the US television networks, the BBC) (van Ginneken, 1998; Williams, 2011). As recently as 2015, more than a quarter of 6,641 foreign correspondents based in 27 European countries came from the same seven countries – Canada (estimated 0.5 per cent), Germany (7.6 per cent), US (6.8 per cent), UK (5.7 per cent), France (3 per cent), Japan (2.55 per cent) and Italy (2.1 per cent) (Terzis, 2015). Using London as their example, Bromley, Tumber and Fritsch (2015, p. 293) concluded that at the level of reporting a 'historical Western dominance of international news flows' remained intact.

The NWICO debates were of particular significance. At the core of the NWICO proposals, mentioned in Chapter 3, and global debates at varying levels of intensity over media policy from the 1970s, was a dissatisfaction with the way in which mass communication exerted a global hegemony of the politically liberal democratic West and industrialized North – which controlled the vast bulk of the means of communication and shaped the messages they carried – over the politically authoritarian East and economically emerging South. In other words, global communication and its contents flowed largely uni-directionally from the West and North to the rest with few, if any, opportunities for any significant contra-flows. Consequently, not only did global mass communication over-represent its Western and Northern origins and values, it also reflected Eastern and Southern interests through a Western and Northern prism. In conditions in which those with communication power could effectively monopolize global information flows, what was the value of 'freedom of information' for everyone else? In reaching for a definition of NWICO, the 1980 UNESCO general conference resolved, inter alia, in favour of:

* 'elimination of the imbalances and inequalities' in existing global mass communication
* 'elimination of the negative effects of certain monopolies ... and excessive concentrations' of communication capacity
* 'wider and better balanced dissemination of information and ideas'
* 'plurality of sources and channels of communication'
* 'respect for each people's cultural identity and the right of each nation to inform the world public about its interests, its aspirations and its social and cultural values'
* 'respect for the right of all peoples to participate in international exchanges of information on the basis of equality, justice and mutual benefit'
* 'respect for the right of the public, of ethnic and social groups and of individuals to have access to information sources and to participate actively in the communication process'.

Crucially, this (eventually temporary) consensus was founded on an acceptance of the principle of the 'free flow' of information, expressed through a commitment to:

* 'freedom of the press and information'
* 'the freedom of journalists and all professionals in the communication media, a freedom inseparable from responsibility' (UNESCO, 1980).

News Values

In terms of journalism, the status quo was demonstrated by the news values of the West and North in determining global news media content. In a subsequently much-referenced analysis, Galtung and Ruge (1965) proposed that (a) events had features (news factors) which made them intrinsically newsworthy as what they called 'foreign news', and (b) journalists brought their news values to bear on events as they constructed this 'foreign news'. Their argument was that news factors were culture-free, whereas news values were cultural expressions. However, by applying values to factors, events were culturally determined (deemed to be newsworthy). The more a perceived set of circumstances met the interrelated criteria, the more likely it would become news (and, of course, of particular importance to the global South, the less it conformed, the more likely it was *not* to be considered news). Furthermore, once something had been selected as being news, the attributes which were considered to make it news would be emphasized, resulting in distortion. Thereby, the view of the world presented by journalists was shaped by these newsworthiness tests (see Figure 4.1).

This led to global news which addressed the world outside the West and North focused on 'visuals, drama and conflict' and reinforcing 'simplistic explanations, stereotypes and clichés' (Williams, 2011, p. 150). The US journalist Mort Rosenblum (1979) coined the term 'coups and earthquakes syndrome' (standing for political violence and natural disasters) to describe this way of reporting the world. In turn, this 'filter' led to inherent biases favouring disruption and deviance (protests and government abuses) based on newsworthiness criteria of 'novelty, conflict, proximity and drama' (Baum & Zhukov, 2015, p. 14). Similarly, ideologically Western news values privileged a shared democratic culture (Sheafer et al., 2012). Consequently, journalism differentiated between human experiences: 'not all casualties are covered equally', *The Atlantic* magazine acknowledged in 2014 (Urist, 2014). Frayn (1965, p. 69) sardonically reviewed the British application of these values:

> Even a rail crash on the Continent [of Europe] made the grade [as news] provided there were at least five dead. If it was in the United States the minimum number of dead rose to 20; in South America 100; in Africa 200; in China 500. But people really preferred an air crash. Here, curiously enough, people showed much less racial discrimination. If the crash was outside Britain, 50 dead Pakistanis or 50 dead Filippinos were as entertaining as 50 dead Americans.

NWICO challenged the belief that these Western/Northern, including communist, news values were unproblematically universal and beneficial.

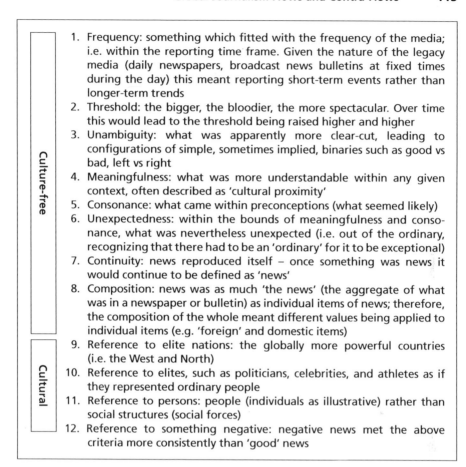

1. Frequency: something which fitted with the frequency of the media; i.e. within the reporting time frame. Given the nature of the legacy media (daily newspapers, broadcast news bulletins at fixed times during the day) this meant reporting short-term events rather than longer-term trends
2. Threshold: the bigger, the bloodier, the more spectacular. Over time this would lead to the threshold being raised higher and higher
3. Unambiguity: what was apparently more clear-cut, leading to configurations of simple, sometimes implied, binaries such as good vs bad, left vs right
4. Meaningfulness: what was more understandable within any given context, often described as 'cultural proximity'
5. Consonance: what came within preconceptions (what seemed likely)
6. Unexpectedness: within the bounds of meaningfulness and consonance, what was nevertheless unexpected (i.e. out of the ordinary, recognizing that there had to be an 'ordinary' for it to be exceptional)
7. Continuity: news reproduced itself – once something was news it would continue to be defined as 'news'
8. Composition: news was as much 'the news' (the aggregate of what was in a newspaper or bulletin) as individual items of news; therefore, the composition of the whole meant different values being applied to individual items (e.g. 'foreign' and domestic items)
9. Reference to elite nations: the globally more powerful countries (i.e. the West and North)
10. Reference to elites, such as politicians, celebrities, and athletes as if they represented ordinary people
11. Reference to persons: people (individuals as illustrative) rather than social structures (social forces)
12. Reference to something negative: negative news met the above criteria more consistently than 'good' news

(left margin labels: *Culture-free* for items 1–8; *Cultural* for items 9–12)

Figure 4.1 *Newsworthiness* (Galtung & Ruge, 1965)

Rather they were ideologically constructed (van Ginneken, 1998). Western news values drew on the liberal precept of being free from state control, while Northern news values were based on the operation of markets, as exploited by the media, and together they constituted the idea of the 'free flow' of news (mentioned in the UNESCO resolution cited above) based on corporate production and individual consumption, and sometimes referred to as the 'free marketplace of ideas' (Herman & McChesney, 1997, p. 25; Nordenstreng, 2016, p. 62; van Ginneken, 1998, p. 138). On the other hand, Soviet news values were founded in journalism operating as an arm of the state to propagate communism (Thussu, 1998). NWICO aimed to deliver a different freedom, as a human right both in and of itself, and for the attainment of wider non-commercial global objectives, such as self-determination, modernization, economic reform, justice, cultural awareness and, above all, greater equality through the widening and deepening of 'the freedom of information by increasing its balance and diversity on a global scale' (Nordenstreng, 2013 translation, p. 66; Nordenstreng, 2016, p. 62; Thomas, 2010a, p. 29; Williams, 2011, pp. 36–37). It was perhaps most adequately summed up in the title of the McBride Report, which formed the basis of the UNESCO declaration cited above – *Many Voices, One World* (van Ginneken, 1998, p. 139). Behind NWICO was the belief that '[t]he right to information is often the basis for the enjoyment of other human rights' (Thomas, 2010b, p. 180).

The idea was received with extreme hostility in the global West and North, however. First of all, NWICO was supported by the communist bloc which was seen as undermining its status as a project of the non-aligned nations. Secondly, authoritarian regimes were not limited to the Soviet bloc: a majority of the 25 countries which comprised the non-aligned grouping from 1961, including Egypt, Indonesia, Iraq, Morocco, Saudi Arabia and Syria, were seen at the time to be authoritarian, particularly in relation to the press. Two (Cuba and Yugoslavia) were communist and others were simply condemned as 'corrupt dictatorships' (Herman & McChesney, 1997, p. 24; Siebert, 1963, pp. 29–33). Journalism was used to promote state objectives such as the formation of national identity (Pakistan) (Jabir, 2013); development (Nigeria) (Edean, 1993); independence (Ghana) (Asante & Ogawa, n.d.), and national integration and unity (Malaysia) (Rudra, 2012). 'Proponents of the NWICO were characterized as tinhorn dictators who wanted to censor the press to keep the truth from their peoples and the world' (Herman & McChesney, 1997, p. 25).

From the 1980s the industrialized and democratic states, led by the US and UK, mounted a 'counter offensive', based in neo-liberal economics, of 'aggressive global pro-market policies' which favoured the formation of a global corporate media hegemony (Herman & McChesney, 1997, pp. 25–27; van Ginneken, 1998, p. 139). In this environment, 'independent media', as promoted by organizations such as the WTO, the International Monetary Fund (IMF) and the World Bank, threw off state and government control by means of economic liberalization – privatization and exposure to global competition through 'free trade' (Herman & McChesney, 1997, pp. 28–31). As a result, 'many of the limits to corporate media expansion' were removed, leading to media corporations becoming some of 'the largest firms in the world' (Hoyler & Watson, 2013, p. 90). Those in the news business manoeuvred to control the whole process from the definition of what constituted news (defining news values) to the platforms which distributed it (see Sreberny, 2006, p. 610). This represented NWICO in 'reverse' (Nordenstreng, 2010, p. 21).

Yet, the technologies (initially, satellite broadcasting) which facilitated an oligopolistic presence in global news also presented the possibility of contra-flows. The success of CNN in providing news globally of the 1991 US attack on Iraq, not least among Arab audiences, encouraged the development of Arab satellite TV stations with the potential both to increase the flow of news across borders and to circumvent state controls and censorship in any one country. In this instance, the development remained a potential rather than an attainment, as it was widely argued that the only Arab satellite television broadcaster to offer a news contra-flow was Al Jazeera (PBS, 2007; Sakr, 1999) (see Case Study 4.1).

It could be argued that, prior to the extensive take-up of the internet, satellite television broadcasting began to change global journalism. The number of truly global stations remained limited and predominantly American and British (see Table 4.1). However, from 1996 Al Jazeera progressively positioned itself as a global news provider, broadcasting in several languages from multiple locations. Others from outside North America and Western Europe with a more global focus included:

- RT (Russia) – broadcasting in English, Arabic and Spanish with RT America and RT UK channels
- China Global Television Network (CGTN) (PRC) broadcasting in English, French, Spanish, Arabic, Russian and Japanese
- i24news (Israel) broadcasting in French, English and Arabic
- NDTV (India) broadcasting in English and Hindi
- NHK World (Japan) – broadcasting in English with a focus on North America and Europe

Nevertheless, as satellite news channels proliferated, often leveraging additional reach through cable services and websites, the greater tendency was to provide regional, national and sub-national services (down to individual city level) in a process of 'localization' (Rai & Cottle, 2016, p. 151). Insofar as UNESCO, as noted above, promoted intra-regional news flows, satellite television appeared to have delivered these to an extent not achieved by news agencies with as many as 20 regional channels operating in the Americas, Europe, the Middle East and South and East Asia (Rai & Cottle, 2016, pp. 145–50). These channels largely remained separate from Western/Northern media and also marginally increased the amount of news flowing northwards from the global South. Similarly, a mixed economy of broadcasters funded by states both directly (Al Jazeera, CGTV, RT), albeit with differing levels of editorial independence, and indirectly

(NHK World), and by commercial entities (iNews24, NDTV) appeared to have enhanced diversity, pluralism and freedom of news flows globally (Rai and Cottle, 2016).

Case Study 4.1: Al Jazeera

Al Jazeera's influence on global news flows has been based on two main factors: an underpinning of the adoption of standard Western news practices and values, adapted to the context within which the station operates but without overtly countermanding Western journalistic traditions, and an overlay of recognizing and expressing Arab identities and cohesiveness. This mix has allowed it to develop a distinctive capacity to innovate and challenge by adopting Western journalistic approaches, such as holding the powerful to account, investigating and broaching controversial topics, and to apply those specifically to the Arab region, the Arab diaspora, the global Muslim community and the global South more widely. As a Western-style broadcaster, Al Jazeera has sought 'scoops', posted staff to so-called 'trouble spots', employed Western-trained journalists, and used orthodox journalistic reporting techniques.

Credited with remapping global news flows (Casara, 2014), Al Jazeera began broadcasting in 1996, part-funded by the emir of Qatar and owned by the Qatari government. It stepped in when the BBC withdrew its Arab service. Originally an Arab language terrestrial, cable and satellite television news channel directed at the Persian Gulf area of the Arab region, by 2017 it was one of the largest news organizations in the world with 80 bureaux, broadcasting in multiple languages through six channels (notably Al Jazeera English from 2006) and the internet in English (2003). It uniqueness lay in its willingness to be controversial and to give air time to people, topics and opinions otherwise not available through the media in Arab countries. It began broadcasting 24/7 in 1999.

Its embeddedness in the Arab world, its journalistic ambitions to be first with the news, and its preparedness to be controversial was evident in its broadcasting of recordings made by Osama bin Laden when he was wanted for terrorist offences. As a result, while Al Jazeera was condemned by some for giving air time to terrorists, it also meant that its reports were widely circulated around the world. This led to formal agreements with other broadcasters on content sharing.

One American journalist commended Al Jazeera as 'a feast of vivid, pathbreaking coverage from all continents ... a visually stunning, deeply reported description of developments in dozens upon dozens of countries simultaneously ... focus[ed] equally on all four corners of the Earth rather than on just the flash points of any imperial or post-imperial interest' (Kaplan, 2009). The American politician and former presidential candidate Hillary Clinton famously described Al Jazeera as offering 'real news' (Folkenflik, 2011). Seib (2008) went so far as to claim there was an 'Al Jazeera effect' by which it provided an outlet for those otherwise unheard (Seib, 2008).

Al Jazeera rapidly established itself as the news channel of choice across the MENA region (Seib, 2008, p. 20). However, it was not without problems. It ran into trouble over its content with a number of countries, and Al Jazeera America, a cable operation, lasted less than three years, closing in 2016.

Nordenstreng (2010, pp. 6–25) usefully suggested that attempts to establish a new world order went through five stages:

- Stage 1 (1970–76): decolonization offensive
- Stage 2 (1976–78): Western counter-attack
- Stage 3 (1978–80): truce
- Stage 4 (1980–90): corporate offensive
- Stage 5 (1991–2010): globalization

He argued that the primary objectives of the initiative were not information and communication purely in themselves, but long-term objectives to promote democratization; foster human rights, including the right to information; support decolonization, independence and self-reliance; counter propaganda; develop professional integrity and standards (ethics) among journalists; and further reciprocal international cooperation through cultural exchange (Nordenstreng, 2010). NWICO 'was ... first and foremost a political exercise in taking stock of the socio-economic forces in the world at that time' (Nordenstreng, 2010, p. 1).

Case Study 4.2: TeleSUR

TeleSUR (La Nueva Televisora del Sur) was founded largely at the behest of the then president of Venezuela, Hugo Chavez. Venezuela held a 51 per cent stake in the channel. Subsequently, the governments of Bolivia, Cuba, Ecuador, Nicaragua and Uruguay have provided additional support. It began broadcasting in 2005 and in 2017 was available across Latin America and in the US, Western Europe and North Africa as a 24/7 news channel. It is transmitted chiefly by satellite but also via cable and terrestrially. In 2014 it started an English language channel. It also has an English language website.

The inspiration for TeleSUR is said to have come from Al Jazeera in providing a regional service and fostering Latin American identity. As a 'platform' for the global South, it professes to promote 'the struggles of peoples for peace, self-determination, respect for Human Rights and Social Justice' (www.telesurtv.net). It is credited with extending the coverage of Latin America beyond the news agenda of the major wire services and global television broadcasters. It is widely viewed in Latin America as an alternative to CNN's Spanish language service, and is seen as being critical of the global West, the US in particular (Kozloff, 2011). However, it was also designed as a counter to the large, privately owned media in Latin America which were overwhelmingly rightist.

In 2016 Argentina, also a founding member, withdrew from the controlling consortium of governments, claiming its more right-of-centre views had been denied air time on the leftist channel. TeleSUR countered by saying that the

move had been prompted by the channel's criticisms of the Argentinian government (Wyss, 2016).

As Al Jazeera itself noted, views are divided between regarding TeleSUR as
'either a pioneering and much needed media voice or a mere propaganda tool ...
TeleChavez in disguise' (*The Listening Post*, 2012). The director of HRW Americas
opposed the establishment of TeleSUR on the grounds that sponsorship by the
government of Cuba, which had 'no basic concept of free speech', was inimical
to the operation of a news medium (Fischlin & Nandorfy, 2007, p. 176).

Nevertheless by 2016 it was Latin America's largest news channel, employing
1,000 people including 40 foreign correspondents.

Flows and Contra-Flows in Countries in Transition

Global flows and contra-flows of news were closely associated with the contexts
of their production. As a generalization, it was reasonably safe to assert that
global flows (from the North to the rest) were based in the commitments
of the liberal ideology of the global West and the economic rationale of the
global North supporting the hegemonic concept of a free market in ideas.
That did not preclude challenging the dominant news hegemony. France 24
was established to provide a (Francophone) journalistic counter-perspective
to that of the likes of the (Anglo) BBC and CNN (Painter, 2008). Similarly,
Fox News countered the orthodoxy of liberal journalistic impartiality (Painter,
2008). Contra-flows (emanating from the rest) were more complexly derived,
however. The historical default position of most of the global South (and the
former global East) was to restrict information flows through mechanisms of
control and censorship. Thus, any contra-flows of news from the global South
were based, at least in part, in accepting the 'free flow' hegemony (Painter,
2008, pp. 4–5). The extent of such acceptance varied considerably. As we
have seen, Al Jazeera largely reproduced Western concepts of journalism,
including news values, practices and personnel, and PSB-type funding, but
focused its journalistic attention on parts of the world and topics poorly
covered, or even ignored, by the dominant global media, adopting a far less
Western-centric approach (see Case Study 4.1). Furthermore, Al Jazeera
Arabic previously initiated Western-style adversarial journalism in the Arab
region (Painter, 2008). TeleSUR, while offering a regional news focus, also
adopted standard journalistic practices, simply inverting the North–South
perspective which led to a focus on social movements, which had more
relevance in Latin America and the global South generally, rather than political
and economic elites who tended to monopolize Northern news agendas (see
Case Study 4.2). Others, such as IPS, extended the deployment of mainly

Western and Northern journalism practices and editorial independence to embrace communication activism with the objective of fostering civil society in the global South. Elsewhere, such journalism was mobilized not only internally but, by developing an international reach, globally, in support of governments; in Singapore, where the *Straits Times* published international editions and operated a multimedia website:

> Editors and journalists are free to exercise their discretion in the preparation of local newspapers. However, they are regularly reminded of their responsibility to society, and reports or articles that arouse the displeasure of the Singapore Government give rise to pressure. (Rieger, 1989, p. 1034)

The example of Singapore illustrated the extent to which democracy came in many guises. As more states professed to transition from autocracy to democracy, many occupied 'the misty zone between liberal democracy and close authoritarianism' (Rizal, 2015, p. xix). The variations included (with some examples), as well as the authoritarian democracy of Singapore with its 'compliant' media echoing the dominant ruling political party's discourse, and eschewing 'rigorous debates and analyses' (Rahim, 2015):

- managed democracy (Russia) – criticism confined to marginal media (small circulation newspapers) but not mainstream television; regime opponents largely silenced (Benyumov, 2016; Kendall, 2017)
- Islamic democracy (Iran) – limits on public expression and 'no questioning of the basic principles of the Islamic revolution and of the republic' (Lewis, 1993)
- neo-patrimonial democracy (Ghana) – access to information curtailed; state-owned media staffed by supporters of political leaders, issuing political propaganda (Brobbey, 2013)
- proto-democracy (Egypt) – popular demand and support for and contribution to free expression preceded (and calls for) wider formal democratization with varying degrees of success (Hafez, 2010).
- illiberal democracy (Hungary) – protection of freedom of expression is abandoned even though it may be constitutionally guaranteed and governments are democratically elected (Puddington, 2017).

Thus it could not be assumed that a transition to democracy meant the complete abandonment of authoritarian approaches to journalism, or that contra-flows of news were always founded in a journalistic counter-hegemony. Rather than producing new ways of doing journalism (a world of many journalisms), they often re-focused established journalism – or simply repeated (state) propaganda.

Freedom of Expression, Pluralism and Diversity

It was not just dedicated 24/7 television news channels that leveraged global reach out of internet connectivity. Print media (newspapers and magazines), traditionally available only in hard copies within distribution distance from their publication locations, exploited the web to establish global presences, as did mainstream broadcasters previously limited to national relay. According to otechworld.com, the top ten news media websites in May 2018 were:

- Google News
- Yahoo! News
- CNN News
- BBC News
- *New York Times*
- *The Guardian*
- Mail Online (*Daily Mail*)
- *Washington Post*
- IndiaTimes
- *Huffington Post*

The most popular social media and blog news sites included *AdWeek*, Bloomberg, Boing Boing, BuzzFeed, CNN, *Forbes*, Fox, *Huffington Post*, *The Guardian* and Mashable. The top news providers specifically on Facebook were BuzzFeed, *Huffington Post*, ABC(US), *The Guardian, New York Times* and *Daily Mail*; on Twitter: BBC, CNN, Fox News, *New York Times, Time, The Guardian* and *Forbes*. However, social media allowed users not only to receive news but to make it, too, by submitting stories, articles, videos and pictures. As a consequence, social media 'scooped' the mainstream media on some of the major global events: the death of Michael Jackson; the Sichuan earthquake in 2008; and the killing of Osama bin Laden in 2011. Digital connectivity also enabled the production of user-generated content: in 2005 the BBC led its main evening news bulletin with videos sent in by the public of the terrorist attacks in the City. This provided the background to the emergence of citizen journalism, addressed in Chapter 6. Summarizing the effects, Alejandro (2010, p. 12) wrote:

> the web is becoming more sociable than searchable or probably both and fulfilling the internet's promise of connecting the world. One thing is for

sure, the power structures are changing. Media organisations do not have the monopoly on journalism anymore. The face of the competition is changing. In less than a decade, the likes of Google, Facebook and Twitter are competing with the *New York Times*, the *Guardian*, CNN and BBC as the news outlet of choice.

All the same, there were some notable presences and absences from such apparently world-connecting journalism. First, 'news' appeared no longer to mean primarily the reporting of the general run of events and discourses but extended to a specialized focus on the digital domain itself. Second, with the exception of the *Times of India*, media from outside the global West and North did not feature at the top of these listings, suggesting that they were having far less global impact (see Table 4.1). The greatest measurable reach was among a number of Indian newspapers' websites (*Dainik Jagran, Indian Express, Economic Times, The Hindu, India Times, Hindustan Times*); papers published in the People's Republic of China (*China Daily, People's Daily, Economic Daily*); the Taiwanese *United Daily News* and *Liberty Times; Hürriyet* and *Milliyet Gazetesi* (Turkey); Zougla (Greece); JPost (*Jerusalem Post*) and Al Arabiya (Saudi Arabia). This suggested that the dominance of English as the language of the web significantly influenced the global reach of news sites, and that the numbers of non-English language web users often remained dependent on indigenous and diasporic communities. Third, news providers included aggregators, such as Yahoo! and Google, who reposted what had appeared elsewhere, rather than originating their own news content. Finally, new exclusively online news media were challenging the traditional legacy media on the web.

Reinventing Journalism in the Digital Domain?

Where did journalism fit in this scenario? First and foremost, there was confusion over who actually counted as a journalist (see Chapter 7). The uncertainty occurred both externally (outside the occupation) and internally within journalism itself. Many of the salient factors have already been addressed in Chapter 2 and are discussed again in the chapters which follow. A lack of global consensus over the roles, values, practices and personnel of journalism, allied to the capacity afforded by digital ICTs for almost anyone to communicate globally, rendered journalism vulnerable. This vulnerability manifested itself in 'fake news' which, as we have seen, became such a feature of public discourse. Aggregators grew in size almost exponentially – by 2017

Google News operated more than 70 country-based websites in almost 40 languages. (Those numbers may be compared with the figures for foreign bureaux operated by legacy media in Table 5.1.) Insofar as they reposted (some said stole) content, much of what they were disseminating was traditionally produced journalism. However, by 2017 67 per cent of Americans were thought to be getting news through social media and most users of Reddit, Facebook and Twitter accessed news from those sites (www.journalism.org). Much of this 'news' was not produced by journalists, or even citizen journalists, but by ordinary users (see Chapters 6 and 8) (Alejandro, 2010, p. 9).

There were many examples of egregious journalism. In the Philippines, a woman, described as 'a sexy dancer turned self-styled journalist', posted what she asserted was an exclusive interview with president-elect Rodrigo Duterte. It was claimed that she was a Duterte supporter who had done nothing more than meet the anti-media politician (Makabenta, 2016). In many instances, external controls determined who counted as a journalist – who was allowed to join the parliamentary lobby; who received fee waivers for FoI enquiries; who was eligible for accreditation; who was protected by shield laws. In such cases, the definition of 'journalist' was most commonly tied to employment – whether the person was working for the media or freelance. The growth of social media muddied the waters. Consequently, it was argued that what defined a journalist was not employment but activity – what journalism professor Jay Rosen described in a tweet as 'acts of journalism, regardless who does them' (@jayrosen_nyu, 2010). In the UK, this went as far as to provide journalistic exemption in relation to data protection to an NGO on the grounds that the organization's purpose was to publish 'information, opinions or ideas for general public consumption' (Brown, 2015). Reacting to this kind of dilution of the idea of who was a journalist, the American Press Institute argued that 'merely engaging in journalistic-like activity – snapping a cell-phone picture at the scene of a fire or creating a blog site for news and comment – does not by itself produce a journalistic product' (www.americanpressinstitute.org). Definition by employment remained the most common way of determining who was a journalist (Peters & Tandoc, 2013). Nevertheless, if anyone could communicate anything from anywhere to anyone else, even if what they were doing was not formally recognized as journalism, did the meaning of global flows and contra-flows change?

Not unexpectedly, journalists themselves have taken to social media as part of their routine work (Turtola, 2017). However, many journalists were concerned that their core values, and their authority, would be diminished. Were 'tweets and truth' compatible? (Hermida, 2012, p. 659). For many, the situation changed quite fundamentally in 2011 when BuzzFeed, a news aggregator whose site traffic came preponderantly through social media as part of its objective of tracking viral content, hired its own reporters and began originating news (Tandoc & Jenkins, 2017). BuzzFeed described itself as the 'first true social media news organization'. Was BuzzFeed 'a news or entertainment site, or a content-focused publication [merely seeking to attract page views] or [a] technology-focused startup company' (Tandoc & Jenkins, 2017 p. 494)? By 2017, BuzzFeed was operating 'a global news organization' with a presence in 12 major cities around the world (notably except Africa) (www.buzzfeed.com/about). Eventually, BuzzFeed appeared to be accepted as a legitimate journalistic enterprise. However, its mix of viral content, advertorial and journalism, which seemed to be inordinately successful financially, posed more questions than its cross-platform networking. Did it represent the future of journalism (Tandoc & Jenkins, 2017)?

Was this combination, made possible by the wealth of the global North, of orthodox journalism and of other content originating anywhere in the world, a new order of flows and contra-flows?

Summary

Over a period of about 50 years the capacity to determine global flows and contra-flows of news devolved from transnational mass media organizations enabled by the wealth of the global North and motivated by the ideology of the global West with digital capabilities being afforded to regional, national, sub-national and socio-linguistic groups and even individuals. This has contributed to 'a communications landscape that is quite different from what we were familiar with' (Servaes & Lie, 2008, p. 58), and led to at least a partial rectification of the status quo in which the global North and West dictated global news flows and set the global news agenda. Nevertheless, issues remained of whether globally journalism and news were more homogenized or more polarized; whether the corporate media which had dominated the landscape for decades remained preeminent as they undeniably grew in size and potentially in power and influence; whether they were being replaced by new Northern corporate entities; or if the potential proliferation of many journalisms would be realized and presaged the development of a global public sphere – whether the outsider looking in was being replaced by the insider reporting out (Schechter, 2005), and whether in all new conditions of democracy counter-hegemonic forms of journalism would prevail over old ways of propagandizing.

Further Reading

1. Cushion, S. & Lewis, J. (eds) (2010) *The Rise of 24-hour News Television: Global Perspectives* (New York: Peter Lang).
2. Cushion, S. & Sambrook, R. (eds) (2016) *The Future of 24-hour News: New Directions, New Challenges* (New York: Peter Lang).
3. Geniets, A. (2013) *The Global News Challenge: Market Strategies of International Broadcasting Organizations in Developing Countries* (New York: Routledge).
4. Nordenstreng, K. (2013) 'Lessons learned from the NWICO process', *Xiandai Chuanbo* 6, 64–69, in English, www.uta.fi, accessed 1 February 2017.
5. Thussu, D.K. (2007) 'Mapping global media flow and contra-flow', in D.K. Thussu (ed.), *Media on the Move: Global Flow and Contra-Flow*, 11–32 (London: Routledge).
6. van Ginneken, J. (1998) *Understanding Global News: A Critical Introduction* (London: Sage).

5

The Evolution of Global Reporting

Chapter overview

This chapter explores the history and evolution of global reporting by focusing on foreign correspondence and war reporting. It is structured around five key periods: (1) The birth of foreign correspondence in the seventeenth century. (2) The professionalization of foreign correspondence in the nineteenth century. (3) The golden age of foreign correspondence in the twentieth century. (4) The post-Cold War period with a focus on war reporting. (5) Foreign correspondence today: a vanishing species? This final section includes the main reasons for the recent decline of foreign correpondence, such as the economic downturn, the role of new technologies and the rise of infotainment.

Learning outcomes

After having read this chapter you will be able to:

1. Explain what role foreign correspondents play and how interest in foreign news first arose
2. Identify the main periods in the history of foreign correspondence
3. Critically analyse the key factors that have contributed to the evolution of foreign correspondence throughout the centuries and its current decline
4. Define the term 'international journalism' and explain the main characteristics of the different types of foreign correspondents.

'The foreign affairs specialist among Washington correspondents is a cosmopolitan among cosmopolitans, a man in gray flannel who ranks very high in the hierarchy of reporters' (Cohen, 1963, p. 17). 'Correspondents talk to heads of state and dine on the Via Veneto, while colleagues back home toil under the watchful eye of editors' (Hamilton & Jenner, 2004b, p. 98). The image of foreign correspondents portrayed by Cohen more than half a century ago is still evident in both popular and academic discourses. Cohen (1963, p. 18) described foreign correspondents as men with college education who had 'long experience in the field of international affairs'. Hamilton and Jenner (2004b), however, argued that

> this image of foreign correspondents as elites offers an incomplete picture ... [because] traditional foreign correspondents no longer have hegemony over foreign news. Taken as a whole, the new classes of foreign correspondents are neither so elite nor so easily defined in their personal characteristics, outlook, or work habits.

This chapter explores the extent to which foreign correspondence has changed by tracing its evolution over the centuries. It explains how global reporting as such – an important strand of global journalism – has evolved. The history of foreign correspondence mirrors the history of journalism as a whole. The first 'journalistic' articles and publications were almost exclusively devoted to foreign stories. The key changes that we describe when looking at the main periods in the history of foreign correspondence did not just affect the work of foreign correspondents but also transformed the work of all journalists. They are significant because they correspond to important transformations in the respective societies journalists work in or report from. Understanding the present involves exploring the past.

Williams (2011, p. 1) defined international journalism as 'the process by which men and women gather, handle and deliver news and information from around the world', and he argued that 'at the heart of this activity is the foreign correspondent and the process of foreign correspondence'. Most dictionary definitions define a foreign correspondent as 'a reporter who sends news reports or commentary from a foreign country' (*American Heritage Dictionary of the English Language*, 2011). Williams (2011, p. 1) added that 'he or she is the node of a system of international news gathering which provides media outlets around the world with a regular, reliable and rapid flow of information'. We will stick to this definition because it covers the wide range of global reporting that foreign correspondents engage in. The main difference between foreign correspondents and home reporters is the fact that foreign correspondents report from abroad.

The Birth of Foreign Correspondence

When and how did it all start? Historical accounts of the early days of foreign correspondence are rare (for an overview see Cole & Hamilton, 2008; Williams, 2011). Williams (2011, p. 45) claimed that foreign stories appeared in the very first newspapers established in the early seventeenth century mainly in response to the interest in the wars of religion and the early explorations of Asia, Africa and the Americas. 'Europe's first newspapers were full of stories or hearsay about events across the length and breadth of the continent and beyond' (Williams, 2011, p. 45). Licensing and censorship contributed to the prevalence of foreign news in newspaper coverage in Western Europe 'well into the eighteenth century and beyond' (Williams, 2011, p. 47). 'Reporting foreign news was less risky than covering domestic affairs', because the European monarchs at the time did not want their subjects to know about their affairs (Williams, 2011, p. 45). He argued that the reporting of foreign news played a political role from its onset. Information gathering from foreign lands 'was an element in the economic and industrial exploitation of the world by Europeans' (Williams, 2011, p. 46). The precursors to newspapers – the so-called *corantos* – were 'periodical news pamphlets issued between 1621 and 1641, containing foreign intelligence taken from foreign papers' (Birch, 2009). The first *corantos* were published in England and the Netherlands. Plagiarism of stories from rival publications was very common but some stories, especially in the British press, were based on first-hand accounts or letters from diplomats and soldiers or information from the official government newspaper *The London Gazette*. Williams (2011, p. 49) argued that 'these accounts were often either bland or highly dubious in their veracity', and newspapers relied so much on foreign papers that any disruptions due to bad weather could result 'in empty pages, stories printed in a larger type face or extraneous accounts'. As a whole, up until the nineteenth century foreign news was 'collected in a casual and haphazard way' (Williams, 2011, p. 49).

Cole and Hamilton (2008) outlined similar trends in the US. They identified six eras in the evolution of foreign correspondence. The first was that of 'the casual correspondents' from 1700 to 1840. American newspapers also reprinted numerous stories from the European newspapers they received by ship with even longer delays than in Europe. As Cole and Hamilton (2008, p. 800) explained, 'a news item about Italy could be two or three months old because the British paper from which it was taken had to wait weeks to get the original report'. The first foreign correspondents were 'friendly souls in London or Paris who wrote letters home as well as passengers and crew who hove into port with newspapers from abroad and their own stories to tell' (Cole & Hamilton, 2008, pp. 799–800).

Three main types of foreign stories appeared in the early days of foreign news. First, 'phantasmagoria', such as 'tales of monsters', serpents and other scary creatures relayed by seafarers and born out of 'fear of the unknown, of lands unexplored and peoples undiscovered' (Williams, 2011, p. 47). Second, business and financial news, such as 'information about exchange rates, insolvencies and prices' as well as rumours about general events and developments, including 'battles, disasters, plots, miracles, royal births, deaths and marriages', executions, etc. (Williams, 2011, p. 48). Third, news about wars and conflicts. Americans were particularly interested in the Seven Years' War in the eighteenth century, which 'spilled over to the colonies in the form of the French and Indian War ... [because] a central issue in that conflict was which European nation would control North America' (Cole & Hamilton, 2008, p. 801).

The Professionalization of Foreign Correspondence

Foreign news reporting became much more professional in the nineteenth century. As Williams (2011) pointed out, the Industrial Revolution, the rise of the modern nation and subsequent cataclysmic events led to an increasing interest in foreign news. Travel (the steamship) and reporting (the telegraph) also became easier. The French Revolution attracted international interest. The London *Morning Post* sent 'an occasional correspondent' to France in 1789 but 'through a lamentable error in judgment, he missed the fall of the Bastille on July 14, the beginning of the great revolt that transformed Europe' (Hohenberg, 1993, p. 3). 'The whole business is over', concluded the reporter before going home (Hohenberg, 1995, p. 3). The practice of actually sending a journalist to a foreign country with the aim of dispatching reports back home developed in the early nineteenth century. The British newspaper *The Times* pioneered the practice by appointing Henry Crabb Robinson as its first foreign correspondent in 1807 (Hohenberg, 1995). Hohenberg (1995) argued that Robinson was not the first foreign correspondent in the world because other foreign newspaper reporters had arrived in Hamburg and Altona before him, but it was impossible to establish who the first one was. Nonetheless, even Robinson was not a conventional reporter in the modern-day sense of the word. He was 'a leisurely writer who sent letters on foreign affairs to his paper when he felt moved to do so' (Hohenberg, 1995, p. 4). Instead of 'chasing' Napoleon, he had an arrangement with a German newspaper to use their reports. He was in no rush to cover Napoleon's actions immediately and often sent important news home with a significant delay. As Hohenberg (1995, p. 4) put it, Robinson 'didn't perceptibly worry about covering Napoleon at long range but satisfied himself, as less-enterprising correspondents still do, by forwarding easily written pieces about the gossip and rumours of the era'. As a result, he only lasted in this post for six months. Back in London Robinson played an instrumental role in setting up a network of foreign correspondents at *The Times*, thus making the newspaper a market leader in the first half of the nineteenth century and contributing to its longstanding reputation as a quality newspaper (Hohenberg, 1995; Williams, 2011).

Other newspapers in Europe and the US also started investing in foreign news, and Cole and Hamilton (2008) described the second era of foreign correspondence in the US from 1840 to 1900 as the era of 'the specials'. The era was marked by the proliferation of specialist reporters, including foreign correspondents. The first foreign correspondents were either volunteers or worked part-time as they had other jobs. One of the most famous early foreign correspondents was Karl Marx who wrote articles from Europe for the *New-York Daily Tribune* from 1852 to 1861. This changed with the gradual commercialization of journalism. Hohenberg (1995) gave examples of three other newspapers, which like *The Times* were deeply committed to foreign reporting, and developed their own networks of foreign correspondents – the Swiss newspaper *Neue Zürcher Zeitung*, and the American *New York Herald* and *The Tribune*. *The Herald* had a network of foreign correspondents, most of whom were based in Europe.

Hohenberg (1995) argued that one of the best foreign specials at *The Tribune* was a woman – Margaret Fuller (Case Study 5.1). She went abroad in 1845 and most of her early work was social and literary criticism – articles on Goethe and other cultural and literary figures, travel sketches, etc. From 1848 onwards, however, she focused more on the revolutions in Europe. She wrote 'a lively and detailed description of the fall of Rome' (Hohenberg, 1995, p. 21) – a battle in which her own husband fought and she served as a nurse. Fuller and her family lost their lives in a storm on their way back to the US. A lot of the prominent foreign correspondents at the time also played an important activist role, or in Hohenberg's (1995, p. 45) words they had 'a crusading spirit'. They often exposed atrocities or injustice and their reporting not only raised awareness but also led to social change.

William Howard Russell, for example, was one of the most influential British foreign correspondents of the nineteenth century. To illustrate his importance, Hohenberg (1995, p. 26) gave an example of how US President Abraham Lincoln welcomed Russell into the White House: 'The London Times is one of the greatest powers in the world – in fact, I don't know anything which has more power than the Mississippi. I am glad to know you

Case Study 5.1: Female foreign correspondents

Margaret Fuller's experience is significant because she was arguably the first female foreign war correspondent and a champion for women's rights. Nearly two centuries later the role of female war correspondents is still hotly contested as memoirs of and interviews with women foreign correspondents demonstrate. Wu and Hamilton (2004) argued that the percentage of American women foreign correspondents rose dramatically during the 1980s and subsequently levelled off in the previous decade to about a quarter of the total number of foreign correspondents. Academic accounts on this topic are rare but women foreign correspondents themselves had focused on three key issues in their memoirs: (1) The extent to which the role of women as foreign correspondents and war reporters in particular has been 'normalized'. Most accounts suggested that female correspondents still encountered a range of prejudices. (2) The focus on potential dangers, especially sexual abuse. In Matloff's (2007) view, this was 'one area where they differ from the boys – sexual harassment and rape' because 'female reporters are targets in lawless places where guns are common and punishment rare'. A 2010 survey with 31 female war reporters showed that half of them had been sexually harassed or abused (International News Safety Institute, 2010). (3) 'Concerns' about the impact of their job on their families, especially if they have children. Asquith (2016) argued that despite the growing number of female foreign correspondents, perceptions about their role had not changed as much as they should have. She claimed that 'when it comes to winning prizes for their work, for example, female foreign correspondents are stuck in the last century' because most of the prestigious prizes for foreign reporting went to men. This in turn 'feeds a cycle that perpetuates the relative authority of men's voices over women's' and 'reinforces the notion that reporting on combat, mission strategy, and violent conflict qualifies as "hard news," while coverage of human rights, maternal health, sexual assault, and education – which women more frequently cover – is "soft" news' (Asquith, 2016).

as its Minister'. Russell's work came into the limelight in 1854–55 during the Crimean War. His reports exposed the sufferings of the British Army by showing how neglected and poorly resourced soldiers were and how they were dying from cholera and malaria. His reports were not well received by Queen Victoria and Prince Albert. Prince Albert called him 'one miserable scribbler … despoiling the country' (Simkin, 1997) but despite their criticisms, Russell was instrumental in bringing down the government (Hohenberg, 1995; Simkin, 1997). He was welcomed back as a hero in London – 'the man who had saved an army' (Hohenberg, 1995, p. 27). Russell also covered the US Civil War. His critical reports were met with hostility by the Northern press in the US and he turned into the 'best abused man in America, caricatured, insulted, threatened, shot at in the streets' (Hohenberg, 1995, p. 30). The situation deteriorated and the War Department refused to accredit him. He returned to London and retired soon after.

Another defining characteristic of that era was the general increase in the proportion of local news at the expense of foreign news in US newspapers due to the development of journalism as a business (Cole & Hamilton, 2008). A similar trend was evident in British newspapers but foreign news dominated in the French and German press until the early 1900s (Williams, 2011). Foreign news also appeared in the newspapers founded on other continents outside Europe and North America. As Williams explained, most of the first newspapers that were established in the colonies were set up by settlers from Europe – either missionaries or the colonial authorities. Therefore, they largely 'served the interests of the European community as well as the native elites who were co-opted into European culture in order to run the colony under the metropolis and the colonial administration' (Williams, 2011, p. 57).

Another key development during the nineteenth century was the establishment of news agencies on both sides of the Atlantic. The three current biggest news agencies – AP, Reuters and AFP – were all set up then. The first news agency – Agence Havas which later became AFP – was founded in France in 1835 by Charles Havas. Havas used trains and pigeons initially, and his business grew quickly as the first 'successful wholesaler of news' (Hohenberg, 1995, p. 7). In the meantime, five New York City newspapers got together in 1846 'to fund a pony express route through Alabama in order to bring news of the Mexican War north more quickly than the U.S. Post Office could deliver it' (Associated Press, 2016). They formed AP.

Shortly after, two other news agencies were established in Germany and in England. A former employee of Havas – Bernhard Wolff – set up Wolffs Telegraphisches Bureau (WTB) in Berlin in 1849. Another German, Paul Julius Reuter, established Reuters in 1851 in London. Reuter started off by transmitting stock market quotations and news between London and Paris over the new Dover–Calais submarine telegraph cable. The three European agencies even signed an agreement in 1856 to exchange stock prices and later political news as well. Their early clients were mainly financial bodies but newspapers also gradually started buying their packages from 1859 onwards. The rise in subscription fees was indicative of the rapid success of the news agencies. Reuters initially charged £30 per month but within ten years the fee went up to £1,000 a year (Hohenberg, 1995). Reuters in particular established a reputation for providing a quick, reliable and objective service to its clients. Its operations spread beyond the European continent and the agency was the first in Europe to announce the assassination of Lincoln in 1865 (Hohenberg, 1995). The international news agencies developed a style of writing, which later became known as "agency copy", placing 'their emphasis on their being first with the news, providing short accounts of action in plain language' (Williams, 2011, p. 51).

The invention of the telegraph put pressure on newspapers and agencies to deliver news with speed. The four agencies eventually formed the 'Four Power' cartel in 1870 in which they divided the world in four zones of exclusive news gathering and dissemination (Hohenberg, 1995) and agreed to freely exchange news between themselves. The divisions were Reuters: the British Empire, Turkey and the Far East; Havas: France, Switzerland, Italy, the Iberian Peninsula, Central and South America, and Egypt (in association with Reuters); WTB: Germany, Austria, Scandinavia, Russia, the Balkans and the Netherlands; AP: the US (Hohenberg, 1995). The cartel lasted until 1937. Williams (2011, p. 61) argued that three main reasons contributed to its collapse: the favourable position Reuters enjoyed at the expense of the American agencies (AP and later UPA) and the various national news agencies; the demise of WTB as a news agency; and the wartime blockade of news from Europe in 1914 as well as the 'rise of America as a world power'. Moreover, the European news agencies also played a controversial political role by perpetuating colonialism and/or their countries' national interests (Williams, 2011).

The Golden Age of Foreign Correspondence

The rise of America as a world power led to a reconsideration of the role of foreign news in the US. The Spanish-American War at the end of the nineteenth century was a decisive moment in that respect. Cole and Hamilton (2008, p. 802) argued that the first 30 years of the twentieth century were the era of 'the foreign service', which saw 'a much more systematic approach to news' as opposed to the focus on sensationalism and episodic coverage prior to that. Owners and editors were no longer happy to rely predominantly on agency copy, and they acknowledged that they needed more in-depth reports written by American reporters for the American public. 'If public opinion is to conduct our foreign affairs wisely, it must be rightly informed, by expert observers', an internal memo from the *Chicago Daily News* read (Cole & Hamilton, 2008, p. 803). The late nineteenth and early twentieth centuries were also a time when some important historical and literary figures such as Winston Churchill and Ernest Hemingway made their debuts as foreign correspondents. Churchill was a 'soldier-correspondent' – sending reports from countries such as Cuba, India and Sudan while also serving in the military (Hohenberg, 1995, p. 55). Hemingway was a foreign correspondent based in Paris during the 1920s. He covered events in other parts of Europe as well.

Morrell (1988) and Cole and Hamilton (2008) defined the era that followed as 'the golden age of foreign correspondence'. Cole and Hamilton (2008) called the period between 1930 and 1970 the era of 'the compleat correspondents'. The period between the two world wars was a particularly important chapter in the history of foreign correspondence, not just in the US but also in Europe. As Sambrook (2010, p. 5) argued

> the ideological battles of the early twentieth century, with the rise of communism and fascism, and two world wars, cemented the necessity for international reporting for most Western news organizations and led to the establishment of international bureaux and staff correspondents to guarantee the provision of reliable news.

Hamilton (2009, p. 194) argued that 'news was momentous. News outlets were plentiful. Living costs abroad were low … In no era have so many correspondents travelled so widely and so freely, many as highly independent freelancers'. The proliferation of foreign reporting was also aided by the development of magazines and broadcast media – radio in particular, but during later wars television as well. Foreign correspondents started writing books and memoirs, too, about their experiences (Cole & Hamilton, 2008). According to Sambrook (2010), two of the most powerful voices in foreign reporting during the Second World War were those of the CBS correspondent Ed Murrow, who was reporting from London, and the BBC journalist Richard Dimbleby reporting from Germany with his very powerful accounts of the Nazi concentration camps. Both of them focused on the human interest angle of the war – the civilian victims. Sambrook (2010, p. 6) argued that

> foreign reporting in the 1930s and 1940s … offered a narrative of conscience, a focus on victims and the humanitarian consequences of big events which still informs much international reporting today. They consolidated in the minds of editors and readers the core importance of bearing witness to unfurling events.

The end of the Second World War did not bring an end to the interest in foreign news, because it was superseded by the beginning of the Cold War between the West and the communist East. Hess (1996, p. 98) claimed that 'from the Truman presidency [1945–53] to the early 1990s the cold war spared editors the necessity for deep thinking about what information their consumers needed to know about the rest of the world'. The focus was very clearly placed on the countries and events that were perceived as potentially endangering the security of their own state. Sambrook (2010, p. 6) argued that the resources devoted 'reflected the politics of the time, with major bureaux in Moscow, Eastern Europe and Asia, and teams deployed to cover the proxy conflicts generated by the Cold War, in Africa, Central America and elsewhere'. Television also started playing a growing role in the process of foreign correspondence, especially at pivotal moments during the Cold War. The US President John F. Kennedy used the medium to address the nation during the Cuban Missile Crisis of 1962. The Vietnam War that ended in the mid-1970s was allegedly the first televised war (Mandelbaum, 1982).

The fall of the Berlin wall in 1989, however, brought about a diminishing interest in foreign news in the West. As Franks (2005, pp. 92–93) explained, 'wars and fighting continued, but they were no longer explicable in a colonial or Cold War framework and so were often dismissed as "tribal" or "ethnic" conflicts, neither comprehensible nor worthy of much interest'. The lack of coverage of the 1994 genocide in Rwanda best exemplified this trend. In spite of nearly a million people losing their lives, there was hardly any coverage of it in Western media in part due to the fact that 'most international news organizations initially misunderstood the nature of the killing in Rwanda, portraying it as the result of tribal warfare, rather than genocide' (Thompson, 2007, p. 2). Thompson (2007, p. 3) even argued that the lack of international coverage 'contributed to the behaviour of the perpetrators of the genocide – who were encouraged by the world's apathy and acted with impunity'.

Cole and Hamilton (2008) calculated that this downward trend in foreign correspondence started in the early 1970s. They called the period between 1970 and 2000 'the corporate correspondent' (Cole & Hamilton, 2008, p. 805) era. The number of foreign correspondents went down and they were generally 'far less free-wheeling and flamboyant, less likely to spend decades overseas' (Cole & Hamilton, 2008, p. 805). Corporate owners were increasingly more interested in attracting bigger audiences and making profits, and foreign news was generally more expensive. The advancement of technology led to the immediacy and proliferation of news, which in turn put foreign correspondents under more pressure and made in-depth reporting more difficult.

The Post-Cold War Period with a Focus on War Reporting

The coverage of the Balkan wars (1991–2001) and the first Gulf War in the early 1990s exemplified a trend towards increased mediatization of conflict, which continued in the post 9/11 'war(s) on terror'. Cottle (2006) argued that the media 'do not simply report or represent diverse situations of conflict', but actively 'enact' and 'perform' them (back cover). The advent of

24/7 news channels brought about live coverage of wars and crises. Robinson (1999, p. 301) even used the phrase the 'CNN effect' – 'the idea that real-time communications technology could provoke major responses from domestic audiences and political elites to global events'. The purpose of this chapter is not to evaluate theoretical assumptions about the role of the media (see Chapter 3) but it is worth briefly exploring some of the practical implications of the increased mediatization of conflict for foreign correspondents.

As already mentioned, these men and women are under increased pressure to transmit news fast, even while events unfold in front of their eyes. There are many recent examples of reporters who appear to expose themselves to danger, especially in pieces-to-camera when bombs explode behind their backs or viewers can hear shots fired in the distance. In addition to that, as already indicated in Chapter 2, NGOs, such as the CPJ, claim that terrorist groups have launched 'jihad against journalists'. Iraq and Syria, where ongoing large-scale conflicts/wars have taken place, were also the two most dangerous countries for journalists, and the majority of journalists who lost their lives in these two countries were war reporters. Feinstein and Sinyor's (2009) study of 218 frontline journalists, who had worked in conflict zones for 15 years on average, also showed that 'exposure to life-threatening events creates potential risk for conditions such as post-traumatic stress disorder (PTSD), depression and substance abuse'. They 'revealed rates of PTSD five times higher than those found in the general population' (Feinstein & Sinyor, 2009). However, by focusing too much on the potential dangers that war reporters face, commentators run the risk of idealizing their work and potentially ignoring some of the main issues surrounding it.

In his anthropological book about the international press pack during the civil war in San Salvador in the late 1980s and early 1990s, Pedelty (1995) argued that two contrasting images of war reporters prevailed. On the one hand, in their autobiographies war correspondents presented themselves as heroes in 'an endless dance with death' with rare mentions of the controversial practice of pack journalism or indeed the 'countless hours spent sitting in press conferences, interviews, taxis, and offices waiting for something "big" to happen' (Pedelty, 1995). On the other hand, solidarity workers viewed foreign correspondents as 'mindless agents of US foreign policy' who 'did little more than attend US embassy functions and get drunk' in hotel lobby bars (Pedelty, 1995). Neither of these two accounts was entirely correct. Pedelty (1995) claimed that 'the autobiographic discourse of war correspondence is not, for the most part, a representation of normal routine, but instead an aggregate of exceptional moments'. While the dangers of war reporting should not be underestimated, it is vital for us to acknowledge that this is not the most common cause of death for journalists and that some measures have been taken to address these safety issues (see Case Study 5.2). 296 out of a total of 1,310 journalists have been killed in crossfire since 1992 (Committee to Protect Journalists, 2018a).

A controversial development that has gained prominence since the early 1990s is the practice of embedded journalism – placing journalists under the control of a specific military unit and allowing them to accompany troops into combat zones. This practice was widely used during the Second World War,

---

Case Study 5.2: Embedded journalism

Embedded journalism is 'the practice of placing journalists within and under the control of one side's military during an armed conflict' by attaching them to a military unit and allowing them to 'accompany troops into combat zones' (Löffelholz, 2016). The practice was introduced by the US Department of Defense during the Iraq War (2003–11) as 'a strategic response to criticisms about the low level of access granted to reporters during the Persian Gulf War (1990–91) and the early years of the Afghanistan War (which began in 2001)' (Löffelholz, 2016). As many as 700 journalists were embedded during the invasion of Iraq. The practice has, however, been widely criticized since by both academics and journalists. The main argument against it is that it leads to a 'distorted view of war' (Cockburn, 2010). Cockburn (2010) argued that embedded journalism earned a bad name during the wars in Iraq and Afghanistan because 'the phrase came to evoke an image of the supposedly independent correspondent truckling to military mentors who spoon-feed him or her absurdly optimistic information about the course of the war. To many, the embedded journalist is a grisly throwback to First World War-style reporting, when appalling butchery in the trenches was presented as a series of judiciously planned advances by British generals'. Critics claimed that embedded journalists were subjective by default because they inevitably gave undue representation to the views of the side they were embedded with. In Tuosto's (2008, p. 20) view, embedded journalism has led to 'an unprecedented media-military collaboration', which 'allows for a pro-war propaganda machine disguised as an objective eyewitness account of the war effort in Iraq'. One of the key disadvantages of the practice was that in their reporting journalists focused predominantly on the military operations and ignored important political developments or indeed some of the key issues such as the rise in the number of civilians who lost their lives in military conflicts (Cockburn, 2010). Tuosto (2008, p. 22) described a process of 'an unprecedented hyper-dramatization of war'. She claimed that there was a general trend towards preoccupying the public with 'stories of war correspondents rather than stories of war' as well as 'an overall desensitization to the horrors of warfare' (Tuosto, 2008, pp. 27–28). Nonetheless, the practice had its benefits, perhaps best summed up by journalist Marjorie Miller (quoted in Tuosto, 2008, p. 21) who said: 'We didn't want to be in bed with the military, but we certainly wanted to be there.' A record number of journalists had unprecedented access to military operations in conflict zones. Moreover, some of the reports they sent back home or in fact the documentaries they produced years later contributed to the important debate about potential cases of abuse or extreme and unjustified violence by soldiers.

but was labelled 'embedded journalism' when it was introduced by the US Department of Defense during the second Iraq War (2003–11). It has been widely criticized due to the ethical and safety implications.

Another trend in war reporting has been towards the 'foxification' of news coverage. The term denotes journalistic practices emulating Fox News's controversial style of reporting and presenting, which promotes 'news values that run counter to public service traditions, with the emphasis on sensationalism, a tabloid style, speculation rather than factual reporting and partisanship rather than balance and objectivity' (Cushion & Lewis, 2009, p. 132). Cushion and Lewis (2009) stated that this trend was particularly evident during the second Iraq War when Fox News achieved impressive commercial success with their 'patriotic' coverage of the war. Moreover, they also claimed that other channels, such as MSNBC, adopted a similar style of coverage by branding their news with patriotic symbols, such as the US flag, and encouraging their viewers to send photos of "America's Bravest" soldiers (Cushion & Lewis, 2009, p. 133). Cushion and Lewis's (2009, p. 132) analysis showed that the drive behind this trend was 'both commercial and ideological – to gain greater audience share and present a partial view of the world – rather than embrace a more public service ethos, which is traditionally associated with promoting audience understanding and democratic participation'.

Case Study 5.3: The journalism of attachment

The journalism of attachment was first proposed by the BBC foreign and war correspondent Martin Bell. He argued that the 'tradition of objective and dispassionate journalism' (Bell, 1998, p. 10) and the requirement for journalists to adopt a pose of 'distance and detachment' (Bell, 1997, p. 8), which were prevalent in Western journalism orthodoxy, were outmoded. They asked journalists to treat all parties, causes and conditions as essentially equal: there could be no distinction between 'good and evil, right and wrong, the victim and the oppressor'. However, journalists should not be 'bystanders', somehow 'neutered' in the face of events, 'indifferent' to consequences (Bell, 1997, pp. 10, 15). Journalism should care as well as know (Bell, 1997, p. 8). All facts/factors, while being adhered to and represented, were not equal. It was necessary to distinguish, as Hume (1997, p. 4) put it, between 'the innocent and the forces of darkness'.

His view ignited a debate which both became 'heated and acrimonious' (McLaughlin, 2016, p. 33) and continued long after Bell retired from journalism (O'Neill, 2012a). The initial response came from Hume (1997, p. 4–5) who argued that journalists were being encouraged to take a moral position which led to them deciding who was worthy of a good or bad press, 'slaying monsters' of their own making, as unaccountable arbiters of values engaged on 'a self-appointed mission'. Reporting became one-sided, bordering on propaganda (McLaughlin, 2016, p. 46).

On a practical note, commenting on the death of an adherent of the journalism of attachment, Marie Colvin, in Syria in 2012, O'Neill (2012a) asked, 'if journalists allow themselves to become moral combatants, crusaders against "evil" rather than mere reporters of fact, is there not a danger that they will be treated as combatants?' There was also the possibility that journalists would themselves become the story: Michael Nicholson, a senior foreign correspondent for the UK's Independent Television News, intervened when he discovered an orphanage under military threat, and eventually adopted one of the children. He wrote about this in a book, *Natasha's Story* (1994) which formed the basis of a film, *Welcome to Sarajevo* (1997) (McLaughlin, 2016).

Why did the journalism of attachment emerge in the mid-1990s? McLaughlin (2016) pointed out that, although it was a new term, the idea was far from novel. However, in the 1990s it was becoming more apparent that there was an omission in international law. Although the idea of 'crimes against humanity' had been raised as early as 1915, it had not been codified or applied. Then in the 1990s it was revisited in relation to events in Yugoslavia (1993), Rwanda (1994) and Cambodia (1997). At the same time, the capacity of journalists to comprehensively cover unjust wars, genocides, ethnic cleansing, massacres, campaigns of terror, state oppression, and so on had increased exponentially, particularly through television. Journalists, imbued with the ethic of truthfulness and suspicious of 'official sources', looked, and were able, to experience first-hand things which in a previous era they had only been told about second-hand, and cameras brought those events directly to publics (Bell, 1997, p. 12; Tumber & Webster, 2006, p. 17).

Many journalists – not just those who were sympathetic to the journalism of attachment – were concerned about how to represent 'truth' in circumstances which were often confused, and in which manipulation of journalists was commonplace and misinformation was rife, but the power to report was enormous. As one correspondent told Tumber and Webster (2006, p. 74): 'How can you balance something when you're watching a village of Muslims being wiped out in Serbia? ... you report what you see. That's the best you can do'.

Foreign Correspondents Today: a Vanishing Species?

As a whole, the technological, economic and political changes in the last few decades have led commentators to consider the extent to which foreign correspondents are becoming 'an endangered species' (Hamilton & Jenner, 2004a, p. 302; Willnat & Martin, 2012, p. 495) or whether they are becoming 'redundant' (Sambrook, 2010). Enda (2011) argued 18 newspapers and two chains in the US closed down all their foreign bureaux between 1998 and 2010, and 'many other papers and chains reduced their coterie of foreign correspondents, meticulously choosing which bureaux to close. A 2011 *American Journalism*

Review census showed that while there were 307 full-time foreign correspondents in 2003, in 2011 this number was down to 234. A recent Tyndall report (quoted by Wadekar, 2015) demonstrated that when the Berlin Wall fell in 1989, the US networks ABC(US), CBS and NBC devoted a collective 4,828 minutes to international news but 'by 2000, after ten years of declining coverage, the same three networks aired only 2,127 minutes of international news'. Similarly, Moore's (2010) study indicated that the number of international stories in the British press fell by 40 per cent from 1979 to 2009. His analysis showed that 'international politics has been the biggest loser', because 'there is less of it and it tends to be more focused on the UK'. Political reporting of the two superpowers of the Cold War had not been replaced by 'a substantial growth in coverage of some of the world's emerging superpowers – such as China, India and Brazil' (Moore, 2010, p. 25).

We already briefly alluded to some of the reasons that have contributed to the decline in foreign correspondence but let us now explore the three key factors. According to Sambrook (2010), these were technology, globalization and economics. The advent of the internet and a range of digital technologies in the past few decades have fundamentally changed the way people produce, disseminate and receive news. Legacy media are not the main news providers any more and lots of online media produce and/or aggregate news. The role of foreign correspondents has inevitably changed as a result of the technological innovations and we already mentioned some of the most prominent changes. News is instantaneous and ongoing, the news cycle is 24/7, and citizen journalists also post reports online. As Sambrook (2010, p. 28) pointed out, foreign reporting has become 'more productive – in terms of quantity at least', and more personal to an extent with some foreign correspondents also publishing blogs online. One consequence is that 'opinion-led journalism is drowning out fact or evidence-based journalism' (Sambrook, 2010, p. 31). The diversity of platforms has not necessarily led to a diversity of agendas or opinions because the big news media still provide a good proportion of the coverage (Sambrook, 2010). The number of freely available eyewitness reporters has undoubtedly increased but the availability of unverified information poses considerable ethical challenges. Another key change is the enhanced opportunities for 'the public to contribute to, partake in and consume international news and information in deeper ways than ever before' (Sambrook, 2010, p. 43).

A second key process that goes hand-in-hand with the advent of technology is globalization. Sambrook (2010) argued that the end of the Cold War also brought about the process of globalization and the overall fragmentation of politics. Put simply, the world is now much more interconnected than before, and 'the clear framework' (Willnat & Martin, 2012, p. 495) for covering international affairs that existed during the Cold War is not in place any more. Sambrook (2010, p. 53) quoted media columnist William Powers who argued that 'new foreign news is diffuse, many-layered, sprawling, chaotic and terribly complicated … like the world itself'. Moreover, the very definition of foreign news has changed because 'what was once "foreign" is better known' (Sambrook, 2010, p. 47). Big organizations such as Reuters employ considerably more local reporters than before as local staff provide 'instant expertise and cultural context' (Sambrook, 2010, p. 56).

Journalists are under increased pressure because 'globalisation has forced greater levels of transparency around international news – with a consequent pressure to deliver greater accuracy, fairness and accountability' (Sambrook, 2010, p. 48). In the absence of a clear framework for reporting international news, the general trend observed around the world is: a definite focus on Western Europe and the US at the expense of the rest of the world and coverage of stories closer to home. Williams (2011, p. 95) argued that the declining numbers of foreign correspondents were 'associated with the concentration of staff in certain parts of the world', while 'certain parts of the world have virtually disappeared off the global map of foreign news coverage'. A continent such as Africa is of little interest to Western media, judged by the number of foreign bureaux based in African countries (see Table 5.1). Bunce (2015, p. 16)

Table 5.1 News media with the highest number of foreign bureaux

News organization	No. of foreign bureaux	Geographical spread
AP	90	Europe – 30 Asia – 28 Americas – 21 Africa – 8 Australia – 3
AFP	112	Europe – 36 Asia – 34 Americas – 25 Africa – 15 Australia – 2
BBC	44	Asia – 19 Americas – 10 (6 in the USA) Europe – 10 (6 in Western Europe) Africa – 5
CNN	31	Asia – 16 (including Istanbul) Europe – 6 Americas – 5 Africa – 4

Table 5.1 (continued)

News organization	No. of foreign bureaux	Geographical spread
Wall Street Journal	35	Asia – 19 (including Istanbul and Jerusalem) Europe – 9 (7 in Western Europe) Americas – 5 Africa – 2
Al Jazeera	'Close to 70'	Asia – 12 Europe – 6 Americas – 5 Africa – 5 Australia – 1
Reuters	200	
Dow Jones		Americas – 13 Europe – 22 Asia – 22 Australia – 4 Africa – 2
Bloomberg	124	Europe – 38 Asia – 30 Americas – 14 Africa – 6 Australia – 5
Xinhua News Agency	106	Middle East – 22 Asian Pacific – 22 Europe – 18 Africa – 13 Latin America – 13 North America – 4 (Dong, 2012)

Note: The information is derived from the news organisations' websites unless otherwise specified. The bureaux the organization has in the country in which it is officially based are not included in the count. The information about Al Jazeera is incomplete because the list of continents covered is based on the list of field correspondents published by Al Jazeera in 2008 while the number of current bureaux was updated in 2014. The AFP website claimed that the agency had 200 bureaux but the actual list on the website included 112 bureaux. Reuters' website claimed that it covered the news from 200 locations but no detailed information was available. Xinhua's website claimed that it had 106 overseas bureaux and 36 domestic bureaux and sub-bureaux but the full list was not included. The information about its list of bureaux is based on Dong's (2012) study.

claimed that the 'big three' news agencies were the main providers of news from Africa. The number of foreign correspondents based on the continent is very low – 'a small number of "elite" outlets tend to have one or perhaps two correspondents covering a very large, complex and expensive-to-manoeuver continent'. Junghanns and Hanitzsch's (2006) study of German foreign correspondents showed a similar trend – only 6.3 per cent covered Africa while 44.9 per cent covered Europe.

Obijiofor and Hanusch (2011, p. 126) actually argued that not much had changed in that respect because it was still very much the case that

> the only time developing countries receive prominence in Western news media ... is when there are issues that tie developing countries to the interests of the First World ('elite') countries, or, more commonly, when extraordinary events such as natural disasters and political instability occur in non-elite countries.

Moreover, their brief review of existing studies on the topic showed that even in non-Western countries, 'the West and the United States enjoyed unique prominence as a news superpower', although some studies showed a general tendency towards regionalism – 'African countries were most concerned with African affairs, South American countries with Latin American news, and so on' (Obijiofor & Hanusch, 2011, p. 121).

Moreover, this trend has also been exacerbated by a second very important factor – the economic situation and the collapse of the traditional business model of legacy media. The financial woes of news media have been extensively discussed both in popular and academic literature. Dwindling advertising revenues and profits, the economic recession and overall greater financial pressures have led to reduced investments in foreign news not just because of the diminishing interest in international stories, but also because 'original foreign reporting is an expensive business' (Moore, 2010, p. 31; Sambrook, 2010). Cutting back on foreign bureaux is 'a quick way to save money' (Franks, 2005, p. 94). Moore (2010) quoted the 2007 Harvard Shorenstein Center's cost estimates according to which a basic foreign bureau, without capital expenditure, cost $200,000–$300,000 a year, and considerably more in war zones. Murrell (2014) cited CNN's Michael Ware who argued that a single journalist in Baghdad cost between $750,000 and $1,000,000. If sending a reporter, with a translator and/or fixer, a single story could cost £5,000–£6,000 a trip (Moore, 2010). Sambrook (2010, p. 12) also pointed out that 'the revenue directly generated by international news (advertising on the foreign pages for example) has never been sufficient to cover these costs'.

These three key factors have led to a general 'shrinking' of foreign news and traditional foreign correspondence. The 'profit-driven agenda' (Obijiofor & Hanusch, 2011, p. 112) has generally led to a stronger focus on cheaper and lighter stories – infotainment at the expense of more serious investigative or foreign reporting. One alternative increasingly seen in the age of 24/7 news has been the so-called firefighter reporting (Franks, 2005, p. 94) or 'parachute journalism', the practice of sending journalists 'to cover foreign events as and when events occur' (Obijiofor & Hanusch, 2011, p. 114) as opposed to having a permanently based foreign correspondent in a country or a city. The practice has been widely criticized (for a summary, see Obijiofor & Hanusch, 2011) because parachute journalists lacked in-depth knowledge of the context and they often turned into a 'dish monkey' – 'someone stuck next to a dish for hours on end is the last creature on earth to have learned anything new, and probably unaware of a corpse twenty yards away' (Adie, 2002 as quoted in Franks, 2005, p. 94).

Not all researchers shared the view that foreign correspondence was in decline or indeed dying. Archetti (2013, p. 419) argued that foreign correspondence was evolving rather than becoming redundant and these 'changes are not necessarily for the worse'. In her view, 'the heavy use of new communication technologies – rather than leading to superficial and low-quality reporting – also supports the pursuit of exclusive news-story angles and a fuller delivery of the correspondent's value'. Cole and Hamilton (2008, p. 806) claimed that foreign correspondents were a 'surviving species' entering into a 'confederacy of correspondences' era, which involved 'a system of multiple models co-existing and collectively providing information'. Their argument was that 'the overall result is a broader, more variegated class of foreign correspondents that, if still imperfect, ensures continued foreign news flow and forms a basis for improvement' (Cole & Hamilton, 2008, p. 807). Similarly, Hamilton and Jenner (2004, p. 303) stated that although the traditional foreign correspondent was 'endangered', foreign correspondence was actually 'flourishing in new environments'. Therefore, the term used should be 'evolution', not 'extinction'.

It should be pointed out that some beats such as the Brussels/EU beat have been growing. Terzis and Harding (2015, pp. 18–19) tracked the growth as the EU expanded from 12 to 28 members – 259 correspondents in 1976; 480 in 1987; 783 in 1995; 929 in 2004, and 1022 in 2013. This included 'a spectacular rise' in the number of Chinese correspondents to 43, equal to the number of Americans (Terzis & Harding, 2015, p. 22). Also, the economic troubles of Western media (especially print media) are not necessarily shared by non-Western media. As already stated in Chapter 2, there has been a boom in newspaper readership in India and China, for example. Does this mean that Asian media have invested more money in foreign correspondents? There is no easy answer to this question due to the dearth of studies on the topic. Academic research published in English suffers from a similar problem as foreign correspondence in general – Western-centrism. Sambrook (2010, p. 71) argued that 'unlike the West, China is expanding its international journalism, from America to Zimbabwe'. In 2009 the Chinese government announced its intention to spend $US7bn on the international expansion of its news media with a particular focus on CCTV (now CGTN) and Xinhua (Sambrook, 2010). Dong's (2012) study showed that the Chinese news agency

Xinhua had quadrupled its number of foreign bureaux from 28 in 1950 to 123 in 2010. In March 2017, Xinhua had 106 overseas bureaux and by July 2018 it was reported that it had 180 overseas bureax. Also notable was its expansion of foreign clients – from 56 in 1996 to more than 200 in 2010. The number of news items it produced had substantially grown as well – from 8,400 per year in 1996 to 110,000 in 2010 (Dong, 2012). However, the Chinese government's media expansion intentions appear to be driven by a propagandist agenda and as such Xinhua's role is also used as an instrument of soft power (similar to Russia's investment in RT). As Dong (2012, p. 56) pointed out,

> the transition of Xinhua from a pure propaganda machine with Communist ideology, to a partially capitalized media group performing more informational functions … is under the control of the government, with the purpose of strengthening China's power in the international arena. Fundamentally, Xinhua is supposed to perform its oppressive propaganda function during China's global development strategy.

Therefore, while these investments appear to bring more foreign news to Chinese audiences and potentially greater exposure to Chinese news for Western audiences, their contribution to the development of a more diverse and plural public sphere and the informational purposes they serve are highly arguable.

Foreign Correspondents Today

What kind of foreign correspondents do media organizations deploy in the early twenty-first century? Boyd-Barrett identified three types of foreign correspondents in Britain in 1979: staff correspondents who work for one news organization only, general reporters who are sent abroad to cover stories occasionally, and stringers – local contributions who have an agreement with one or more news media. Hamilton and Jenner (2004a) and Cole and Hamilton (2008) recognized that these traditional types of foreign correspondents still existed but they also argued that due to the recent technological changes, other 'species' had also emerged. Hamilton and Jenner (2004a, pp. 313–14) proposed a new typology of foreign correspondents which included: traditional foreign correspondents, parachute journalists, foreign foreign correspondents, local foreign correspondents, foreign local correspondents, in-house foreign correspondents, premium service foreign correspondents, amateur correspondents (later defined by Cole and Hamilton as citizen foreign correspondents). Table 5.2 summarizes the main characteristics of each type of foreign correspondent.

Table 5.2 Hamilton and Jenner's (2004) typology of foreign correspondents, later further developed by Cole and Hamilton (2008)

Type of foreign correspondent	Main characteristics
Traditional foreign correspondent	Permanently based in a location abroad, covering events for one news medium
Parachute journalist	Sent to cover events in a foreign country if and when events occur, e.g., embedded reporters within the army
Foreign foreign correspondent	'The hired foreign national' (Hamilton & Jenner, 2004a, p. 313)
Local foreign correspondent	Local reporters covering foreign news 'from home' (Hamilton & Jenner, 2004a, p. 313)
Foreign local correspondent	A reporter for a foreign news organization 'whose news is available worldwide on the internet or via satellite' (Hamilton & Jenner, 2004a, p. 313)
In-house foreign correspondent	An employee 'of a non-news organization whose exclusive job is to provide updated and high-quality news and information related to the organization's mission' (Cole & Hamilton, 2008, p. 806)
Premium service foreign correspondent	Working for 'gated', high-cost news services such as Bloomberg News and the Dow Jones News
Amateur/ citizen foreign correspondent	Amateur (not professional) journalists sending news reports (mainly online)

Summary

Global reporting has significantly evolved from its initial incarnations in the early seventeenth century – in the form of letters from travellers, merchants and soldiers and war reports with significant delays as well as stories about monsters and serpents in unknown lands – to its contemporary version of instantaneous, 24/7 live coverage, including from combat zones. Nonetheless, some trends appear to have perpetuated over the centuries. Foreign correspondence was born in the advanced Western countries and despite the range of financial difficulties experienced by journalists in these countries in recent decades, Western-centrism is still very much the norm both in terms of regions covered by foreign correspondents and also in terms of topics that appear on the 'global agenda'. The number of countries, regions and continents with no permanent foreign bureaux based in them is increasing – ironically at a time when we evidence a rise of disturbing developments, including public health threats (the Ebola outbreak) and military conflicts. Mainly stringers and parachute journalists cover Africa, Latin America and parts of Asia, and the implications of this development concern many. The economic crisis of journalism, the end of the Cold War, globalization and the advent of new technologies have brought about a shrinking in the number of foreign correspondents and have led commentators to debate whether we are evidencing an 'extinction' of foreign correspondence as such. While conventional foreign reporting by men and women permanently based in a locale and dispatching stories to their home countries has indeed changed, the evidence presented in this chapter suggests that foreign correspondents are not a vanishing species, and while the nature of foreign correspondence has indisputably transformed, the need for in-depth and well-informed reports is more acute than ever. In the age of infotainment, news fragmentation and with no clear geo-political framework for reporting foreign news, audiences need competent professional journalistic reports to make sense of developments in distant lands. New types of foreign correspondents have appeared throughout the world. Moreover, countries outside of the Western world, especially on the Asian continent, are showing an increased interest and investment in foreign news. In addition to that, citizen/amateur journalists have also made their contributions to the field (Chapter 6).

Further Reading

1. Cohen, B.C. (1963) *The Press and Foreign Policy* (Princeton, NJ: Princeton University Press).
2. Cole, J. & Hamilton, J.M. (2008) 'The history of a surviving species', *Journalism Studies* 9(5), 798–812.
3. Cottle, S. (2006) *Mediatized Conflict: Developments in Media and Conflict Studies* (Maidenhead: Open University Press).
4. Hamilton, J.M. & Jenner, E. (2004b) 'Foreign correspondence: evolution, not extinction', *Nieman Reports* 58/3, 98–100.
5. Hohenberg, J. (1995) *Foreign Correspondence: The Great Reporters and Their Times* (Syracuse, NY: Syracuse University Press).
6. O'Neill, B. (2012a) 'Dangers of the "journalism of attachment"', *The Drum* (24 February), www.abc.net.au, accessed 7 March 2017.
7. Sambrook, R. (2010) *Are Foreign Correspondents Redundant?* (Oxford: The Reuters Institute for the Study of Journalism).
8. Williams, K. (2011) *International Journalism* (London: Sage).

6

From Them to Us: Alternative and Citizen Journalism

Chapter overview

This chapter explores the role of citizen and alternative journalists, activists and social media. It provides definitions and maps out the history of alternative and citizen journalism by focusing on case studies and projects from around the world, including ones whose significance spans across national contexts. It also investigates the relationship between legacy media and citizen journalism by asking whether this relationship resembles a forced marriage.

Learning outcomes

After having read this chapter you will be able to:

1. Define the terms 'citizen journalism' and 'alternative journalism' by also unpacking existing definitions
2. Discuss the key developments in the history of citizen and alternative journalism
3. List specific examples of citizen journalism projects and platforms, and reflect upon their key features
4. Explore the relationship between legacy media and citizen journalism.

'Helicopter hovering above Abbottabad at 1AM (is a rare event).' 'A huge window shaking bang here in Abbottabad Cantt. I hope its not the start of something nasty :-S' These tweets were posted by a 33-year-old IT consultant who later became known as 'the man who live-tweeted Osama's death'. Sohaib Athar unknowingly tweeted details of the US-led raid on the terrorist's compound as it happened – hours before Barack Obama officially announced the news about Osama bin Laden's death. Since then Athar's tweets have often been given as a prime example of citizen journalism. However, citizen journalism needs to be defined, and its evolution tracked in order to determine how that may have influenced its definition. Furthermore, what relationship (historical or current) has citizen journalism had with a pre-existing form of journalism – alternative journalism – which set itself in opposition to professional/industrial/mass media journalism? What characteristics do various citizen journalism projects demonstrate, and how do they help with defining the concept?

Although much citizen journalism is hyperlocal (Williams, 2016a), the focus here is on developments and projects in citizen journalism whose significance spans national contexts. Particular attention is paid to alleged 'online revolutions' such as the Arab Spring, and to the emergence of forms of alternative and citizen journalism in countries governed by both hard and soft authoritarian regimes (specifically in Asia, such as South Korea and North Korea). Various case studies illustrate the potential impact of alternative and citizen journalism on mainstream media and society and the common issues and challenges both for amateur and traditional journalists, but also the seemingly different practices they engage in and their varied contexts – from Occupy New York City bloggers and Brazilian ninja citizen journalists to North Koreans sharing their videos about the regime in the country by smuggling them into South Korea. Finally, we examine the relationship between legacy media/'industrial journalism' and citizen journalism.

Legacy media have reacted in different ways to the advent of citizen journalism – from introducing dedicated user-generated content (UGC) units (e.g. the BBC) to developing separate platforms aimed at encouraging citizen participation in news reporting (e.g. CNN's iReport). In analysing the nature of these relationships, can we genuinely talk about 'networked journalism' (Beckett, 2010, p. 1) or even a forced marriage? Examples of citizen journalism projects aided or to a great extent run by professional journalists seem to indicate an increasing blurring of the boundaries between citizen and professional journalists.

What is Citizen Journalism? Terms of Reference

Waisbord (2014, p. 186) argued that citizen journalism was 'a relatively straightforward concept', and it referred to '"random acts of journalism"' 'practised by ordinary people. Stuart Allan (2013, p. 9) provided a slightly more detailed definition:

[A] type of first-person reportage in which ordinary individuals temporarily adopt the role of a journalist in order to participate in newsmaking, often spontaneously during a time of crisis, accident, tragedy or disaster when they happen to be present on the scene.

He explained that the term was fairly new – it 'gained currency' in the aftermath of the South Asian tsunami at the end of 2004. Gillmor (2004) also claimed that this was a pivotal moment in the history of citizen journalism – 'This is one of those before and after moments. There will be before the tsunami and after the tsunami.' Other terms used to describe similar processes are: 'user-generated content'; 'grassroots journalism'; 'open source journalism'; 'participatory journalism'; 'hyperlocal journalism'; 'distributed journalism'; and 'networked journalism' (Allan, 2013, p. 9). Key to these definitions are two factors: (1) citizen journalism is a type of journalism, and (2) as Waisbord (2013, p. 185) pointed out, it is 'non-professional journalism', namely it is different from 'industrial journalism' – 'produced by news bureaucracies – it doesn't follow standard rules, isn't produced by paid labor, and isn't housed in news companies'.

Cottle (2014, p. x) argued that citizen journalism materialized in different forms – from 'deliberately pursued and circulated images by activists' to 'contingent scenes witnessed by bystanders'. He believed that there was much more to citizen journalism 'than the media industry's preferred term of "user-generated content"'. He objected to the use of the term 'user-generated content' because 'it doesn't do justice to the more radical, pluralizing or mobilizing forms of communications that coalesce under the umbrella term of "citizen journalism"'. He praised the 'expanding rise of citizen journalism within major crises and conflicts around the world', particularly in states run by authoritarian regimes. Moreover, in his view UGC as a term 'offers a particularly stunted and proprietorial view of "its" user audience and the corporate utility of "their" generated content'. While acknowledging 'the continuing need for further refined conceptualization and theorization', he defined citizen journalism as 'a more active, participatory and responsible sense of "being in the world", one that variously enacts and brings alive a sense of civic duty or civil society in action, whether as moral witness or agent of change' (Cottle, 2014, p. xi).

Cottle's conceptualization of citizen journalism with an emphasis on social activism particularly in non-democratic countries moves more into the realm of a particular type of citizen journalism – what Atton and Hamilton (2008, p. 1) defined as 'alternative journalism'. In their view, alternative journalism 'can include the media of protest groups, dissidents, fringe political organisations, even fans and hobbyists'. Similar to citizen journalism, alternative journalism was produced by amateurs who 'report from their position as citizens, as members of communities, as activists or as fans' (Atton & Hamilton, 2008, p. 2). This type of journalism 'proceeds from dissatisfaction not only with the mainstream coverage of certain issues and topics, but also with the epistemology of news' – conventions of news writing, values and norms, the professional, elite basis of journalism, and the 'subordinate role of audience as receiver' (Atton & Hamilton, 2008, p. 1). Alternative journalism is not just the domain of social activists because it 'may be home to explorations of individual enthusiasm and sub-cultural identity just as much as to radical visions of society and the polity' (Atton & Hamilton, 2008, p. 2).

Towards a History of Citizen Journalism and Alternative Journalism

The 2004 Boxing Day (26 December) tsunami in South Asia prompted an eruption of citizen reports – witness accounts, photos, video footage, blogs – and as a result was seen as 'a decisive moment ... when citizen journalism became a prominent feature on the journalistic landscape' (Allan, 2009, p. 18). What made this particular disaster so important in the history of journalism? To start with, because of its geographical remoteness (relative to Western media), there were no foreign reporters there at the time when the disaster happened. As the then head of Reuters explained, none of the agency's 2,300 journalists or 1,000 stringers was on the beaches the moment the wave struck. However, tourists who were there at the time of the disaster were actively relaying first-hand accounts and visuals of what had happened. 'For the first 24 hours the best and only photos and video came from tourists' (Glocer, 2006). This meant that news and visuals about the tsunami spread not only on social media; legacy media also had to increasingly rely on citizen reports and footage. The importance of these citizen reports became newsworthy in itself with numerous media publishing articles on this topic. The term 'citizen journalism' became a permanent feature of both academic and media discourses.

This connection between crisis reporting and citizen journalism still very strongly dominates the narrative (Allan, 2009; Cottle, 2014). Even before the term came into use, there were instances of eyewitness accounts appearing on the web in crisis situations. Contributions by non-journalists to news reports were not new. Particularly from the 1980s, domestic quality electronic goods, such as still and video cameras and sound recorders, could capture images and sound suitable for broadcast (Bromley, 2012, p. 27).

There were millions in use in industrialized countries. The 1991 beating by police of Rodney King in Los Angeles was filmed by a local resident who sent the footage to a news station. Even before that, Frank Zapruder caught the assassination of President John F. Kennedy on camera in 1963. As noted in Chapter 5 some of the early foreign correspondents were non-journalist citizens, albeit privileged ones. These contributions may be more accurately described as 'amateur' and UGC rather than citizen journalism (Wardle & Dubberley, 2014).

Using blogs and other Web 1.0 facilities, citizens, groups and non-media organizations exchanged information and views on, among other news events, the Oklahoma bombing in the US (1995); the TWA flight 800 explosion and crash off New York (1996); the death of Princess Diana (1997); the Kosovo war ('the first web war' – 1998–1999) and the Columbine school shootings (1999) (Bromley, 2010; Bromley, 2012). The 9/11 attacks in the US in 2001 coincided with the early emergence of Web 2.0 with its greater orientation to social media. The combination of the enormity of the event and technological capability led to the demand for online reports being so high that Google even posted an advisory note warning that: 'If you are looking for news, you will find the most current information on TV or radio. Many online news services are not available, because of extremely high demand.'

The war blog of a 29-year-old Iraqi citizen during the Iraq war was yet another example of the potential of citizen journalism prior to the pivotal 2004 tsunami. Writing under the pseudonym Salam Pax on his site 'Where is Raed' (http://dear_raed.blogspot.co.uk), the Baghdadian architect documented the strikes and their aftermath. His reports included both extremely detailed accounts of the bombings and his very critical analysis of the situation. The posts were addressed to a friend who was a student in Jordan at the time but gained such prominence that his blog was eventually shut down by the Iraqi authorities, and he himself was dubbed 'the most famous web diarist in the world' (Pax, 2003). Here are a couple of excerpts from his web diary:

> The all-clear siren just went on. The bombing would come and go in waves, nothing too heavy and not yet comparable to what was going on in 91. All radio and TV stations are still on and while the air raid began, the Iraqi TV was showing patriotic songs and didn't even bother to inform viewers that we are under attack.
>
> Remember the time just before the Gulf war when everybody was rushing around and people were doing their perfunctory 'well, we tried but … blah

blah blah' speeches? This is what it looks like now. This is "the re-run of a bad movie" Bush was talking about in one of his speeches; believe me I don't want to sit thru it either, watching the world get in line after yet another Bush and his magical flute. (Salam's diary, 24 March 2003)

What these excerpts demonstrate is that Salam's blog posts were different from conventional reporting because they blended fact reporting with subjective commentary – an approach most Western journalists educated/ indoctrinated in the objective/balanced reporting tradition would not be allowed to adopt. As Blaagaard (2013, p. 187) pointed out, 'citizen journalism is often characterised as subjective and contextual'. While clearly playing an important role in breaking 'the narrow ideological parameters of much Western news coverage' (Allan, 2009, p. 28), blogs such as Salam's were more the exception than the norm in the early years of citizen journalism. War blogs proliferated in subsequent years, and as Allan (2009, p. 28) explained, two big crises in 2005 consolidated the importance of citizen journalism, 'effectively dispensing with claims that it was a passing "fad" or "gimmick" for all but its fiercest critics'. The 7/7 bombings in London and Hurricane Katrina in the US in 2005 demonstrated the increasing significance citizen reports played especially at times of major crises. In both cases professional journalists' access to the scene of the crisis was limited and because of the newsworthiness and emotional impact of these events, journalists had to rely on citizen reports. A lot of citizens who were caught up in the midst of these tragic events used their mobile phones to capture the moment. The BBC alone received 22,000 emails and text messages about the London tube and bus bombings, includ- ing 300 photos, 50 of which were sent within an hour of the first bomb going off (Douglas, 2006). Sommers (2015) even argued that the 7/7 bombings 'marked a journalism "tipping point" that caught news gatherers offguard'.

The situation in the US the following month exemplified similar trends but only to an extent. Citizen reports were not only providing eyewitness accounts and original reports but often an alternative discourse to the one dominating mainstream media. Petersen (2014) identified two main frames in mainstream US media's coverage of the disaster – looting and lawlessness. Moreover, these two frames also had a racial dimension to them (Johnson et al., 2010; Petersen, 2014; Sommers et al., 2006). Petersen (2014, p. 42) illustrated how the racial dimension was used by giving an example of CNN footage repeatedly shown of

Black men in shorts and no shirts carrying stacks of clothes on their backs running down a street littered with debris; footage of what appeared to be a Black family picking their way through debris with full bags across their backs.

Sommers et al. (2006, p. 39) provided a similar example – of 'the widely circulated photo captions that described a Black man as "looting" and a seemingly comparable White couple as "finding food"'. Petersen (2014, p. 43) argued that the framing in terms of looting 'relied not only on racial discourses and news routines that link blackness and crime ... but also on the conceptual apparatus of the "urban underclass"'. New media, on the other hand, provided a range of resources and were particularly useful for sharing information and fact finding and checking. Citizens were posting photographs and reports online, blogs with personal accounts and commentary, missing persons' registers, Wikinews items, including original reporting, etc. (Vis, 2009).

The Hurricane Katrina example presents a logical transition to consideration of alternative journalism, which emanates from citizen accounts but functions in opposition to professional journalism. Bruns (2016, pp. 32–33) linked the initial emergence of citizen journalism with the development of the Independent Media Center (IMC) network. Wall (2015, p. 803) labelled these types of projects 'The Resistance'. The history of alternative journalism can be traced back long before the emergence of the internet and the development of citizen journalism but we mainly focus on its online incarnations. Atton and Hamilton (2008) provided a useful summary of the history of alternative journalism in the West but it is worth bearing in mind that what can be labelled as 'alternative journalism' in the West (for example, development journalism) might actually be the norm elsewhere.

Atton and Hamilton (2008, p. 79) argued that 'the most prevalent function of alternative news is to fill the gaps that its reporters believe have been left by the mainstream media' due to 'the increasingly conglomerated nature of commercialized news production' and 'the professionalized nature of journalism, where newsgathering and assessments of newsworthiness are routinized to such an extent that news production relies on repeated formulas'. Harcup (2014, p. 11) explained that this rejection of mainstream journalism might mean that

> alternative journalists may see themselves as working to different news values, covering different stories, giving access to a different cast of news actors and sources, operating to an alternative set of ethics, and in effect operating as a form of watchdog on mainstream journalistic organisations that like to portray themselves as watchdogs.

Atton and Hamilton (2008) argued that the internet had presented opportunities for two main types of alternative journalism: sites that monitor news input and then analyse, evaluate, discuss and critique this information. Bruns (2005) called this process 'gatewatching'. Alternative journalism is, therefore, a form of participatory journalism but it is not a form of participation 'through the media' but 'in the media' (Giraud, 2014, p. 423).

Indymedia is a prime example of this type of participatory alternative journalism (Atton & Hamilton, 2008; Giraud, 2014). It is 'a network of individuals, independent and alternative media activists and organisations, offering grassroots, non-corporate, non-commercial coverage of important social and political issues' (Indymedia, 2003). The first website was set up in 1999 when media activists came together during the anti-WTO protests in Seattle, protesting against neo-liberalism, war and environmental destruction. Indymedia's (2003) mission was to provide 'an interactive platform for reports from the struggles for a world based on freedom, cooperation, justice and solidarity, and against environmental degradation, neoliberal exploitation, racism and patriarchy'. The main guiding principle was that of open publishing – anyone could upload content on to the websites. It claimed that its moderators were 'collective members' and it worked on a non-hierarchical basis, opposing any forms of domination and discrimination. Moreover, the UK website stated that 'Indymedia UK does not attempt to take an objective and impartial standpoint: Indymedia UK clearly states its subjectivity'. Indymedia UK included a number of collectives in the country but as of July 2018 most of the local websites advertised on their main website were either no longer active or had not been updated recently.

Giraud (2014, p. 420) acknowledged a dramatic decline in the network in recent years, which, in her view, 'does not necessarily amount to a failure'. She argued that Indymedia was still thriving in Latin America, Oceania, Western Europe and some parts of the US. A range of factors had contributed to the general decline of Indymedia such as 'problems of informal hierarchies … resulting in some IMCs becoming what John Downey and Natalie Fenton dubbed "radical ghettos" relevant only to activists' as well as a general 'erosion of the radical participatory principles which were originally central to Indymedia' (Giraud, 2014, p. 420). In addition to that, there were authority-related issues such as police seizure of servers. The Bristol Indymedia website was closed down in 2014 after the police obtained a court order for access to the website's servers. The police request was prompted by posts on the website claiming responsibility for crimes in the region such as an arson.

Indymedia's success and then decline or even failure are important moments in the history of online alternative journalism, because they exemplify two key trends. On the one hand, as Giraud (2014) acknowledged, Indymedia's initial success showed the participatory potential of digital media. Indymedia paved the way for a different type of citizen journalism and for other participatory forms of journalism that gained prominence later on such as the

Occupy movement and the Arab Spring (Wall, 2015). On the other hand, the network's current decline demonstrates the potent role of the capitalist forces Indymedia set out to criticize and undermine. The decline of radical participatory media took place in parallel with another process – the development and subsequent thriving of other participatory projects that were either commercially driven or as Wall (2015, p. 803) noted, 'showed less concern about using social media tools produced by corporate entities such as Twitter'.

The Occupy movement was a case in point because it relied heavily on commercial, mainstream platforms such as Twitter, Livestream and Storify (Wall, 2015). The Occupy Wall Street movement started in New York in 2011 when the first protests against social inequality and the decline of democracy were launched, and subsequently spread to 82 countries. Social media were so widely used at the time that the high volume of online traffic on the topic forced legacy media to put the issue on their agenda much more prominently than they had done initially. However, as Giraud (2014, p. 425) pointed out, this 'commercialization of "participation" had resulted in the emergence of a counter-narrative, which pointed to capitalism's ability to recuperate dissent in the communicative realm to the extent that communication is argued to be totally "captured" by capital'. This prompted some commentators to question the extent to which 'resistant'/alternative citizen journalism can be clearly distinguished from traditional news media (Wall, 2015).

The Arab Spring was considered by many as a revolutionary point not just in the history of citizen journalism but also in terms of demonstrating social media's potential to drive social change. The Arab Spring was a series of anti-government protests and uprisings that took place in the Middle East in 2010–12 that led to significant changes in some of the regimes in the region. The long-term consequences and the extent to which these uprisings were indeed an Arab 'spring' have been hotly contested but the short-term significance of these events should not be underestimated. As Al-Ghazzi (2014) pointed out, the Arab uprisings generated a lot of discourse about citizen journalism because digital media were widely used at the time not just by activists, rebels and ordinary citizens but also by the authorities, soldiers and even the torturers. Echoing the dominating discourse on the topic, Al-Ghazzi (2014, p. 436) acknowledged that digital media 'were instrumental in efforts to mobilize political action against brutal dictatorships, but they were also used as a weapon of war and tool of torture'.

Al-Ghazzi (2014) actually argued against the use of citizen journalism as a concept in the context of the Arab Spring because it concealed the complexity of these processes. His main point was that citizen journalism was a Western concept and as such could not be applied by default in such a different context as the Arab world. 'The larger point is that citizenship and journalism are not universal categories and that the agency of digital media users should not be assumed as citizen or journalist, when the meanings of both concepts are contextual' (Al-Ghazzi, 2014, p. 437). The meaning of citizenship in the Arab context, for example, can only be understood in relation to 'the contentious and ongoing debate about the political legacy of Islam within the nation-state' (Al-Ghazzi, 2014, p. 445). Thus, the practices associated with citizen journalism can only be comprehended if local context and history are taken into account. Al-Ghazzi (2014, p. 449) concluded that:

> The Arab uprisings, particularly in Syria, demonstrate how digital media use on the ground complicates our assumptions about their relation to political and social agency. The citizen journalism frame circumscribes the critical imagination. It prescribes rather than describes what these digital practices signify. As such, it inadvertently imposes the reference points of its own historical formation. This is not then simply a call to coin another neologism instead of citizen journalism. Rather, it is a criticism of the need to capture the myriad kinds of digital media practices in an all-encompassing concept.

While it is important to acknowledge the limitations of Western concepts and theories, it is beyond the scope of this chapter to theorize further on the issue. An overarching theme across all chapters in this book is the need to appreciate the complexities of the different contexts journalists operate in, and the importance of contextual factors in relation to journalistic practices. A few other examples from beyond the global North further demonstrate the importance of context.

Citizen Journalism Beyond the Global North

A wave of protests 'erupted' in Brazil in the summer of 2013. Protesters were demonstrating against a range of issues: from high public transport fares to reckless public spending on the Rio Olympics to government corruption. Davis (n.d.) argued that 'one of the most common claims was an intense dissatisfaction with the way the nation's news media were failing to represent the views of the Brazilian citizenry'. By contrast, the Brazilian protesters 'offered what many international journalists called the "beginning of an alternative media sphere in Brazil"' (Davis, n.d.). Mídia NINJA was a citizen journalism project that gained particular prominence during the protests. NINJA was a decentralized communication network that produced and disseminated content based on collaborative work and online sharing. It claimed that its work was 'where the fight for social justice, cultural, political, economic and environmental change takes place' (NINJA, 2016).

NINJA citizen journalists (or Ninjas as they referred to themselves) used their mobile phones to film footage of the protests, especially police violence and arrests, which they often broadcasted live via social media (Davis, n.d.). The organization used a range of online platforms such as TwitCasting, Twitter, Facebook and Instagram as well as the group's websites. NINJA grew out of For a do Fixo – 'a network of cultural political grassroots organizations spread all over Brazil' (NINJA, 2016). On its website, NINJA claimed that 'it aims to highlight, in communications, what FdE have already demonstrated in the cultural field: the old mediators can no longer see the new'. NINJA journalists were also activists and as Davis (n.d.) pointed out, 'NINJA reporters were on the front lines of every major protest' since. However, one criticism the organization has faced was its funding strategy, especially the source of funding and the allocation of resources. NINJA has been criticized for receiving funding from big companies such as Coca-Cola as well as allegedly from political parties (Davies, n.d.).

The state of citizen journalism in the world's most secretive society – North Korea – has attracted no known academic study. The account below is based on a range of other predominantly popular sources. Journalists face numerous restrictions in North Korea but in recent years a network of citizen journalists has allegedly been developed in the country. Some of these journalists operate as part of the Asia Press International network – a small group of photo-video-journalists who work and support each other by following the model of the Yui Cooperative – an Asian agricultural group. The members of this network claimed that they 'strive to be free from any dependence on capital and authority' (asiapress.org). The group has offices and local networks in a number of Asian countries. It issues an online North Korean magazine, which is also available in English – *Rimjin-gang*. The magazine exposes a range of wrongdoings in North Korea. The website also featured an article in which the journalists talked about some of the dangers they faced:

We are often asked, 'Isn't this dangerous for the reporters?' When thinking about the situation in North Korea today, the only answer we can give is, 'Of course. It is extremely dangerous.' … North Korean authorities would most likely view as espionage or treason the reporters' spiriting of secretly taken videos and reports outside North Korean borders for distribution to the outside world. Reporters take these risks because they have a strong will to let the world know the reality in North Korea and inspire a desire to improve the situation there ... The main constituents of Rimjin-gang are the citizens of North Korea who have had their freedom of expression completely taken away from them. Since such people are our reporters, there are some sections in the reports that show lack of experience. However, as the saying goes, 'The citizen's heart is the heart of the heavens.' We believe we will be able to find the voice of the nation, which will provide the strength to change North Korean society. We would also like to point out that in a society where citizens cannot openly express their feelings and thoughts, people are beginning to express their true feelings through the efforts of the reporters in North Korea. (www.asiapress.org)

It is clear from the outline above that the online magazine was run by citizen, not professional, journalists. They mentioned eight contributors on their website who appeared to come from different walks of life – from stay-at-home mums to a labourer, a company driver, an economist and a trade supervisor. Each citizen journalist had to either physically smuggle his/her reports into China or send weekly news updates via mobile phones over the Chinese networks. In an interview for the UK's *Independent* newspaper, Ishimaru Jiro, the network's only outside contact, explained how the scheme worked: 'Each undercover North Korean citizen journalist must cross over rugged land or gushing rivers in the dark of night to meet with Ishimaru at a pre-arranged point along the 1400km border between China and DPRK to deliver secretly recorded footage' (Mortensen, 2014). *Rimjin-gang* also had a Twitter account that was frequently updated. Some of the most recent news items published in late September 2016 included photos of North Korean middle and high school textbooks idolizing Kim Jong-un and of army officers facing starvation as well as a report about the interrogations families of 'missing persons' had been subjected to.

Another journalistic project devoted to the situation in North Korea is the online publication *Daily NK* which is run from South Korea but has reporters inside North Korea. It allegedly received funding from a number of international organizations. It prides itself on breaking news about public executions and other wrongdoing in North Korea. However, by its own admission, *Daily NK* provides reports and editorials from 'experienced journalists' and cannot therefore be classified as an example of citizen journalism.

Nonetheless, South Korea itself has a history of citizen journalism. Arguably the most famous participatory online project in the country is

OhmyNews. Joyce (2007, p. 3) claimed that OhmyNews was 'a pioneer' in the field of citizen journalism 'not only for being an early player, but for having created a successful model with citizens as journalists and professional editors to filter content'. The website was launched in 2000 with the slogan: 'Every citizen's a reporter' (Gillmor, 2004, p. 110) at a time when the media landscape was dominated by three conservative newspapers with a collective share of 80 per cent of daily circulation (Joyce, 2007). The founder of OhmyNews – Oh Yeon Ho – worked as a journalist himself in South Korea, and then studied for his master's degree in the US where he developed his idea for the website. He launched it shortly after he came back from America. He defined the project as 'open progressivism' (Joyce, 2007, p. 4). In his inaugural article Oh Yeon Ho said: 'OhmyNews declares it is making a complete departure from the media culture of the 20th century. We are going to change the culture of how news is produced, distributed, and consumed, all at one time' (Joyce, 2007, p. 7). The founder of OhmyNews opened the website to contributors by allowing anyone who wanted to send a story to do that. He also argued that the website would be changing the whole definition of newsworthiness by focusing not just on reporting events such as press conferences but also on more human interest stories (Joyce, 2007). However, Joyce (2007) argued that one of the reasons his project was so successful was because he used professional editors. Moreover, his contributors also received financial incentives and were encouraged to respond to readers' comments. The website's interactivity was a key feature of the project (Gillmor, 2004).

Within a year of its launch, the site grew in popularity. In the next five years or so the site had over 26,000 contributors and more than 50 staff members (Gillmor, 2004). OhmyNews gained particular prominence during the 2002 presidential elections in the country and it 'had been credited with having helped elect' President Roh Moo Hyun who ran as a reformer (Gillmor, 2004, p. 110). The development of OhmyNews has not been without its controversies. The online newspaper was accused of being too loyal to President Roh and it also allegedly accepted a government grant for struggling media (Joyce, 2007). OhmyNews has allegedly been struggling to establish a successful business model that does not involve advertising. Moreover, on a few occasions its practices have been ethically questionable, such as the reprinting of the alleged assassination of Bill Gates, which turned out to be a hoax (Joyce, 2007). Since 2010 OhmyNews International has changed the scope of its activities and has rebranded itself as the site that is 'curating the debate on citizen journalism'. This model of participatory collaborative journalism between citizen and professional journalists, sometimes known as pro-am, that OhmyNews pioneered was later appropriated by a number of mainstream media.

Case Study 6.1: Sahara Reporters

The citizen journalism project Sahara Reporters (http://saharareporters.com) is 'Nigeria's answer to South Korea's foremost citizen journalism website, OhmyNews.com' (Dare, 2011, p. 23), or in its own words 'the WikiLeaks of Africa' (SaharaTV, n.d.). Sahara Reporters was launched in 2006 as 'an online community of international reporters and social advocates dedicated to bringing you commentaries, features, news reports from a Nigerian-African perspective'. It defined itself as: 'A unique organization, founded in the spirit of Article 19 of the Universal Declaration of Human Rights, comprising of ordinary people with an overriding commitment to seeking the truth and publishing it without fear or favor. Because its core members are unapologetic practitioners of advocacy journalism, Sahara Reporters also serves as an umbrella outlet for objective reporting of verifiable and accurate news and untainted social commentaries for anyone wishing to exercise their freedom of speech in the public interest and common good' (Sahara Reporters, n.d.).

In 2011 it also launched SaharaTV – a broadcast outlet. The Reporters' motto is 'Report yourself'. The main website is very popular in Nigeria – ranked 37th by the number of visitors in December 2010 (Dare, 2011), and 137th in July 2018 (Alexa.com, 2018). SaharaReporters.com was established by a New York-based Nigerian blogger and activist, Omoyele Sowore, who explicitly defined himself as a citizen journalist. His desire to launch such a website was born out of his own personal experience of trying to find online platforms to expose corruption practices such as stories about the properties owned by Nigerian government officials in the US and the UK.

Dare (2011, p. 32) argued that the 'eureka moment' for Sowore was when he interviewed the son of the then President Gbenga Obasanjo in which he revealed 'corrupt dealings' of very senior politicians, including the vice president, and 'deep family and government secrets'. The presidential son later 'said that the frank conversation was down to his desire to get even with his father for wrecking his marriage' (Dare, 2011, p. 33). Dare (2011) argued that although Sowore eventually found a platform for the interview, he felt a pressing need to set up his own website and provide a platform for other citizens to report stories.

The website quickly became famous for its investigative reports exposing corruption practices by high-profile politicians and breaking news stories (Dare, 2011). 'Every Governor, Cabinet Minister, key government official and close aides and advisers of the President reckon with Sahara Reporters and of times have made direct threats, trashed them in the media or sued them' (Dare, 2011). The website has significantly expanded its activities both in terms of the number of stories published and the number of contributors. It claimed that it had a verification process in place as well (Dare, 2011). Its main sources of funding were donations from supporters and advertisements.

Legacy Media and Citizen Journalism – 'Networked Journalism' or a Forced Marriage?

The examples explored so far show that citizen journalism fulfils a number of important functions that legacy media are either unwilling or unable to fulfil. What is the relationship, however, between legacy media and citizen journalism? Does it resemble a forced marriage or can we genuinely talk about 'networked journalism', which Beckett (2010, p. 1) defined as 'a synthesis of traditional news journalism and the emerging forms of participatory media enabled by Web 2.0 technologies such as mobile phones, email, websites, blogs, micro-blogging, and social networks'? Wall and El Zahed (2015, p. 165) argued that citizen journalism had made 'its largest impact … in its incorporation into mainstream news media culture'. Wall (2015, p. 798) provided a useful summary of existing research on the topic. She argued that mainstream's media's approach to citizen journalism had been reactive and especially in the early days there was 'a less-than enthusiastic embrace by many traditional news outlets, as a "clash of cultures" erupted in which amateur content, fuelled by a growing participatory ethos, conflicted with the perceived needs of professional journalists to maintain their authority'. While incorporating interactive elements into their websites had become a must for most media organizations, a minority had been relatively proactive in the process. However, there were some more innovative projects and approaches.

CNN's iReport is a pioneering citizen journalism project run by a mainstream media organization. It is a citizen journalism platform accessed via CNN's main website, which encourages citizens to submit their stories to CNN. Citizens can submit stories on topics of interest to them or can choose one of the topics assigned by the producers. The FAQ section explained that 'stories submitted to CNN iReport were not edited fact-checked or screened before posted, and 'only stories marked "CNN iReport" had been verified and cleared by CNN'. The stories verified by CNN could also be used on their other platforms. One of the FAQs was 'What counts as "news" here?'. The answer was revealing: 'We'll decide that together. One of the goals of CNN iReport is to expand the current definition of news.' CNN also offered community guidelines and a toolkit with story tips for its contributors. The main rules were: the stories must be original, true, new and interesting. The toolkit had a telling slogan: 'Tell your story like a pro' (CNN iReport, 2016).

Kperogi (2011, p. 314) argued that CNN iReport was an example of the 'hegemonic co-optation of citizen journalism' because by mainstreaming citizen journalism, the corporation 'is seeking to contain, or at least negotiate, its potentially disruptive effect on mainstream journalism'. CNN did that by simultaneously opening the gates to citizen journalists and by asking them to abide by the conventions of professional journalism by 'making its news values seem like, as Gramsci would say, the "common sense" values of all and then by legitimizing these values not so much by manipulation as by active consent' (Kperogi, 2011, p. 324). The process of hegemonic cooptation was not passive, however, but involved constant negotiation and renegotiation (Kperogi, 2011; Palmer, 2012).

This process is fundamentally linked to a wider issue, namely the role citizen journalism plays in society and how it impacts on mainstream journalism. One of the key discourses dominating the debate on citizen journalism is about the extent to which citizen journalism has a deliberative democratic potential. At the heart of this debate is the question of whether the advent of citizen journalism has led to the emergence of a Habermasian alternative virtual public sphere or in fact a counter public sphere or spheres (Downey & Fenton, 2003). As Wall and El Zahed (2015, p. 165) put it, the fundamental issue was 'whether mainstream news usage of amateur content actually signifies any truly new changes to journalism'. In Kperogi's (2011, p. 315) view, this potential has not been realized. He claimed that

> while the vigorous profusion of web-based citizen media has the potential to inaugurate an era of dynamic expansion of the deliberative space and even serve as a counterfoil to the suffocating dominance of the discursive space by the traditional media, we are now witnessing a trend toward the aggressive cooptation of these citizen media by corporate media hegemons.

Other legacy media on both sides of the Atlantic had followed in the footsteps of CNN and adopted similar platforms for citizen journalists. GuardianWitness in the UK, for example, also has a strong focus on the assignments set by the newspaper's editorial staff.

This blending of citizen reports within the structural and ideological confines of mainstream/legacy media has led some commentators such as Williams, Wardle and Wahl-Jorgensen (2011) to claim that not much has changed in professional journalism, because eyewitness accounts were nothing new and the processing of audience material followed a long-established protocol of newsgathering and sourcing. By contrast, Wall and El Zahed (2015, p. 165) argued that the fact that legacy media attempted to incorporate citizen content 'suggests in fact professionals see citizen contributions as disruptive enough as to threaten their own authority'. However, in their view this assimilation of citizen journalism within the confines of mainstream media was dangerous because 'in this way, the potential of citizen journalism may never be realized' (Wall & El Zahed, 2015, pp. 165–66).

Another example of this phenomenon is the BBC's approach to citizen content. The BBC established a dedicated UGC Hub in 2005 based in its newsroom in London and responsible for managing the user-generated and social media content sent to the BBC. They also set up the so-called 'Have Your Say' webpage where members of the public were encouraged to send their stories to the BBC. The BBC has received a high number of submissions from the public, but Wardle and Williams (2010, p. 782) argued that news workers at the corporation 'are enthusiastic about certain types of audience material … which fit the traditional model of journalism: audience footage, audience comments and experiences'. Incidentally, the BBC has always received and used these types of material (Wardle & Williams, 2010). Wardle and Williams (2010, p. 782) claimed that 'for the majority of newsworkers, therefore, nothing had changed significantly, apart from the technological advances, which has meant that the BBC receives much larger amounts of content, at much faster speeds'. Harrison (2010, p. 253) also argued that

> overall moderation ensures that there is little sign of UGC changing or challenging the BBC's editorial values and UGC is now systematically used to enhance or provide value added to news stories by conforming to predetermined BBC news selection processes and styles.

The wider implication of this development is that 'the participatory and democratizing possibilities of UGC are often an afterthought, if they are mentioned at all' (Wardle & Williams, 2010, p. 783). UGC's democratizing potential is not realized because citizen input is used in a conventional way mainly as a news source. As Wardle and Williams (2010, p. 792) argued, 'overwhelmingly, journalists have remained journalists and audiences have remained audiences. Until this mindset is challenged the possibilities for truly collaborative and networked journalism at the BBC will remain on the margins'. Wall and El Zahed (2015, p. 166) saw all these processes as an example of 'boundary maintenance' by mainstream media in their attempts to 'maintain control over the overall narrative and more broadly journalistic authority'.

Another accusation that professional journalists frequently level at citizen journalists is over a lack of ethical standards and rigorous fact-checking procedures. Attempts have been made for codes of ethics for citizen journalists to be developed and citizen journalists contributing to mainstream media (as the CNN iReport and GuardianWitness examples showed) also have to follow ethical guidelines. Moyo (2015, p. 125) argued, however, that citizen journalists should not abide by professional journalists' standards because journalism ethics especially in crisis reporting was 'ambivalent, nascent, fluid, individualised, situational, and sometimes contradictory'. He argued instead for a move away from professional codes of conduct to 'individual moral impulses in a complex melange of the deontic, virtuous and teleological, that is informed by higher-order ethics of freedom, human rights, social justice, media pluralism and citizen participation'. (Moyo, 2015, p. 125)

Summary

Citizen journalism as a form of random non-professional acts of journalism practised by citizens has firmly secured its place on the media landscape throughout the world – from within repressive dictatorial regimes in the global South, including in countries such as North Korea, to the advanced democracies of the global North. Historically, citizen journalists have most significantly contributed to the newsmaking process in breaking news and supplying eyewitness accounts and footage during times of major crises, born out of natural or man-made disasters. A number of innovative pioneering projects have paved the way for collaborations between citizen and professional journalists but although it takes two to tango, professional journalists appear to lead in the global North. In the global South, however, especially in some authoritative regimes, citizen journalists/activists have arguably played an important (at least short-term) progressive role as a force for social and/or political change.

The few examples used in this chapter clearly suggest that we have to be very careful when making attempts to generalize whether citizen journalism plays a wider democratizing role, because appreciating the importance of context is of key significance. It very much appears to be the case that although no respectful traditional newsroom in the global North can ignore citizen content anymore, the full democratic potential of citizen journalism has not been realized. Day-to-day journalistic practices might have changed to an extent but it is highly arguable whether the overarching role journalists play in democratic societies has changed. While some alternative journalism projects such as Indymedia have tried to break the practical and ideological conventions of traditional journalism, their long-term sustainability is problematic. Founded in opposition to capitalism and its forces, most of these projects have either struggled to sustain themselves financially or have adapted to such an extent that they now rely on the same commercial forces they once set out to challenge and undermine. Trends have been different in other parts of the world, such as the Arab World; however, long-term sustainability of both citizen journalism projects and democratic developments is a major issue there as well.

Further Reading

1. Al-Ghazzi, O. (2014) '"Citizen journalism" in the Syrian uprising: problematizing Western narratives in a local context', *Communication Theory* 24(4), 435–54.
2. Allan, S. (2013) *Citizen Witnessing: Revisioning Journalism in Times of Crisis* (Cambridge: Polity).
3. Atton, C. & Hamilton, J.F. (2008) *Alternative Journalism* (London: Sage).
4. Bruns, A. (2005) *Gatewatching: Collaborative Online News Production* (New York: Columbia University Press).
5. Gillmor, D. (2004) *We the Media: Grassroots Journalism by the People, for the People* (Sebastopol, CA: O'Reilly Media).
6. Thorsen, E. and Allan, S. (eds) (2014) *Citizen Journalism: Global Perspectives* (New York: Peter Lang).
7. Wall, M. (2015) 'Citizen journalism', *Digital Journalism* 3(6), 797–813.
8. Wardle, C. & Williams, A. (2010) 'Beyond user-generated content: a production study examining the ways in which audience material is used at the BBC', *Media, Culture & Society* 32(5), 781–99.

7

Women and Journalism – A Global Transformation?

Chapter overview

This chapter addresses the issue of the identity of journalists globally. Who makes up the personnel of the occupation – and does it matter who they are? For some, it is far more important to identify journalism as a set of practices – what it is, and what it is not – rather than know about the journalists themselves. However, it is clear that over the past 30 years or so, the global journalism population has changed to include more women. The chapter presents comprehensive data from more than 150 countries on the presence of women in journalism. This feminization of the journalism workforce has in turn raised questions about whether journalism has changed as a result.

Learning outcomes

After having read this chapter you will be able to:

1. Arrive at a determination about whether the composition of the journalism population – who journalists are – impacts on journalism as an occupation
2. Critically analyse the feminization of journalism, paying particular attention to the relationship between presence and participation
3. Compare and contrast the relative circumstances of women journalists in the global North and the global South
4. Collect and collate data on the journalism population in a country or countries, or region.

The hostility or supportiveness of the contexts in which journalists practised, arising from politics, economics, society or culture; journalists' own orientations to and practices of journalism, whether determined relatively autonomously as an expression of a form of professionalism or as a result of external pressure and direction; and the actual or imagined dilution of journalism as a distinctive activity consequent on the near-universal diffusion of digital communication capacity – conditions addressed so far in this book – might logically be seen to bear most acutely on the journalism population itself. However, globally, there is little by way of basic information about exactly who these journalists are. As we have seen, foreign correspondents and their contemporary successors achieved a degree of attention, even if this waxed and waned over time, and many were relatively well-known. As representatives of the journalist population, foreign correspondents were exceptional, though, and estimates were that this status of journalist constituted no more than about 10 per cent of the occupation (Tunstall, 1971, 1983, 1996). The rest, the largely anonymous majority, enjoyed more mundane status: they were not A-listers (Caves, 2000).

Where journalists figured in studies (mainly in the global North and West) they were largely viewed as operatives, socialized into a shared occupational ideology, subsumed within a system of routinized bureaucratic news production (Cottle, 2000). As journalists, individuals were less important (Shoemaker & Vos, 2009). There may be good reasons for this, but it has had the effect of limiting studies largely to aggregates of journalists in a narrow range of settings, commonly the newsrooms of the mainstream legacy media. Journalists have traditionally subjugated their identities to that of the newsroom or news organization, hiding behind a shield of 'professionalism' as employees rather than individuals. This might have been changing with the use of social media by writers and on-air 'talent' (Canter, 2015, p. 890; Hanusch & Bruns, 2017), but many journalists, especially those engaged in print production or behind the microphone or camera, remained overwhelmingly anonymous. Furthermore, although we may have got to know a considerable amount about journalists per se at, say, the *New York Times* (Usher, 2014), we still know far less about journalists working for the approximately 7,500 small-town weekly newspapers in the US (Muller, 2011). That concentration has become increasing untenable even within the global North and West as the news media landscape has changed and diversified, making it more obvious that journalists comprise 'differentiated "tribes"' and mainstream legacy newsrooms no longer are as representative of the occupation (Cottle, 2000, p. 23). This realization may be even more applicable to the variegated global journalism population.

The number of journalists globally, however, is still unknown as we approach the third decade of the twenty-first century (see Tamam et al., 2012; Zhang & Su, 2012). The majority of the numbers in this chapter were produced over an extended period from the 1990s to 2016. During this time, the IFJ claimed to represent about 600,000 members through trade unions in 140 countries (www.ifj.org). However, trade union membership among journalists varied widely (for example, from around 95 per cent in Finland to 1.5 per cent in Turkey). At the individual national level there was uncertainty. The numbers in Australia and the US were based on estimates, even though both the Australian Bureau of Statistics (2011, 2014) and United States Department of Labor, Bureau of Labor Statistics (2015a, 2015b) published figures. In 2016 the American Society of News Editors (ASNE) stopped estimating the size of the newspaper workforce (ASNE, 2015; Jackson, 2013; Williams, 2016b). The problem was that the categories used were only loosely comparable. This was recognized by the European Security, Research & Innovation Forum (2009) in trying to calculate the number of journalists in the EU. (It arrived at a final estimate of between 220,000 and 300,000 – a variation of more than a third.) The only organization believed to collect statistical information on the global journalism population was WAN-IFRA which had numbers for journalists working in newspapers.

Photographers and Camera Operators

One category of journalists who have found it difficult at times to be accepted as such both inside and outside the occupation are photographers (and camera operators from the early days of the silent newsreels to contemporary video-journalists) (Anderson, 2014; Gopsill & Neale, 2007; Johnsen, 2004; Schlesinger, 1978; Zelizer, 1995). Their numbers were not inconsiderable: around 2016, the National Press Photographers Association (NPPA) in the US claimed more than 12,000 members. The first such organization of press photographers, established in Denmark in 1912, had more than 800 members, as did the White House News Photographers Association (WHNPA) which began in 1921. There were associations in other places, including the UK, the Republic of Ireland, Sweden, Canada and Norway. Photographers began appearing routinely as members of editorial staffs from the mid-1920s following technical developments in printing, cameras and film: *Asahi Shimbun* established its photography division in 1929. In the 1930s pictorial magazines (*Life, Picture Post, Stern, Paris-Match*) specialized in publishing photographs (Anderson, 2014).

News camera operators, introduced through the production of news films in the 1890s, became more numerous with the introduction of television from the 1940s: the NPPA introduced a 'newsfilm cameraman (*sic*) of the year' award in 1954 (Underwood, 2007, pp. 7, 15–16). Press photographers and news camera operators were essentially news gatherers (Magar, 2011). Photojournalism was arguably a different, more documentary and cinematic genre, shaped not by mundane 'spot news' but 'the desire to witness and record historical events and important people, the belief in photography's power to advance social justice, and the embrace of a universal humanism' (Cookman, 2009, p. 15). Video began to supplant film from the 1970s. By the 1990s video journalism had come to mean one person working for either television or online, and either news gathering or producing documentaries (Lancaster, 2013).

Even among press photographers themselves, women were the object of discrimination (Hermann, 2015). A woman was not admitted to active membership of the WHNPA until the 1940s (www.whnpa.org), and as late as 1961 there were only three female members of the New York Press Photographers Association. Women photographers were more routinely employed by Australian daily newspapers only from the 1980s (Darian-Smith, 2016). Even as recently as 2014 a book, albeit a memoir, appeared sub-titled 'code of *the* news camera*man*' (Schoepp, 2014 – emphasis added).

Locating the Journalist Population

At its simplest, journalists may be employed, self-employed or unemployed (a) as journalists working in orthodox (news) media environments (known as 'specialists'), (b) working in non-media environments either as journalists or in some related role ('embedded'), and (c) in what the CPJ called 'media support work' (Potts & Shehadeh, 2014, p. 50) (although Bridgstock and Cunningham (2014) found that among their sample of recent Australian graduates, those with journalism degrees were most likely to be 'specialists'). The widespread uptake of ICTs, the use of social media and the emergence of citizen journalism, which have been scoped in earlier chapters, have only added to the imprecision of who actually was recognized as a journalist (see Figure 8.1).

It was largely left to individual researchers to define what they meant by 'journalist'. As a consequence, who did the counting impacted on the numbers (Josephi & Richards, 2012; North, 2014). In some places, governments effectively decided who was a journalist (Conseil de Presse (Luxembourg), 2014; Herscovitz, 2012; McMane, 2012). Many surveys, however, as noted, sampled only employees in news organizations and institutional newsrooms – sometimes in a limited number of urban settings, and/or, as also noted, only mainstream, legacy media – and worked from constrained definitions of 'journalist' (Beasley, 2001; for examples, see Herscovitz, 2012; Kirat, 2012; Mitchell, 2011; Tsfati & Meyers, 2012; Weischenberg et al., 2012; Zhang & Su, 2012). These were potentially unrepresentative of a diversified and multiplex occupation where atypical working was commonplace (Bonfadelli et al., 2012; European Security, Research & Innovation Forum, 2009; Pasti et al., 2015). Some surveys explicitly excluded many categories of journalists (Skovsgaard et al., 2012); in others such exclusions were more implied as if somehow 'natural' (Vasarhelyi, 2012; Son et al., 2012). Chan et al. (2012, p. 25) omitted 'sports, photo-, and entertainment journalists' and an Israeli survey similarly discounted 'journalists who concentrate on soft news, such as sports, travel, and fashion' (Tsfati & Meyers, 2012, p. 447). By definition the unemployed were largely overlooked, as sampling was confined mainly to 'working journalists' (Brownlee & Beam, 2012, p. 349; Jyrkiäinen & Heinonen, 2012, pp. 173–74; Skovsgaard et al., 2012, p. 157). Sometimes freelancers were not counted either (Edstrom & Ladendorf, 2012; Raeymaekers et al., 2012).

Women in Journalism

It was broadly agreed, however, that over a period of about 20–30 years there had been a general increase globally in the presence of women in journalism (Gallagher, 2001b; UNESCO, UN Women & International Federation of Journalists 2014). This was explained in a number of usually interconnected ways including younger women entering the occupation replacing older men who were retiring or whose jobs in declining legacy media were discontinued; higher educational attainments of women; a demand for more journalists as the media generally expanded; the proliferation of television (and, to a lesser extent, radio) channels; buoyancy in the magazine sector; the availability of sex discrimination legislation which allowed women to challenge unfair employment practices (Djerf-Pierre, 2007; Saitta, 2013; Steiner, 2000). This led to a continuing debate over the feminization of journalism – whether women's presence in journalism (measured by head counts) was reflected in their participation in journalism (status, remuneration, power, opportunities, security of employment, influence, leadership, etc. – were they 'underpaid and under-promoted' (Williams, 2016c))? (Case Study 7.1).

Almost everywhere, even in recent times women were hugely underrepresented in the higher echelons of the occupation; for example, in 2012 the number of female national newspaper editors in the UK – just one – was lower than it had been in the 1980s (Martinson, 2012). In the US the number of top female editors at the biggest dailies fell from seven to three between 2004 and 2014 (Griffin, 2014). In the US, three-quarters of freelancers, whose roles were obviously more precarious, with less job security, usually lower pay and fewer health and welfare benefits, were believed to be women (Massey & Elmore, 2011); up to 70 per cent in Uganda (Kaija, 2013). In Canada, France and Norway it was estimated that women comprised a half or more of freelancers (Austenå, 2004; Saitta, 2013; Salamon, 2016). Freelancing was popular among women in Saudi Arabia (Sakr, 2004). There was evidence that the proportion of female freelancers globally was rising (Pleijter et al., 2012; Weaver & Willnat, 2012).

Case Study 7.1: The Alliance for Women in Media

The Alliance for Women in Media (AWM) was formed in 1951 as American Women in Radio and Television, the women's division of the National Association of Broadcasters. It changed its name in 2010. Its mission is to connect, recognize and inspire women in the media. It last declared about 7,000 members, and had local affiliates around the US.

Unlike many women's groups in the global South promoting basic rights and protections for journalists, AWM is comprised of 'influential media professionals' (Kaplan, 2013). In 2016 its leadership programme honoured seven women – three company presidents, one vice president, a chief executive officer, a founder and chair, and an editorial director. Its women in media series invited 'high-profile' participants (allwomeninmedia.org).

Its finances were comprised chiefly of corporate sponsorship.

In 1975 AWM initiated annual awards which in 1997 were named The Gracies after Gracie Allen, the comedian, and are handed out at a glitzy event in Los Angeles, followed by a lunch in New York.

The Alliance's foundation supports female students with bursaries worth almost $US20,000 as they enter the workplace as well as offering other smaller scholarships.

One of AWM's slogans – 'We've come a long way, ladies' – summarized its role in addressing residual gender discrimination in a largely egalitarian society in the global North.

Employment precarity appeared to contribute to the abuse of women journalists in the workplace: many of those who responded to a *Newsweek* survey in the US said they had been sexually harassed while on internships (Westcott, 2016). The most high-profile incidence involved the founder, chairman and chief executive officer of Fox News and the Fox Television Stations Group, Roger Ailes, who was forced to resign in 2016 after being sued for sexual harassment; more than 20 women claimed they had been abused over a 30-year period (Sherman, 2016). In January 2017 it was revealed that Fox News had settled a second claim against the network's host Bill O'Reilly, following a reported previous pay-out in 2004 (Steel & Schmidt, 2017). A wider, global survey confirmed that the most common intimidation, threat or abuse suffered by female journalists came in the newsroom from those in power in the form of harassment (Barton & Storm, 2014).

Physical attacks and sexual violence were much more likely to occur while female journalists were working in the field, with the consequence that news organizations often limited women's opportunities to report globally from what were considered to be difficult, dangerous or just different locations (Barton & Storm, 2014; Simon, 2016). In some cultures it was simply considered wrong for women to work as journalists (Khalid, 2015), and those who did faced extreme social pressures, including threats to their families (Anon, 2016c). Nevertheless, women were less likely than male journalists to be killed or imprisoned because of their work: women made up no more than 7 per cent of those killed since 1992, and 3 per cent of journalists in prison in 2016 – nine, of whom three were in China and two in Iran (Radsch, 2016).

By the start of the twenty-first century, it was estimated that almost 40 per cent of the world's journalists were women (Ran, 2012), having begun to constitute majorities in journalism in some places from the 1980s. By the mid-1990s they had done so in a range of countries including Finland, Estonia, Latvia, Serbia and Slovakia (Strong, 2007; Tytarenko 2011). Our own collection of global figures suggested that by 2016 in 43 states and territories for which there were statistics available (almost one in three of the total), women had either equal presence or comprised a majority in journalism. In ten, women accounted for at least two-thirds of journalists, suggesting something of a dominance in the occupation there (see Table 7.1). (However, in line with the imprecision in data collection already noted, the situation in Bulgaria was unclear: the Bulgarian National Statistical Institute data indicated that 53.5 per cent of journalists (3,100 out of 5,800) were women but in the WoJ survey women comprised 64.6 per cent; our own sources indicated 67.5 per cent).

The presence of women among the world's journalism students increased in this period, forming a 'new majority' (Beasley, 1988). The trend started in the US in the 1970s (Becker et al., 2003). By the mid-1990s women accounted for 50 per cent of journalism students in the Netherlands; 52 per cent in the UK, and 55 per cent in Norway (van Zoonen, 1998). About ten years later, they made up at least 50 per cent of student bodies in Austria, Cyprus, Finland, France, Germany, Lithuania, Poland, Portugal, Romania, Slovakia, Spain and Sweden, too (Terzis, 2009). By the second decade of the twenty-first century around the world they accounted for up to 95 per cent of enrolments in some places; greater majorities in the global North; and new majorities in global South countries such as Lebanon, Palestine, South Africa, Tanzania and Zambia (Avadani, 2002; Becker et al., 2010; Franks, 2013; Grenby et al., 2009; Melki, 2009; Mfumbusa, 2010; North, 2010; Nyondo, 2011; Splichal & Sparks, 1994; Thawabteh, 2010). The preponderance of women studying journalism was still not fully reflected in the numerical presence of women in the occupation (Franks, 2013).

Presence or Participation?

In the global West and North, and most notably the US, there was 'an avalanche' of studies of women in journalism from the 1960s (Klos, 2013), while elsewhere female journalists were often ignored (van den Wijngaard, 1992). Interest in them in places like Africa, the Arab region, China, Bangladesh and Pakistan developed only as more women entered the occupation in the 1990s and the 2000s (Ali, 2015; Bubul, 2010; Duwe & White, 2011; Gadzekpo, 2011; Pintak & Ginges, 2012; Zhang & Su, 2012). The ways in which female journalists were studied were also distinctive. More recent scholarship has concentrated on how women experienced journalism through 'the more general and deeper structures of patriarchy, regardless of local cultures and traditions' (de Bruin, 2014, pp. 43–44; Rush et al., 2005, pp. 249–50). Gallagher (2001a, 2002, 2005) summarized the main concerns (power, values, identity, ideology, politics, discrimination, oppression, role, exclusion, sexual harassment – and, she might have added, particularly in reference to places outside the global West, physical violence (Barton & Storm, 2014; Sreberny, 2014)). Scholarship, Gallagher (2002, 2005, 2014) argued, had moved on from concerns with 'numerical redistribution' to a 'struggle for visibility, voice and influence'. Auditing the proportion of women working as journalists was seen as merely a 'preparatory phase' (Ross, 2001, p. 531) to tackling journalism as an inherently 'en-gendered practice' (Ross, 2001). The idea that the numerical presence of women in journalism could reach a 'tipping point' to give women 'strategic power' no longer had currency (Obijiofor & Hanusch, 2011, p. 91; Ross, 2001, p. 542; Steiner, 2012, pp. 211–13).

Case Study 7.2: Women Journalists Without Chains/Munazzamat Ṣaḥafīyāt Bilā Quyūd

Women Journalists Without Chains (WJWC) was formed in Yemen in 2005, largely through the inspiration of Tawakkul Karmān, the daughter of a former Yemeni government minister, and a leading member of the Al-Iṣlāḥ (Reform) party. After graduating, she started a career in journalism, writing and producing documentary films. She was possibly the first Yemini journalist to use the internet as an outlet. However, she ran into difficulties with the Yemeni government, at which point, along with colleagues, she formed WJWC.

Since then the organization has agitated for women's rights, civil rights more broadly, justice, anti-corruption and freedom of expression. She was arrested several times as a result of pursuing non-violent protests in the Yemeni capital Sanaa. During the so-called Arab Spring she led pro-democracy mass demonstrations against the Yemeni regime, helping to set up a protest encampment in the grounds of Sanaa University which lasted for several months.

Despite WJWC's efforts, the organization reported that 2016 was the worst year on record for press freedom in Yemen, with nine journalists and media workers killed and another 199 subjected to human rights abuses (World Summit of Nobel Peace Laureates, 2017).

In an interview in 2014 Karmān explained the rationale behind WJWC: [W]e are aiming for a situation where women are no longer chained down in society … We came up with the name 'without chains' to convey our aim of removing the fetters binding free speech, human rights, and women's rights. We played an important role, as female journalists, in leading demonstrations. The demonstrations that we led did not aim to exclude men, however, and they participated alongside us. Our organization Women Journalists Without Chains ended up playing an extremely important part within the movement to protect individual freedom and the right to free expression (Joji, 2014).

In 2011 Karmān, who was then 32, was awarded the Nobel Peace Prize, the youngest laureate to date. The award was welcomed by a number of journalists' organizations worldwide. However, questions have been raised about the funding of such NGOs. WJWC received financial support from the US National Endowment for Democracy (Gershman, 2011).

On the other hand, it was also argued that 'Gender balance is an obvious prerequisite for pluralistic media reflecting the diversity of any given population' (Joseph, 2013; see also Byerly, 2014; Djerf-Pierre, 2011; Kitch, 2015, p. 35; Rauhala et al., 2012). The Global Alliance on Media and Gender, formed in 2013, included in its declaration 'gender equality in and through media by 2030', making a commitment to increased numbers of women in journalism, and UNESCO's ongoing global survey on media and gender asked governments to provide information on actions taken to promote gender equality of presence in journalism (UNESCO, 2015). Presence, it seemed, did still matter – at least to some (Joyce, 2014; UNESCO, 2015; UNESCO, UNESCO Women & International Federation of Journalists, 2014). It was difficult to argue that a quantitative presence could unproblematically cross 'a critical threshold' to effect qualitative difference (Carneiro, 2000), or that there was some number beyond which somehow gender ceased to be an issue (Djerf-Pierre, 2011). Nevertheless, the numerical distribution globally of female journalists could be a potential factor in shaping women's experiences of journalism (Djerf-Pierre, 2011). And, in turn, those experiences were likely to help illuminate the global condition of journalism.

The place of women in journalism has drawn scholarly, occupational and popular attention for at least a century, focused chiefly on participation in the means of production of journalism through ownership, management and access to employment, and the associated representation of women in the products of journalism (Byerly, 2013b; Lonsdale, 2012). All the same, and reflecting the point made above, the 'baseline information' of the numbers of women journalists in the world has provided limited scope for global study because of a concentration on a narrower rather than broader range of contexts (Byerly, 2013a; de Bruin, 2014; Ross, 2001) and a somewhat piecemeal approach to data collection, based largely on nations, regions and sub-regions as the primary defining contexts (Byerly, 2013b; Cushion, 2014; Hanitzsch et al., 2012; Mellado et al., 2012; Örnebring, 2012). Even within (sub) regions some national contexts have received more attention than others (Mellado, 2012). Djerf-Pierre (2011) has even argued that 'Feminist media research has … been uninterested in … extensive data collections in a very large number of countries'. In summary, we know very little about the presence of women in journalism globally.

Back to Head Counts?

The most comprehensive global study specifically of women working as journalists, produced by the International Women's Media Foundation (IWMF), used survey data collected in 59 countries (Byerly, 2011), representing fewer than 30 per cent of the states and territories in full and associated membership of UNESCO. UNESCO's own collection of data provided even fewer annual head counts of women journalists – in 55 countries for one or other of the years 1999–2006 (UNESCO Institute for Statistics, 2011, 2014). The WoJ survey over the period 2012–16 noted the gender make-up of its samples from 67 countries (www.worldsofjournalism.org). Gallagher with von Euler (1995) included data from 43 countries, and Weaver and Willnat (2012) from 31. The Global Media Monitoring Project audited 114 countries; however, it gathered only proxy information from on-air appearances and print by-lines (Macharia, 2015). The IREX Media Barometers (2007–15) also incidentally collected some information on numbers of female journalists in individual countries (IREX, 2015). Head counts have figured (purposely or incidentally), too, in studies at the

* regional level (for example, Eastern African Journalists' Association, 2008; European Federation of Journalists, 2012; International Federation of Journalists, 2010; Joseph, 2015; Witt-Barthel, 2006)
* sub-regional level (for example, Joof, 2013; Mellado et al., 2012; Pintak & Ginges, 2012; Seshu, 2014)
* national level (including Bailie & Azgin, 2012; Isaeva et al., 2007; Kunthear, 2008; Lobo et al., 2015; North, 2014; Pinto & Sousa, 2003; Radu & Chekera, 2014; South African National Editors' Forum, 2007; Tsui & Lee, 2012; Weaver & Willnat, 2012).

However, Gallagher with von Euler (1995) ignored the Middle East (Sakr, 2004). Africa was under-represented in all these surveys. North America was largely confined to the US and Canada.

To try to present a more globally representative sample of the presence of women in journalist occupations we collated secondary data from 153 states and territories representing three-quarters of the UNESCO membership. The presence of countries in Asia and Middle East and North Africa (MENA) was enhanced, with that of the global North (represented by Europe and North America) correspondingly reduced.

Finding Female Journalists

There were dozens of sources of figures covering the period 1999 to 2016, and these showed many differences. Even within the same records there were apparent discrepancies; for example, three surveys conducted almost simultaneously in the UK produced figures purporting to show the presence of women in journalism which diverged by close to 30 per cent (Delano, 2003). Sampling, sampling methods and sample sizes varied, too, and were probably the main source of disagreements.

Women appeared not to be equally distributed across the occupation. Ross and Carter (2011) noted that in the UK the proportion of women in news roles was 15 percentage points lower than the percentage of women in

Table 7.1 The presence of women in journalism (153 states and territories)

Category	Numerical presence	States and territories	N (%)
1. Women in a clear majority	>66%	Albania; Armenia; Bulgaria; Cabo Verde; Cuba; Fiji; Liechtenstein; Lithuania; Suriname; Tajikistan	10 (6.5%)
2. Gender parity	50–66%	Anguilla; Australia; Bermuda; Bhutan; Bosnia; Cayman Isles; Chechnya; Czech Rep; Finland; Georgia; Ghana; Iceland; Latvia; Malaysia; Moldova; Montenegro; Myanmar; New Zealand; Palau; Papua New Guinea; Puerto Rico; Romania; Russia; Serbia; Singapore; Slovakia; Slovenia; South Africa; Sri Lanka; Sweden; Thailand; Trinidad; US	33 (21.4%)
3. Making progress towards gender parity	34–49%	Austria; Azerbaijan; Belarus; Belgium; Bolivia; Botswana; Brazil; Canada; Chile; China; Costa Rica; Croatia; Cyprus; Denmark; Dominican Rep; Ecuador; Egypt; El Salvador; Estonia; France; Germany; Greece; Hong Kong; Hungary; Israel; Jamaica; Kyrgyzstan; Lebanon; Luxembourg; Madagascar; Malta; Mauritius; Mexico; Monaco; Morocco; Netherlands; Nigeria; Norway; Philippines; Poland; Portugal; Spain; St. Lucia; St. Vincent; Switzerland; Taiwan; Tanzania; Tunisia; Uganda; UK; Ukraine; Venezuela	52 (33.8%)

Table 7.1 (Continued)

Category	Numerical presence	States and territories	N (%)
4. 'Glass wall'	25–33%	Algeria; Argentina; Benin; Burundi; Cambodia; Colombia; Congo; Djibouti; Kenya; Kosovo; India; Indonesia; Ireland; Italy; Macao; Marshall Isles; Mozambique; Namibia; Niue; Palestine; Peru; Sudan; Swaziland; Turkey; Vietnam	25 (16.2%)
5. Women unwelcome	<25%	Afghanistan; Angola; Bahrain; Bangladesh; Cameroon; Chad; DR Congo; Ethiopia; Iran; Iraq; Japan; Jordan; Kurdistan; Kuwait; Laos; Liberia; Malawi; Mali; Nepal; Oman; Pakistan; Qatar; Rwanda; Senegal; Sierra Leone; Somalia; South Korea; South Sudan; Togo; UAE; Yemen; Zambia; Zimbabwe	33 (22%)
Total			153 (100%)

journalism as a whole. As mentioned above, the gender distribution of the journalism population also varied considerably by sector (newspaper, magazine, broadcast, online) and role (reporter, editor, commentator, freelance, etc.) (Byerly, 2011; Delano, 2003; Mitchell, 2011; Lo, 2012; Pasti et al., 2012; Ross & Carter, 2011; Stepinska et al., 2012).

Measuring presence was – and still is – never straightforward; for example, in Pakistan the proportion of women in the occupation fell marginally from 5 per cent to 4.2 per cent between 2002 and 2014 but the number of female journalists rose more than sevenfold (Seshu, 2014). In Bahrain in 2010 women comprised 50 per cent of print journalists; 20 per cent of broadcast employees (not just journalists); and 15 per cent of trade union members (International Federation of Journalists, 2010). In some places, while anecdotal evidence suggested a substantial presence of women in journalism – even parity or beyond – the figures were simply not available (Bethel, 1993; El Issawi, 2014).

The IWMF report included categories of occupation which did not commonly describe journalists, including members of governing boards; publishers; chief executives; chief financial officers; camera, sound and lighting technicians; graphic designers; wardrobe designers; sales, finance and administration personnel; and consultants.

In sum, serious questions should be raised as to the extent to which any of the data accurately represented 'the profession as a whole', including the women in it (Lealand & Hollings, 2012, p. 129; UNESCO, 2014, p. 58), and how it was – and still is – distributed across the world. Therefore, our aggregation of the available figures was no more than the presentation of best estimates and an indication of the presence of women globally in journalism. Consequently, rather than offering individual percentages, we clustered the figures in broad categories (see Table 7.1). Nevertheless, the increased presence of women in journalism globally was an important factor in shaping the occupation into, and following, the turn of the century.

The Count

Figures existed for:

* 33 African countries (excluding MENA)
* 28 Asian states and territories
* 19 Central and Eastern European states (including Georgia but not the Baltic states)
* 17 Western European countries (including Cyprus but not the Nordic states)
* 17 MENA nations
* 15 Latin American nations (including Cuba)
* nine countries in North America (including the Caribbean)
* seven Pacific and Oceanic countries
* all five Nordic countries, and
* three Baltic States.

Some places (notably a large number of relatively small, geographically dispersed and culturally variegated Caribbean and Pacific islands) remained under-represented. Layton (1995) noted the wide variation in the presence of women in journalism across Pacific small island nations in the early 1990s – from 11 per cent to 75 per cent – which the current data failed to capture completely (see also Higgins et al., 2008). In the most recently available report on the state of the media in the Caribbean four out of 14 countries reported no figures for the numbers of journalists and the rest provided estimates which varied as widely as 50–100 and 125–40 (Association of Caribbean Mediaworkers, 2013).

In allocating the numbers we drew on the R^3 thesis proposed by Rush, Oukrop and Sarikakis (2005) which suggested that women were confined by a 'glass wall' which restricted their participation in journalism to between 25 per cent and 33 per cent of the occupation's population, and Robinson and Buzzanell (2012, p. 149) who argued that when women comprised between 34 per cent and 49 per cent of journalists they were 'making progress' towards parity of presence. Thus, in Table 7.1:

- Category 1 drew on the R^3 thesis but applied inversely. This grouping included the countries where the presence of men in journalism ranged between 25 per cent and 33 per cent, indicating that women were in a clear majority
- Category 2 included all the states where the proportion of women in journalism had reached parity but did not exceed 65 per cent. The World Bank estimated that women had reached at least 50 per cent of the general labour force in only eight countries in the world by 2016
- Category 3 was based on women making 'progress' towards parity in numerical presence (34–49 per cent). World Bank data showed that women's participation in the general labour force globally in 2016 was at 39.4 per cent
- Category 4 reflected the R^3 thesis and included places where women's presence in journalism ranged between 25 per cent and 33 per cent suggesting that a 'glass wall' was preventing their greater presence
- Category 5 accounted for countries where the presence of women in journalism had not reached the lower R^3 threshold of 25 per cent, indicating that women were still unwelcome in journalism.

In more than a quarter of states and territories women had either equal presence or constituted a majority in journalism. In ten of these, women accounted for at least two-thirds of journalists. In a further third of places, the number of women in journalism was progressing towards parity (above 33 per cent but below a half). Therefore, in six out of ten states and territories, women appeared to have broken through the 'glass wall'. However, in more than a fifth women were barely present, and seemed to be unwelcome, in journalism. In about a sixth of states women had restricted access to journalism as an occupation in line with the R^3 thesis.

Among the places where women's presence had reached at least parity, just under half were in Europe, the US and Canada, and these countries were mostly among those where women fell short of a two-thirds majority. That was especially the case in Western Europe. In the group where women's presence was dominant were countries as diverse as Cuba, Fiji and Tajikistan. Only Lithuania of the Baltic nations, Albania and Bulgaria in Central and Eastern Europe and Liechtenstein in Western Europe appeared here. Two

Western European countries – Ireland and Italy – demonstrated levels of women's presence in journalism below 33 per cent, although the WoJ returns were different.

In the Nordic states, where Byerly (2011, p. 12) noted 'a relatively high degree of gender equality', the presence of women in journalism was no more than parity (Finland, Iceland and Sweden) and 'making progress' towards parity (Denmark and Norway). Similarly in the Baltic states the presence of women in journalism ranged from a clear majority (Lithuania) through parity (Latvia) to 'making progress' towards parity (Estonia). The Eastern and Central European countries, supposedly with 'strong tendencies toward gender egalitarianism' (Byerly, 2011), also demonstrated variable presences of women, from a majority situation (Albania and Bulgaria) to less than 33 per cent (Kosovo). In more than half these places there was parity.

The UNESCO data suggested women were at least equally present in US journalism. This was at odds with Byerly's (2011, p. 13) conclusion that in America there was 'a pervasive pattern of women's under-representation' in journalism. That most surveys of US journalists included only employees in news organizations (Brownlee & Beam, 2012; Gray, 2014; Willnat & Weaver, 2014) may explain why the generally accepted figure of about 36–39 per cent for women in journalism was at odds with the 60 per cent reported by UNESCO's Institute for Statistics (2014) which relied on census returns. Canadian journalism was still in the process of progressing towards parity. All the same, all the European states plus the two major North American countries were over-represented among countries where women's presence in journalism was at parity or greater. Although they made up less than 28 per cent of the total sample, they accounted for almost 44 per cent of the countries where this was the case.

Patterns of women's presence in journalism elsewhere in the world indicated less of a negative situation than has perhaps been previously suggested.

- In Asia, where Byerly (2011, p. 11) noted 'a general pattern of exclusion' of women from journalism with some exceptions, almost half of states and territories reported gender parity and above, or women as making progress towards parity.
- In MENA, in five of 17 states (including Israel) women were 'making progress' towards parity, although in more than half women made up less than 25 per cent of journalists (Byerly, 2011, p. 10).
- In African states, excluding MENA, where again in almost half of places women's presence in journalism fell below 25 per cent, they had reached parity and above in three and were progressing towards parity in a further five (a total of 26 per cent of the sample).

- In Latin America, women had reached at least parity (21 per cent) or were progressing toward parity (57 per cent) in more than three-quarters of countries.
- In ten countries (BRICS plus Hungary, Indonesia, Mexico, Nigeria and Turkey) identified as emerging economies in which institutional transformation accompanied industrialization and the development of markets (Vercueil, 2012), although women were nowhere in a clear majority they had reached parity in 20 per cent of places and were making progress towards parity in a further 50 per cent.

Only in Asia and Africa, including the MENA states, were women still unwelcomed in journalism. In the Baltic and Nordic countries and North America they were no longer stranded on the wrong side of a 'glass wall' restricting their entry into the occupation. However, even in Western Europe (excluding the Baltic and Nordic states) and Central and Eastern Europe, the 'glass wall' continued to be evident. Women were at parity or in a majority in North America (but nowhere here did they constitute a clear majority). In Central and Eastern Europe the same was the case in 91 per cent of places. The 'norm' in Central and Eastern Europe was parity. In Western Europe outside the Baltic and Nordic countries women were making progress rather than having achieved parity or more.

Summary

The data presented here challenges the totality of the proposition that a 'glass wall' restricted women's presence in journalism to between 25 per cent and 33 per cent (Rush et al., 2005) as this was now exceeded in 60 per cent of countries. We might also question whether women's presence in journalism globally has been previously underestimated. This might partially explain why the number of women counted as present in the occupation fell below the numbers graduating from journalism education and training programmes in the past 30–40 years. It may be that many surveys bypassed places where female journalists were to be found, such as online platforms or blogs, when mainstream media opportunities were closed to them (Al-Najjar, 2013; Bernardi, 2010). There was an over-reliance on surveying newsrooms and employment in predetermined news (often legacy) media (Herscovitz, 2012), and too narrow a definition of 'journalist' was used (Weischenberg et al., 2012). Women's historical engagement with journalism did not necessarily follow the same patterns as men's (Robinson & Buzzanell 2012).

Women's presence in journalism appears to be more complex than hitherto demonstrated. The idea that a group of states in geographical proximity formed a coherent regional context was challenged; for example, while communist ideology promoted the idea of a uniformity of egalitarianism in Central and Eastern Europe, it was argued that this was largely mythical and that the former states of the Soviet empire did not constitute a single context (Nastasia & Nastasia, 2013a; Nastasia and Nastasia, 2013b; Nastasia et al., 2013; Smirnova, 2013). Of course, by reflection, this applied to male journalists, too. So did the skewing of samples in which parts of the world were over- and under-represented. Thus, being alert to the varieties of journalism cultures and practices in, as well as across, geographical – as well as political, economic, social and cultural – contexts, as explored in Chapter 2, applies also to who formed the global journalism population itself – a group about which we appear still to know too little.

It is evident that over a period of 20–30 years the composition of the global journalism population was changing, and that it seems likely to continue to change into the foreseeable future. What this means for journalism, its practices, values, status and distinctiveness, is less certain.

Further Reading

1. Byerly, C.M. (ed.) (2013a) *The Palgrave International Handbook of Women and Journalism* (Basingstoke: Palgrave Macmillan).
2. Chambers, D., Steiner, L. & Fleming, C. (2004) *Women and Journalism* (London: Routledge).
3. European Federation of Journalists (2012) *Survey Report on Women in Journalists' Unions in Europe* (Brussels: International Federation of Journalists).
4. Franks, S. (2013) *Women and Journalism* (London: I.B. Taurus).
5. Gillespie, E. (ed.) (2003) *Changing the Times: Irish Women Journalists 1969–1981* (Dublin: Lilliput Press).
6. Montiel, A.V. (ed.) (2014) *Media and Gender: A Scholarly Agenda for the Global Alliance on Media and Gender* (Paris: UNESCO).
7. Robin, M. (2001) *Intersecting Places, Emancipatory Spaces: Women Journalists in Tanzania* (Trenton, NJ: Africa World Press).
8. Whitt, J. (2008) *Women in American Journalism: A New History* (Urbana & Chicago, IL: University of Illinois Press).

8

The Future of Global Journalism

Chapter overview

This chapter explores conjectures about the foreseeable future of global journalism. It asks more questions than it answers, given that the future is uncertain. What does the so-called post-truth era hold for journalism? Is the idea of post-truth eliding the differences between 'free' and 'unfree' journalism environments? How can journalism respond? And, given that the future of journalism is dependent on the reproduction of the occupation, how will university journalism education cope with what appears to be a shifting paradigm, layered on top of the disruption caused by digitization? Where will the sustainable future of journalism lie if, as is almost certainly the case, it is not exclusively in the traditional journalism of the mass media of the global North?

Learning outcomes

After having read this chapter you will be able to:

1. Evaluate the challenges to journalism of the 'post-truth era'
2. Analyse approaches to the education and training of journalists
3. Imagine journalism's global future.

In November 2016 during the global panic over 'false' or 'fake' news which, it was contended, had influenced the outcome of that month's election for the presidency of the United States, mis- and disinformation was mostly spread through social media (Wingfield et al., 2016). In the last three months of the election campaign the 20 false stories attracting most attention on Facebook generated almost a fifth more interest than the same number of top items posted on mainstream media web pages (Silverman, 2016). Social media and the search engine Google were accused of facilitating 'a host of faux-journalistic players to pollute the democracy with dangerously fake news items' (Rutenberg, 2016). Such items went viral in the digital domain, but were also taken up by mainstream media, and even cited by politicians, thus gaining widespread traction. Supporters of the Republican candidate Donald Trump appeared to be more likely to believe and recirculate such sensational 'news' (Silverman & Alexander, 2016).

The purpose of this 'fake news' seemed to be two-fold: for many years purveyors had been creating and posting it as part of a culture of satire and send-up. This 'spoof news' was intended as a joke and was associated with sites such as *National Report* (http://nationalreport.net) which labelled its 'news' as 'fiction', and *The Onion* which began online publication in 1996. Perhaps the greatest impact in blending journalism with comedy was achieved by the US cable and satellite television channel Comedy Central's *The Daily Show with Jon Stewart* which surprising numbers of younger Americans turned to as their primary source of news (Anon, 2008). One American 'impresario of a fake news empire', allegedly earning $US10,000 a month through it, argued that his 'news' was (intentionally) obviously 'fake'. The US was not the only place to find such 'news'. The Indian site *FakingNews* confessed that it was 'a website that has news content with no reliable sources. We simply fake news to attract your attention' (www.fakingnews.firstpost.com). Similarly, UK's *The Daily Mash* declared itself 'a satirical website which publishes spoof articles, i.e. it is all made-up and is not intended, *in any way whatsoever*, to be taken as factual (www.thedailymash.co.uk – original emphasis). However, many users confused this with 'real' news, and simply accepted it as accurate without checking its veracity (Dewey, 2014, 2016; Woolf, 2016).

Second, about 140 'fake news' websites dedicated to US politics were found to have originated in one town in the Former Yugoslav Republic of Macedonia. These were driven instrumentally by their capacity to garner ad revenues in US dollars as gullible Americans trended their contents (Silverman & Alexander, 2016). To some extent, this audience may have been primed by the so-called supermarket tabloids which gained popularity in the US from the 1970s with 'bizarre' headlines like 'Woman turns into wild dog after being forced to eat pet food for 3 years' (Bird, 1992, p. 43). This kind of 'journalism' (not everyone believed it was truly journalism) had been published through-out the modern era of the mass media (possibly from the 1880s, and certainly from the 1920s) (Bird, 1992).

'False' or 'fake' news was a complex concept. It appeared in at least three interrelated versions:

- *Reactive*: the organization Article 19 noted that the category of 'false news' was prevalent (and its dissemination punishable) mostly in 'the laws of repressive countries', where it marked out what was unacceptable to publish as opposed to officially sanctioned information, and curtailed legitimate reporting by journalists through creating a chilling effect by criminalizing opinions, and privileging 'official' facts over any information journalists sourced (Anon, 2016a). In 2017 the human rights activist Nabeel Rajab was imprisoned in Bahrain awaiting trial for 'broadcasting false news' (Bahrain Center for Human Rights, 2017).
- *Subversive*: partly as a consequence, satirical news outlets in places such as the Arab region, Turkey, the Caribbean, Australia, Hungary and Italy used parodies of mainstream news media practices and news values to put otherwise under-reported topics into the public domain, and to highlight alternative, often (radical and populist) oppositional, views. This content also played into longstanding folklore, conspiracy theories and urban legends which, in turn, influenced mainstream popular journalism (for an exploration of this complex relationship, see Conboy (2002)).
- *Proactive*: publishing 'propaganda as fact' and fabricating news reports was first practised on a modern state scale by the UK during World War One. This was different from censorship, which sought to hide the facts by either refusing to provide journalists with information or forbidding them to publish (Greenslade, 2014). In the 1930s 'fake news' became routine state practice in Nazi Germany, Fascist Italy and Stalinist Russia but was also evident in the US, Japan, France and the UK (Brendon, 2017). From about 2008 Russia engaged in a 'special operations' campaign of spreading disinformation (*dezinformatsiya*), planting 'fake news', in Germany, Sweden, Finland, the UK and the US (MacFarquhar, 2016). Two essentially Russian state-controlled media, the television broadcaster RT (started in 2005) and the web/radio/news agency organization Sputnik International (2014), were accused of spreading 'fake news' (Rapoza, 2016).

Thus 'fake news' appeared in its various forms, not only in social media but also in orthodox mainstream media in environments which were classified both as 'free' and 'unfree' in terms of journalism culture.

The US President, Barack Obama, urged discrimination:

> If we are not serious about facts and what's true and what's not, if we can't discriminate between serious arguments and propaganda, then we have problems ... If everything seems to be the same and no distinctions are made, then we won't know what to protect. We won't know what to fight for. And we can lose so much of what we've gained in terms of the kind of democratic freedoms and market-based economies and prosperity that we've come to take for granted. (Quoted in Solon, 2016)

This was surely a reference to the distinguishing characteristic of the liberal model of journalism: 'the gathering of facts, obtained via a range of identifiable and verifiable sources'. Circumventing this process was viewed as 'professional failure' (Phillips, 2015a, p. 40). Journalism supposedly presented '*factual*, rather than fictional, artistic, or scientific' information. Consistently, in 1981, 1996 and 2007, Francophone Québecois journalists listed accurate reporting as their number one professional value (Pritchard & Bernier, 2010). Getting at 'truth', therefore, was at the core of this kind of journalism and journalism education, where students learnt 'reporting techniques and discursive strategies to discover truth and mirror this in a comprehensible way to a general audience', even if hesitantly in post-1990s China, and not always perfectly put into practice elsewhere (Broersma, 2012; Duffy, 2010; Mfumbusa, 2010; UNESCO, 2007; Wu, 2006; Zhongshi, 2010). 'To have value as information, journalism has to be accepted as *true*' (McNair, 2005, p. 30 – original emphasis).

However, one researcher argued that 'fake news' had turned the role of journalism on its head: it no longer mattered if journalists exposed phoney 'facts' (Tambini, 2016). Had the world entered a 'post-truth era' (Keyes, 2004)? In 2016 Oxford Dictionaries named 'post-truth' as their international word of the year (Flood, 2016). Public belief in journalistic truthfulness was at a low ebb: in the US trust in the media to report accurately fell from 73 per cent to 32 per cent between 1972 and 2016, and in 2016 in the UK only 25 per cent of people trusted journalists to tell the truth (Preston, 2016). To some extent, the legacy mainstream media in the global North (especially those that could be described as 'tabloid') had subverted their own authority by themselves 'faking it' with concocted stories published over many years (Hargreaves, 2003, pp. 113–20). Furthermore, in pursuit of online 'clicks', some websites invented 'news' in order to cash in on public prejudice (Solomon, 2017). It seemed to be a global problem, with fake news reported by 2018 in Australia, Austria, Brazil, Canada, China, the Czech Republic, Eritrea, Finland, France,

Germany, Hong Kong, India, Indonesia, Italy, Kenya, Malaysia, Myanmar, Nigeria, Pakistan, Philippines, Poland, South Africa, South Korea, Sweden, Thailand, Taiwan, Ukraine and the UK as well as the US (Anon, 2017b; Biswas, 2018; Eun-Young, 2017; Lee, 2016; Leetaru, 2016; Saldanha, 2016).

Journalism Education as an Antidote to 'Fake News'

Could journalism education act as a bulwark against forces seemingly eroding journalism by providing a route to professionalism and more secure relative autonomy (Tumber & Prentoulis, 2005)? Not all interested parties believed so: a 2013 study of journalism education in the US found that only just over a half of practitioners thought that a journalism degree was important or very important for understanding the value of journalism (Finberg, 2013). Three broad views on what a liberal journalism education should entail were found not only between journalism schools but often within them:

* Traditionalists – in the modern era journalists served the public by serving the media; as the media changed and adapted, journalists must do so, too, but in line with the media (Picard, 2015)
* Reformers – led by Kovach and Rosensteil (2001): the media have veered sharply away from their traditional roles and journalists must reassert their fundamental occupational, rather than organizational, skills and values
* Innovators – journalists need to adapt to the times; to the decline and deviation of legacy media; and to seize opportunities for truly independent journalism, not bound by the impositions of the traditional mainstream media, using discovery, enterprise and creativity to connect directly with publics (Lynch, 2015).

Such disagreements suggested fissure in the near-monolith of the Western liberal and Northern industrial model of journalism education, and that there was room for the far more nuanced categorization of journalisms (plural) introduced in Chapter 3. Certainly, it was an ambition of NWICO that journalism capacity should be diffused far more widely across the world acknowledging localized cultures as well as democratic rights (see also Anon, 2016b). In the second decade of the twenty-first century journalists were clearly not the same all over the world; for example, the presence of women (60 per cent plus in Russia; around 10 per cent in Bangladesh – see Chapter 7) varied, as did the length of experience, and, crucially, feelings of autonomy (worldsofjournalism.org). Despite assumptions that globalization has led to 'convergence in journalistic orientations and practices' (Hanitzsch, 2007, p. 367), the evidence was inconclusive. Dueze (2005) believed that journalists were unified globally by five shared orientations – to public service; impartiality; autonomy; immediacy; and ethics – and, as explored in Chapter 2, Hanitzsch (2011) identified four occupational milieux (detached watchdog; populist disseminator; critical change agent; opportunist facilitator) (see Tables 2.1–2.10). However, all of these could be located within any national or regional cohort of journalists: it was the quantitative distribution which gave rise to a more or less dominant milieu in any one place. These were not immutable categorizations; for example, although UK journalists appeared to Hanitzsch to adhere principally to the traditional liberal watchdog role, Örnebring (2016) found them to be oriented to the populist disseminator role. This apparent discrepancy possibly reflected the immediate context of working for, say, the 'impartial' public service BBC as opposed to the partisan commercial newspaper sector. Hanitzsch (2007) proposed a seven-part test to ascertain both the external constraints working on, and internal values of, journalists (and their relationships) including commitments to objectivity; associations with external power; place in the market; and idealistic notions of the occupation.

Case Study 8.1: The J-school in the twenty-first century

As he was installed as president of Columbia University in 2002, Lee Bollinger stunned the closed and somewhat esoteric world of journalism education by announcing a review of the institution's prestigious Journalism School (one of, if not the most respected in the world) and challenging its near-century-old tradition of focusing on practical training for careers in the news media.

In his inaugural address, he referred to Pulitzer's vision in endowing the school 'for educating a noble profession (journalism) not simply about the practical side of being journalists but also in the knowledge a great university can offer: "Why not teach," he [Pulitzer] asked rhetorically, "politics, literature, government, constitutional principles and traditions (especially American), history, political economy; also the history and the power of public opinion and public service, illustrated by concrete examples, showing the mission, duty and opportunity of the Press as a moral teacher?" He was criticized for this "visionary" scheme – by many in the press, no less' (Bollinger, 2002).

Bollinger suspended the search for a new dean, and established a taskforce with the remit 'to push the Journalism School to upgrade itself intellectually'

(Sonderman, 2012). This almost instantaneously ignited a debate among journalism faculty and journalists around age-old dualisms – craft or profession; skills or understanding; practice or theory; training or education; trade schools or university departments (Atkins et al., 2002).

Bollinger appeared not to be prepared to compromise: 'To teach the craft of journalism is a worthy goal but clearly insufficient in this new world and within the setting of a great university,' he said.

In 2003 Nicholas Lehmann, a task force member, was appointed the school's dean. He was clearly on-side: 'The professional education of a journalist should include intellectual content. ... to understand the world we are supposed to cover,' he argued. In 2005 the school introduced a new journalism MA concentrating not on practice but on other fields – science, economics, public health, politics, arts, culture, etc. This ran alongside the existing MS in basic practical journalism skills which had been cut from two years to one in 1935 (Patterson, 2013; Sonderman, 2012).

When Lehmann stepped down in 2012, unusually, Bollinger himself led the search for another new dean (Sonderman, 2012). Steve Coll was appointed to the role in 2013. Coll had a reputation as a journalist who married knowledge with practice. It was uncommon among American journalists: 'Coll's method is not the way most journalists work' (Patterson, 2013, p. 94). Patterson called it 'knowledge-based journalism'.

The idea that the formation of journalists should involve more than 'the tricks and machinery of the trade' was asserted by the Commission on Freedom of the Press in 1947 (p. 78).

A six-year, $US20m future of journalism education initiative, involving 11 journalism schools in America (including Columbia), was launched in 2005 focused on curriculum change and substituting for declining (mainly local) journalism (Newton, 2011). Those behind the initiative believed that journalism schools were 'stuck in the past' (Patterson, 2013, p. 96).

The initiative was 'rooted in a sense that journalism was in trouble. Even before the full impact of digital technology was apparent and the economic model for journalism had collapsed, there was a growing sense that a complex world needed a deeper journalism and better-trained journalists.' Its objectives were to advance 'journalistic excellence' through 'curriculum enrichment' by exposing students to the intellectualism of universities (Donsbach & Fielder, 2008, p. 2; https://knightfoundation.org).

Many J-schools followed Columbia in introducing more subject matter instruction (Patterson, 2013, pp. 97–98). In Patterson's view (2013, pp. 99–100):

> For the first time in their history, journalism schools are positioned to play a major part in setting the standards for quality journalism. News outlets have traditionally set the standards, which journalism schools have then used as the benchmark for their training programs ... if knowledge-based reporting is to be a significant part of journalism's future, the university rather than the newsroom is the logical place to develop it. ... False choices can blind journalism schools to their options. Should they focus on skills training? Or on knowledge training? The answer is that their training would be strengthened by integrating the two.

The relationship between education and practice in journalism, and the socialization of entrants into the occupation, appeared to be primarily unidirectional – from the contextual conditions and the internalized values of established practice to education – with the result that the longer a student was exposed to journalism education the more they started to 'think like journalists' practising in the same cultural context (Hanusch et al., 2015, pp. 15–16). Thus journalism education tended, not always exclusively nor necessarily even consciously, but often both, to reproduce the labour force shaped by the established context(s) and habits of practice (Curran, 2000, p. 41). However, research in the US found that many respondents 'singled out the need to raise the degree of mastery that journalists bring to the field and a new level of analytical skills that are needed to explain a complex world' (Knight Foundation, 2011). This was a decades-old concern (Political and Economic Planning, 1938).

An Ideal Education?

Not surprisingly, when the Communication and Information Sector of UNESCO published *Model Curricula for Journalism Education for Developing Countries & Emerging Democracies*, it included in 'professional standards' the rubric that 'Journalists question the accuracy of most everything ... A competent journalist develops effective techniques for ensuring accuracy' (UNESCO, 2007, p. 31). The document's so-called 'Foundations of Journalism' included instructions on assessing the credibility of evidence, and identifying 'bogus or misleading information' (UNESCO, 2007, pp. 40–41). An earlier manual, designed primarily for journalists in the Asia Pacific region, urged them to check and re-check 'the facts' (Henshall & Ingram, 1991, pp. 14–15). Journalists learnt to develop 'a reverence for the facts' (Mindich, 1998, p. 142). Fabrication was an egregious professional error (Willis, 2010). Believing journalism to be under attack from other forms of public communication, the first of Kovach and Rosenstiel's (2001, pp. 12–13) fundamental principles (elements) of journalism (as noted in Chapter 3) was 'Journalism's first obligation is to the truth', and the third was 'Its essence is a discipline of verification'. The standards editor of AP argued:

> nothing ... has changed the journalist's fundamental job of reporting facts from the ground up – conducting original reporting, day after day, in a disciplined and consistent way. The result is a methodically built credibility that cannot be created by other means. (Kent, 2013a)

The model curricula were devised by two dozen academics coordinated by a working group established following a UNESCO-hosted meeting of journalism educators in 2005 (UNESCO, 2007). They were presented first at the inaugural World Journalism Education Congress (WJEC) held in Singapore. By 2013, UNESCO claimed that the curricula were being used by 70 journalism education institutions in 60 developing countries (Karkins, 2013). The decision to write the curricula was prompted by the rapid development of 'independent media' associated with democratization processes outside the global West (UNESCO, 2007, p. 4). In 2007 it was estimated that worldwide there were 1,859 institutions offering journalism programmes. Just over a quarter were in North America, with a fifth each in Latin America, Europe and Asia. Fewer than one in eight were in Africa and the Middle East (Hume, 2007). By 2010 the total had risen to 2,338, an increase of more than a quarter, and the proportion in North America, Asia and Europe had grown to 80 per cent, meaning that the rate of growth was uneven across the world (Oliver, 2010; Banda, 2013). The influence of the liberal norm of journalism (also explored in Chapter 3) seemed evident; for example, in Taiwan it was noted that 'political democratization, economic prosperity, educational progress and mass media modernization' were accompanied by a 'well-developed' journalism education system (Wang, 2006, p. 159), while Clarke (2000; 2010) counted 40 outside organizations, including those from the US, UK, France, Australia, Denmark, Sweden, Canada and Germany, which had delivered journalism education in Cambodia.

The publication of the model curricula was complemented by a declaration of principles adopted in Singapore by 27 journalism education bodies (see Figure 8.1). Perhaps not surprisingly, the declaration did not meet with unanimous acclaim. Objections pivoted chiefly around four interrelated, if not always wholly compatible, arguments:

- Despite origins which seemed to lie mainly in the US, some felt that the failure to mention basic liberal ideals such as freedom of expression, resistance to censorship and a commitment to a journalistic truth was a serious oversight.
- Others believed that the ideas behind the project were dated; anchored in legacy practices (journalistic and educational); reformist rather than evolutionary; defensive; and averse to the kind of experimentation necessary in the contemporary global context.
- A third view was that in striving to identify uniform, universalist principles, what had emerged was the lowest common denominator rather than the highest common factor.

- Finally, many argued that the original anchorage in the global West informed the entire project, and represented an attempt to impose Western values.

In 2013, UNESCO published a revised version of the model curricula intended principally to address most of these objections through 'a strategic rethink' prompted by the crisis facing journalism particularly made manifest by the onset of the global financial crash in 2008 (Banda, 2013; Karkins, 2013, p. 5; Nistor, 2013, p. 61). The new version embraced innovation, cultural sensitivity, rights and a still unabated global demand for journalism education (Banda, 2013). UNESCO also recognized that model curricula were not just for developing countries and emerging democracies, as if there were an unmet need for, and an unproblematic transfer of, capability from the West to the rest (Self, 2015).

From Media to Universities

At the end of the twentieth century in many places (from the liberal democratic UK to the communist People's Republic of China) the education and training of journalists were systematically relocated from the media to universities – from hit-and-miss learning in the, often partisan, even politically controlled, workplace to structured study in more autonomous, scholarly driven higher education institutions (Self, 2015). This shift brought not only relative independence but also better access to various technologies as universities could amortize the development, adoption and promotion of, as well as experimentation with, technological innovation across a wide range of fields and disciplines; intercultural penetration fostered by global student and faculty mobility and collaboration; a capacity feedback loop in which practitioners joined faculty and media organizations hired graduates; and a better amalgam of theory and practice when practitioners and scholars worked together (Self, 2015).

> We, the undersigned representatives of professional journalism education associations, share a concern and common understanding about the nature, role, importance, and future of journalism education worldwide. We are unanimous that journalism education provides the foundation as theory, research, and training for the effective and responsible practice of journalism. Journalism education is defined in different ways. At the core is the study of all types of journalism. Journalism should serve the public in many important ways, but it can only do so if its practitioners have mastered an increasingly complex body of knowledge

and specialized skills. Above all, to be a responsible journalist must involve an informed ethical commitment to the public. This commitment must include an understanding of and deep appreciation for the role that journalism plays in the formation, enhancement and perpetuation of an informed society.

We are pledged to work together to strengthen journalism education and increase its value to students, employers and the public. In doing this we are guided by the following principles:

1. At the heart of journalism education is a balance of conceptual, philosophical, and skills-based content. While it is also interdisciplinary, journalism education is an academic field in its own right with a distinctive body of knowledge and theory.

2. Journalism is a field appropriate for university study from undergraduate to postgraduate levels. Journalism programs offer a full range of academic degrees including bachelors, masters and Doctor of Philosophy degrees as well as certificate, specialized, and mid-career training.

3. Journalism educators should be a blend of academics and practitioners; it is important that educators have experience working as journalists.

4. Journalism curriculum includes a variety of skills courses and the study of journalism ethics, history, media structures/institutions at national and international level, critical analysis of media content, and journalism as a profession. It includes coursework on the social, political, and cultural role of media in society and sometimes includes coursework dealing with media management and economics. In some countries, journalism education includes allied fields like public relations, advertising, and broadcast production.

5. Journalism educators have an important outreach mission to promote media literacy among the public generally and within their academic institutions specifically.

6. Journalism program graduates should be prepared to work as highly informed, strongly committed practitioners who have high ethical principles and are able to fulfill the public interest obligations that are central to their work.

7. Most undergraduate and many masters programs in journalism have a strong vocational orientation. In these programs experiential learning, provided by classroom laboratories and on-the-job internships, is a key component.

8. Journalism educators should maintain strong links to media industries. They should critically reflect on industry practices and offer advice to industry based on this reflection.

9. Journalism is a technologically intensive field. Practitioners will need to master a variety of computer-based tools. Where practical, journalism education provides an orientation to these tools.

10. Journalism is a global endeavor; journalism students should learn that despite political and cultural differences, they share important values and professional goals with peers in other nations. Where practical, journalism education provides students with first-hand experience of the way that journalism is practiced in other nations.

11. Journalism educators have an obligation to collaborate with colleagues worldwide to provide assistance and support so that journalism education can gain strength as an academic discipline and play a more effective role in helping journalism to reach its full potential.

Figure 8.1   Declaration of Principles of Journalism Education, World Journalism Education Conference, 2007

In sum, the academization of journalism led to its incremental profes-sionalization, in which journalism strove to be recognized globally, like law and medicine, as a single, if variable, occupation based on formalization and standardization. This was a stated ambition of Pulitzer when he endowed Columbia University's journalism school (Harris, 2008 – see Case Study 8.1). While a number of models of education and training survived from the past, the drift towards two in particular was evident – the university model and a mixed economy of university schools and separate specialized institutions. This did not assuage anxieties over Western hegemony, as the West's insti-tutions dominated global higher education as well as global media (Ibold & Deuze, 2012).

Notwithstanding the global trend towards the formalization of journalism as a profession by means of the establishment, recognition and implemen-tation of independent standards and agreed practices, most journalists were identified not by their qualifications but by their employment (see Chapter 7), leading to tensions between different professionalisms – occupational (internal values and skills) and organizational (meeting the criteria set by employers) (Örnebring, 2016). In some cases a distinction was drawn between education (in educational settings) and training which occurred in the workplace (Mfumbusa, 2010). Some employment was directly in the service of the state (Central China Television; Syrian Arab Television and Radio Broadcasting); or by statal organizations (such as the BBC in the UK, ABC(Aus) and RT). Across the world, a large number were in the employ of private sector, corporate media. In a few countries (examples have included Belgium, Brazil, Costa Rica, Egypt, Italy, Portugal and Zambia) attempts (some successful) have been made to restrict who constituted a journalist to either membership of a syndicate, professional body or trade union, or through compulsory licensing and/or the attainment of educational quali-fications. Behind these were legal provisions, often based in constitutional commitments to freedom of expression, whether observed or not, and written into statute.

In many places, including the US, university education was supported by employers as a means of determining 'the quality and the prestige of journalism' as a relatively autonomous practice (Waisbord, 2013, p. 23). Yet completing a university course in journalism was not necessarily the exclusive way to qualify as a journalist as defined by working in a newsroom. Even in the US, where formal journalism higher education was first established, 72 per cent of those working in news media organizations considered what they did to be journalism, but only 42 per cent of those with journalism degrees believed they were working in journalism (Rosenstiel et al., 2015). The American Press Institute argued that 'asking who is a journalist is the wrong question because journalism can be produced by anyone' (www.americanpressinstitute.org). The US Senate agreed: it proposed untying journalism from the news media or (self-) employment – a pay cheque test – and instead linking it to the activities of gathering, processing and disseminating journalistic content, particularly with a public interest intent (Kent, 2013b; Reynolds, 2013). Thereby lay what Hargreaves (2003, pp. 15–16) identified as a paradox: although, on the one hand, journalism sought to establish its specific credentials through mechanisms such as formal qualifications and standardization, on the other hand, journalism was 'philosophically and practically beyond regulation by any body associated with the state'. That was because:

> The core democratic right to free expression gives every citizen the right to be a journalist, to report a fact, and to publish an opinion … Even to place too heavy an emphasis upon training or professional standards can diminish this necessary freedom … The alternative is to turn journalism into another branch of established power.

The education of journalists, then, was a site of contestation over the definition of what constituted journalism through the reproduction of the journalistic labour force (Starck, 2000). At the core of this tussle was the idea of a journalistic equivalent of medicine's clinical practice – the domain over which the qualified practitioner held sway and prioritized the best interests of their patient (or client) through their expertise in accessing and interpreting evidence and accumulated professional practice: in journalistic terms 'people rather than power', whether that power was internal or external to the media (Phillips, 2015a, pp. 60, 79). This often set journalism education at odds with media norms and state requirements moderated by political environments and constitutional and statutory legal oversight. As a result, the commitment to 'editorial independence' was often observed more in the breach than its effective implementation (Phillips, 2015a, pp. 63–64). The education of journalists was a key determinant of what was identified as journalism as it expanded globally by acting as an attempt at 'shoring up the autonomy of journalists' (Phillips, 2015a, p. 78). Journalism education had to negotiate disparate cultural contexts, therefore. However, two specific intervening and mutually supportive factors were evident globally at the beginning of the twenty-first century – citizen participation and rapid technological change.

Classroom and Newsroom

Ongong'a (2010, pp. 146–47) noted starkly that in Kenya, 'A wide gap exists between what is learned at journalism schools and what is … done in … newsrooms'. This was an almost universal experience although it manifested itself in different ways, in different places, at different times (Clarke, 2010; Dickson & Brandon, 2000; Duhe & Zukowski, 1997; Lago & Romancini, 2010; Vlad & Balasescu, 2010; Winch, 2012). Nyarota (2006) believed that as a graduate he was overqualified to enter the cadet training scheme (apprenticeship) at the Rhodesian Printing and Publishing Company (in what was later to become Zimbabwe). The curriculum consisted chiefly of addressing the 5 Ws and H: 'the basic skills of interviewing, story construction, how to establish a comprehensive network of contacts and sources, and how to develop a hound's nose for news' (Nyarota, 2006, pp. 52–57). That may be compared to the principles of journalism university education adopted in Russia with their emphasis on concepts such as 'public significance', 'social responsibility', 'cultural and educative value', 'interdisciplinary knowledge', mastering 'a semantically complex linguistic system' and 'large-scale sociocultural communication' calling for command of 'foreign languages, cultural phenomena and regional studies' (Vartanova et al., 2010, pp. 205–06). Josephi (2010) identified a widespread disconnect between idealized journalism education and media practice (captured in outline in Table 8.1).

Robie (2014) provided a positive explanation for the disconnects between academia and the media: the critical nature of university study produced

> vastly more talented innovative and investigative journalists, critical thinkers who are challenging the mainstream and producing new media models or making their mark in the mainstream. Also, journalist graduates end up in media-related careers and more involved in debating the future trajectories of the industry in crisis.

Table 8.1 Journalism values in education and practice

Classroom	Newsroom
Ideas	Reality
Diversity	Monopoly
Professional	Practitioner
Creative	Mundane
Truth seeking	Propaganda
News values	'Good/bad news'
Opposition	Oppression

Source: Zhongshi (2010, pp. 16, 22).

This was as opposed to vocational journalism schools which were 'far more focused on fodder for replicating the local industry with little engagement for the journalism of change'. Others were more negative, claiming that journalism courses were ineffective at producing graduates who were 'job-ready' (Winch, 2012).

The traditional (US) journalism university education was an amalgam of both general (commonly, liberal arts) learning supplemented by a fixed proportion (usually, no more than 25 per cent) of technical instruction in journalism (Merrill, 2010). Nevertheless, on the whole, there was 'a consistency in journalism education to be characterised by a dominant professional orientation, motivated in part by attracting students to the field through its occupational promises ... the need to produce employable graduates' for legacy mainstream media (Loo, 2000, p. 3). The uptake of digital ITCs impacted on even this narrow vocational orientation. What Picard (2014, p. 277) called 'a craft mode of news production' began to emerge.

> In this mode, news is produced by individual entrepreneurial journalists and small-scale journalistic cooperatives ... Most are providing news directly to consumers ... These journalists act as suppliers and partners in a business relationship that is very different from that of freelance journalists ... these new production modes have important implications for how journalists work, the resources available to them, how they organize their careers, ... and how they construct their professional identities, values, and behavioural norms.

Starting in the mid-1980s, journalism schools in America began to change albeit slowly, reflecting the relative decline of legacy news media; the ubiquity of digitization; the need for innovation; the rise of the information society; and globalization (Folkerts, 2014).

What to Do?

Simons (2007) noted a paradox: in Australia journalists appeared to be better educated (more professional) yet more unethical (less professional). The Leveson Inquiry in the UK was founded on a similar belief that as British journalists became more formally qualified, ethical standards slipped (Leveson, 2012). Josephi (2010, p. 1) also pointed out that while journalism education had 'expanded exponentially around the world', media freedom hadn't. Furthermore, Saleh (2010, pp. 124–25) argued that in Egypt, 'The increasing quantity of journalism programs is not matched by an equivalent care for the quality of the education'. Finally, Boczkowski and Mitchelstein

(2013, pp. 46–47) found that the education and training of journalists, insofar as it had become more similar around the world, contributed to a convergence of journalists' news values but a significant divergence from what the public was interested in as news, creating what they called 'the news gap'. In other words, arguments were made which claimed that the journalism which was reproducing chiefly through journalism education was itself deficient in many ways.

Nevertheless, a counter-offensive against fake news and the undermining of liberal journalism began in the early 2000s. By 2016 more than 100 independent fact-checking groups had been started in about 50 countries. More than 90 per cent were established after 2010, and just less than a half between 2014 and 2016. Outside the US, the majority were not affiliated with mainstream media (Graves & Cherubini, 2016). In Europe, almost three-quarters identified themselves as predominantly journalism enterprises (Graves & Cherubuni, 2016). Ninety per cent focused on checking the claims made by politicians and other political actors: only a small number checked the media (Graves & Cherubini, 2016). However, by 2016 that had begun to change. Governments, mainstream media and social media platforms, such as Google, Facebook, WeChat and Weibo, began monitoring and 'outing' fake news and disinformation, particularly when it appeared online (Anon, 2017a; Colborne, 2016; Joseph, 2017; Nicas & Seetharaman, 2016; Zhou, 2016). The organization Fake News Watch usefully listed fake/hoax news sites; satire websites; and clickbait websites to avoid (www.facebook.com/fakenewswatch). However, what appeared to be a novel problem in the global North had been evident for years in the global South (Mozur & Scott, 2016). Moreover, younger Americans were sceptical about journalistic objectivity and 'facts', and associated being informed less with mainstream media (which they mistrusted as establishment institutions) and more with 'fake news, "snarky" talk radio, and opinionated [TV] current events shows', savouring 'ideological clashes' based on the expression of diverse opinions and popular participation (Marchi, 2012, pp. 257–58). In these ways, distinctions in the news consumption of the (liberal) global North, with its predominantly 'free' flows of news which were supposed to be trustworthy, and the (authoritarian) global South, where news flows were traditionally constrained and more fraudulent than honest, appeared to be dissolving.

The global challenge for journalism appeared to be both its continued relevance to the 13 per cent of the world's population living in cultures with a 'free' press (as the consumption of and trust in mainstream journalism in these domains continued to decline) and its status elsewhere where it was still struggling to achieve a foothold – and in the interstices between 'the West and the rest' in processes of democratization. At the same time, media development has been uneven across the world in terms of both decline and growth and the popularity of platforms. While it is evident that Web 2.0 stimulated a global expansion of the use of the internet and in particular social media, newspaper reading increased significantly in China and Japan, television usage grew in India and both commercial and community radio stations proliferated in Africa. Of all of these, the internet had most facilitated access to news. This led legacy media to colonize the web as multimedia 'brands', utilizing pod- and vod-casts, apps, sites and aggregators, alongside and sometimes in conjunction with social media. In a relatively short period of time, the concept of global journalism appeared to have been recast from a small number of privileged media institutions (mainly in the global North) employing professionalized journalists to report internationally within top-down mass communication flows (see Chapter 5) to a worldwide network of actors, platforms and practices in which each had to (re)establish its authority and authenticity in a peer-to-peer asymmetrical system (Beckett, 2010) (see Chapter 6).

The Fifth Estate and the End of a Paradigm?

The changes in journalism coinciding with the adoption of digital ICTs have been considerably (see Chapter 4). Negatively, taking the UK as an example, the number of journalism jobs generally across all media, and in particular the number of newspaper titles in circulation, have fallen markedly, as noted in Chapter 3 (Ponsford, 2016). Furthermore, the initial response of legacy mainstream media to digital challenges was often to hire 'a room full of young, badly paid people with basic computing skills', thereby diluting any professional sense of journalism founded in traditional skills and values (Phillips, 2015a, p. 72). On a more positive note, digital ICTs also facilitated a greater range of opportunities for journalists in gaining more jurisdiction over the whole journalistic process (from conception to closing feedback loops with users); greater immediacy; wider scope; and enhanced scale; as well as control over the tools of mediation: social media, web publishing systems and video hosting platforms allowed journalists to 'build' audiences (Scanlon, 2012). Outside the global West and North opportunities arose not only through the development of indigenous journalism but additionally by meeting the journalistic needs of the West and North through outsourcing (Aram & Paul 2009).

Given Hargreaves' (2003) comment it was not surprising that people who were not formally journalists – 'the people formerly known as the audience' in Rosen's (2006) celebrated phrase – turned their hand to journalism. When the modern mainstream media controlled access, most of those who traditionally practised journalism from outside the ranks of journalists but within these media were privileged figures, such as politicians, historians and other academics, athletes, celebrities, and so on. Any others tended to be confined to the so-called 'alternative' and 'community' media (Hyde-Clarke, 2010, pp. 2–3). For many, this version of journalism was directly opposed to the professional kind, and was often dismissed as 'unprofessional'. As Conboy (2011) pointed out, however, using the UK as an example, this was hardly always the case, with what might be called recognized journalists producing media for and with a wide range of non-media interests, including the women's movement, workers, political parties, single-issue groups, the homeless, and local communities. At the same time, 'alternative' journalism produced from outside the formal mainstream journalistic community had a vibrant history (Atton, 2003) (see Chapter 6).

From the mid-1990s digitized ICTs began to open up access beyond the control of all traditional forms of media, giving rise to the advent of citizen journalism which some have called 'the fifth estate' (Al-Rodhan, 2007; Cooper, 2006; Dutton, 2009). To reinforce the observation about the long tradition of citizen-based journalism as a form of Fifth Estate, the magazine *fifth estate*, first published in Detroit in 1965, was still going in 2018 (www.fifthestate. org). (Symbolically, the title *The Fifth Estate* was also given to a 2013 movie about Wikileaks.) Citizen journalism is explored specifically in Chapter 6. It is worth noting here, however, that the scale and scope of the change has had considerable implications for the formation of journalism. As Jones and Pitcher (2010, pp. 99–100) succinctly put it, 'Journalism has shifted from the practice of professionals to the engagement of writers with society.' One consequence of this was the creation and transmission of 'fake news' when citizens, thinking they were practising a form of journalism, posted information without checking their facts. In one instance, an American tweeted an unverified, and as it turned out, erroneous story, which he believed would be seen by only about 40 personal followers, but which 'fueled a nationwide conspiracy theory' when it was re-tweeted at least 16,000 times and shared more than 350,000 times on Facebook (Maheshwari, 2016). Evidence of 'fake news' being circulated (by states, the media and politicians as well as ordinary people) was found in many places, including Indonesia, Germany, Hong Kong, France, Spain, Myanmar, Colombia, Italy, Sierra Leone, China, Brazil, India and the Philippines (Connolly et al., 2016; Mozur & Scott, 2016).

How, in the face of a tsunami of popular participation, could journalism be sustained, particularly where it was still a relatively new practice, as a standardized 'profession' certificated by higher education institutions applying restrictive entry criteria? Moreover, as citizens brought their own traditional communication practices into play, what future was there for an exclusionary universalist approach to journalism managed through higher education or the media? Rather than thinking of journalism as a profession, akin to medicine, the law or engineering, was it not more a literary activity like novel-writing (Tumber & Prentoulis, 2005)?

As we have seen, in some places there was an ongoing debate over who might be designated a journalist (see Figure 4.4). In others, such as Egypt and a number of Arab countries, journalists were legally defined as such by membership of an approved syndicate which left those working for broadcast and online media and overseas correspondents, as well as 'citizen journalists', technically only posing as journalists (a criminal offence), thus effectively criminalizing the practice of journalism (Kuttab, 2015). Caught in a kind of pincer movement, with 'citizen journalists' encroaching on one side, and authoritarian states imposing restrictions on the other side, how might journalism clarify its role and function as a globally expanding independent occupation in the twenty-first century?

Summary

To return to the theme with which this chapter began, collecting contributions from 40 US journalists following the presidential election campaign of 2016 the British *Guardian* newspaper and the American *Columbia Journalism Review* found that, alongside the orthodox fact-checking, revelations and challenges which marked out liberal watchdog journalism, journalists had:

* uncritically used social media content because it made 'ratings-friendly headlines'
* provided 'unhealthily generous, inflated coverage' in line with the treatment of TV personalities not politicians
* routinely failed to hold those who made claims to account for what they professed
* effectively provided free advertising
* treated all claims as equal, even when some were clearly lies
* been partisan
* normalized deviant behaviour (Pilkington, 2016).

The chief international correspondent for CNN believed that this journalism was facing 'an existential crisis, a threat to the very relevance and usefulness of our profession', and she sought to rally journalists to 'protect journalism' by re-committing to 'robust fact-based reporting without fear or favour' – 'real reporting'; 'basic good journalism' (Amanpour, 2016). A former British newspaper editor who taught in a journalism school for many years argued that 'impartiality tools just don't work any longer' when social media spread information rapidly and indiscriminately: false news had currency before the mainstream media could correct it (Greenslade, 2016). Almost a quarter of a century before, journalists in Australia had accepted the responsibility for protecting and promoting the watchdog function, and believed that the news media were undermining it (Schultz, 1998).

The supposed paradigmatic global model of media freedom, editorial independence and autonomous 'professional' journalism has demonstrated a remarkable degree of fragility. Freedom House noted in its 2017 report on media freedom that 'Global press freedom declined to its lowest point in 13 years in 2016 amid unprecedented threats to journalists and media outlets in major democracies and new moves by authoritarian states to control the media', and RWB expressed 'concern about the sustainability of the "European model"'. Erosions of these freedoms were recorded not only in places where they had long struggled to gain a foothold (Africa, Latin America, the Middle East and North Africa) but also in emerging and even established democracies such as Australia, Canada, France, Greece, India, Japan, South Korea, the UK and the US (Dunham, 2016; Dunham et al., 2015; Farrell, 2016). Cohen (2016) characterized countries such as Hungary, Poland, Russia and South Africa, which were supposedly transitioning to democratic status, as 'deformed democracies' because of their denials of journalistic freedom, and Simon (2016) devised the neologism 'democratators' to describe popularly elected autocratic governments which curtailed these freedoms in places such as Ecuador, Philippines, Singapore, Turkey and Venezuela. A World Forum for Democracy (2015, p. 7) organized by the Council of Europe urged journalists to respond by re-asserting the 'European' liberal model of investigative journalism; 'reporting from the scene'; professional ethics; evidence-based, considered analysis; an exclusive focus on journalism rather than lucrative sidelines, and adaptation to 'new formats'. Nevertheless, the adoption globally of this model ignored the 'difference and variability' which flowed from the contextual determination of journalism (Curran & Park, 2000, p. 15).

As explored in detail in Chapter 2, the taxonomies of journalism mentioned above were no more than rough guides. Although the watchdog orientation was associated with (neo-) liberal democracies (US, UK, Australia) it was also found in democratic corporatist countries (Austria, Germany, Switzerland). The popular disseminator role was prevalent in polarized pluralist states (Spain, Italy) but also in a regulated democracy (Israel). Within regions there was diversity: journalists in the former communist states of Eastern Europe oriented to both the popular disseminator (Bulgaria, Romania) and opportunist (Russia) roles. Again, it appeared that it might be more appropriate to consider journalisms (in the plural) conditioned by the specificities of context with a veneer of shared understanding, rather than a single universal practice glossed by cultural diversity (Curran & Park, 2000; Hallin & Mancini, 2004; Hanitzsch, 2011; Jakubowicz, 2008).

The question which arose then was what this might mean for the sustainability of the universality of human rights as declared by the UN as 'a common standard of achievements for all peoples and all nations', and in particular Article 19 – 'Everyone has the right to freedom of opinion and expression; this right includes freedom to hold opinions without interference and to seek, receive and impart information and ideas through any media and regardless of frontiers.' Could the universality of the right to freedom of expression be promoted without imposing a uniformity of culture and allowing a thousand journalisms to bloom (Tharoor, 1999)? Whose version of journalism might prevail? Considering particularly the relationship between mass media organizations, citizens and technology, the Dutch Journalism Fund/Stimuleringfonds voor de Journalistiek (2015) scoped four possible scenarios for journalism in 2025:

1. Wisdom of the crowd: 'A world in which the economy and society will be dominated by start-ups and virtual collaborations. Using the latest technology (radical developments) citizens will organise themselves (do it yourself), and remove any requirement for large organisations. Media brands no longer decide what news is, the crowd will do that now'.

2. A handful of apples: 'A world in which a handful of organisations dominate the market and technological changes are accelerating (radical development). Consequently, the CEOs of Ali Baba, Apple, Baidu, Facebook and Google are more powerful than many heads of state. Small initiatives struggle, and citizens are happy because large corporations take care of everything for them (do it for me). Technology is everywhere, privacy is a rare phenomenon and ... journalistic organisations are suppressed'.

3. The shire: 'A world in which large organisations disappear and more and more citizens organise themselves (do it yourself) and are reluctant to make use of new technology (reluctance). ... The citizen claims the power'.

4. Darwin's game: 'A society in which citizens still depend on large companies and organisations (do it for me) and citizens show (reluctance) to make use of new technology'.

For the Fund the most important dimension of its vision of a possible future for journalism was 'the new – very important role – that users play in the [news] process', captured in the do-it-yourself and do-it-for-me projections, and how they utilize or reject digital communication capacity, and the impact that may have on media institutions (Ireton, 2015). A Google search in March 2017 using the term 'future of journalism in a digital world' produced more than 4 million results. There was far less thought given to the question of 'To what extent are changes in journalist work practices country specific or are there differences in practices within and between Europe, America, the BRIC nations, and the global South?' (Rottwilm, 2014, p. 16), and how configurations of technology, media and citizenry might be differently mobilized impacting on those practices and journalism more generally. Boczkowski (2016) observed:

> We celebrate the new [digital] infrastructure when it helps undermine information practices of oppressive governments, and denounce it when it contributes to misinforming the citizens of liberal democratic states. But unfortunately, it seems unrealistic to have one without the other, since they are the two sides of the same coin. This does not mean that truthful accounts of oppressive governments are equivalent to untruthful accounts about democratic candidates, but that the information infrastructure that contributes to the spread of both types of accounts is one and the same. Ambivalence about this infrastructure might tempt us to call for policing its destabilizing capabilities in some cases, but this might have the unintended consequence of curtailing its emancipatory potential in others.

Digital capacity allowed the substitution of 'foreign reporting for U.S. [or any domestic] audiences … [with] local stories initially written for a local audience that are also adaptable for and relevant to a global audience' (the international with the global) (Tran, 2016). That capacity was available, as we have seen, to about 50 per cent of the world's population, and spreading. How it might be used – and by whom – was by no means clear but it seemed unlikely to be exclusively through forms of journalism historically practised in the global North. Sustainable forms of journalism, and how they might serve the world's diverse populations both separately and together, may already exist and need only to be identified, or have yet to be found. Where they might be remained an open question, too.

Further Reading

1. Banda, F. (ed.) (2013) *Model Curricula for Journalism Education: A Compendium of New Syllabi* (Paris: UNESCO).
2. Dutch Journalism Fund. (2015) 'The journalistic landscape in 2025', www.journalism2025.com, accessed 23 March 2017.
3. Peters, C. & Broersma, M. (eds) *Rethinking Journalism: Trust and Participation in a Transformed News Landscape* (Abingdon: Routledge).
4. UNESCO (2007) *Model Curricula for Journalism Education for Developing Countries & Emerging Democracies* (Paris: UNESCO).
5. Zelizer, B. (2017) *What Journalism Could Be* (Cambridge: Polity).

9

Conclusion

Making Sense of Global Journalism

Chapter overview

This chapter summarizes, synthesizes and analyses the main themes and issues addressed in this book. Many of those overlap and recur in different forms and configurations. The core challenge is to try to answer the six questions posed in the Preface – the what, who, where, when, how and why of global journalism – at the macro, mezzo and micro levels. To do so satisfactorily, we have argued, requires critical, systematic and independent enquiry and the application of abstract principles to evidence, taking into account a wide range of factors both external (context) and internal (practices, personnel) to journalism.

Learning outcomes

After having read this chapter you will be able to:

1. Distinguish trends and issues in global journalism occurring at the macro, mezzo and micro levels
2. Compare and contrast trends and issues in global journalism occurring in a range of political, economic, social and cultural contexts
3. Apply abstract principles to evidence
4. Evaluate what journalism is (in context).

In many ways, considering global journalism hitherto has raised the issue addressed by Zelizer (2017) as to 'what journalism could be'. Zelizer (2017, p. 2) was concerned with the condition of journalism as a product and manifestation of 'narrow understandings of modernity and reason, an identity that highlights its preoccupation with realism, an institutional neighbour-hood whose most proximate residents … privilege truth-telling … a university environment that accommodates its relevance for the public good' lodged in Western ideology and systemized and spread more or less globally through Northern economic power. Broadening the scope of enquiry as much as possible to the global, acknowledging and trying to take account of the extent of global activity in the domain called 'journalism' in many places, invariably exposed a more 'complex and nuanced enterprise', as well as 'the complexity under which journalism operates' (Zelizer, 2017, pp. 7, 214) (see Chapter 2). Moreover, both liberal democracy and capitalism relied heavily on stability and on journalism as a contribution to managing disruption and reinforcing solidarity, consensus and shared identity by providing a 'safety valve' to relieve social tensions arising out of – and to correct – inequality, injustice and curtailments of freedom (Bromley, 2010, p. 195; Zelizer, 2017, p. 243). Journalists were, as Ettema and Glasser (1998, pp. 3–4) found, 'custodians of conscience … engag[ing] the public's sense of right and wrong'.

These were neither the orientation, nor the conditions, which necessarily prevailed in other parts of the world: even as the forces of democratization took hold, they could 'lead anywhere' (Rizal, 2015, p. xviii). Furthermore, as the twenty-first century headed towards the end of its second decade, these approaches appeared to be in decline in the global West and North. Consequently, whereas authoritarian forces were accused of pursuing a 'jihad against journalists' (see Chapters 2 and 5), in the liberal global North there was, according to some, a parallel 'war on journalism' (Fowler, 2015). In-between, some countries supposedly transitioning to, or reinforcing, democracy turned to so-called illiberalism, impacting negatively on journalism (Stiglitz, 2017). Taken together they straddled the global North, South and former East, including in their number Egypt, Hungary, Israel, Myanmar, Poland, Russia, Serbia and Turkey (see Chapter 8). This combined 'assault on journalism' (Carlsson & Pöyhtäri, 2017, p. 12) was truly global, including the global West, and involving 'censorship and repression, self-censorship, surveillance, monitoring and control, gatekeeping, propaganda – disinformation, acts of terror, anti-terror laws, criminalization of encryption and/or anonymity, hate speech and harassment, and organized crime'. For women journalists, harassment could be sexual, too (Steiner, 2016). Even within the member states of the Council of Europe, 69 per cent of journalists surveyed reported experiences of 'psychological violence, mainly at the hands of public authorities' (Clark & Grech, 2017, p. 223). (The killing, including murder, of journalists is referred to in the Introduction and a number of subsequent chapters.)

Zelizer's observations problematized what could appear to be an inexorable march of journalism globally, opposed only by feudalists and authoritarians protective of their (corrupt) power in the face of popular expectations of freedom, equity, fairness and transparency in public life, and the development of civil society and civil liberties. Journalism, as an essential contribution to 'free media', was seen by organizations such as the WTO as underpinning economic development and global prosperity, too (see Chapter 3). The supposed exemplar was the global West. Carey (1997, p. 332) went so far as to argue that 'journalism as a practice is unthinkable except in the context of democracy; in fact, journalism is usefully understood as another name for democracy' (a thought echoed by Josephi as referred to in Chapter 3). However, Schudson (2010, p. 8) countered with examples of where journalism existed 'outside democracy'. In his view, journalism served seven purposes:

1. Providing 'full and fair' information
2. Investigating power
3. Analysing 'a complex world'
4. Sharing social experiences
5. Acting as a 'public forum'
6. Advocating and mobilizing
7. '[E]ncouraging a fuller, richer vision of liberal democracy' (Schudson, 2010, pp. 8ff)

He wrote:

> Journalism ... cannot produce democracy where democracy does not exist, but it can do more to help democracies along if it recognizes the multiple services it affords democracy, encourages the virtues that endow those services, and clarifies for journalists and the public the many gifts news offers to humane self-government. (Schudson, 2010, p. 21)

Yet there were many types of democracy (as explored in Chapter 8), some of which appeared to preclude journalism from pursuing objective 7 and circumscribing its effectiveness on delivering the other objectives on Schudson's list. Moreover, if journalism was unanchored from liberal democracy, human rights, the separation of powers, the rule of law, and freedom of expression, was the project itself at risk of destruction?

Similarly, '[i]nquisitive, daring and influential media outlets willing to take a strong stand against economic power are essential in a competitive capitalist society', but falling incomes from advertising, and/or public support and an accompanying decline in user interest, as noted in Chapter 5 as impacting particularly on how journalism scoped the world, severely inhibited the freedom of the press to pursue this kind of journalism in the global North (Zingales, 2015). The commercial imperative of the news media (whether sustaining profitability or responding to cuts in public funding) led to less journalism being produced by these media, and journalism which more routinely failed to interrogate, instead serving to please and, above all, designed to be sellable – a consumer rather than a public good, clumsily captured in the online term *clickbait* by which sensational and eye-catching material, irrespective of its value, was posted merely to draw in users (Lewis, 2013, pp. 94–97). Furthermore, it has been argued that the link between democracy and capitalism had been 'broken', and market economies (with marketable media) thrived in undemocratic states (Zizek, 2015), while media with public service foci declined in democracies. Thus Steiner (2009) suggested making a distinction between journalism and the media, with their self-interest in industrial, commercial, statal or non-profit 'business models'.

> [J]ournalism refers to consistent institutionalized and even, dare I say it, professionalized news processes. Journalists are the ones who are educated into the responsibilities, ethics, and needs for collectively producing comprehensive journalism on a daily basis. They commit themselves to undertaking long and often tedious investigative projects. They have a sense of journalism history, and an appreciation for the varied news needs, both on-going and long-term, of democratic societies.
>
> … As story-tellers, as the bards of contemporary society, journalists need to demonstrate the value they 'add' in providing stories that are comprehensive, insightful, broad and deep. Journalism needs to do some of what it has always distinctively achieved, and perhaps figure out how to do more, and do better, in order to sustain itself. Society will not need newspapers that merely provide information products. Journalism's survival lies in helping the whole of society understand where we have come from and where we are going, as well as how our problems have come to be and how to solve them. (Steiner, 2009, p. 383)

However, journalists could perhaps be too 'professionalized' (as we have seen in Chapters 5 and 6), losing their connection with the mass of the population. They became 'insiders' with a stake in 'the system', rather than outsiders representing the disempowered (Fowler, 2015, p. 264–65). At the same time (as noted in Chapter 4), the bulk of the news media in the US and the rest of world were owned and controlled by a largely Western- and Northern-based global oligopoly of corporate entities run mainly by extremely wealthy proprietors or managers invested in globalization and with conservative and neo-liberal views and political associations (see McChesney, 2001). One study calculated that 'economic élites' (including 'powerful business organizations') were highly influential in shaping US government policy (Gilens & Page, 2014). Among those business interests lobbying law makers was the wider communications industry which spent $US3.5bn on lobbying over a ten-year period (www.represent.us). Thus, it was by no means a stretch for Donald Trump to have adopted the 'watchdog' function idealized in Western journalism for holding politicians and others with power to account, and to have focused it instead on the media and journalists themselves (Grynbaum, 2017) (see Case Study 2.6). Trump argued that 'the corporate media in our country is (*sic*) no longer involved in journalism. They are a political special interest, no different than any lobbyist or other financial entity with an agenda' (Schwartz, 2015). China's state-run *Global Times* argued that Trump's 'war with mainstream media' was part of 'the recession of liberalism' (Phillips, 2017).

Yet there were those who repulsed this movement. The Republican US Senator John McCain told journalists:

> I hate the press. But the fact is we need you. We need a free press. We must have it. ... if you want to preserve democracy as we know it, you have to have a free and many times adversarial press.... . Without it, I am afraid that we would lose so much of our individual liberties over time. ... When you look at history, the first thing that dictators do is shut down the press. (Quoted in Yuhas, 2017).

Others complained that the owners and controllers of the media colluded with states and politicians, espousing free speech only when it suited their purposes, and often supporting the erosion of civil liberties; engaged in propaganda rather than news; and sacrificed journalism to failing business models (Fowler, 2015). It had become too easy to manage public perceptions through the manipulation of information and the media (Fowler, 2015). This line of argument was succinctly put by the *Guardian* journalist Maggie O'Kane's (1996) investigation into the first Gulf War – *How to Tell Lies and Win Wars*. Journalism was neither robust nor honest enough, too often compromising its 'primary role ... in disclosing inconvenient truths ... [the] ... role as a counterweight to the excesses of executive government ... [and] the core journalistic principle to question those in power' (Fowler, 2015, p. 15).

Losing the Plot?

The global condition of journalism was perhaps evident, then, in the confrontation of 'competing narratives' exemplified by the renewed focus from 2016, particularly in the US, on the ambiguities of 'fake news' and 'alternative facts' of the so-called infowars, a label which itself held more than one meaning but drew on the diffusion of digital ICTs which boosted the capacity to facilitate the production and dissemination of counter-information, circumventing state controls and censorship, corporate power, the historical pre-eminence of the mainstream news media, and the professional aspirations of journalists. It appeared that in the face of an uncontrollable flow the traditional managers of information had been outflanked by 'not only by an explosion of information but also a wide range of actors producing competing narratives and viewpoints' (Ojala et al., 2018; Rid & Hecker, 2009, p. 211). Nevertheless, the acquisition of a voice by the voiceless, as in citizen journalism (explored in Chapter 6), was accompanied, too, by opportunities afforded to the powerful which were turned to advantage by states, corporations and politicians (Snegovaya, 2015). As Fowler (2015, p. 17) noted, 'Though the internet has made it easier to disseminate information and for all of us to access libraries of knowledge … it has also handed governments a weapon of extraordinary power.' This beset and undermined chiefly the certainties of normatively construed Western journalism founded in 'objective reporting' and the credibility of its institutional hosts lodged in the economic power of the global North – and wherever this model was to be found in whatever state of development elsewhere in the world (Herd, 2007; Jackson, 2017; Moyo, 2009; Murphy, 2016).

The original meaning of 'fake news' (anything which was not authorized by, and usually discomfited, authoritarian regimes; in other words 'unofficial news' based in fact) and the liberal ideological meaning (lies, deception, dis- and misinformation which had no basis in fact and was exposed as such by the journalistic endeavour acting as a check on power) appeared to be converging (Hernandez, 2017; Phillips, 2017) (see Chapter 8). The emergence of a professionalized 'political class' in liberal democracies and its adoption of commercial marketing and public relations techniques led to the refinement of 'spin' (the kind of 'exaggerations and false claims' and 'pseudo-evidence' associated with dishonest advertising and hucksterism) – in other words, systemic lying – and a progressively disempowered and inhibited journalism failed to apply correctives to such claims (Alterman, 2005; Davies, 2008; Oborne, 2005; Phillips, 2012). It could be argued that 'fake news' was preceded by 'fake leaks' (Fowler, 2015, pp. 50–51). Two of the most egregious examples of Western journalists falling for political 'spin' and disingenuously leaked information were the UK's *Sun* newspaper's repetition of concocted 'evidence' of what occurred during the Hillsborough soccer stadium disaster when 96 people were unlawfully killed, and the *New York Times's* coverage of the supposed development of Iraq's nuclear arsenal prior to the invasion of 2003 (Conn, 2016; Davies, 2008; From the Editors, 2004). In turn, this led from c. 2003 to the growth of fact-checking organizations, as noted in Chapter 8 (Kessler, 2014). The infowars descended into a 'growing inability, and even unwillingness, to separate truth from lies' (Smith, 2017).

In such conditions, 'the authority and status of journalism' became 'questionable' with public trust 'waning … with each country [in the global West and North] able to tell its own story of how the press fails' (Broersma & Peters, 2013, p. 11). The symbiotic accountability and responsibility relationship between journalists, the powerful and citizens appeared to have broken down with none trusting the others (Brants, 2013) in a swirl of misinformation. In 2016 the number of Americans expressing trust and confidence in the media 'to report the news fully, accurately and fairly' fell to its lowest recorded level (32 per cent) since it was first tested in 1972 (Swift, 2016). Even so, trust in the news generally ran higher than trust in journalists in most liberal democracies. The highest level of trust in journalists was returned in Finland (51 per cent): elsewhere in 19 liberal democracies the figures did not reach a half, with Japan (21 per cent) and Sweden (25 per cent) reporting the lowest levels (see Table 9.1) (Dragomir, 2016; Ipsos-MORI, 2016; Newman et al., 2016, pp. 24–25). The crude averages across the sample were just below 48 per cent trusting the news, and just below 36 per cent trusting journalists. Given that higher levels of 'professionalism' supposedly characterized journalism in the North Atlantic and democratic corporatist systems, according to Hallin and Mancini (2004), it might have been expected that the levels of trust in journalists would be significantly higher than in the polarized pluralist system. However, that was not the case.

As noted in Chapter 8, journalism's claim to present truth (within the limits of its practices) underpinned its invitation to be trusted (Broersma, 2013). In the historical heartlands of journalism in these liberal democracies with varying degrees of mixed state and private economies, however, 'fact and opinion are muddied, and truthiness … comes to the fore' (Peters, 2013, p. 186). Initially a term of satire, truthiness came to mean asserted, rather than demonstrated, 'truth'; belief rather than knowledge (Schudson, 2009, p. 106). While there was a certain taken-for-grantedness about journalism in the global West and North, where its worth was historically self-evident and its definition clear and widely accepted, that was not the case elsewhere where journalism had yet to fully establish its credentials (Broersma & Peters, 2013).

Table 9.1 Public trust in the news and in journalists in selected liberal democracies

Liberal democracy*	Country	Trust in news	Trust in journalists
North Atlantic			
	Australia	43%	32%
	Canada	55%	47%
	Ireland	50%	37%
	UK	50%	29%
	USA	33%	27%
	AVERAGE	**46.2%**	**34.3%**
Democratic corporatist			
	Austria	43%	32%
	Belgium	51%	48%
	Denmark	46%	33%
	Finland	65%	51%
	Germany	52%	40%
	Netherlands	54%	49%
	Norway	46%	32%
	Sweden	40%	25%
	Switzerland	50%	35%
	AVERAGE	**49.66%**	**38.33%**
Polarized pluralist			
	France	32%	29%
	Italy	42%	33%
	Portugal	60%	47%
	Spain	47%	35%
	AVERAGE	**45.25%**	**36%**

Source: Newman et al. (2016); * Hallin and Mancini (2004)

Note: Greece was excluded because of special circumstances prevailing there in 2016

Journalism – Procedure, Methodology and Standards

US journalists working within the liberal media system identified by Hallin and Mancini (2004), particularly professed a degree of autonomy, adherence to ethics and a focus on public service in which an idealized 'glass wall' separated the commercial interests of the media from their editorial functions and protected 'editorial independence' (Kurz, 1999) (Case Study 9.1) This assumed an internal control over the occupation (self-regulation) which essentially defined what journalism was by the ways in which it was practised and the standards it kept. Journalists' perceptions of their roles strongly indicated their definitions of journalism (see Tables 2.1–2.10).

Case Study 9.1: CBS and editorial independence

In the 1930s the then radio network, CBS, founded a news division which was independent from the advertising-driven commercial enterprise. Despite the head of CBS, William Paley, being a supporter of Republican presidents, CBS News broadcast items critical of such administrations. Later Paley professed, 'We would not bow to the pressure of anybody. ... I used to say, "Look here, I don't care if it was my brother in the White House, I would not slant the news"' (Gerard, 1990). Editorial independence and editorial integrity were seen as 'inextricably linked', the then chairman of CBS asserted in 1985 (Greenhouse, 1985). As far as news was concerned, CBS was not 'just a business' (Diamond, 1986, p. 37). On the other hand, the business was free to pursue its own self-interest. Sumner Redstone, chairman of CBS and a lifelong Democrat, donated to the Democratic candidate John Kerry's 2004 presidential campaign but supported the election of Republican George W. Bush because his presidency would be more favourable for the company. Similarly, Redstone's successor Leslie Moonves argued that the candidacy of Trump 'may not be good for America, but it's damn good for CBS' (Anon, 2004; Bond, 2016), and Katharine Graham, publisher of the *Washington Post*, oversaw the paper's Watergate investigation into President Richard Nixon, despite being on close terms with both Republican and Democratic political leaders.

Codes of ethics, too, served to spell out what journalists thought journalism was (Figure 9.1). These mechanisms pointed to procedure (an established way of doing, conducted in a particular order); a methodology (a rationalized system of methods derived from, and reflecting purpose; answering the questions, *Who, What, Where, When, Why* and *How*); and standards (agreed correct behaviour) in journalism, and for which journalists were educated and trained (Yeoman, 2013). Each element was intimately related in a complex matrix. (We have addressed these pragmatically rather than philosophically.)

1. Procedure
   * Ideas (concepts of what made news)
   * Research (gathering data, 'facts')
   * Sourcing (using often human sources)
   * Construction (composing meaningful content)
   * Dissemination (making the meaningfulness of content accessible to users) (Broersma, 2010).
   * Positive interaction (engaging in feedback loops with sources, users, et al.).

Preamble

Members of the Society of Professional Journalists believe that public enlightenment is the forerunner of justice and the foundation of democracy. Ethical journalism strives to ensure the free exchange of information that is accurate, fair and thorough. An ethical journalist acts with integrity.
The Society declares these four principles as the foundation of ethical journalism and encourages their use in its practice by all people in all media.

Seek Truth and Report It

Ethical journalism should be accurate and fair. Journalists should be honest and courageous in gathering, reporting and interpreting information.

Minimize Harm

Ethical journalism treats sources, subjects, colleagues and members of the public as human beings deserving of respect.

Act Independently

The highest and primary obligation of ethical journalism is to serve the public.

Be Accountable and Transparent

Ethical journalism means taking responsibility for one's work and explaining one's decisions to the public.

The SPJ Code of Ethics is a statement of abiding principles supported by additional explanations and position papers that address changing journalistic practices. It is not a set of rules, rather a guide that encourages all who engage in journalism to take responsibility for the information they provide, regardless of medium. The code should be read as a whole; individual principles should not be taken out of context.

Figure 9.1 Society of Professional Journalists: Code of Ethics
Source: www.spj.org/ethicscode.asp

2. Methodology (Lamble, 2004)
   * Interviewing (quizzing authority (Schudson, 1994))
   * Observation (engaging with social ('real') life (Deacon et al., 1999, p. 249))
   * Analysis of documents (understanding primary texts in their context (Hannis, 2012, p. 80) and increasingly data-mining (Stray, 2016))
3. Standards
   * Ethics (Hare, 2015; see Figure 9.1)

It was perhaps instructive that many of these points gave rise to disputes; for example, in the confrontation between Trump and US journalists over the use of (anonymous) sources (Helmore, 2017).

Summary

Undoubtedly, in the first quarter of the twenty-first century journalism faced considerable challenges – possibly even to its existence as the broadly recognized modern phenomenon which had evolved over time. Thus, at the moment when the concept of global journalism could be seriously considered, the idea of journalism itself was threatened. Both the mixed motives of oppositional power (democratic and authoritarian) and the paradox of the digital domain were at work. While the majority of threats to journalism were external, however, those which came from within the occupation appeared to be as potentially damaging. Fowler (2015), for one, believed that in the global North journalism had turned on itself, abandoning its 'core' principles. Adherence to those principles, the former British newspaper editor, Peter Preston (2017) argued, was the best defence: 'the problem isn't just fake news. It's failure to share the same world of information … And one certain way to make a bad situation worse is not to report – fair and square, context and all'.

To illustrate Preston's point: Art Cullen, the owner of an independent, small-town newspaper in the largely farming US state of Iowa, the *Storm Lake Times* (circulation 3,300 copies twice weekly), which regularly published mundane news of 'a baby, a dog, a fire and a crash on every front page', won a 2017 Pulitzer Prize for his exceptional coverage of the role of agribusiness in secretly funding defence of a legal suit which claimed farming was polluting public water supplies (Anon, 2017c). Such incidences were usually well documented in the global North, whereas similar acts of journalism in the global South more often went unnoticed: that did not diminish their achievements (Bromley, 2017).

The International Consortium of Investigative Journalists (ICIJ) won its own Pulitzer Prize in 2017 for a collaborative project revealing the off-shore finances of more than 140 politicians in 50-plus countries. About 400 journalists in 80 countries, including Ecuador, Turkey, Ukraine, Venezuela and Hong Kong, worked with the ICIJ on the Panama Papers investigation (Fitzgibbon, 2016). From 2013, Zaina Erhaim, who held a master's degree in journalism from the UK and had worked for the BBC, trained more than 100 citizen journalists in Syria, a third of them women, to provide unique on-the-spot reporting of the civil war after most international journalists had fled the country, and helped establish independent media outlets there. Her work was recognized internationally in 2015 and 2016 (Berkhead, 2015; Fletcher, 2015). The Global Investigative Journalism Network cited investigative journalism projects in a range of 'developing or emerging' states, including

Montenegro, Ukraine, South Africa, Azerbaijan, Pakistan, Brazil, Moldova and Sri Lanka (gijn.org). Knight International Journalism Award winners (entries were confined to journalists working in Africa, Asia, Central and Eastern Europe, Latin America, the Caribbean and the Middle East) included journalists from Mexico, Bosnia, Egypt, Myanmar, China, Democratic Republic of the Congo, Nigeria, Cuba, India and Cambodia.

But a dominant paradigm of detached watchdog journalism exemplified by investigative journalism and characterized by independence, a commitment to scrutiny and exposure, and an adversarial approach, was far from representative, and somewhat idealized. Sabato's (1991, p. 26) and Louw's (2005) categories of journalism, and their relationships with external political, economic, social and cultural power, although devised for political journalism in liberal democracies, offered a perhaps more realistic picture of global journalism (see Chapter 2): as well as watchdog journalism, they proposed the existence of:

- partisan journalism which collaborated with external power
- Fourth Estate journalism that participated by promoting its own agendas (akin to the fourth branch of government) (see Boyce's (1978) argument about the ambiguity of the concept of the Fourth Estate)
- sensational journalism, based on exaggeration and scandal
- lapdog journalism was unquestioningly supportive
- 'junkyard-dog' journalism was 'harsh aggressive and intrusive' and focused on titillation

We conclude then with the questions asked at the outset:

- What do journalists do?
- Who is recognized as a journalist, and does recognition authenticate what they do?
- Where do journalists practise (narrowly in media channels and more broadly in political, social, economic and cultural systems)?
- Are those outlets and contexts supportive of journalism, and if so what kind of journalism?
- What do the public think about journalism, or as Rosen (1999) put it, what do they think journalists are for?
- Do these conditions change over time, and if so is that to journalism's betterment or worsening?
- How do journalists themselves view their role in society (the role perceptions explored in Chapter 2)?

- Crucially, how does journalism perform in the global environment in which historically news has flowed predominantly from the global North and West to the rest, and what is its function in creating and sustaining contra-flows?

To this list can be added the question: where and how is the evidence to provide answers to be found? This book has attempted to provide at least partial answers to these questions by drawing on a range of academic and non-academic sources, including our own work on these topics. Yet, as was indicated in Chapter 3, aligning critical, systematic and independent enquiry and abstract principles with practice and practical concerns has been, and is likely to continue to be, difficult. Understanding global journalism, we suggest, requires study at many levels – from the level of the individual journalist through collective practices, such as global reporting (addressed in Chapter 5), to ideological geo-political systems – an ongoing task for journalism students and scholars, and for journalists themselves.

Further Reading

1. Berglez, P. (2013) *Global Journalism: Theory and Practice (Global Crises and the Media)* (New York: Peter Lang).
2. Boyce, G. (1978) 'The Fourth Estate: the reappraisal of a concept' in G. Boyce, J. Curran & P. Wingate (eds) *Newspaper History: From the 17th Century to the Present* (London: Constable), pp. 19–40.
3. Clarke, J. & Bromley, M. (eds) (2012) *International News in the Digital Age: East-West Perceptions of a New World Order* (New York: Routledge).
4. de Beer, A.S. (2009) *Global Journalism: Topical Issues and Media Systems*, 5th edn (Boston: Pearson, Allyn and Bacon).
5. Kalyango, Y. & Mould, D.H. (eds) (2014) *Global Journalism Practice and New Media Performance* (London: Palgrave Macmillan).
6. Zelizer, B. (2004) *Taking Journalism Seriously: News and the Academy* (London: Sage).

Glossary of Key Terms

Alternative journalism journalism produced by amateurs (most commonly social activists), which 'proceeds from dissatisfaction not only with the mainstream coverage of certain issues and topics, but also with the epistemology of news' – conventions of news writing, values and norms, the professional, elite basis of journalism, and the 'subordinate role of audience as receiver' (Atton & Hamilton, 2008, p. 1).

Arab Spring a series of anti-government protests and uprisings in the Middle East in 2010–12 that involved the wide use of digital media for political mobilization purposes and led to significant changes in some of the regimes.

Asian value journalism a non-adversarial development type of journalism that endorses Asian values but is criticized for being subservient to those in power.

Audiences consumers of media messages (readers, viewers, online users, etc.).

Authoritarian journalism journalism supervised by the state and its agencies that might include prohibitions on news believed to counter the state's position.

Banal nationalism a term coined by Michael Billig that explains the powerful role the media play in the daily, mundane and banal reinforcement of nation-states and their symbols.

Brown envelope journalism the practice of sources giving cash to journalists in brown envelopes to ensure (usually favourable) coverage even of the most routine events.

Citizen journalism journalism practised by ordinary people/amateurs who do not abide by the norms and rules of professional journalism.

Censorship the suppression of freedom of expression through the imposition of various restrictions by state authorities in non-democratic countries that deprive journalists of their freedom to decide what stories to work on and publish.

CNN effect 'the idea that real-time communications technology could provoke major responses from domestic audiences and political elites to global events' (Robinson, 1999, p. 301).

Convergence journalism the interconnection between the various forms of journalism (print, broadcast, online, photo) that has led to an increasing demand for journalists to produce content for different platforms and in different formats.

Corantos the precursors of modern-day newspapers, periodical news pamphlets published in the seventeenth century which contained foreign stories.

Coups and earthquakes syndrome a term coined by the US journalist Mort Rosenblum (1979) to describe Western journalists' tendency to focus on natural disasters and dramatic political events when reporting on the rest of the world (mainly the global South).

Detached watchdog journalism the dominant role perception for journalists from the global North (and arguably globally), placing an emphasis on values such as objectivity, balance and impartiality and advocating journalists' responsibility to be watchdogs of political and business elites.

Development journalism journalism that promotes positive news and advocates collaboration between the state and the media for the purpose of nation building and development, practised mainly in Africa and Asia.

Digital divide the belief that instead of reducing the gap between rich and poor and empowering disadvantaged communities, the advent of digitally based ICTs has actually widened that gap.

Embedded journalism 'the practice of placing journalists within and under the control of one side's military during an armed conflict' by attaching them to one military unit and allowing journalists to 'accompany troops into combat zones' (Löffelholz, 2016).

Fake news the opposite of 'true' news, namely the publication of completely made-up stories, not based on facts. The use of this term in authoritarian countries is different – it refers to news unauthorized by the state.

Flows and contra-flows of news the processes of collection, creation, distribution and reception of news from the global North to the rest of the world and from the global South to the global North.

Foreign correspondent 'a reporter who sends news reports or commentary from a foreign country' (*American Heritage Dictionary of the English Language*, 2011).

Foxification journalistic practices emulating Fox News's controversial style of reporting and presenting, which promotes 'news values that run counter to public service traditions, with the emphasis on sensationalism, a tabloid style, speculation rather than factual reporting and partisanship rather than balance and objectivity' (Cushion & Lewis, 2009, p. 132).

Freedom of expression 'the power or right to express one's opinions without censorship, restraint, or legal penalty' (Oxford Dictionaries, 2017).

Free press the belief that the flow of news should be unhindered by both external (political and economic pressures) and internal (editorial interference by owners and advertisers) factors.

Glocalism/Glocalization a process of adapting global forces and trends in the process of adopting them at a local level and in response to local conditions.

Globalization an all-encompassing term referring 'to the rapidly developing process of complex interconnections between societies, cultures, institutions and individuals world-wide' (Tomlinson, 1991, p. 165).

Global journalism the notion that due to globalization journalism is practised and disseminated on a worldwide basis rather than just in any nation-state or a group of nation-states.

Global North Europe, Northern America and Oceania.

Global South Asia, Africa, Latin America and the Caribbean.

Hegemony '(especially of countries) the position of being the strongest and most powerful and therefore able to control others' (*Cambridge Dictionary*, 2017).

Ideology 'a set of beliefs or principles, especially one on which a political system, party, or organization is based' (*Cambridge Dictionary*, 2017).

Impunity exemption from punishment or recrimination, especially for perpetrators of crimes against journalists.

International journalism a process of producing 'foreign news' (Williams, 2011, p. 1); that is, information originating somewhere other than the nation-state in which it is being disseminated.

Internet penetration rate the percentage of the total population of a given country or region that uses the internet.

Legacy media 'old' media that predated the internet – radio, newspapers and TV.

Media regulation the process of control of the media by state rules, procedures and regulations, most often prescribed by statute. Self-regulation is regulation by the industry itself.

Mediatization 'the processes by which social change in particular (or all) fields of society has been shaped by media' (Livingstone & Lunt, 2014, p. 704).

Networked journalism 'a synthesis of traditional news journalism and the emerging forms of participatory media enabled by Web 2.0 technologies' (Beckett, 2010, p. 1).

News values the factors and attributes that make certain events and developments newsworthy. The first typology of news values was developed by the Norwegian academics Galtung and Ruge who compiled a list of news values used by journalists in the selection of foreign news.

Normative liberal theory arguably a dominant theory in the Western world, underpinned by liberal values such as freedom of expression, plurality, transparency and accountability and emphasizing the ideal functions of journalism – most notably the belief that the media should be the 'Fourth Estate'.

Parachute journalism, also known as firefighter reporting (Franks, 2005, p. 94) – the practice of sending journalists 'to cover foreign events as and when events occur' (Obijiofor & Hanusch, 2011, p. 114) as opposed to having a permanently based foreign correspondent in a country or a city.

Participatory collaborative journalism a model pioneered by the South Korean OhmyNews website that involves collaborations between citizen and professional journalists.

Pluralism 'the scope for a wide range of social, political and cultural values, opinions, information and interests to find expression through the media' (Dohnanyi, 2003, p. 27).

Post-truth era the period after the Brexit referendum in the UK and the election of Donald Trump in the US in which objective facts were 'less influential in shaping public opinion than appeals to emotion and personal belief' but actually dating from 1992 (*Oxford Dictionaries*, 2016).

Propaganda model a model proposed by Herman and Chomsky (1988) which suggested that the media in the global West and North, partially through ownership and the drive to be profitable, promoted the interests of the powerful, thus marginalizing opposing views.

Public service broadcasting 'broadcasting made, financed and controlled by the public, for the public. It is neither commercial nor state-owned, free from political interference and pressure from commercial forces' (UNESCO, n.d.)

Public sphere a term originally coined by Jürgen Habermas (1997, p. 105) to denote 'a domain of our social life in which such a thing as public opinion can be formed' after rational debate and argumentation.

Stringer a local contributor who has an agreement with one or more news media to send news reports from his/her locality.

Totalitarian journalism journalism practised mainly in communist, fascist or Islamist states whereby journalists are regarded as servants of 'the people' (that is, the state which represents 'the people') and as a tool for eliminating 'wrong' thinking and facilitating emancipation.

Transnational journalism a process that became noticeable in the 1980s with journalists producing and disseminating news in more than one country, and news organizations being based in more than one country.

Web 2.0 the second stage of the development of the World Wide Web, which involves a much greater degree of interactivity and the advent of social media.

References

4 International Media & Newspapers. (2016) '2016 newspaper web rankings', www.4imn.com/top200, accessed 20 January 2017.

Agren, D. (2018) '"They went to execute him": fourth Mexican journalist killed so far in 2018', *The Guardian* (15 May), www.theguardian.com, accessed 18 May 2018.

Ahmed, A. (2017) 'In Mexico, "it's easy to kill a journalist"', *The New York Times* (29 April), www.nytimes.com, accessed 18 May 2018.

Alejandro, J. (2010) *Journalism in the Age of Social Media*, Reuters Institute Fellowship Paper, University of Oxford.

Alexa. (2018) 'saharareporters.com Traffic Statistics', www.alexa.com, accessed 10 July 2018.

Al-Ghazzi, O. (2014) '"Citizen journalism" in the Syrian uprising: problematizing Western narratives in a local context', *Communication Theory* 24(4), 435–54.

Ali, N.S. (2015) 'Women in the news', *Dawn* (6 December), www.dawn.com, accessed 9 January 2016.

Allan, S. (1997) 'News and the public sphere: towards a history to objectivity and impartiality' in M. Bromley & T. O'Malley (eds) *A Journalism Reader* (London: Routledge), pp. 296–329.

Allan, S. (2009) 'Citizen journalism and the rise of "mass self-communication": reporting the London bombings', *Global Media Journal Australian Edition* 1(1), 1–20.

Allan, S. (2013) *Citizen Witnessing: Revisioning Journalism in Times of Crisis* (Cambridge: Polity).

Al-Najjar, A. (2013) 'Jordan: towards gender balance in the newsrooms' in C.M. Byerly (ed.) *The Palgrave International Handbook of Women and Journalism* (Basingstoke: Palgrave Macmillan), pp. 419–31.

Al-Rodhan, N.R.F. (2007) *The Emergence of Blogs as a Fifth Estate and their Security Implications* (Geneva: Geneva Centre for Security Policy).

Alterman, E. (2005) *When Presidents Lie: A History of Official Deception and its Consequences* (New York: Penguin).

Amanpour, C. (2016) 'In this dangerous new world, journalism must protect itself', *The Guardian* (23 November), www.theguardian.com/commentisfree, accessed 23 November 2016.

American Heritage Dictionary of the English Language. (2011) 'Foreign correspondent', www.thefreedictionary.com, accessed 10 February 2017.

American Society of News Editors. (2015) 2015 Census, asne.org, accessed 7 March 2017.

Anderson, B. (2006 edn.) *Imagined Communities: Reflections on the Origin and Spread of Nationalism* (London: Verso).

Anderson, F. (2014) 'Photography' in B. Griffen-Foley (ed.) *A Companion to the Australian Media* (North Melbourne: Australian Scholarly Publishing), pp. 337–40.

Anon. (2004) 'Guess who's a GOP booster? The ceo of CBS's parent company endorses President Bush', *Asian Wall Street Journal* (24 September), https://web.archive.org, accessed 22 February 2017.

Anon. (2008) 'Journalism, satire, or just laughs? *The Daily Show with Jon Stewart* examined', Pew Research Center (8 May), www.journalism.org, accessed 19 November 2016.

Anon. (2016a) 'False news', Article 19, www.article19.org, accessed 18 November 2016 & 10 February 2017.

Anon. (2016b) 'How the west extends its control over journalism worldwide', *New Atlas* (30 July), www.thenewatlas.org, accessed 21 November 2016.

Anon. (2016c) 'Women journalists commitment and challenges', Reporters Without Borders (25 January), http://rsf.org, accessed 14 March 2017.

Anon. (2017a) 'Fake news: how can African media deal with the problem? BBC News (16 February), www.bbc.co.uk, accessed 23 March 2017.

Anon. (2017b) 'McCain attacks Trump administration and inability to "separate truth from lies"', *The Guardian* (18 February), www.theguardian.com, accessed 18 February 2017.

Anon. (2017c) 'Tiny, family-run Iowa newspaper wins Pulitzer for taking on agriculture businesses', *The Guardian* (11 April), www.theguardian.com, accessed 11 April 2017.

Appadurai, A. (1990) 'Disjuncture and difference in the global cultural economy', *Theory, Culture & Society* 7, 295–310.

Aram, A. & Paul, S. (2009) 'Challenges facing media education in India' in C-K. Cheung (ed.) *Media Education in Asia* (Heidelberg: Springer), pp. 121–30.

Archetti, C. (2013) 'Journalism in the age of global media: the evolving practices of foreign correspondents in London', *Journalism Studies* 13(5–6), 847–56.

Asante, F. & Ogawa, F.J. (n.d.) 'The role of Ghanian media towards achieving independence', www.ghana.gov.gh, accessed 18 February 2017.

Ash, T.G. (n.d. a) 'Journalism', Free Speech Debate, http://freespeechdebate.com, accessed 29 June 2016.

Ash, T.G. (n.d. b) 'Free expression in an interconnected world', Free Speech Debate. http://freespeechdebate.com, accessed 29 June 2016.

Asogwa, B.E. and Ezema, I.J. (2017) 'Freedom of access to government information in Africa: trends, status and challenges', *Records Management Journal* 27(3), 318–38.

Asquith, C. (2016) 'The world according to men', *The Atlantic* (7 March), www.theatlantic.com, accessed 28 March 2017.

Associated Press. (2016) 'Our story', www.ap.org, accessed 10 February 2017.

Association of Caribbean Mediaworkers. (2013) *The Looming Storm*, acmpress.org, accessed 11 March 2017.

Atkins, A., O'Hehir, A. & Rosen, J. (eds) (2002) *Zoned for Debate* 1 & 2, https://journalism.nyu.edu, accessed 15 March 2017.

Atton, C. (2003) 'What is alternative journalism?', *Journalism* 4(3), 267–72.

Atton, C. & Hamilton, J.F. (2008) *Alternative Journalism* (London: Sage).

Austenå, A.-M. (2004) Notes on women journalists in Norway. Copy held by authors.

Australian Bureau of Statistics. (2011) Arts and culture in Australia: a statistical overview, 2011, Employment, www.abs.gov.au, accessed 10 March 2017.

Australian Bureau of Statistics. (2014) Arts and culture in Australia: a statistical overview, 2014, Literature and Print Media, www.abs.gov.au, accessed 10 March 2017.

Avadani, I. (2002) 'From fashion to profession: education of journalists in Romania' in T. Jusic & M. Dedovic (eds) *Education of Journalists in Southeast Europe: A Step Closer to Professionalism* (Sarajevo: Media Online), pp. 120–35.

Bahrain Center for Human Rights. (2017) 'Updates: arrest and detention of BCHR's president Nabeel Rajab' (22 March), www.bahrainrights.org, accessed 30 March 2017.

Bailie, M. & Azgin, B. (2012) 'Disturbing the peace: gender, journalism and the Cypriot press', *Journalism Studies* 12(5), 689–704.

Bakker, G. (2007) 'Trading facts: Arrow's fundamental paradox and the emergence of global news networks, 1750–1900', *Working Papers on the Nature of Evidence: How Well do Facts Travel?* 17(07), Department of Economic History: London School of Economics.

Balaraman, R.A., Hashim, N.H., Hasno, H., Ibrahim, F. & Arokiasmy, L. (2015) 'New media: online citizen journalism and political issues in Malaysia', *Social Sciences & Humanities* 23, 143–54.

Banda, F. (ed.) (2013) *Model Curricula for Journalism Education: A Compendium of New Syllabi* (Paris: UNESCO).

Barber, J. (2015) 'Canada's anti-terror legislation faces legal challenge by free speech advocates', *The Guardian* (21 July), www.theguardian.com, accessed 10 February 2017.

Bárd, P. & Bayer, J. (2016) 'A comparative analysis of media freedom and pluralism in the EU member states', *European Parliament*, www.europarl.europa.eu, accessed 12 September 2017.

Barton, A. & Storm, H. (2014) *Violence and Harassment against Women in the News Media: A Global Picture* (Washington, DC: International Women's Media Foundation).

Baum, M.A. & Zhukov, Y.M. (2015) 'Filtering revolution: reporting bias in international newspaper coverage of the Libyan civil war', *Journal of Peace Research* 52(3), 1–17.

Beasley, M.H. (1988) *The New Majority: A Look at What the Preponderance of Women in Journalism Education Means to the Schools and the Profession* (Lanham, MD: University Press of America).

Beasley, M. (2001) 'Recent directions for the study of women's history in American journalism', *Journalism Studies* 2(2), 207–20.

Beck, U., Sznaider, N. & Winter, R. (2003) *Global America? The Cultural Consequences of Globalization* (Liverpool: Liverpool University Press).

Becker, L.B., Huh, J., Vlad, T. & Mace, N.R. (2003) 'Monitoring change in journalism and mass communication faculties 1989–2001: supplemental report to the annual survey of journalism & mass communication enrollments' (James M. Cox Jr. Center for International Mass Communication Training and Research, Grady College of Journalism & Mass Communication University of Georgia).

Becker, L.B., Vlad, T. & Desnoes, P. (2010) 'Enrollments decline slightly and the student body becomes more diverse', *Journalism & Mass Communication Educator* 65(3&4), 224–49.

Beckett, C. (2010) *The Value of Networked Journalism* (London: POLIS, London School of Economics and Political Science).

Bell, M. (1997) 'TV news: how far should we go?' *British Journalism Review* 8(1), 7–16.

Bell, M. (1998) 'The truth is our currency', *Press/Politics* 3(1), 102–09.

Benson, R. (2008) 'Journalism: normative theories' in W. Donsbach (ed.) *The Inter-national Encyclopedia of Communication*, vol. VI (Chichester: Wiley-Blackwell), pp. 2591–97.

Benyumov, K. (2016) 'How Russia's independent media was dismantled piece by piece', *The Guardian* (25 May), www.theguardian.com, accessed 22 March 2017.

Bercovici, J. (2011) 'The most influential news orgs, according to Google', *Forbes* (25 March), www.forbes.com, accessed 28 January 2017.

Berger, G. (2017) 'Expressing the changes: international perspectives on evolutions in the right to free expression' in H. Tumber & S. Waisbord (eds) *The Routledge Companion to Media and Human Rights* (Abingdon: Routledge), pp. 17–29.

Berglez, P. (2013) *Global Journalism: Theory and Practice (Global Crises and the Media)* (New York: Peter Lang).

Berkhead, S. (2015) 'Q&A with Zaina Erhaim: teaching citizen journalists to survive in Syria', International Journalists' Network (2 November), https://ijnet.org, accessed 12 April 2017.

Bernardi, C. (2010) 'Saudi bloggers, women's issues and NGOs', *Araba Media & Society* 11, www.arabmediasociety.com, accessed 25 January 2016.

Bethel, N. (1993) 'Bahamian kinship and the power of women', MPhil thesis, University of Cambridge.

Billig, M. (1995) *Banal Nationalism* (London: Sage).

Birch, D. (2009) 'Coranto' in D. Birch (ed.) *The Oxford Companion to English Literature* (Oxford: Oxford University Press), p. 250.

Bird, S.E. (1992) *For Enquiring Minds: A Cultural Study of Supermarket Tabloids* (Knoxville, TE: University of Tennessee Press).

Birkinbine, B.J., Gómez, R. & Wasko, J. (2017) 'Introduction' in B.J. Birkinbine, R. Gómez & J. Wasko (eds) *Global Media Giants* (New York: Routledge), pp. 1–6.

Biswas, S. (2018) 'On the frontline of India's WhatsApp fake news war', *BBC News* (20 August), https://www.bbc.co.uk, accessed 5 September 2018.

Blaagaard, B.B. (2013) 'Shifting boundaries: objectivity, citizen journalism and tomorrow's journalists', *Journalism* 14(8), 1076–90.

Blackshaw, T. (2013) 'Contemporary community theory and football' in A. Brown, T. Crabbe & G. Mellor (eds) *Football and Community in the Global Context: Studies in Theory and Practice* (Abingdon: Routledge), pp. 23–43.

Blum, R. (2005) 'Bausteine zu einer theorie der mediensysteme', *Medienwissenschaft Schweitz* 2(1–2), 5–11.

Boczkowski, P. (2016) 'Fake news and the future of journalism', NiemanLab (19 December), www.niemanlab.org, accessed 23 March 2017.

Boczkowski, P.J. & Mitchelstein, E. (2013) *The News Gap: When the Information Preferences of the Media and the Public Diverge* (Cambridge, MA: MIT Press).

Bollinger, L.C. (2002) Inaugural address, Columbia University (3 October), www.columbia.edu, accessed 14 March 2017.

Bond, P. (2016) 'Leslie Moonves on Donald Trump: "It may not be good for America, but it's damn good for CBS"', *Hollywood Reporter* (29 February), www.hollywood-reporter.com, accessed 22 February 2017.

Bonfadelli, H., Keel, G., Marr, M. & Wyss, V. (2012) 'Journalists in Switzerland: structure and attitudes' in D.H. Weaver & L. Willnat (eds) *The Global Journalist in the 21st Century* (New York: Routledge), pp. 320–30.

Boyce, G. (1978) 'The Fourth Estate: the reappraisal of a concept' in G. Boyce, J. Curran & P. Wingate (eds) *Newspaper History: From the 17th Century to the Present* (London: Constable), pp. 19–40.

Boyd-Barrett, O. (1997) 'Global news wholesalers as agents of globalization' in A. Sreberny-Mohammadi, D. Winseck, J. McKenna & O. Boyd-Barrett (eds) *Media in Global Context – A Reader* (London: Arnold), pp. 131–44.

Boyd-Barrett, O. & Rantanen, T. (eds) (1998) *The Globalization of News* (London: Sage Publications).

Bourgault, L.M. (1995) *Mass Media in Sub-Saharan Africa* (Bloomington: Indiana University Press).

Brants, K. (2013) 'Trust, cynicism, and responsiveness: the uneasy situation of jour-nalism in democracy' in C. Peters & M. Broersma (eds) *Rethinking Journalism: Trust and Participation in a Transformed News Landscape* (Abingdon: Routledge), pp. 15–28.

Brendon, P. (2017) 'Death of truth: when propaganda and "alternative facts" first gripped the world', *The Guardian* (11 March), www.theguardian.com/media, accessed 14 March 2017.

Bridgstock, R.S. & Cunningham, S.D. (2014) 'Graduate careers in journalism, media and communications within and outside the sector: early career outcomes, trajectories and capabilities' in G. Hearn, R. Bridgstock, B. Goldsmith & J. Rogers (eds) *Creative Work Beyond the Creative Industries: Innovation, Employment and Education* (Cheltenham: Edward Elgar), pp. 226–44.

Brislin, T. (1997) 'An update on journalism ethics in Asia: values and practices as context for meaning in Japan, China and Korea', paper presented to the annual meeting of the Association for Practical and Professional Ethics, Washington, DC (6–8 March).

Brobbey, C.A.-B. (2013) 'Neopatrimonialism and democratic stability in Africa: a case of Ghana's 1992 re-democratization', *European Scientific Journal* 2, 98–108.

Broersma, M. (2010) 'Journalism as performative discourse: the important of form and style in journalism' in V. Rupar (ed.) *Journalism and Meaning-Making: Reading the Newspaper* (Cresskill, NJ: Hampton Press), pp. 15–35.

Broersma, M. (2013) 'A refractured paradigm: journalism, hoaxes and the challenge of trust' in C. Peters & M. Broersma (eds) *Rethinking Journalism: Trust and Participation in a Transformed News Landscape* (Abingdon: Routledge), pp. 28–44.

Broersma, M. & Peters, C. (2013) 'Rethinking journalism: the structural transformation of a public good' in C. Peters & M. Broersma (eds) *Rethinking Journalism: Trust and Participation in a Transformed News Landscape* (Abingdon: Routledge), pp. 1–12.

Bromley, M. (2003) 'The media' in J. Hollowell (ed.) *Britain since 1945* (Malden, MA: Blackwell), pp. 211–37.

Bromley, M. (2010) 'Anyone can be a reporter: citizen journalism, social change and OhmyNews' in P. Thomas & M. Bromley (eds) *An Introduction to Communication and Social Change* (St. Lucia: Centre for Communication and Social Change, The University of Queensland), pp. 187–201.

Bromley, M. (2012) 'From spotlight to echo chamber? Citizen journalism and international news' in M. Bromley & J. Clarke (eds) *International News in the Digital Age: East-West Perspectives on a New World Order* (New York: Routledge), pp. 23–40.

Bromley, M. (2016) 'Televisual newspapers? When 24/7 television news channels join newspapers as "old media"' in S. Cushion & R. Sambrook (eds) *The Future of 24-hour News: New Directions, New Challenges* (New York: Peter Lang), pp. 129–41.

Bromley, M. (2017) 'Investigative journalism and human rights' in H. Tumber & S. Waisbord (eds) *The Routledge Companion to Media and Human Rights* (Abingdon: Routledge), pp. 220–28.

Bromley, M. & Clarke, J. (2012) 'Continuity and change in international news: an introduction' in J. Clarke & M. Bromley (eds) *International News in the Digital Age: East-West Perspectives of a New World Order* (New York: Routledge), pp. 3–20.

Bromley, M., Tumber, H. & Fritsch, J. (2015) 'Foreign correspondents in the UK: London – a city "bathed in light"' in G. Terzis (ed.) *Mapping Foreign Correspondence in Europe* (New York: Routledge), pp. 281–96.

Brown, H. (2015) 'Who is a journalist now?' Farrer & Co, www.farrer.co.uk/news/briefings/who-is-a-journalist-now-, accessed 14 December 2017.

Brownlee, B.J. & Beam, R.A. (2012) 'US journalists in the tumultuous early years of the 21st century' in D.H. Weaver & L. Willnat (eds) *The Global Journalist in the 21st Century* (New York: Routledge), pp. 348–62.

Bruns, A. (2005) *Gatewatching: Collaborative Online News Production* (New York: Columbia University Press).

Bruns, A. (2007) 'Produsage: towards a broader framework for user-led content creation', *Proceedings Creativity & Cognition* 6, http://eprints.qut.edu.au, accessed 18 February 2017.

Bruns, A. (2016) '"Random acts of journalism" redux: news and social media' in J.L. Jensen, M. Mortensen & J. Ørmen (eds) *News Across Media: Production, Distribution and Consumption* (New York: Routledge), pp. 32–47.

Bubul, P. (2010) 'Women in media in Bangladesh', *The Daily Star* (11 August), http://ijnet.org, accessed 9 January 2016.

Bühlmann, M. & Kriesi, H. (2013) 'Models for democracy' in H. Kriesi, D. Bochsler, J. Matthes, S. Lavenex, M. Bühlmann & F. Esser, F. (eds) *Democracy in the Age of Globalization and Mediatization* (London: Palgrave Macmillan), pp. 44–68.

Bunce, M. (2010) '"This place used to be a white British boys' club": reporting dynamics and cultural clash at an international new bureau in Nairobi', *The Commonwealth Journal of International Affairs* 99(410), 515–28.

Bunce, M. (2015) 'Africa in the click stream: audience metrics and foreign correspondents in Africa', *African Journalism Studies* 36(4), 12–29.

Burbidge, D. (2012) 'How "brown envelope journalism" holds back sub-Saharan Africa', Free Speech Debate (7 August), freespeechdebate.com, accessed 2 June 2018.

Bussiek, H. (n.d.) *Freedom of Expression and Media Regulation: A Media Regulation Manual* (Windhoek: Friedrich Ebert Stiftung).

Byerly, C.M. (2011) *Global Report on the Status of Women in the News Media* (Washington, DC: International Women's Media Foundation).

Byerly, C.M. (ed.) (2013a) *The Palgrave International Handbook of Women and Journalism* (Basingstoke: Palgrave Macmillan).

Byerly, C.M. (2013b) 'Introduction' in C.M. Byerly (ed.) *The Palgrave International Handbook of Women and Journalism* (Basingstoke: Palgrave Macmillan), pp. 1–10.

Byerly, C.M. (2013c) 'Factors affecting the status of women journalists: a structural analysis' in C.M. Byerly (ed.) *The Palgrave International Handbook of Women and Journalism* (Basingstoke: Palgrave Macmillan), pp. 11–26.

Byerly, C.M. (2014) 'Women and media control: feminist interrogations at the macro-level' in C. Carter, L. Steiner & L. McLaughlin (eds) *The Routledge Companion to Media & Gender* (London: Routledge), pp. 105–15.

Cagé, J. (2014) 'The economics of the African media' in C. Monga and J.Y. Lin (eds) *The Oxford Handbook of Africa and Economics*, vol. 2 (Oxford: Oxford University Press), https://spire.sciencespo.fr, accessed 2 June 2018.

Cambridge Dictionary. (2017) 'Hegemony; ideology'. http://dictionary.cambridge.org, accessed 12 September 2017.

Canter, L. (2015) 'Personalised tweeting', *Digital Journalism* 3(6), 888–907.

Carey, J.W. (1997) 'Afterword: the culture in question' in E.S. Munson & C.A. Warren (eds) *James Carey: A Critical Reader* (Minneapolis: University of Minnesota Press), pp. 308–39.

Carlsson, U. (2016) 'Freedom of media in a time of uncertainty: a brief introduction' in U. Carlsson (ed.) *Freedom of Expression and Media in Transition: Studies and Reflections in the Digital Age* (Göteborg: Nordicom), pp. 9–18.

Carlsson, U. & Pöyhtäri, R. (2017) 'Words of introduction' in U. Carlsson & R. Pöyhtäri (eds) *The Assault on Journalism: Building Knowledge to Protect Freedom of Expression* (Götebor: Nordicom), pp. 11–17.

Carneiro, R.L. (2000) 'The transition from quantity to quality: a neglected causal mechanism in account for social evolution', *PNAS* 97(23), 12926–31.

Casara, C. (2014) 'Al Jazeera remaps global news flows' in R.S. Fortner & P.M. Facker (eds) *The Handbook of Media and Mass Communication Theory* (Malden, MA: John Wiley).

Castells, M. (2004) *The Network Society: A Cross-cultural Perspective* (Cheltenham, UK: Edward Elgar).

Caves, R.E. (2000) *Creative Industries: Contracts Between Art and Commerce* (Cambridge, MA: Harvard University Press).

Chan, J.M., Lee, F.L.F. & So, C.Y.K. (2012) 'Journalists in Hong Kong: a decade after the transfer of sovereignty' in D.H. Weaver & L. Willnat (eds) *The Global Journalist in the 21st Century* (New York: Routledge), pp. 22–35.

Chapman, A. (2018) 'Pluralism under attack: The assault on press freedom in Poland' *Freedom House*, https://freedomhouse.org, accessed 14 May 2018.

Cheeseman, N. (2015) *Democracy in Africa: Successes, Failures, and the Struggle for Political Reform* (Cambridge: Cambridge University Press).

Choi, C. (2014). 'PR101: journalism with Chinese characteristics', *PR Week* (26 November), www.prweek.com, accessed 21 February 2017.

Chapman, A. (2018) 'Pluralism under attack: The assault on press freedom in Poland' *Freedom House*, https://freedomhouse.org, accessed 14 May 2018.

Christiano, T. (2015) 'Democracy' in E.N. Zalta (ed.) *The Stanford Encyclopedia of Philosophy*, http://plato.stanford.edu, accessed 1 July 2016.

Clark, M. & Grech, A. (2017) 'Unwarranted interference, fear and sel-censorship among journalists in Council of Europe member states' in U. Carlsson & R. Pöyhtäri (eds) *The Assault on Journalism: Building Knowledge to Protect Freedom of Expression* (Götebor: Nordicom), pp. 221–26.

Clarke, J. (2000) 'Training journalists in an emerging democracy: the case of Cambodia', *AsiaPacific Media Educator* 8, 82–98.

Clarke, J. (2010) 'Cambodia: educating journalists in a world of poverty, corruption, and power abuse' in B. Josephi (ed.) *Journalism Education in Countries with Limited Media Freedom* (New York: Peter Lang), pp. 53–70.

CNN iReport. (2016). 'iReport Toolkit tell your story like a pro', http://ireport.cnn.com, accessed 17 February 2017.

Cockburn, P. (2010). 'Embedded journalism: a distorted view of war', *The Independent* (23 November), www.independent.co.uk, accessed 15 March 2017.

Cockburn, P. (2017) 'Donald Trump and the US media are in a fight to the finish – and they're both guilty of peddling alternative facts', *The Independent* (17 February), www.independent.co.uk, accessed 21 February 2017.

Cohen, B.C. (1963) *The Press and Foreign Policy* (Princeton, NJ: Princeton University Press).

Cohen, N. (2016) 'How our laws inspired Trump's attack on free speech', *The Guardian* (3 December), www.theguardian.com/commentisfree, accessed 3 December 2016.

Colborne, M. (2016) 'Meet the Czechs fighting back against Russia's (dis)information war', *Sydney Morning Herald* (19 December), www.smh.com.au, accessed 23 March 2017.

Cole, J. & Hamilton, J.M. (2008) 'The history of a surviving species', *Journalism Studies* 9(5), 798–812.

Commission on Freedom of the Press. (1947) *A Free and Responsible Press* (Chicago, IL: University of Chicago Press).

Committee to Protect Journalists. (2015). 'Getting away with murder', www.cpj.org, accessed 10 February 2017.

Committee to Protect Journalists. (2016a) 'Critics are not criminals: comparative study of criminal defamation laws in the Americas', www.cpj.org, accessed 13 February 2017.

Committee to Protect Journalists. (2016b) '2016 prison census: 259 journalists jailed worldwide', www.cpj.org, accessed 21 February 2017.

Committee to Protect Journalists. (2016c) 'Global impunity index', www.cpj.org, accessed 21 February 2017.

Committee to Protect Journalists. (2017) '1229 journalists killed since 1992', www.cpj.org, accessed 10 February 2017.

Committee to Protect Journalists. (2018a) '1304 journalists killed since 1992', www.cpj.org, accessed 14 May 2018.

Committee to Protect Journalists. (2018b) 'Military court in Egypt sentences journalists to 10 years in jail', www.cpj.org, accessed 2 June 2018.

Conboy, M. (2002) *The Press and Popular Culture* (London: Sage).

Conboy, M. (2011) *Journalism in Britain: A Historical Introduction* (London: Sage).

Conn, D. (2016) 'How the *Sun*'s "truth" about Hillsborough unravelled', *The Guardian* (26 April), www.theguardian.com, accessed 22 February 2017.

Connolly, K., Chrisafis, A., McPherson, P., Kirchgaessner, S., Haas, B., Phillips, D., Hunte, E. & Safi, M. (2016) 'Fake news: an insidious trend that's fast becoming a global problem', *The Guardian* (2 December), www.theguardian.com/media, accessed 16 March 2017.

Conseil de Presse [Luxembourg] (2014) Liste des journalistes officiellement reconnus au Grand-Duché de Luxembourg.

Cook Islands Government Portal. (2017) 'About the Cook Islands situation', http://government.whupi.com, accessed 8 March 2017.

Cookman, C. (2009) *American Photojournalism: Motivations and Meanings* (Evanston, IL: Northwestern University Press).

Cooper, S.D. (2006) *Watching the Watchdog: Bloggers as the Fifth Estate* (Phoenix, AZ: Marquette).

Cottle, S. (2000) 'New(s) times: towards a "second wave" of news ethnography', *Communications* 25(1), 19–41.

Cottle, S. (2006) *Mediatized Conflict: Developments in Media and Conflict Studies* (Maidenhead: Open University Press).

Cottle, S. (2008) *Global Crisis Reporting: Journalism in the Global Age* (Maidenhead: Open University Press).

Cottle, S. (2009) 'Journalism and globalization' in K. Wahl-Jorgensen & T. Hanitzsch (eds) *The Handbook of Journalism Studies* (New York: Routledge), pp. 341–56.

Cottle, S. (2014) 'Series editor's preface' in E. Thorsen & S. Allan (eds) *Citizen Journalism: Global Perspectives* (New York: Peter Lang), pp. ix–xii.

Cozma, R. (2012) 'From Murrow to mediocrity? Radio foreign news from World War II to the Iraq war' in J.M. Hamilton & R.G. Lawrence (eds) *Foreign Correspondence* (Abingdon: Routledge), pp. 38–53.

Cozma, R. & Hamilton, J.M. (2009) 'Film portrayals of foreign correspondents', *Journalism Studies* 10(4), 489–505.

Craft, S. & Davis, C.N. (2016) *Principles of American Journalism: An Introduction*, 2nd edn (New York: Routledge).

Curran, J. (2000) 'Press reformism 1918–98: a study of failure' in H. Tumber (ed.) *Media Power, Professionals and Policies* (London: Routledge), pp. 35–55.

Curran, J. & Park, M-J. (2000) 'Beyond globalization theory' in J. Curran & M-J. Park (eds) *De-Westernizing Media Studies* (Abingdon: Routledge), pp. 3–18.

Cushion, S. (2014) 'Do public service media (still) matter? Evaluating the supply, quality and impact of television news in western Europe' in R. Kuhn & R.K. Nielsen (eds) *Political Journalism in Transition: Western Europe in a Comparative Perspective* (London: I.B. Taurus), pp. 151–70.

Cushion, S. & Lewis, J. (2009) 'Towards a "Foxification" of 24-hour news channels in Britain? An analysis of market-driven and publicly funded news coverage', *Journalism* 10(2), 131–53.

Daly, C.B. (2012) *Covering America: A Narrative History of a Nation's Journalism* (Amherst and Boston, MA: University of Massachusetts Press).

Dare, S. (2011) The rise of citizen journalism in Nigeria – a case study of Sahara Reporters, Reuters Institute Fellowship Paper (Oxford: Reuters Institute for the Study of Journalism).

Darian-Smith, L. (2016) 'The "girls": women press photographers and the representation of women in Australian newspapers', *Media International Australia* 161(1), 48–58.

Davies, N. (2008) *Flat Earth News* (London: Chatto & Windus).

Davies, N. (2014) *Hack: How the Truth Caught up with Rupert Murdoch* (London: Chatto & Windus).

Davis, S. (n.d.) 'MÍDIA NINJA and the rise of citizen journalism in Brazil'. http://civicmediaproject.org, accessed 10 February 2017.

Deacon, D., Pickering, M., Golding, P. & Murdock, G. (1999) *Researching Communications: A Practical Guide to Methods in Media and Cultural Analysis* (London: Arnold).

Dearden, L. (2014) 'Isis issues rules for journalists forcing them to "swear allegiance as subjects of the Islamic State"', *The Independent* (7 October), www.independent. co.uk, accessed 17 February 2017.

de Beer, A. (ed.) (2008) *Global Journalism: Topical Issues and Media Systems* (Boston, MA: Pearson).

Debevoise & Plimpton LLP. (2016) 'Critics are not criminals: Comparative study of criminal defamation laws in the Americas', https://cpj.org, accessed 27 April 2018.

de Bruin, M. (2014) 'Gender and newsroom cultures' in A.V. Montiel (ed.) *Media and Gender: A Scholarly Agenda for the Global Alliance on Media and Gender* (Paris: UNESCO), pp. 41–46.

Delano, A. (2003) 'Women journalists: what's the difference?' *Journalism Studies* 4(2), 273–86.

Denyer, S. (2016) 'China's scary lesson to the world: censoring the internet works', *Washington Post* (23 May), www.washingtonpost.com, accessed 22 January 2017.

Deuze, M. (2005) 'What is journalism? Professional identity and ideology of journalists reconsidered', *Journalism* 6(4), 46–64.

Dewey, C. (2014) 'This is not an interview with Banksy', *Washington Post* (22 October) www.washingtonpost.com, accessed 18 November 2016.

Dewey, C. (2016) 'Facebook fake-news writer: "I think Donald Trump is in the White House because of me"', *Washington Post* (17 November) www.washington-post.com, accessed 18 November 2016.

Diamond, E. (1986) 'The Tisch touch', *New Yorker* (26 May), pp. 32–37.

Dickson, T. & Brandon, W. (2000) 'Media criticisms of US journalism education: unwarranted, contradictory', *AsiaPacific Media Educator* 8, 42–58.

Djerf-Pierre, M. (2007) 'The gender of journalism: the structure and logic of the field in the twentieth century', *Nordicom Review*, 81–104.

Djerf-Pierre, M. (2011) 'The difference engine', *Feminist Media Studies* 11(1), 43–51.

Dorer, J., Götzenbrucker, G. & Hummel, R. (2009) 'The Austrian journalism education landscape' in G. Terzis (ed.) *European Journalism Education* (Bristol: Intellect), pp. 79–92.

Dobek-Ostrowska, B. (2012) 'Italianization (or mediterraneanization) of the Polish media system? Reality and perspective' in D.C. Hallin & P. Mancini (eds) *Comparing Media Systems beyond the Western World* (Cambridge: Cambridge University Press), pp. 69–108.

Dobek-Ostrowska, B. (2015) '25 years after communism: four models of media and politics in Central and Eastern Europe' in D. Ostrowka & M. Glowacki (eds) *Democracy and Media in Central and Eastern Europe 25 years on* (New York: Peter Lang), pp. 11–46.

Dohnanyi, J. (2003) *The Impact of Media Concentration on Professional Journalism* (Vienna: Representative on Freedom of Media, Organization for Security and Co-operation in Europe).

Domatob, J.K. & Hall, S.W. (1983) 'Development journalism in black Africa', *International Communication Gazette* 31, 9–33.

Dong, J. (2012) 'A comparative study of Xinhua and CNN's overseas news bureaus', MA Thesis, University of Florida, USA, http://ufdc.ufl.edu, accessed 27 March 2017.

Donsbach, W. & Fielder, T. (2008) *Journalism School Enrichment: A Midterm Report of the Carnegie-Knight Initiative on the Future of Journalism Education* (Harvard University: Joan Shorenstein Center).

D'Orazio, F. (2015) 'Journey of an image: from a beach in Bodrum to twenty million screens across the world' in F. Vis & O. Goriunova (eds) *The Iconic Image on Social Media: A Rapid Research Response to the Death of Aylan Kurdi* (Sheffield: Visual Social Media Lab), pp. 11–18.

Douglas, T. (2006) 'How 7/7 "democratised" the media' *BBC News* (4 July) http://news.bbc.co.uk, accessed 13 February 2017.

Douglass, F. (1860) 'A plea for free speech in Boston', repro ThisNation.com, www.thisnation.com, accessed 25 June 2016.

Downey, J. & Fenton, N. (2003) 'New media, counter publicity and the public sphere', *New Media & Society* 5(2), 185–202.

Dragomir, M. (2016) 'Trust in journalists and media sinks to new lows', Media-PowerMonitor (5 June), mediapowermonitor.com, accessed 22 February 2017.

Duffy, A. (2010) 'Shooting rubber bands at the stars: preparing to work within the Singapore system' in B. Josephi (ed.) *Journalism Education in Countries with Limited Media Freedom* (New York: Peter Lang), pp. 33–51.

Duhe, S.F. & Zukowski, L.A. (1997) 'Radio-TV journalism curriculum: first jobs and career preparation', *Journalism & Mass Communication Educator* 52(1), 4–15.

Dunham, J. (2016) 'Press freedom in 2015: the battle for the dominant message', Freedom House, https://freedomhouse.org, accessed 17 February 2017.

Dunham, J., Nelson, B. & Aghekyan, E. (2015) 'Harsh laws and violence drive global decline', Freedom House, https://freedomhouse.org, accessed 17 February 2017.

Dutch Journalism Fund. (2015) 'The journalistic landscape in 2025', www.journalism2025.com, accessed 23 March 2017.

Dutton, W.H. (2009) 'The Fifth Estate emerging through networks of networks', *Prometheus* 27(1), 1–15.

Dutton, W.H., Dopatka A., Hills, M., Law, G. & Nash, V. (2011) *Freedom of Connection – Freedom of Expression: The Changing Legal and Regulatory Ecology Shaping the Internet* (Paris: UNESCO, Division for Freedom of Expression, Democracy and Peace).

Duwe, I. & White, R. (2011) 'How successful are media women's associations in Africa? A case study of the Tanzanian Association of Media Women (TAMWA)', *African Communication Research* 4(3), 515–35.

Eastern African Journalists' Association. (2008) *Enhancing Gender Equality in the Media in Eastern Africa* (Djibouti: Eastern Africa Journalists' Association).

eBizMBA Guide. (2017) 'Top 15 most popular news web sites', www.ebizmba.com, accessed 4 February 2017.

Edean, D.O. (1993) 'Role of development journalism in Nigeria's development', *Gazette* 52, 123–43.

Edstrom, M. & Ladendorf, M. (2012) 'Freelance journalists as a flexible workforce in media industries', *Journalism Practice* 6(5–6), 711–21.

Egorov, G., Guriev, S. & Sonin, K. (2009) 'Media freedom in dictatorships', *American Political Science Review* 103(4), 645–68.

Ehrlich, M.C. (2010) *Journalism in the Movies* (Urbana & Chicago, IL: University of Illinois Press).

Eke, I.W. (2014) 'Brown envelope syndrome and the future of journalism in Nigeria', *International Interdisciplinary Journal of Scientific Research* 1(1), 148–56.

El Issawi, F. (2014) 'Women and media: Libyan female journalists from Gaddafi media to post-revolution: case study', *CyberOrient* 8(1), www.cyberorient.net, accessed 25 January 2016.

Enda, J. (2011) 'Retreating from the world', *American Journalism Review* (December–January), http://ajrarchive.org, accessed 18 February 2017.

Ettema, J.S. & Glasser, T.L. (1998) *Custodians of Conscience: Investigative Journalism and Public Virtue* (New York: Columbia University Press).

Eun-Young, K. (2017) 'Asian struggling with fake news', *Huffington Post* (9 March), www.huffingtonpost.com, accessed 23 March 2017.

European Federation of Journalists. (2012) *Survey Report on Women in Journalists' Unions in Europe* (Brussels: International Federation of Journalists).

European Security, Research & Innovation Forum. (2009) *Final Report* (Brussels: ESRIF).

Farrell, P. (2016) 'The AFP and me: how one of my asylum stories sparked a 200-page police investigation', *The Guardian* (11 February), www.theguardian.com/media, accessed 4 December 2016.

Feinstein, A. & Sinyor, M. (2009) 'Women war correspondents: They are different in so many ways', *Nieman Reports*, http://niemanreports.org, accessed 28 March 2017.

Felle, T. (2015) 'Freedom fighting: why FOI is important for democracy' in T. Felle & J. Mair (eds) *FOI 10 years on: Freedom Fighting or Lazy Journalism?* (Bury St. Edmunds: Abramis), pp. 29–39.

Finberg, H. (2013) *State of Journalism Education 2013* (St. Petersburg, FL: Poynter).

Fischlin, D. & Nandorfy, M. (2007) *The Concise Guide to Global Human Rights* (Montreal: Black Rose).

Fishman, M. (1980) *Manufacturing the News* (Austin, TX: University of Texas Press).

Fitzgibbon, W. (2016) 'Journalists hang tough in the face of backlash against Panama Papers reporting', International Consortium of Investigative Journalists (1 December), https://panamapapers.icij.org, accessed 12 April 2017.

Fletcher, M. (2015) 'Why I am going back to live in Aleppo', *Times* (15 September), www.thetimes.co.uk, accessed 12 April 2017.

Flood, A. (2016) '"Post-truth" named word of the year by Oxford Dictionaries', *The Guardian* (15 November), www.theguardian.com, accessed 19 November 2016.

Folkenflik, D. (2011) 'Clinton lauds virtues of Al Jazeera: "It's real news"', National Public Radio (3 March), www.npr.org, accessed 6 March 2017.

Folkerts, J. (2014) 'History of journalism education', *Journalism & Communication Monographs* 16(4), 277–99.

Forsdick, S. (2018) 'Former Phnom Penh Post journalist describes state of press freedom in Cambodia as "dire"', *PressGazette* (17 May), pressgazette.co.uk, accessed 9 July 2018.

Fowler, A. (2015) *The War on Journalism: Media Moguls, Whistleblowers and the Price of Freedom* (North Sydney: William Heinemann).

Foy, H. (2016) 'Lunch with the FT: Andrej Babiš', *Financial Times* (19 February), www.ft.com,accessed 27 April 2018.

Franks, S. (2005) 'Lacking a clear narrative: foreign reporting after the Cold war', *Political Quarterly* 76 (S1), 91–101.

Franks, S. (2013) *Women and Journalism* (London: I.B. Taurus).

Frayn, M. (1965) *The Tin Men* (London: Collins).

Freedom House. (2015a) 'Freedom of the press 2015: country reports, https://freedomhouse.org, accessed 17 February 2017.

Freedom House. (2015b) Freedom on the net 2015, https://freedomhouse.org, accessed 3 June 2018.

Freedom House. (2016) 'Freedom of the press: country reports', https://freedom-house.org, accessed 17 February 2017.

Freedom House. (2017a) 'Freedom of the press 2017: Press freedom's dark horizon report and country reports', https://freedomhouse.org, accessed 14 May 2018.

Freedom House. (2017b) 'Freedom on the net 2017', https://rsf.org, accessed 3 June 2018.

From the Editors. (2004) '*The Times* and Iraq' (26 May), www.nytimes.com, accessed 22 February 2017.

Gadzekpo, A. (2011) 'Battling old ghosts in gender and African media research', *African Communication Research* 4(3), 389–410.

Gallagher, M. (2001a) 'The push and pull of action and research in feminist media studies', *Feminist Media Studies* 1(1), 11–15.

Gallagher, M. (2001b) 'Reporting on gender in journalism', *Nieman Reports* (Winter), niemanreports.org, accessed 8 March 2017.

Gallagher, M. (2002) 'Women, media and democratic society: in pursuit of rights and freedoms', United Nations Division for the Advancement of Women, expert group meeting (12–15 November) Beirut.

Gallagher, M. (2005) 'Feminist media perspectives' in A.N. Valdivia (ed.) *A Companion to Media Studies* (Oxford: Blackwell), pp. 19–39.

Gallagher, M. (2014) 'Feminist scholarship and the debates on gender and communication' in A.V. Montiel (ed.) *Media and Gender: A Scholarly Agenda for the Global Alliance on Media and Gender* (Paris: UNESCO), pp. 11–14.

Gallagher, M. with von Euler, M. (1995) *An Unfinished Story: Gender Patterns in Media Employment*, Reports and Papers on Mass Communication 110 (Paris: UNESCO).

Galtung, J. & Ruge, M.H. (1965) 'The structure of foreign news', *Journal of Peace Research* 2(1), 64–91.

Garcia, J. (2015) 'Media freedom and plurality is struggling in Eastern Europe', Euractiv (18 November), www.euractiv.com, accessed 25 February 2017.

Garrido, M. (2016) 'Freedom of expression under threat in Zambia', Peace & conflict monitor (14 August), www.monitor.upeace.org, accessed 23 December 2016.

George, C. (2012) 'The myth of the online bypass', Singapore Management University Law School (3 September), www.airconditionednation.com, accessed 25 January 2017.

Gerard, J. (1990) 'William S. Paley, who built CBS into a communications empire, dies at 89', *New York Times* (28 October), www.nytimes.com, accessed 22 February 2017.

Gershman, C. (2011) '21st century media: new frontiers, new barriers', World Press Freedom Day symposium (3 May), www.ned.org, accessed 13 March 2017.

Gilens, M. & Page, B.I. (2014) 'Testing theories of American politics: elites, interest groups, and average citizens', *Perspectives in Politics* 12(3), 564–81.

Gillmor, D. (2004) *We the Media: Grassroots Journalism by the People, for the People* (Sebastopol, CA: O'Reilly Media).

Giraud, E. (2014) 'Has radical participatory online media really "failed"? Indymedia and its legacies', *Convergence* 20(4), 419–37.

Glocer, T. (2006) 'Old media must embrace the amateur' *Financial Times* (8 March), www.ft.com, accessed 18 February 2017.

Gopsill, T. & Neale, G. (2007) *Journalists: 100 Years of the NUJ* (London: Profile).

Graves, L. & Cherubini, F. (2016) *The Rise of Fact-Checking Sites in Europe* (Oxford: Reuters Institute for the Study of Journalism).

Gray, K. (2014) *The Status of Women in the US Media 2014* (Washington, DC: Women's Media Center).

Greenidge, K., McIntyre, M.A. & Yun, H. (2016) *Structural Reform and Growth: What Really Matters? Evidence from the Caribbean*, IMF Working Paper WP/16/82.

Greenslade, R. (2014) 'First World War: how State and press kept truth off the front page', *The Guardian* (27 July), www.theguardian.com/media, accessed 14 March 2017.

Greenslade, R. (2016) 'Here's the truth: "fake news" is not social media's fault', *The Guardian* (23 November), www.theguardian.co/media, accessed 23 November 2016.

Grenby, M., Kasinger, M., Patching, R. & Pearson, M. (2009) 'Girls, girls, girls. A study of the popularity of journalism as a career among female teenagers and its corresponding lack of appeal to young males', *Australian Journalism Monographs* 11(1), 1–44.

Griffin, A. (2014) 'Where are all the women: why we need more female newsroom leaders', *Nieman Reports* (11 September), http://niemanreports.org, accessed 4 January 2016.

Grynbaum, M.M. (2017) 'Trump calls the news media the "enemy of the American people"', *New York Times* (17 February) www.nytimes.com, accessed 18 February 2017.

Guerlin, O. (2018) 'Crushing dissent in Egypt', *Assignment*, World (22 February), www.bbc.co.uk, accessed 2 June 2018.

Guttal, S. (2016) 'Interrogating the relevance of the Global North-South divide', *CETRI* (3 February), www.cetri.be, accessed 26 April 2018.

Habermas, J. (1989) *The Structural Transformation of the Public Sphere*, trans. T. Burger (Cambridge: Polity Press).

Habermas, J. (1997) 'The public sphere' in R.E. Goodin & P. Pettit (eds) *Contemporary Political Philosophy: An Anthology* (Oxford: Blackwell Publishers), pp. 103–06.

Hafez, K. (2009) 'Global journalism: myth or reality? In search of a theoretical base', paper presented to the annual meeting of the International Communication Association, Chicago, IL (23 May).

Hafez, K. (2010) *Radicalism and Political Reform in the Islamic and Western Worlds*, trans. A. Skinner (Cambridge: Cambridge University Press).

Hallin, D.C. & Mancini, P. (2004) *Comparing Media Systems: Three Models of Media and Politics* (Cambridge: Cambridge University Press).

Hallin, D.C. & Mancini, P. (eds) (2011) *Comparing Media Systems Beyond the Western World* (Cambridge: Cambridge University Press).

Hamilton, J.M. (2009) *Journalism's Roving Eye: A History of American Foreign Reporting* (Baton Rouge, LA: Louisiana State University Press).

Hamilton, J.M. (2012) 'Foreign correspondence: one age ends, another begins' in J. Clarke & M. Bromley (eds) *International News in the Digital Age: East-West Perspectives of a New World Order* (New York: Routledge), pp. 211–22.

Hamilton, J.M. & Jenner, E. (2004a) 'Redefining foreign correspondence', *Journalism* 5(3), 301–21.

Hamilton, J.M. & Jenner, E. (2004b) 'Foreign correspondence: evolution, not extinction', *Nieman Reports* 58/3, 98–100.

Hanitzsch, T. (2007) 'Deconstructing journalism culture: toward a universal theory', *Communication Theory* 17(4), 367–85.

Hanitzsch, T. (2011) 'Populist disseminators, detached watchdogs, critical change agents and opportunist facilitators: professional milieus, the journalistic field and autonomy in 18 countries, *International Communication Gazette* 73(6), 477–94.

Hanitzsch, T., Hanusch, F., Mellado, C., Anikina, M., Berganza, R., Cangoz, I., Coman, M., Hamada, B., Hernandez, M.E., Karadjov, C.D., Moreira, S.V., Mwesige, P.G., Plaisance, P.L., Reich, Z., Seethaler, J., Skewes, E.A., Noor, D.V. & Yuen, K.W. (2011) 'Mapping journalism cultures across nations: a comparative study of 18 countries', *Journalism Studies* 12(3), 273–93.

Hanitzsch, T., Seethaler, J., Skewes, E.A., Anikina, M., Berganza, R., Cangol, I., Coman, M., Hamada, B., Hanusch, F., Karadjov, C.D., Mellado, C., Moreira, S.V., Mwesige, P.G., Plaisance, P.L., Reich, Z., Noor, D.V. & Yuen, K.W. (2012) 'Worlds of journalism: journalistic cultures, professional autonomy, and perceived influences across 18 nations' in D.H. Weaver & L. Willnat (eds) *The Global Journalist in the 21st Century* (New York: Routledge), pp. 473–94.

Hannis, G. (2012) 'Enhancing students' critical thinking in journalism education: an approach using historical primary journalism texts', *Journalism Education* 1(2), 76–86.

Hanusch, F. (2013) 'Journalists in times of change: evidence from a new survey of Australia's journalistic workforce', *Australian Journalism Review* 35(1), 27–40.

Hanusch, F. & Bruns, A. (2017) 'Journalistic branding on Twitter: a representative study of Australian journalists' activities and profile descriptions', *Digital Journalism* 5(1), 26–43.

Hanusch, F., Clifford, K., Davies, K., English, P., Fulton, J., Lindgren, M., O'Donnell, P., Price, J., Richards, I. & Zion, L. (2015) 'Australian journalism students' professional views and news consumption: results from a representative study', *Australian Journalism Review* 37(1), 5–19.

Hanusch, F. & Upal, C. (2015) 'Combining detached watchdog journalism with development ideals: an exploration of Fijian journalism culture', *International Communication Gazette* 77(6), 557–76.

Harcup, T. (2014) *A Dictionary of Journalism* (Oxford: Oxford University Press).

Hardy, J. (2010) *Western Media Systems* (London: Routledge).

Hardy, J. (2014) 'Critical political economy of communications: a mid-term review', *International Journal of Media & Cultural Politics* 10(2), 189–202.

Hare, K. (2015) 'You can now search through more than 400 media ethics codes', Poynter (17 November), www.poynter.org, accessed 11 April 2017.

Hargreaves, I. (2003) *Journalism: Truth or Dare?* (Oxford: Oxford University Press).

Harris, R.J. (2008) *Pulitzer's Gold: Behind the Prize for Public Service Journalism* (London: University of Missouri Press).

Harrison, J. (2010) 'User-generated content and gatekeeping at the BBC hub', *Journalism Studies* 11(2), 243–56.

Hayes, M. (2005) 'On being Tuvaluan *tino tusitala*: reporting from the frontlines of global warming' in E. Papoutsaki & U.S. Harris (eds) *South Pacific Islands Communication: Regional Perspectives, Local Issues* (Singapore: Asia Media, Information and Communication Centre), pp. 254–73.

Hegedüs, D. (2018) 'Nations in Transit: Hungary', *Freedom House*, https://freedomhouse.org, accessed 14 May 2018.

Helmore, E. (2017) 'Trump's media war threatens journalists globally, protection group warns', *The Guardian* (25 February), www.theguardian.com, accessed 11 April 2017.

Henry, N. (2007) *American Carnival: Journalism under Siege in the Age of New Media* (Berkeley, CA: University of California Press).

Henshall, P. & Ingram, D. (1991) *The News Manual: Volume Three – Ethics and the Law* (Surry Hills: Poroman Press).

Herd, G.P. (2007) 'The "counter-terrorist" operation in Chechnya: "information warfare" aspects', *The Journal of Slavic Military Studies* 13(4), 57–83.

Herman, E.S. & Chomsky, N. (1988) *Manufacturing Consent: The Political Economy of the Mass Media* (New York: Pantheon Books).

Herman, E.S. & McChesney, R.W. (1997) *The Global Media: the New Missionaries of Global Capitalism* (London: Cassell).

Hermann, M.A. (2015) *Images of America: New York Press Photographers* (Charleston, NC: Arcadia).

Hermida, A. (2012) 'Tweets and truth: journalism as a discipline of verification', *Journalism Practice* 6(5–6), 659–668.

Hernandez, B.A. (2012) 'The top 10 news organizations with the most Google+ engagement', MashableUK (11 January), http://mashable.com, accessed 28 January 2017.

Herscovitz, H.G. (2012) 'Brazilian journalists in the 21st century' in D.H. Weaver & L. Willnat (eds) *The Global Journalist in the 21st Century* (New York: Routledge), pp. 365–81.

Hess, S. (1996) *International News and Foreign Correspondents* (Washington, DC: Brookings Institution Press).

Higgins, V. de M., Correa, T., Flores, M. & Meraz, S. (2008) 'Women and the news: Latin America and the Caribbean' in P. Poindexter, S. Meraz & A.S. Weiss (eds) *Women, Men, and News: Divided and Disconnected in the News Media Landscape* (New York: Routledge), pp. 262–92.

Hjarvard, S. (1995) 'TV news flow studies revisited', *Electronic Journal of Communication* 5(2–3), www.cios.org, accessed 5 April 2018.

Hjarvard, S. (2008) 'The mediatization of society: a theory of media as agents of social and cultural change', *Nordicom Review* 29(2), 105–34.

Hohenberg, J. (1995) *Foreign Correspondence: The Great Reporters and Their Times* (Syracuse, NY: Syracuse University Press).

Holland, P. (2001) 'Authority and authenticity: redefining television current affairs' in M. Bromley (ed.) *No News is Bad News: Radio, Television and the Public* (Harlow: Pearson), pp. 80–95.

Hooke, P. (2012) 'Why newspaper markets are growing in China and India, while they decline in the US and UK', *eJournalist* 12(1), ejournalist.com.au, accessed 17 February 2017.

Hopkin, G. (2014) 'The Grenada revolution – 1979–1983' (13 March), www.facebook.com/gerry.hopkins1, accessed 5 July 2016.

Howard, P.N., Duffy, A., Freelon, D., Hussain, M.M., Mari, W. & Maziad, M. (2011) *Opening Closed Regimes: What Was the Role of Social Media During the Arab Spring?* Working paper 2011.1, University of Washington: Project on Information Technology & Political Islam.

Høyer, S. (2005) 'The idea of the book: introduction' in S. Høyer & H. Pöttker (eds) *The Diffusion of the News Paradigm 1850–2000* (Göteborg: Nordicom), pp. 9–16.

Hoyler, M. & Watson, A. (2013) 'Global media cities in transnational media networks', *Tijdschrift voor Economische en Sociale Geografie* 104(1), 90–108.

Hu, Z. & Ji, D. (2013) 'Retrospection, prospection and the pursuit of an integrated approach for China's communication and journalism studies', *Javnost – the Public* 20(4), 5–16.

Human Rights Watch. (2018) 'Mexico: Events of 2017', hrw.org, accessed 27 April 2018.

Hume, E. (2007) *University Journalism Education: A Global Challenge*, a report to the Center for International Media Assistance, Washington, DC: National Endowment for Democracy.

Hume, M. (1997) *Whose War is it Anyway? The Dangers of the Journalism of Attachment, Living Marxism Special* (London: Informinc).

Hwang, Y. & Jeong, S.-H. (2009) 'Revisiting the knowledge gap hypothesis: a meta-analysis of thirty-five years of research', *Journalism & Mass Communication Quarterly* 86(3), 513–32.

Hyde-Clarke, N. (2010) 'Introduction' in N. Hyde-Clarke (ed.) *The Citizen in Communication: Re-visiting Traditional, New and Community Media Practices in South Africa* (Claremont, SA: Juta), pp. 1–8.

Ibelema, M. & Bosch, T. (2009) 'Sub-Saharan Africa' in A. de Beer & J. Merrill (eds) *Global Journalism: Topical Issues and Media Systems* (Boston, MA: Pearson), pp. 293–336.

Ibold, H. & Deuze, M. (2012) 'Comparing experiences in journalism education: the Netherlands and the United States' in B. Dernbach & W. Loosen (eds) *Didaktik der Journalistik: Konzepte, Methoden und Beispiele aus der Journalistenausbildung* (Wiesbaden: Springer Fachmedien), pp. 405–17.

Indymedia. (2003) 'Indymedia UK', www.indymedia.org.uk, accessed 3 October 2017.

International Federation of Journalists. (2010) *Women Journalists – Partners in Trade Union Leadership* (Brussels: International Federation of Journalists).

International News Safety Institute. (2010) 'Women reporting war', http://newssafety.com, accessed 28 March 2017.

Internet Live Stats. (2016) 'Singapore internet users', www.internetlivestats.com, accessed 3 June 2018.

Internet World Stats. (2016) 'Internet users in the world by regions: June 2016', www.internetworldstats.com, accessed 14 February 2017.

Internet World Stats. (2017) 'Internet users in the world by regions' (31 December), www.internetworldstats.com, accessed 6 March 2017.

Inter Press Service. (2017) 'About us', www.ipsnews.net/about-us, accessed 14 December 2017.

Ipsos-MORI. (2016) Ipsos-MORI Veracity Index 2015: trust in professions, www.ipsos-mori.com, accessed 22 February 2017.

Ireton, C. (2015) 'Thinking about 2025: scenarios for the future of journalism', *World News Publishing Focus* (9 July), https://blog.wan-ifra.org, accessed 23 March 2017.

IREX. (2015) Media sustainability index, www.irex.org, accessed 3 January 2016.

Isaeva, T., Kumasaki, S. & Fuchinoue, H. (2007) *Why Did Women Become Journalists in Chechen?* HiPEC International Peace Building Conference, Hiroshima (8 and 9 March).

Jabir, J. (2013) 'Role of media in national development in the 21st century', *Criterion Quarterly* 2(2),www.criterion-quarterly.com, accessed 18 February 2017.

Jackson, J. (2017) 'Fact-checkers are weapons in the post-truth wars, but they're not all on one side', *The Guardian* (15 February), www.theguardian.com/media, accessed 15 February 2015.

Jackson, S. (2013) 'Journalist jobs drop 16pc in year', *Australian* (4 November), www.theaustralian.com.au, accessed 10 March 2017.

Jakubowicz, K. (2008) 'The eastern European/post-communist media model countries: introduction' in G. Terzis (ed.) *European Media Governance: National and Regional Dimensions* (Bristol, UK: Intellect), pp. 303–13.

Jakubowicz, K. & Sükösd, M. (2008) *Finding the Right Place on the Map: Central and Eastern European Media Change in a Global Perspective* (Bristol: Intellect).

Jebril, N., Stětka, V. & Loveless, M. (2013) *Media and Democratisation: What is Known about the Role of Mass Media in Transitions to Democracy* (Oxford: Reuters Institute for the Study of Journalism).

Jefferson, T. (1787, 1903) Letter to Colonel Edward Carrington (16 January) in A.A. Lipscomb & A.E. Bergh (eds) *The Writings of Thomas Jefferson*, vol. 6 (Washington, DC: The Thomas Jefferson Memorial Association), p. 57.

Johnsen, S.S. (2004) 'News technology: deconstructing and reconstructing news', *Nordicom Review* 1(2), 237–57.

Johnson, K.A., Dolan, M.K., Johnson, L., Sonnett, J. & Reppen, R. (2010) 'Interjournalistic discourse about African Americans in television news coverage of Hurricane Katrina', *Discourse & Communication* 4(3), 243–61.

Joji, H. (2014) 'Unchaining the potential of women worldwide: an interview with Nobel laureate Tawakkol Karman', Nippon Communications Foundation (12 September), www.nippon.com, accessed 13 March 2017.

Jones, A. (2009) *Losing the News: The Future of the News that Feeds Democracy* (Oxford: Oxford University Press).

Jones, N. & Pitcher, S. (2010) 'Traditions, conventions and ethics: online dilemmas in South African journalism' in N. Hyde-Clarke (ed.) *The Citizen in Communication: Re-visiting Traditional, New and Community Media Practices in South Africa* (Claremont, SA: Juta), pp. 97–112.

Joof, A. (2013) 'Gender equality and communication in Africa', WACC (17 November), www.waccglobal.org, accessed 4 January 2016.

Joseph, A. (2013a) 'Media pluralism and gender: not just a question of number', WACC (16 November), www.waccglobal.org, accessed 11 March 2016.

Joseph, A. (2015) 'Executive summary', *Inside the News: Challenges and Aspirations of Women Journalists in Asia and the Pacific* (Paris: UNESCO), pp. 10–17.

Joseph, R. (2017) 'Do we really know what "fake news" is? *Global News* (14 January), globalnews.com, accessed 23 March 2017.

Josephi, B. (2005) 'Journalism in the global age', *Gazette: The International Journal for Communication Studies* 67(6), 575–90.

Josephi, B. (2010) 'Introduction' in B. Josephi (ed.) *Journalism Education in Countries with Limited Media Freedom* (New York: Peter Lang), pp. 1–11.

Josephi, B. (2015) 'Journalists for a young democracy', *Journalism Studies*, DOI 10.1080/1461670X.2015.1065199.

Josephi, B. & Richards, I. (2012) 'The Australian journalist in the 21st century' in D.H. Weaver & L. Willnat (eds) *The Global Journalist in the 21st Century* (New York: Routledge), pp. 115–25.

Joyce, A. (2014) 'Is journalism really a male-dominated field? The numbers say yes', *Washington Post* (20 May), www.washingtonpost.com, accessed 26 January 2016.

Joyce, M. (2007) 'The citizen journalism web site "OhmyNews" and the 2002 South Korean presidential election', *Berkman Center Research Publication No. 2007–15*, http://dx.doi.org/10.2139/ssrn.1077920, accessed 17 February 2017.

Joye, S. (2009) 'Raising an alternative voice: assessing the role and value of the global alternative news agency Inter Press Service', *Javnost – the Public* 16(3), 5–20.

Junghanns, K. & Hanitzsch, T. (2006) 'Deutsche Auslandskorrespondenten im Profil', *Medien & Kommunikationswissenschaft* 3, 412–29.

Jyrkiäinen, J. & Heinonen, A. (2012) 'Finnish journalist: the quest for quality amidst new pressures' in D.H. Weaver & L. Willnat (eds) *The Global Journalist in the 21st Century* (New York: Routledge), pp. 171–86.

Kaija, B. (2013) 'Uganda: women near parity but still leaving newsrooms' in C.M. Byerly (ed.) *The Palgrave International Handbook of Women and Journalism* (Basingstoke: Palgrave Macmillan), pp. 315–29.

Kaplan, M.D.G. (2013) 'The innovators: the big embrace', Associations Now (1 February), associationsnow.com, accessed 13 March 2017.

Kaplan, R.D. (2009) 'Why I love Al Jazeera', *The Atlantic* (October), www.theatlantic.com, accessed 6 March 2017.

Karikari, K. (2007) 'African media since Ghana's independence' in E. Barratt & G. Berger (eds) *50 Years of Journalism: African Media since Ghana's Independence* (Johannesburg: The African Editors' Forum, Highway Africa and Media Foundation for West Africa), pp. 10–20.

Karkins, J. (2013) 'Foreword' in F. Banda (ed.) *Model Curricula for Journalism Education: A Compendium of New Syllabi* (Paris: UNESCO), pp. 5–6.

Keller, B. (2013) 'It's the golden age of news', *New York Times* (3 November), www.nytimes.com, accessed 25 February 2017.

Kelly, S., Truong, M., Shahbaz, A. & Earp, M. (2016) 'Silencing the messenger: communication apps under pressure', *Freedom on the Net 2016*, Freedom House, https://freedomhouse.org/report/freedom-net/freedom-net-2016, accessed 22 January 2017.

Kemp, S. (2016) 'Digital in 2016', We Are Social (27 January), http://wearesocial. com, accessed 28 January 2017.

Kendall, B. (2017) 'Foresight in journalism' in L.W. Sherman & D.A. Feller (eds) *Foresight* (Cambridge: Cambridge University Press), pp. 32–57.

Kendo, O. (2010) 'Media and responsibility' in C. Mwita & L.G. Franceschi (eds) *Media and the Common Good: Perspectives on Media, Democracy and Responsibility* (Nairobi: LawAfrica), pp. 89–96.

Kent, T. (2013a) 'A whole new kind of journalism? A dissenting view', *The Huffington Post* (16 September), www.huffingtonpost.com, accessed 18 November 2016.

Kent, T. (2013b) 'Who's a journalist? Closing in on a definition', *The Huffington Post* (3 October), www.huffingtonpost.com, accessed 2 October 2016.

Kessler, G. (2014) 'The global boom in political fact checking', *Washington Post* (13 June), www.washingtonpost.com, accessed 22 February 2017.

Keyes, R. (2004) *The Post-Truth Era: Dishonesty and Deception in Contemporary Life* (New York: St. Martin's Press).

Khalid, S. (2015) 'Bangladeshi group orders firing of female journalists', Al Jazeera (22 October), www.aljazeera.com, accessed 14 March 2017.

Khalil, J. & Kraidy, M. (2009) *Arab Television Industries* (London: Palgrave Macmillan).

Kirat, M. (2012) 'Journalists in the United Arab Emirates' in D.H. Weaver & Lars Willnat (eds) *The Global Journalist in the 21st Century* (New York: Routledge), pp. 458–69.

Kircher, L. (2012) 'Seven lessons Scandinavian media can teach us', *Columbia Journalism Review* (2 July), http://archives.cjr.org, accessed 21 February 2017.

Kitch, C. (2015) 'Women in the newsroom: status and stasis', *Journalism & Mass Communication Quarterly* 92(1), 35–38.

Klos, D.M. (2013) *The Status of Women in the US Media 2013* (Washington, DC: Women's Media Center).

Knight Foundation. (2011) 'Carnegie-Knight initiative on the future of journalism education', www.knightfoundation.org, accessed 15 March 2017.

Kovach, B. & Rosenstiel, T. (1999) *Warp Speed: America in the Age of Mixed Media* (New York: Century Foundation Press).

Kovach, B. & Rosenstiel, T. (2001) *The Elements of Journalism: What Newspeople Should Know and the Public Should Expect* (New York: Crown).

Kovach, B. & Rosenstiel, T. (2010) *Blur: How to Know What's True in the Age of Information Overload* (New York: Bloomsbury).

Kozloff, N. (2011) 'Middle Eastern and Latin American media: a thorn in the side of US military in Haiti', *Huffington Post* (24 March), www.huffingtonpost.com, accessed 7 March 2017.

Kperogi, F.A. (2011) 'Cooperation with the corporation? CNN and the hegemonic cooptation of citizen journalism through iReport.com', *New Media & Society* 13(2), 314–29.

Kraidy, M.M. (2000) 'Transnational television and asymmetrical interdependence in the Arab world: the growing influence of the Lebanese satellite broadcasters', *Transnational Broadcasting Studies* 5, http://repository.upenn.edu, accessed 19 June 2016.

Kunthear, M. (2008) 'Female journalist plans ladies only club', *Phnom Penh Post* (12 June), www.phnompenhpost.com, accessed 3 January 2016.

Kurz, H. (1999) '"Ethical iceberg" seen in L.A. Times scandal probe', *Washington Post* (21 December), www.washingtonpost.com, accessed 22 February 2017.

Kuttab, D. (2015) 'Who is a journalist?' Doha Centre for Media Freedom (7 September), www.dc4mf.org, accessed 14 November 2016.

Lago, C. & Romancini, R. (2010) 'Aspects of journalism education in Brazil' in B. Josephi (ed.) *Journalism Education in Countries with Limited Media Freedom* (New York: Peter Lang), pp. 175–95.

Lamble, S. (2004) 'Documenting the methodology of journalism', *Australian Journalism Review* 26(1), 85–106.

Lancaster, K. (2013) *Video Journalism for the Web: A Practical Introduction to Storytelling* (New York: Routledge).

Landemore, H. (2013) *Democratic Reason: Politics, Collective Intelligence, and the Rule of the Many* (Princeton, NJ: Princeton University Press).

Lanzillo, A. (2011) 'Iran and the Green Movement: changes in media and censorship capabilities', Changing Communications, https://changingcommunications.wordpress.com, accessed 23 December 2016.

Layton, S. (1995) 'The demographics of diversity: profile of Pacific Island journalists', *Australian Studies in Journalism* 4, 101–21.

Lealand, G. & Hollings, J. (2012) 'Journalists in New Zealand' in D.H. Weaver & L. Willnat (eds) *The Global Journalist in the 21st Century* (New York: Routledge), pp. 126–37.

Lee, S. (2016) 'How South Korea's fake news hijacked a democratic crisis', Gizmodo (3 October), gizmodo.com, accessed 23 March 2017.

Leetaru, K. (2016) 'The global perspective on fake news', *Forbes* (11 December), www.forbes.com, accessed 23 March 2017.

Levada-Center. (2015) 'Putin's approval rating', www.levada.ru/en, accessed 17 February 2017.

Leveson, B. (2012) *An Inquiry into the Culture, Practices and Ethics of the Press: Executive Summary and Recommendations*, HC 799 (London: The Stationery Office).

Lewis, B. (1993) 'Islam and liberal democracy', *The Atlantic* (February), www.theatlantic.com, accessed 20 February 2017.

Lewis, D. (2010) 'Foreign correspondents in a modern world The past, present and possible future of global journalism', *The Elon Journal of Undergraduate Research in Communications* 1(1), 119–27.

Lewis, J. (2013) *Beyond Consumer Capitalism: Media and the Limits to Imagination* (Cambridge: Polity)

Liebling, A.J. (1960) 'The wayward press: do you belong in journalism?' *The New Yorker* (14 May), 105, 109.

Livingstone, S. & Lunt, P. (2014) 'Mediatization: an emerging paradigm for media and communication studies' in K. Lundby (ed.) *Mediatization of Communication. Handbooks of Communication Science (21)* (Berlin: De Gruyter Mouton), pp. 703–724.

Lo, V-h. (2012) 'Journalists in Taiwan' in D.H. Weaver & L. Willnat (eds) *The Global Journalist in the 21st Century* (New York: Routledge), pp. 104–12.

Lobo, P., Silveirinha, M.J., Torres da Silva, M. & Subtil, F. (2015) 'In journalism, we are all men', *Journalism Studies*, DOI: 10.1080/146167X.2015.1111161.

Löffelholz, M. (2016) 'Embedded journalism', *Encyclopaedia Britannica*, www.britannica.com, accessed 15 March 2017.

Lonsdale, S. (2012) '"We agreed that women were a nuisance in the office anyway": the portrayal of women journalists in early twentieth-century British fiction', *Journalism Studies* 14(4), 461–75.

Loo, E. (2000) 'In this issue', *AsiaPacific Media Educator* 8, 3.

Louw, E. (2005) *The Media and Political Process* (London: Sage).

Lugo-Ocando, J. (2008) *The Media in Latin America* (Maidenhead: Open University Press).

Lynch, D. (2015) *Above & Beyond: Looking at the Future of Journalism Education*, Knight Foundation, www.knightfoundation.org, accessed 21 November 2016.

MacFarquhar, N. (2016) 'A powerful Russian weapon: the spread of false stories', *New York Times* (28 August), www.nyt.com, accessed 14 March 2017.

Macharia, S. (2015) *Who Makes the News? Global Media Monitoring Project 2015* (Toronto, ON: World Association for Christian Communication).

Macpherson, C.B. (1977) 'Do we need a theory of the State?' *European Journal of Sociology* 18(2), 223–44.

Magar, G. (2011) *Kiss Me Quick before I Shoot: A Filmmaker's Journey into the Lights of Hollywood and True Love* (Seattle, WA: Sea Script).

Maheshwari, S. (2016) 'How fake news goes viral: a case study', *New York Times* (20 November) www.nytimes.com, accessed 20 November 2016.

Makabenta, Y. (2016) 'Who is a journalist?' *The Manila Times* (6 July) www.manila-times.net, accessed 2 October 2016.

Mandelbaum, M. (1982) 'Vietnam: The television war', *Daedalus* 111(4), 157–169.

Marchi, R. (2012) 'With Facebook, blogs, and fake news, teens reject journalistic "objectivity"', *Journal of Communication Inquiry* 36(3), 246–62.

Martin, S.E. & Hansen, K.A. (1998) *Newspapers of Record in a Digital Age: From Hot Type to Hot Ink* (Westport, CT: Praeger).

Martinson, J. (2012) 'Why are there so few female national newspaper editors', *The Guardian* (31 May), www.theguardian.com, accessed 8 March 2017.

Massey, B.L. & Elmore, C.J. (2011) 'Happier working for themselves?' *Journalism Practice* 5(6), 672–86.

Masterton, M. (1996) *Asian Values in Journalism* (Singapore: Asia Media, Information and Communication Centre).

Mastrini, G. & Becerra, M. (2011) 'Structure, concentration and changes of the media system in the southern cone of Latin America', *Communicar* XVIII, 51–59.

Matloff, J. (2007) 'Unspoken: foreign correspondents and sexual abuse', *Columbia Journalism Review*, http://archives.cjr.org, accessed 28 March 2017.

Matos, C. (2012) 'Mass media' in G. Ritzer (ed.) *The Wiley-Blackwell Encyclopaedia of Globalization, Vol. III* (Chichester: Wiley-Blackwell), pp. 1329–38.

McChesney, R.W. (2001) 'Global media, neoliberalism, and imperialism', *Monthly Review* 52(10), https://monthlyreview.org, accessed 21 February 2017.

McChesney, R.W. (2014) 'Liberalism and the media', openDemocracy (12 August), www.opendemocracy.net, accessed 29 April 2018.

McIntosh, T. (2014) 'Paraguay is 100th nation to pass FOI law, but struggle for openness goes on', *The Guardian* (19 September) www.theguardian.com, accessed 14 December 2016.

McLaughlin, G. (2016) *The War Correspondent,* 2nd edn (London: Pluto Press).

McLuhan, M. (1962) *Gutenberg Galaxy: The Making of Typographic Man* (Toronto: University of Toronto Press).

McLuhan, M. & Fiore, Q. (1967) *The Medium is the Massage* (London: Penguin).

McMane, A.A. (2012) 'The French journalist' in D.H. Weaver & L. Willnat (eds) *The Global Journalist in the 21st Century* (New York: Routledge), pp. 187–204.

McNair, B. (2005) 'What is journalism?' in H. de Burgh (ed.) *Making Journalists* (London: Routledge), pp. 25–43.

McQuail, D. (2010) *McQuail's Mass Communication Theory*, 6th edn (London: Sage).

Masterton, M. (ed.) *Asian Values in Journalism* (Singapore: Asian Media, Information and Communication Centre).

Meade, A. (2016) 'ABC closes opinion website the Drum with immediate effect', *The Guardian* (5 July), https://theguardian.com/media, accessed 5 July 2016.

Media Reform Coalition. (2014) *The Elephant in the Room: A Survey of Media Ownership and Plurality in the United Kingdom* (London: Media Reform Coalition).

Melki, J. (2009) 'Journalism and media studies in Lebanon', *Journalism Studies* 10(5), 672–90.

Mellado, C. (2012) 'The Chilean journalist' in D.H. Weaver & L. Willnat (eds) *The Global Journalist in the 21st Century* (New York: Routledge), pp. 382–99.

Mellado, C. & Lagos, C. (2013) 'Redefining comparative analyses of media systems from the perspective of new democracies', *Communication & Society* 26(4), 1–24

Mellado, C., Moreira, S.V., Lagos, C. & Hernandez, M.E. (2012) 'Comparing journalism cultures in Latin America: the case of Chile, Brazil and Mexico', *International Communication Gazette* 74(1), 60–77.

Mellor, N. (2011) *Arab Journalists in Transnational Media* (New York: Hampton Press).

Mendel, T. (2008) *Freedom of Information: A Comparative Legal Survey*, 2nd edn (Paris: UNESCO).

Menon, V. (1996) 'Preface' in M. Masterton (ed.) *Asian Values in Journalism* (Singapore: Asian Media, Information and Communication Centre), pp. vii–ix.

Merrill, J.C. (2010) 'Training or education?' in J.C. Merrill & R.L. Lowenstein (eds) *Viva Journalism! The Triumph of Print Media in the Media Revolution* (Bloomington, IN: AuthorHouse), pp. 99–112.

Mfumbusa, B. (2010) 'Tanzania's journalism education at crossroads: western models, local realities' in B. Josephi (ed.) *Journalism Education in Countries with Limited Media Freedom* (New York: Peter Lang), pp. 155–72.

Michaelson, R. (2018) 'Egypt's Sisi is sworn in for a second term, amid crackdown on dissent', *The Guardian* (2 June), www.theguardian.com, accessed 2 June 2018.

Mihelj, S. (2013) 'Television entertainment in socialist Eastern Europe: between Cold War politics and global developments' in T. Havens, A. Imre & K. Lustyik (eds) *Popular Television in Eastern Europe during and since Socialism* (New York: Routledge), pp. 13–28.

Mill, J.S. (1859, 1997) 'Of the liberty of thought and discussion' in M. Bromley & T. O'Malley (eds) *A Journalism Reader* (London: Routledge), pp. 22–27.

Milton, J. (1644) *Areopagitica: A Speech of Mr. John Milton for the Liberty of Unlicens'd Printing to the Parliament of England*, London, www.dartmouth.edu, accessed 18 February 2017.

Mindich, D.T.Z. (1998) *Just the Facts: How 'Objectivity' Came to Define American Journalism* (New York: New York University Press).

Mindich, D.T.Z. (2005) *Tuned Out: Why Americans under 40 Don't Follow the News* (New York: Oxford University Press).

Mitchell, A., Gottfried, J., Barthel, M. & Shearer, E. (2016) 'Pathways to news', *The Modern News Consumer* (Washington, DC: Pew Research Center).

Mitchell, B. (2011) 'Women journalists aren't increasing overall', Poynter (2 March), www.poynter.org, accessed 30 November 2012.

Mohan, K. (2014) 'Factsheet: freedom of information in Africa', Africa Check, https://africacheck.org, accessed 15 February 2017.

Mollick, E.R. & Nanda, R. (2015) 'Wisdom or madness? Comparing crowds with expert evaluation in funding the arts', Harvard Business School Working Paper No. 14–116.

Molnar, H. & Meadows, M. (2001) *Songlines to Satellites: Indigenous Communication in Australia, the South Pacific and Canada* (Annandale, NSW: Pluto).

Molnar, H. & Meadows, M. (2001) *Songlines to Satellites: Indigenous Communication in Australia, the South Pacific and Canada* (Annandale, NSW: Pluto).

Moore, M. (2010) 'Shrinking world: the decline of international reporting in the British press', Media Standards Trust, http://mediastandardstrust.org, accessed 15 February 2017.

Morrell, H. (1988) *Transatlantic Vistas: American journalists in Europe, 1900–1940*, (Kent: Kent State University Press).

Mortensen, A. (2014) 'Voices in danger: North Korea is no place for citizen journalists, but this hasn't stopped Ishimaru Jiro', *The Independent* (29 October), www.independent.co.uk/voices/comment, accessed 15 February 2017.

Mowlana, H. (1985) *International Flow of Information: A Global Report and Analysis*, Reports and Papers on Mass Communication No. 99 (Paris: UNESCO).

Mowlana, H. (1997/2005) *Global Information and World Communication: New Frontiers in International Relations*, 2nd edn (London: Sage).

Moyo, D. (2009) 'Citizen journalism and the parallel market of information in Zimbabwe's 2008 election', *Journalism Studies* 10(4), 551–67.

Moyo, L. (2015) 'Digital age as ethical maze: citizen journalism ethics during crises in Zimbabwe and South Africa', *African Journalism Studies* 36(4), 125–44.

Mozur, P. & Scott, M. (2016) 'Fake news in US election? Elsewhere, that's nothing new', *New York Times* (17 November) www.nytimes.com, accessed 20 November 2016.

Muller, J. (2011) *Emus Loose in Egnar: Big Stories from Small Towns* (Lincoln, NE: University of Nebraska Press).

Murphy, P.D. (2003) 'Without ideology? Rethinking hegemony in the age of transnational media' in L. Artz & Y.R. Kamalipour (eds) *The Globalization of Corporate Media Hegemony* (Albany, NY: State University of New York Press), pp. 55–78.

Murphy, T. (2016) 'How Donald Trump became conspiracy theorist in chief: he's made the paranoid style of American politics go mainstream', *Mother Jones* (November/December) www.motherjones.com, accessed 15 February 2017.

Murrell, C. (2014) *Foreign Correspondents and International Newsgathering: The Role of Fixers* (New York: Routledge).

Nastasia, D.I. & Nastasia, S. (2013b) 'Poland: women journalists and "the Polish mother" mentality' in C.M. Byerly (ed.) *The Palgrave International Handbook of Women and Journalism* (Basingstoke: Palgrave Macmillan), pp.151–63.

Nastasia, D.I., Pilvre, B. & Tampere, K. (2013) 'Estonia: women journalists and women's emancipation in Estonia' in C.M. Byerley (ed.) *The Palgrave International Handbook of Women and Journalism* (Basingstoke: Palgrave Macmillan), pp. 39–50.

Nastasia, S. & Nastasia, D.I. (2013a) 'Bulgaria: Cinderella went to market, with consequences for women journalists' in C.M. Byerley (ed.) *The Palgrave International Handbook of Women and Journalism* (Basingstoke: Palgrave Macmillan), pp. 27–38.

Neff, G. (2015) 'Learning from documents: applying new theories of materiality to journalism', *Journalism* 16(1), 74–78.

Newman, N. with Fletcher, R., Levy, D.A. & Nielsen, R.K. (2016) *Reuters Institute Digital News Report 2016* (Oxford: Reuters Institute for the Study of Journalism).

News Media Association. (2015) 'The BBC's role in the news media landscape: the publishers' view' (London: News Media Association).

Newton, E. (2011) 'Journalism schools can be leaders in innovation and news', Nieman Lab (13 October), www.niemanlab.org, accessed 15 March 2017.

Nicas, J. & Seetharaman, D. (2016) 'Google and Facebook take aim at fake-news sites', *Wall Street Journal*, www.wsj.com, accessed 23 March 2017.

NINJA. (2016). About us, https://ninja.oximity.com, accessed 17 February 2017.

Nistor, C. (2013) 'Journalism education and professional practices', *Proceedings of the International Conference Literature, Discourse and Multicultural Dialogue* 1, 58–64.

Nordenstreng, K. (2010) 'MacBride Report as culmination of NWICO', keynote at International Colloquium *Communication et changement social en Afrique*, Université Stendhal, Grenoble 3 (27–29 January), www.uta.fi, accessed 19 February 2017.

Nordenstreng, K. (2013) 'Lessons learned from the NWICO process', *Xiandai Chuanbo* 6, 64–69, in English, www.uta.fi, accessed 1 February 2017, 1–14.

Nordenstreng, K. (2016) 'Liberate freedom from its ideological baggage!' in U. Carlsson (ed.) *Freedom of Expression and Media in Transition: Studies and Reflections in the Digital Age* (Gothenburg: Nordicom), pp. 61–65.

Norris, P. (2006) 'The role of the free press in promoting democratization, good governance and human development', paper for the Midwest Political Science Association annual meeting, 20-22 April, Chicago, https://pdfs.semanticscholar.org, accessed 29 April 2018.

North, L. (2010) 'The gender "problem" in Australian journalism education', *Australian Journalism Review* 32(2), 103–15.

North, L. (2014) 'Still a "blokes club": the motherhood dilemma in journalism', *Journalism*, DOI 10.1177/1464884914560306.

Nwaubani, A.T. (2015) 'Nigeria's "brown envelope" journalism', BBC News (5 March), www.bbc.co.uk, accessed 2 June 2018.

Nyarota, G. (2006) *Against the Grain: Memoirs of a Zimbabwean Newsman* (Cape Town: Zebra).

Nyondo, R. (2011) *Audit of Gender in Media Education and Training in Southern Africa* (Johannesburg: Gender Links).

Obijiofor, L. & Hanusch, F. (2011) *Journalism Across Cultures: An Introduction* (Basingstoke: Palgrave Macmillan).

Oborne, P. (2005) *The Rise of Political Lying* (Sydney: Simon & Schuster).

Ojala, M., Pantti, M. & Kangas, J. (2018) 'Professional role enactment amid information warfare: war correspondents tweeting on the Ukraine conflict', *Journalism* 19(3), 297–313.

O'Kane, M. (1996) *Riding the Storm: How to Tell Lies and Win Wars*, dir. Ron Orders (London: Cinécontact).

Oliver, L. (2010) 'Census charts the world's journalism education programmes', journalism.co.uk (5 July), www.journalism.co.uk, accessed 7 October 2016.

O'Malley, T. (2001) 'The decline of public service broadcasting in the UK, 1979–2000' in M. Bromley (ed.) *No News is Bad News: Radio, Television and the Public* (Harlow: Pearson), pp. 28–45.

O'Neill, B. (2012a) 'Dangers of the "journalism of attachment"', *The Drum* (24 February), www.abc.net.au, accessed 7 March 2017.

O'Neill, O. (2012b) 'So, what is a free press?' *The Guardian* (23 November), www.theguardian.com/commentisfree, accessed 23 June 2016.

Ongong'a, S.O. (2010) 'The challenges for Kenya's journalism education' in B. Josephi (ed.) *Journalism Education in Countries with Limited Media Freedom* (New York: Peter Lang), pp. 137–54.

O'Reilly, L. (2016) 'The 30 biggest media companies in the world', *Business Insider UK* (31 May), http://uk.businessinsider.com, accessed 28 January 2017.

Örnebring, H. (2012) 'Comparative journalism research – an overview', *Sociology Compass* 6(10), 769–80.

Örnebring, H. (2016) *Newsworkers: A Comparative European Perspective* (London: Bloomsbury).

Owen, J. & Purdey, H. (2009) *International News Reporting: Frontlines and Deadlines* (Chichester: Wiley-Blackwell).

Oxford Dictionaries. (2016) 'Post-truth', https://en.oxforddictionaries.com, accessed 12 September 2017.

Oxford Dictionaries. (2017). 'Freedom of expression', https://en.oxforddictionaries.com, accessed 12 September 2017.

Painter, J. (2008) *Counter-Hegemonic News: A Case Study of Al-Jazeera English and TeleSUR* (Oxford: Reuters Institute for the Study of Journalism).

Palmer, L. (2012). '"iReporting" an uprising: CNN and citizen journalism in network culture', *Television & New Media* 14(5), 367–85.

Papoutsaki, E. & Harris, U.S. (2008) 'Unpacking "Islandness" in South Pacific islands communication' in E. Papoutsaki & U.S. Harris (eds) *South Pacific Islands Communication: Regional Perspectives, Local Issues* (Singapore: Asia Media, Information and Communication Centre), pp. 1–12.

Pasti, S., Chernysh, M. & Svitich, L. (2012) 'Russian journalists and their profession' in D.H. Weaver & L. Willnat (eds) *The Global Journalist in the 21st Century* (New York: Routledge), pp. 267–82.

Pasti, S., Ramaprasad, J. & Ndlovu, M. (2015) 'BRICS journalists in global research' in K. Nordenstreng & D.K. Thussu (eds) *Mapping BRICS Media* (Abingdon: Routledge), pp. 205–26.

Paterson, C. (2011) *The International Television News Agencies: the World from London* (New York: Peter Lang).

Patterson, T.E. (2013) *Informing the News: The Need for Knowledge-Based Journalism* (New York: Vintage).

Pavli, D. (2010) 'Berlusconi's chilling effect on Italian media', Open Society Foundations (30 March), www.opensocietyfoundations.org, accessed 3 June 2018.

Pax, S. (2003) '"I became the profane pervert Arab blogger"', *The Guardian* (9 September), theguardian.com, accessed 9 July 2018.

PBS (2007) 'Stories from a small planet' (27 March), www.pbs.org, accessed 5 April 2018.

Pedelty, M. (1995) *War Stories: The Culture of Foreign Correspondents* (Oxon: Routledge).

Perse, E.M. & Lambe, J. (2017) *Media Effects and Society*, 2nd edn (New York: Routledge).

Peters, C. (2013) '"Even better than being informed": satirical news and media literacy' in C. Peters & M. Broersma (eds) *Rethinking Journalism: Trust and Participation in a Transformed News Landscape* (Abingdon: Routledge), pp. 173–88.

Peters, J. & Tandoc, E.C. (2013) '"People who aren't really reporters at all, who have no professional qualifications": defining a journalist and deciding who may claim the privileges', *New York University Journal of Legislation and Public Policy Quorum* 34, 33–63.

Petersen, J. (2014) 'Risk and the politics of disaster coverage in Haiti and Katrina', *Communication, Culture & Critique* 7(1), 37–54.

Pew Research Center (26 May), www.journalism.org, accessed 10 July 2018

Phillips, A. (2015a) *Journalism in Context: Practice and Theory for the Digital Age* (London: Routledge).

Phillips, K. (2015b) 'The history of media ownership in Australia', *Rear Vision*, ABC Radio National (6 October), www.abc.net.au/radionational, accessed 29 June 2016.

Phillips, T. (2012) 'Why the truth doesn't matter (to the candidates)', *Huffington Post* (29 October), www.huffingtonpost.com, accessed 22 February 2017.

Phillips, T. (2017) 'Trump's media attacks play into China's hands, says Beijing press', *The Guardian* (18 February), www.theguardian.com, accessed 18 February 2017.

Picard, R.G. (2014) 'Twilight or new dawn of journalism? *Digital Journalism* 2(3), 273–83.

Picard, R.G. (2015) 'Deficient tutelage: challenges of contemporary journalism education' in G. Allen, S. Craft, C. Waddell & M.L. Young (eds) *Toward 2020: New Directions in Journalism Education* (Toronto, ON: Ryerson Journalism Research Centre), pp. 4–10.

Pilger, J. (2007) 'The invisible government', johnpilger.com (16 June), http:// johnpilger.com, accessed 29 June 2016.

Pilkington, E. (2016) 'Trump v the media: did his tactics mortally wound the fourth estate?' *The Guardian* (22 November), www.theguardian.com/media, accessed 23 November 2016.

Pintak, L. & Ginges, J. (2012) 'Arab journalists' in D.H. Weaver & L. Willnat (eds) *The Global Journalist in the 21st Century* (New York: Routledge), pp. 429–42.

Pinto, M. & Sousa, H. (2003) 'Journalism education at universities and journalism schools in Portugal' in R. Fröhlich & C. Holtz-Bacha (eds) *Journalism Education in Europe and North America* (Cresskill, NJ: Hampton Press), pp. 169–86.

Pleijter, A., Hermans, L. & Vergeer, M. (2012) 'Journalists and journalism in the Netherlands' in D.H. Weaver & L. Willnat (eds) *The Global Journalist in the 21st Century* (New York: Routledge), pp. 242–54.

Political and Economic Planning. (1938) *The British Press* (London: PEP).

Pompeo, J. (2010) 'The top 20 most influential news media Twitter feeds', *Business Insider*, 3 September, www.businessinsider.com, accessed 5 April 2018.

Ponsford, D. (2016) 'Former daily editor says up to 80 per cent of local newspaper journalism jobs have gone since 2006', *Press Gazette* (25 April), www.pressgazette. co.uk, accessed 15 August 2016.

Postoutenko, K. (2010) 'Prolegomena to the study of totalitarian communication' in K. Postoutenko (ed.) *Totalitarian Communication: Hierarchies, Codes and Messages* (New Brunswick, NJ: Transaction), pp. 11–44.

Potts, J. & Shehadeh, T. (2014) 'Compensating differentials in creative industries and occupations: some evidence from HILDA' in G. Hearn, R. Bridgstock, B. Goldsmith & J. Rogers (eds) *Creative Work Beyond the Creative Industries: Innovation, Employment and Education* (Cheltenham: Edward Elgar), pp. 47–60.

Preston, P. (2015) 'Foreword' in T. Felle & J. Mair (eds) *FOI 10 Years on: Freedom Fighting or Lazy Journalism?* (Bury St Edmunds: Abramis), pp. 1–4.

Preston, P. (2016) 'Trust in the media is the first casualty of a post-factual war', *The Guardian* (25 September), www.theguardian.com/media, accessed 19 November 2016.

Preston, P. (2017) 'In the fake news era, we need the bigger picture', *The Guardian* (9 April), www.theguardian.com, accessed 11 April 2017.

Price, M. (2001) 'The transformation of international broadcasting', *Razón Y Palabra* 23, www.razonypalabra.org.mx, accessed 2 June 2016.

Primo, A. & Zago, G. (2015) 'Who and what do journalism?' *Digital Journalism* 3(1), 38–52.

Pritchard, D. & Bernier, M-F. (2010) 'Media convergence and changes in Québec journalists' professional values', *Canadian Journal of Communication* 35(4), 595–607.

Puri, S. (2014) *The Grenada Revolution in the Caribbean Present: Operation Urgent Memory* (New York: Palgrave Macmillan).

Radsch, C.C. (2016) 'On International Women's Day, CPJ recognizes nine female journalists jailed for their work', Committee to Protect Journalists (7 March), https://cpj.org, accessed 14 March 2017.

Radu, W.S. & Chekera, Y.T. (2014) *Power, Patriarchy and Gender Discrimination in Zimbabwean Newsrooms* (Johannesburg: Media Monitoring Africa).

Raeymaekers, K., Paulussen, S. & De Keyser, C. (2012) 'A survey of professional journalists in Flanders (Belgium)' in D.H. Weaver & L. Willnat (eds) *The Global Journalist in the 21st Century* (New York: Routledge), pp. 141–54.

Rahim, L. (2015) 'Fear, smear and the paradox of authoritarian politics in Singapore', *The Conversation* (28 September), theconversation.com, accessed 20 February 2017.

Rai, M. & Cottle, S. (2016) '24-hour news channels about the globe: continuity or change?' in S. Cushion & R. Sambrook (eds) *The Future of 24-hour News: New Directions, New Challenges* (New York: Peter Lang), pp. 143–62.

Ran, M. (2012) 'Foreword' in *Gender Pay Gap in Journalism: Wage Indicator Global Report 2012*, Central European Labour Studies Institute (Amsterdam: Wage Indicator Foundation), p. 4.

Rapoza, K. (2016) 'Fake news in Russia: "Obama threatens sanctions due to Russia's role in Syria"', *Forbes* (7 December), www.forbes.com, accessed 14 March 2017.

Rash, J. (2011) 'International news coverage after 9/11'. *StarTribune* (9 September), www.startribune.com, accessed 25 February 2017.

Rauhala, A., Lindgren, A. & Fatima, S. (2012) *Women in the Field: What do You Know? A Snapshot of Women in Canadian Journalism* (Ryerson Journalism Research Centre, Ryerson University).

Rawls, J. (2001) *Justice as Fairness: A Restatement*, ed. E. Kelly (Cambridge, MA: Belknap Press).

Reese, S. (2016) 'The new geography of journalism research: levels and spaces', *Digital Journalism*, DOI: 10.1080/21670811.2016.1152903.

Reporters Without Borders. (2014) 'World press freedom index 2014', https://rsf.org, accessed 16 February 2017.

Reporters Without Borders. (2016) '2016 World press freedom index: a "deep and disturbing" decline in media freedom', https://rsf.org, accessed 16 February 2017.

Reporters Without Borders. (2017a) 2017 World Press Freedom Index, http://rsf.org, accessed 3 June 2018.

Reporters Without Borders. (2017b) 'Mexico', http://rsf.org, accessed 21 February 2017.

Reynolds, G.H. (2013) 'Who's a journalist?' *New York Post* (8 July), http://nypost.com, accessed 2 October 2016.

Rid, T. & Hecker, M. (2009) *War 2.0: Irregular Warfare in the Information Age* (Westport, CT: Praeger Security International).

Rieger, H.C. (1989) 'The quality of life in Singapore: a foreigner's reflections' in K.S. Sandhu & P. Wheatley (eds) *Management of Success: The Moulding of Modern Singapore* (Singapore: Institute of Southeast Asian Studies), pp. 1022–48.

Rizal, D. (2015) *The Royal Semi-Authoritarian Democracy of Bhutan* (Lanham, MY: Lexington Books).

Robie, D. (2005) 'South Pacific notions of the Fourth Estate: a collision of media models, cultures and values' in E. Papoutsaki & U.S. Harris (eds) *South Pacific Islands Communication: Regional Perspectives, Local Issues* (Singapore: Asia Media, Information and Communication Centre), pp. 102–16.

Robie, D. (2008) 'Changing paradigms in media education aid in the Pacific' in E. Papoutsaki & U.S. Harris (eds) *South Pacific Islands Communication: Regional Perspectives, Local Issues* (Singapore: The Asian Media Information and Communication Centre), pp. 59–81.

Robie, D. (2013) '"Four Worlds" news values revisited: A deliberative journalism paradigm for Pacific media', *Pacific Journalism Review* 19(1), 84–110.

Robins, M.B. (2000) 'Africa's women/Africa's women journalists: critical perspectives on internet initiatives', Southeastern Regional Seminar in African Studies (14–15 April), Cullowhee, NC.

Robie, D. (2014) 'Lies, media integrity and the new digital environment', Pacific Media Centre (17 March), www.pmc.aut.ac.nz, accessed 29 June 2015.

Robinson, G.J. & Buzzanell, P.M. (2012) 'Comparing gender and communication' in F. Esser & T. Hanitzsch (eds) *The Handbook of Comparative Communication Research* (New York: Routledge), pp. 148–60.

Robinson, P. (1999) 'The CNN effect: can the news media drive foreign policy?' *Review of International Studies* 25(2), 301–09.

Romano, A. (2005) 'Asian journalism: news, development and the tides of liberalization and technology' in A Romano & M. Bromley (eds) *Journalism and Democracy in Asia* (Abingdon: Routledge), pp. 1–14.

Romano, A. & Bromley, M. (2005) 'Preface' in A Romano & M. Bromley (eds) *Journalism and Democracy in Asia* (Abingdon: Routledge), pp. xi–xiv.

Roosvall, A. & Salovaara-Moring, I. (2010) 'Introduction' in A. Roosvall & I. Salovaara-Moring (eds) *Communicating the Nation: National Topographies of a Global Media Landscape* (Göteborg: Nordicom), pp. 9–21.

Rosen, J. (1999) *What are Journalists for?* (New Haven, CT: Yale University Press).

Rosen, J. (2006) 'The people formerly known as the audience', Pressthink (27 June), archive.pressthink.org, accessed 16 March 2017.

Rosenblum, M. (1979) *Coups and Earthquakes: Reporting the World for America* (New York: Harper & Row).

Rosenstiel, T., Ivancin, M., Loker, K., Lacy, S., Sonderman, J. & Yaeger, K. (2015) 'Who is a "journalist" today, where they work and what they do', American Press Institute (6 August) www.americanpressinstitute.org, accessed 2 October 2016.

Ross, K. (2001) 'Women at work: journalism as en-gendered practice', *Journalism Studies* 2(4), 531–44.

Ross, K. & Carter, C. (2011) 'Women and news: a long and winding road', *Media, Culture & Society* 33(8), 1148–65.

Rotheray, B. (2010) *Good News from a Far Country?: Changes in International Broadcast News Supply in Africa and South Asia* (Oxford: Reuters Institute for the Study of Journalism).

Rottwilm, P. (2014) *The Future of Journalistic Work: Its Changing Nature and Implications* (Oxford: Reuters Institute for the Study of Journalism).

Rudra, G. (2012) 'Canons of journalism – the forgotten and unlamented Malaysian version', https://uppercaise.wordpress.com, accessed 2 February 2017.

Rush, R.R., Oukrop, C.E. & Sarikakis, K. (2005) 'A global hypothesis for women in journalism and mass communications', *Gazette* 67(3), 239–53.

Rutenberg, J. (2016) 'Media's next challenge: overcoming the threat of fake news', *New York Times* (6 November), www.nytimes.com, accessed 18 November 2016.

Sabato, L. (1991) *Feeding Frenzy: How Attack Journalism has Transformed American Politics* (New York: Free Press).

Sahara Reporters (n.d.) 'Sahara reporters: about', http://saharareporters.com, accessed 8 March 2017.

SaharaTV (n.d.) 'SaharaTV: about', http://saharareporters.tv, accessed 8 March 2017.

Saitta, E. (2013) 'France: a nuanced feminization of journalism' in C.M. Byerly (ed.) *The Palgrave International Handbook of Women and Journalism* (Basingstoke: Palgrave Macmillan), pp. 238–51.

Sakr, N. (1999) 'Satellite television and development in the Middle East', *Middle East Report* 210, 6–8.

Sakr, N. (2004) 'Women-media interaction in the Middle East: an introductory overview' in N. Sakr (ed.) *Women and Media in the Middle East* (London: I.B. Taurus), pp. 1–14.

Salam's diary. (2003) *The Guardian* (24 March), www.theguardian.com, accessed 18 February 2017.

Salamon, E. (2016) 'Links between freelancing and gender inequality highlighted by *Chronicle Herald* dispute', Story Board (22 January), www.thestoryboard.ca, accessed 30 January 2016.

Saldanha, A. (2016) 'Fake news in review: here are the top 10 forwards Indians (almost) believed in 2016', *FirstPost* (26 December), www.firstpost.com, accessed 23 March 2017.

Saleh, I. (2010) 'Journalism education in Egypt: politically hazed and socially confused' in B. Josephi (ed.) *Journalism Education in Countries with Limited Media Freedom* (New York: Peter Lang), pp. 115–34.

Salwen, M.B. & Garrison, B. (1991) *Latin American Journalism* (London: Routledge).

Sambrook, R. (2010) *Are Foreign Correspondents Redundant?* (Oxford: The Reuters Institute for the Study of Journalism).

Santora, M. & Carter, B. (2006) 'Iraq becomes deadliest of modern wars for journalists', *New York Times* (30 May), www.nytimes.com, accessed 5 February 2017.

Sassen, S. (1991) *The Global City* (New York: W.W. Norton).

Scanlon, C. (2012) 'Why study journalism? Because web audiences want quality, too', *Sydney Morning Herald* (18 July), www.smh.com.au, accessed 29 June 2015.

Schechter, D. (2005) 'Helicopter journalism. ZCommunications (6 January), https://zcomm.org, accessed 29 April 2018.

Schiller, H.I. (1975) 'Communication and cultural domination', *International Journal of Politics* 5(4), 1–12.

Schlesinger, P. (1978) *Putting 'Reality' Together: BBC News* (London: Constable).

Schmidt, E.E. (2014) 'The future of internet freedom', *New York Times* (4 March), www.nytimes.com, accessed 22 January 2017.

Schoepp, H. (2014) *Shoot First: The Code of the News Cameraman* (Pennsauken, NJ: BookBaby).

Schudson, M. (1994) 'Question authority: a history of the news interview in American journalism, 1860s–1930s', *Media, Culture & Society* 16(4), 565–87.

Schudson, M. (1996) 'The sociology of news production revisited' in J. Curran & M. Gurevitch (eds) *Mass Media and Society*, 2nd edn (London: Arnold), pp. 141–59.

Schudson, M. (2008) 'The "Lippmann-Dewey debate" and the invention of Walter Lippmann as an anti-democrat, 1986–1996', *International Journal of Communication* 2, 1031–42.

Schudson, M. (2009) 'Factual knowledge in the age of truthiness' in B. Zelizer (ed.) *The Changing Faces of Journalism: Tabloidization, Technology and Truthiness* (Abingdon: Routledge), pp. 104–13.

Schudson, M. (2010) 'News and democratic society: past, present, and future', *The Hedgehog Review* (Summer), 7–21.

Schudson, M. (2013) 'Would journalism please hold still!' in C. Peters & M. Broersma (eds) *Rethinking Journalism: Trust and Participation in a Transformed News Landscape* (Abingdon: Routledge), pp. 191–99.

Schultz, J. (1998) *Reviving the Fourth Estate: Democracy, Accountability & the Media* (Cambridge: Cambridge University Press).

Schwartz, I. (2015) 'Trump: corporate media Clinton's most powerful weapon, "no longer involved in journalism"', RealClear Politics (13 October), www.realclear-politics.com, accessed 21 February 2017.

Schwarzlose, R.A. (1973) 'Early telegraphic news dispatches: the forerunner of the AP', paper presented to the annual meeting of the Association for Education in Journalism (19–22 August), Fort Collins, CO.

Schweizer, C., Puppis, M., Künzler, M. & Studer, S. (2014) *Public Funding of Private Media*, Media Policy Brief 11 (London: London School of Economics and Political Science).

Scott, C.P. (1921, 1997) 'The *Manchester Guardian*'s first hundred years' in M. Bromley & T. O'Malley (eds) *A Journalism Reader* (London: Routledge), pp. 108–09.

Scott, Z. & Mcloughlin, C. (2014) *Political Systems: Topic Guide* (Birmingham: GSDRC, University of Birmingham).

Seib, P. (2004) *Beyond the Front Lines: How the News Media Cover a World Shaped by War* (New York: Palgrave Macmillan).

Seib, P. (2008) *The Al Jazeera Effect: How the New Global Media are Reshaping World Politics* (Washington, DC: Potomac)

Self, C.C. (2015) 'Global journalism education: a missed opportunity for media development?' *Insights* (June), 1–6.

Sen, A. (1999) 'Democracy as universal value', *Journal of Democracy* 10(3), 3–17.

Seneviratne, K. (2015) 'Asian scholars crafting a non-adversarial approach to journalism', *IDN-InDepthNews*, www.indepthnews.net, accessed 17 February 2017.

Servaes, J. & Lie, R. (2008) 'Media globalization through localization' in J. Servaes (ed.) *Communication for Development and Social Change* (New Delhi: Sage), pp. 58–67.

Seshu, G. (2014) *The Campaign for Justice: Press Freedom in South Asia, 2013–2014* (Brussels: International Federation of Journalists).

Shavit, U. (2009) *The New Imagined Communities: Global Media and the Construction of National and Muslim Identities of Migrants* (Brighton: Sussex Academic Press).

Shaw, I.S. (2009) 'Towards an African journalism model: a critical historical perspective', *International Communication Gazette* 71(6), 491–510.

Sheafer, T., Shenhav, S., Bloom, P.B.N. & Segev, E. (2012 'The roles of political culture, values and identity proximity in international political communication: a comparative analysis, paper presented to the European Consortium for Political Research, University of Antwerp (10–15 April).

Sherman, G. (2016) 'The revenge of Roger's angels: how Fox News women took down the most powerful, and predatory, man in media', *New York* (2 September), nymag.com, accessed 14 March 2017.

Shoemaker, P.J. & Vos, T.P. (2009) *Gatekeeping Theory* (New York: Routledge).

Shrivastava, K.M. (2007) *News Agencies from Pigeon to Internet* (Elgin, IL: New Dawn Press).

Shufiyan, S.L. (2017) 'About us', Citizen Journalists Malaysia (nd), http://cj.my, accessed 25 January 2017.

Siebert, F.S. (1963) 'The authoritarian theory of the press' in F.S. Siebert, T. Peterson & W. Schramm, *Four Theories of the Press: The Authoritarian, Libertarian, Social Responsibility and Soviet Communist Concepts of What the Press Should Be and Do* (Urbana, IL: University of Illinois Press), pp. 9–37.

Siebert, F.S., Peterson, T. & Schramm, W. (1956) *Four Theories of the Press: The Authoritarian, Libertarian, Social Responsibility, and Soviet Communist Concepts of What the Press Should Be and Do* (Urbana, IL: University of Illinois Press).

Silverman, J. (2013) 'Journalists should be equipped with theory as well as practical skills', BBC College of Journalism (24 July), www.bbc.co.uk/blogs/collegeofjournalism.

Silverman, C. (2016) 'Viral fake election news outperformed real news on Facebook in final months of the election', *BuzzFeed News* (16 November), www.buzzfeed.com, accessed 18 November 2016.

Silverman, C. & Alexander, L. (2016) 'How teens in the Balkans are duping Trump supporters with fake news', *BuzzFeed News* (4 November), www.buzzfeed.com, accessed 18 November 2016.

Simkin, J. (1997) 'William Howard Russell', Spartacus Educational, http://spartacus-educational.com, accessed 17 February 2017.

Simon, J. (2016) 'Breaking the silence' in *Attacks on the Press: Gender and Media Freedom Worldwide* (New York: Committee to Protect Journalists), www.cpj.org, accessed 14 March 2017.

Simons, M. (2007) *The Content Makers: Understanding the Media in Australia* (Camberwell: Penguin).

Simpson, J. (1995) 'A joke, a shot, a pool of blood', *The Independent* (14 August), www.independent.co.uk, accessed 5 February 2017.

Simpson, J. (2016) *We Chose to Speak of War and Strife: The World of the Foreign Correspondent* (London: Bloomsbury).

Singer, J.B. (2004) 'Strange bedfellows? Diffusion of convergence in four news organizations', *Journalism Studies* 5(1), 3–18.

Siomos, T. (2009) 'The Greek journalism education landscape' in G. Terzis (ed.) *European Journalism Education* (Bristol: Intellect), pp. 267–75.

Skovsgaard, M., Albæk, E., Bro, P. & de Vreese, C. (2012) 'Media professionals or organizational marionettes? Professional values and constraints of Danish journalists' in D.H. Weaver & L. Willnat (eds) *The Global Journalist in the 21st Century* (New York: Routledge), pp. 155–70.

Slavtcheva-Petkova, V. (2016a) '"We are not fools": Online news commentators' perceptions of real and ideal journalism', *International Journal of Press/Politics* 21(1), 68–87.

Slavtcheva-Petkova, V. (2016b) 'Are newspapers' online discussion boards democratic tools or conspiracy theories' engines? A case study on an Eastern European "media war"', *Journalism & Mass Communication Quarterly* 93(4), 1115–34.

Slavtcheva-Petkova, V. (2017) 'Country report: journalists in Bulgaria', *Worlds of Journalism Study*, www.worldsofjournalism.org

Smirnova, O.V. (2013) 'Women's advancement in journalism: psychological characteristics', *Psychology in Russia: State of the Art* 6(1), pp. 119–27.

Smith, D. (2017) 'Trump press conference: president says team running like "fine-tuned machine"', *The Guardian* (16 February), www.theguardian.com, accessed 16 February 2017.

Smythe, D.W. & Van Dinh, T. (1983) 'On critical and administrative research: a new critical analysis', *Journal of Communication* 33(3), 117–127.

Snegovaya, M. (2015) *Putin's Information Warfare in Ukraine: Soviet Origins of Russia's Hybrid Warfare*, Russia Report 1 (Washington, DC: Institute for the Study of War).

Solomon, S. (2017) 'Fake news, false information stokes xenophobia in South Africa', Voice of America (1 March), www.voanews.com, accessed 23 March 2017.

Solon, O. (2016) 'Barack Obama on fake news: "We have problems" if we can't tell the difference', *The Guardian* (18 November) www.theguardian.com/media, accessed 18 November 2016.

Sommers, J. (2015) '7/7 bombings marked a journalism "tipping point" that caught news gatherers offguard', *The Huffington Post*, www.huffingtonpost.co.uk, accessed 17 February 2017.

Sommers, S.R., Apfelbaum, E.P., Dukes, K.N., Toosi, N. & Wang, E.J. (2006) 'Race and media coverage of Hurricane Katrina: Analysis, implications, and future research questions', *Analyses of Social Issues and Public Policy* 6(1), 39–55.

Son, Y.J., Kim, S.T. & Choi, J. (2012) 'Korean journalists in the 21st century' in D.H. Weaver & L. Willnat (eds) *The Global Journalist in the 21st Century* (New York: Routledge), pp. 66–77.

Sonderman, J. (2012) 'What's next for Columbia's journalism school as dean Nicholas Lehmann steps down?' Poynter (10 October), www.poynter.org, accessed 14 March 2017.

South African National Editors' Forum. (2007) *Glass Ceiling 2: An Audit of Women and Men in South African Newsrooms* (Johannesburg: SANEF).

Spampinato, A. (2016) 'Italy: new Bill proposes heavy jail sentence for defamation', European Centre for Press & Media Freedom, https://ecpmf.eu, accessed 17 February 2017.

Sparks, C. with Reading, A. (1998) *Communism, Capitalism and the Mass Media* (London: Sage).

Spilsbury, M. (2013) *Journalists at Work: Their Views on Training, Recruitment and Conditions* (Essex: National Council for the Training of Journalists).

Splichal, S. & Sparks, C. (1994) *Journalists for the 21st Century* (Norword, NJ: Ablex).

Sreberny, A. (2006) 'The global and the local in international communications' in M.G. Durham & D.M. Kellner (eds) *Media and Cultural Studies Key Works*, revised edition (Malden, MA: Blackwell), pp. 604–25.

Sreberny, A. (2014) 'Violence against women journalists' in A.V. Montiel (ed.) *Media and Gender: A Scholarly Agenda for the Global Alliance on Media and Gender* (Paris: UNESCO), pp. 30–33.

Starck, K. (2000) 'Negotiating professional and academic standards in journalism education', *AsiaPacific Media Educator* 8, 59–69.

Steel, E. & Schmidt, M.S. (2017) 'Fox News settled sexual harassment allegations against Bill O'Reilly, documents show', *New York Times* (10 January), www.nytimes.com, accessed 29 March 2017.

Steensen, S. & Ahva, L. (2015) 'Theories of journalism in a digital age', *Journalism Practice* 9(1), 1–18.

Steiner, L. (2000) 'Gender in the newsroom' in K. Wahl-Jorgensen & T. Hanitzsch (eds) *The Handbook of Journalism Studies* (New York: Routledge), pp. 116–29.

Steiner, L. (2009) 'Disambiguating "the media" and "the media plot"', *Journalism* 10(3), 381–83.

Steiner, L. (2012) 'Failed theories: explaining gender difference in journalism', *The Review of Communication* 12(3), 201–33.

Steiner, L. (2016) 'Bodies at war: the dangers facing women reporters' in B. von der Lippe & R. Ottosen (eds) *Gendering War and Peace Reporting: Some Insights – Some Missing Links* (Göteborg: Nordicom), pp. 33–47.

Stepinska, A., Ossowski, S., Pokrzycka, L. & Nowak, J. (2012) 'The journalists and journalism of Poland' in D.H. Weaver & L. Willnat (eds) *The Global Journalist in the 21st Century* (New York: Routledge), pp. 255–66.

Štětka, V. (2012a) 'From multinationals to business tycoons: media ownership and journalistic autonomy in Central and Eastern Europe', *The International Journal of Press/Politics* 17(4), 433–56.

Štětka, V. (2012b) 'There and back again? media freedom and autonomy in Central and Eastern Europe', openDemocracy, www.opendemocracy.net, accessed 17 February 2017.

Stevenson, N. (1999) *The Transformation of the Media: Globalisation, Morality and Ethics* (Harlow: Longman).

Stiglitz, J. (2017) 'Putin's illiberal stagnation in Russia offers a valuable lesson', *The Guardian* (3 April), www.theguardian.com, accessed 11 April 2017.

Stokes, G. (1993) *The Walls Came Tumbling Down: The Collapse of Communism in Eastern Europe* (New York: Oxford University Press).

Stray, J. (2016) 'What do journalists do with documents?', jonathanstray.com (2 November), accessed 11 April 2017.

Strong, C. (2007) 'Female journalists shun sports reporting: lack of opportunity versus lack of attractiveness', *Communication Journal of New Zealand* 8(2), 7–18.

Surowiecki, J. (2004) *The Wisdom of Crowds: Why the Many are Smarter than the Few* (London: Little Brown).

Sutterer, A. (2017) 'Project exile: Eritrean state media reporter turns critic', *Global Journalist* (2 February), http://globaljournalist.org, accessed 20 February 2017.

Swift, A. (2016) 'American's trust in mass media sinks to new low', Gallup (14 September), www.gallup.com, accessed 22 February 2017.

Tamam, E., Raj, S.J. & Govindasamy, M. (2012) 'Malaysian journalists' in D.H. Weaver & L. Willnat (eds) *The Global Journalist in the 21st Century* (New York: Routledge), pp. 78–90.

Tambini, D. (2016) 'In the new robopolitics, social media has left newspapers for dead', *The Guardian* (18 November), www.theguardian.com/commentisfree, accessed 21 November 2016.

Tan, A. (2017) '7 in 10 Singaporeans use social media on mobile, double global average: survey', *The Business Times* (24 January), www.businesstimes.com.sg, accessed 3 June 2018.

Tandoc, E.C. & Jenkins, J. (2017) 'The Buzzfeediciation of journalism? How traditional news organization are talking about a new entrant to the journalistic field will surprise you!' *Journalism* 18(4), 482–500.

Terzis, G. (2015) 'Conclusions: the "professional strangers" of Europe at the dawn of the 21st century' in G. Terzis (ed.) *Mapping Foreign Correspondence in Europe* (London: Routledge), pp. 297–313.

Terzis, G. & Harding, G. (2015) 'Foreign correspondents in Belgium: Brussel correspondents' struggle to make the important interesting' in G. Terzis (ed.) *Mapping Foreign Correspondence in Europe* (London: Routledge), pp. 18–34.

Tharoor, S. (1999) 'Are human rights universal?' *World Policy Journal* 16(4), 1–16.

Thawabteh, N. (2010) 'Palestinian media map: production congestion and consumption dispersion' in B. Josephi (ed.) *Journalism Education in Countries with Limited Media Freedom* (New York: Peter Lang), pp. 73–93.

The Associated Press/NORC. (2015) 'How Millenials use technology to get news: difference by race and ethnicity', Project Brief, Media Insight Project.

The Constitution of the Republic of Cuba. (1976). www.constitutionnet.org, accessed 21 February 2017.

The Listening Post. (2012) 'Tuning in to Telesur's agenda', Al Jazeera (22 September), www.aljazeera.com, accessed 7 March 2017.

The State Committee for Family, Women and Children Affairs in the Republic of Azerbaijan. (2014) 20th anniversary of the Beijing declaration and platform for action: state report (Baku: Republic of Azerbaijan).

Thomas, P. (2010a) 'Communication and Social Change' in P. Thomas & M. Bromley (eds) *An Introduction to Communication and Social Change* (St. Lucia: Centre for Communication and Social Change, The University of Queensland), pp. 23–35.

Thomas, P. (2010b) 'The right to information movement in India' in P. Thomas & M. Bromley (eds) *An Introduction to Communication and Social Change* (St. Lucia: Centre for Communication and Social Change, The University of Queensland), pp. 179–85.

Thompson, A. (2007) *The Media and the Rwanda Genocide* (London: Pluto Press).

Thussu, D. (1998) *Electronic Empires: Global Media and Local Resistance* (London: Hodder Arnold).

Tomlinson, J. (1991) *Cultural Imperialism: A Critical Introduction* (London: Continuum).

Tran, M. (2016) 'International expansion without colonial overtones', NiemanLab (19 December), www.niemanlab.org, accessed 23 March 2017.

Tsfati, Y. & Meyers, O. (2012) 'Journalists in Israel' in D.H. Weaver & Lars Willnat (eds) *The Global Journalist in the 21st Century* (New York: Routledge), pp. 443–57.

Tsui, C.Y.S. & Lee, F.L.F. (2012) 'Trajectories of women journalists' careers in Hong Kong', *Journalism Studies* 13(3), 370–85.

Tumber, H. & Prentoulis, M. (2005) 'Journalism and the making of a profession' in H. de Burgh (ed.) *Making Journalists* (Abingdon: Routledge), pp. 58–74.

Tumber, H. & Webster, F. (2006) *Journalists Under Fire: Information War and Journalistic Practices* (London: Sage).

Tunstall, J. (1971) *Journalists at Work. Specialist Correspondents: Their News Organizations, News Sources, & Competitor-Colleagues* (London: Constable).

Tunstall, J. (1977) *The Media are American: Anglo-American Media in the World* (London: Constable).

Tunstall, J. (1983) *The Media in Britain* (London: Constable).

Tunstall, J. (1996) *Newspaper Power: The New National Press in Britain* (Oxford: Clarendon Press).

Tuosto, K. (2008) 'The "Grunt Truth" of embedded journalism: the new media/ military relationship', *Stanford Journal of International Relations* 10(1), 20–31.

Turnbull, M. (2014) 'Foreign correspondents, their importance and their future', Lowy Institute Media Awards (13 August), www.malcolmturnbull.com.au, accessed 4 March 2017.

Turner, G. (2000) '"Media Wars": journalism, cultural and media studies in Australia', *Journalism* 1(3), 353–65.

Turner, G. (2001) 'Sold out: recent shifts in television news and current affairs in Australia' in M. Bromley (ed.) *No News is Bad News: Radio, Television and the Public* (Harlow: Pearson), pp. 46–58.

Turtola, I. (2017) *How Do Social Media Build the Professional Identity of Journalists?* Reuters Institute Fellowship paper (Oxford: Reuters Institute for the Study of Journalism).

Tytarenko, M. (2011) 'Feminizing journalism in Ukraine: changing the paradigm' in M.J. Rubchak (ed.) *Mapping Difference: The Many Faces of Women in Contemporary Ukraine* (New York: Berghahn Books), pp. 145–60.

UN. (2012) 'UN Plan of Action on the Safety of Journalists and the Issue of Impunity', www.unesco.org, accessed 12 September 2017.

UN. (2013) 'Composition of macro geographical (continental) regions, geographical sub-regions, and selected economic and other groupings', https://unstats.un.org, accessed 17 February 2017.

Underwood, R. (2007) *Shoot! Shooting TV News: Views from behind the Lens* (Burlington, MA: Focal Press).

UNESCO. (n.d.) 'Public service broadcasting', www.unesco.org, accessed 9 July 2018.

UNESCO. (1980) Records of the General Conference, Twenty-First Session, Belgrade, 23 September–28 October. Volume 1, Resolutions 14/19.

UNESCO. (2007) *Model Curricula for Journalism Education for Developing Countries & Emerging Democracies* (Paris: UNESCO).

UNESCO. (2008) 'Media development indicators: a framework for assessing media development', www.unesco.org, accessed 17 February 2017.

UNESCO. (2012) 'Capacity building for women community radio journalists', IDPC Project, www.unesco-ci.org, accessed 3 January 2016.

UNESCO. (2014a) 'World trends in freedom of expression and media development', www.unesco.org, accessed 17 February 2017.

UNESCO. (2014b) 'World trends in freedom of expression and media development: regional overview of Asia and the Pacific' www.unesco.org, accessed 17 February 2017.

UNESCO. (2014c) 'World trends in freedom of expression and media development: regional overview of Latin America and the Caribbean', www.unesco.org, accessed 17 February 2017.

UNESCO. (2014d) 'World trends in freedom of expression and media development: regional overview of Africa', www.unesco.org, accessed 17 February 2017.

UNESCO. (2015) 'Women make the news', www.unesco.org, accessed 10 January 2016.

UNESCO, UN Women & International Federation of Journalists. (2014) *Inside the News: Challenges and Aspirations of Women Journalists in Asia and the Pacific* (Paris: UNESCO).

UNESCO Institute for Statistics. (2011), http://knoema.com/, accessed 11 March 2014.

UNESCO Institute for Statistics. (2014), http://knoema.com/, accessed 11 January 2016.

UNHCR. (2016) 'Refugees & charities display "lifejacket graveyard" in Parliament Square as world leaders meet at United Nations Migration Summit in New York', www.unhcr.org/uk, accessed 17 February 2017.

United States Department of Labor, Bureau of Labor Statistics. (2015a) 'Reporters, correspondents, and broadcast news analysts', *Occupational Outlook Handbook*, www.bls.gov, accessed 7 March 2017.

United States Department of Labor, Bureau of Labor Statistics. (2015b) Editors, *Occupational Outlook Handbook*, www.bls.gov, accessed 7 March 2017.

Urist, J. (2014) 'Which deaths matter? How the media covers the people behind today's grim statistics', *The Atlantic* (29 September), www.theatlantic.com, accessed 26 January 2017.

Usher, N. (2014) *Making News at the New York Times* (Ann Arbor, MI: University of Michigan Press).

van den Wijngaard, R. (1992) 'Women as journalists: incompatibility of roles?', *Africa Media Review* 6(2), pp. 47–56.

van Ginneken, J. (1998) *Understanding Global News: A Critical Introduction* (London: Sage).

van Zoonen, L. (1998) 'One of the girls? The changing gender of journalism', in: C. Carter, G. Branston & S. Allan (eds) *News, Gender and Power* (London: Routledge), pp. 33-46.

Vartanova, E., Lukina, M., Svitich, L. & Shiryaeva, A. (2010) 'Between tradition and innovation: journalism education in Russia' in B. Josephi (ed.) *Journalism Education in Countries with Limited Media Freedom* (New York: Peter Lang), pp. 199–216.

Vasarhelyi, M. (2012) 'Journalism in Hungary' in D.H. Weaver & L. Willnat (eds) *The Global Journalist in the 21st Century* (New York: Routledge), pp. 234–41.

Vercueil, J. (2012) *Les pays émergents. Brésil - Russie - Inde - Chine... Mutations économiques et nouveaux défis*, 3rd edn (Paris: Bréal).

Vis, F. (2009) 'Wikinews reporting of Hurricane Katrina' in S. Allan & E. Thorsen (eds) *Citizen Journalism: Global Perspectives*, vol. 1 (New York: Peter Lang), pp. 65–74.

Vis, F. & Goriunova, O. (2015) *The Iconic Image on Social Media: A Rapid Research Response to the Death of Aylan Kurdi* (Sheffield: Visual Social Media Lab).

Vlad, T. & Balasescu, M. (2010) 'Few educators, many media and journalism programs: journalism and mass communication education in Romania after the fall of Communism' in B. Josephi (ed.) *Journalism Education in Countries with Limited Media Freedom* (New York: Peter Lang), pp. 217–33.

Volkmer, I. (2002) 'Journalism and political crises in the global network society' in B. Zelizer & S. Allan (eds) *Journalism after September 11* (London: Routledge), pp. 235–46.

Voltmer, K. (2008) 'Comparing media systems in new democracies: East meets South meets West', *European Journal of Communication* 1, 23–40.

Voltmer, K. (2013) *The Media in Transitional Democracies* (Cambridge: Polity).

Wadekar, N. (2015) 'State of the media: international coverage in U.S. journalism', Annenberg Media Center, www.neontommy.com, accessed 17 February 2017.

Waisbord, S. (2013) *Reinventing Professionalism: Journalism and News in Global Perspective* (Cambridge: Polity).

Waisbord, S. (2014) 'Citizen journalism, development and social change: hype and hope' in E. Thorsen & S. Allan (eds) *Citizen Journalism: Global Perspectives*, vol. 2 (New York: Peter Lang), pp. 185–98.

Wall, M. (2015) 'Citizen journalism', *Digital Journalism* 3(6), 797–813.

Wall, M. & El Zahed, S. (2015) 'Embedding content from Syrian citizen journalists: the rise of the collaborative news clip', *Journalism* 16(2), 163–80.

Wang, S-f.S. (2006) 'Journalism and communication education in Taiwan: an observation in a transitional society' in K.W.Y. Leung, J. Kenny & P.S.N. Lee (eds) *Global Trends in Communication Education and Research* (Cresskill, NJ: Hampton Press), pp. 159–76.

Ward, S.J.A. (2017) 'Global media ethics, human rights and flourishing' in H. Tumber & S. Waisbord (eds) *The Routledge Companion to Media and Human Rights* (Abingdon: Routledge), pp. 211–19.

Wardle, C. & Dubberly, S. (2014) *Amateur Footage: A Global Study of User-Generated Content*, towcenter.org, accessed 16 March 2017.

Wardle, C. & Williams, A. (2010) 'Beyond user-generated content: a production study examining the ways in which audience material is used at the BBC', *Media, Culture & Society* 32(5), 781–99.

Wasserman, H. (2006) 'Have ethics, will travel – the glocalization of media ethics from an African perspective', Center for Journalism Ethics, University of Wisconsin (14 September) https://ethics.journalism.wisc.edu, accessed 5 July 2016.

Weaver, D.H. & Willnat, L. (eds) (2012) *The Global Journalist in the 21st Century* (New York: Routledge).

Weischenberg, S., Malik, M. & Scholl, A. (2012) 'Journalism in Germany in the 21st century' in D.H. Weaver & L. Willnat (eds) *The Global Journalist in the 21st Century* (New York: Routledge), pp. 205–19.

Westcott, L. (2016) 'Women journalists share their stories of sexual harassment', *Newsweek* (22 August), europe.newsweek.com, accessed 14 March 2017.

Whipple, M. (2005) 'The Dewey-Lippmann debate today: communication distortions, reflective agency, and participatory democracy', *Sociological Theory* 23(2), 156–78.

Wilder, A.E. (2016) Various postings at *The Grenada Revolution*, www.thegrenadarevolutiononline.com, accessed 6 July 2016.

Williams, A. (2016a) 'Hyperlocal news in the UK: its current state and future prospects', IMPRESS (24 March), impress.press, accessed 16 March 2017.

Williams, A., Wardle, C. & Wahl-Jorgensen, K. (2011) '"Have they got news for us?" Audience revolution or business as usual at the BBC?' *Journalism Practice* 5(1), 85–99.

Williams, A.T. (2016b) 'Employment picture darkens for journalists at digital outlets', *Columbia Journalism Review*, www.cjr.org, accessed 7 March 2017.

Williams, G. (2007) *US-Grenada Relations: Revolution and Intervention in the Backyard* (New York: Palgrave Macmillan).

Williams, K. (2001) 'Demise or renewal? The dilemma of public service television in western Europe' in M. Bromley (ed.) *No News is Bad News: Radio, Television and the Public* (Harlow: Pearson), pp. 9–27.

Williams, K. (2011) *International Journalism* (London: Sage).

Williams, O. (2016c) 'British journalism is 94% white and 55% male, survey reveals', *The Guardian* (24 March), www.theguardian.com, accessed 10 March 2017.

Willis, J. (2010) *The Mind of a Journalist: How Reporters View Themselves, their World, and their Craft* (Thousand Oaks, CA: Sage).

Willnat, L. & Martin, J. (2012) 'Foreign correspondents – an endangered species?' in D.H. Weaver & L. Willnat (eds) *The Global Journalist in the 21st Century* (New York: Routledge), pp. 495–510.

Willnat, L. & Weaver, D.H. (2014) *The American Journalist in the Digital Age: Key Findings* (Bloomington, IN: School of Journalism, Indiana University).

Winch, T. (2012) 'Journalism school a far cry from reality', *The Australian* (14 March), 39.

Wingfield, N., Isaac, M. & Benner, K. (2016) 'Google and Facebook take aim at fake news sites', *New York Times* (14 November), www.nytimes.com, accessed 18 November 2016.

Winseck, D. & Pike, R.M. (2009) 'The global media and the empire of liberal internationalism, *circa* 1910–1930', *Media History* 15(1), 31–54.

Witchel, E. (2018) 'Getting away with murder', Committee to Protect Journalists, www.cpj.org, accessed 10 July 2018.

Witt-Barthel, A. (2006) 'EFJ survey: women journalists in the European integration process', Gender Equality Seminar, Delhi (20–21 May).

Woo. (2015). 'China's media war: censorship, corruption and control', International Federation of Journalists, www.ifj.org, accessed 21 February 2017.

Woolf, N. (2016) 'As fake news takes over Facebook feeds, many are taking satire as fact', *The Guardian* (17 November), www.theguardian.com/media, accessed 18 November 2016.

World Forum for Democracy. (2015) *Freedom vs Control: For a Democratic Response* (Strasbourg: Council of Europe).

World Summit of Nobel Peace Laureates. (2017) 'Women Journalists Without Chains reporting', www.nobelpeacesummit.com, accessed 13 March 2017.

Worlds of Journalism. (2011) 'The WJS 2007–11 pilot study: journalism cultures, influences and trust', www.worldsofjournalism.org, accessed 17 February 2017.

Worlds of Journalism 2012–2016 study. (2017) 'Data and key tables 2012–2016: Aggregated data on key variables', www.worldsofjournalism.org, accessed 26 April 2018.

Wu, D. & Hamilton, J. (2004) 'US foreign correspondents: changes and continuity at the turn of the century', *International Communication Gazette* 66(6), 517–32.

Wu, T. (2006) 'Journalism education in China: a historical perspective' in K.W.Y. Leung, J. Kenny & P.S.N. Lee (eds) *Global Trends in Communication Education and Research* (Cresskill, NJ: Hampton Press), pp. 133–57.

Wyss, J. (2016) 'Argentina pulls plug on Venezuela's Telesur', *Miami Herald* (28 March), www.miamiherald.com, accessed 7 March 2017.

Xu, X. (2005) *Demystifying Asian Values in Journalism* (Singapore: Marshall Cavendish).

Yeoman, F. (2013) 'The value of professional journalism', *The Independent* (4 December), www.independent.co.uk, accessed 11 April 2017.

Yuhas, A. (2017) 'John McCain on Trump: suppressing the free press is "how dictators get started"', *The Guardian* (19 February), www.theguardian.com, accessed 19 February 2017.

Zaffiro, J. (1997) 'African news media and foreign policy: the case of Botswana', in A. Malek (ed.) *News Media and Foreign Relations: A Multifacted Perspective* (Westport, CT: Greenwood), pp. 211–23.

Zelizer, B. (1995) 'Words against images: positioning newswork in the age of photography' in H. Hardt & B. Brennen (eds) *Newsworkers: Towards a History of the Rank and File* (Minneapolis, MN: University of Minnesota Press), pp. 135–59.

Zelizer, B. (2004) 'When facts, truth, and reality are God-terms: on journalism's uneasy place in culltural studies', *Communication and Critical/Cultural Studies* 1(1), 100–19.

Zelizer, B. (2009) 'Journalism and the academy' in K. Wahl-Jorgensen & T. Hanitzsch (eds) *The Handbook of Journalism Studies* (Oxon: Routledge), pp. 29–41.

Zelizer, B. (2017) *What Journalism Could Be* (Cambridge: Polity).

Zelizer, B. & Allan, S. (2010) *Keywords in News and Journalism Studies* (Maidenhead: Open University Press).

Zere, A.T. (2017) 'About me', http://abrahamzere.com, accessed 20 February 2017.

Zhang, H. & Su, L. (2012) 'Chinese media and journalists in transition' in D.H. Weaver & L. Willnat (eds) *The Global Journalist in the 21st Century* (New York: Routledge), pp. 9–21.

Zhongshi, G. (2010) 'Through barbed wires: context, content, and constraints for journalism education in China' in B. Josephi (ed.) *Journalism Education in Countries with Limited Media Freedom* (New York: Peter Lang), pp. 15–32.

Zhou, V. (2016) 'How China's highly censored WeChat and Weibo fight fake news … and other controversial content', *South China Morning Post* (16 December), www.scmp.com, accessed 23 March 2017.

Zingales, L. (2015) 'A strong press is best defence against crony capitalism', *Financial Times* (18 October), www.ft.com, accessed 20 February 2017.

Zizek, S. (2015) 'Capitalism has broken free of the shackles of democracy', *Financial Times* (1 February), www.ft.com, accessed 20 February 2017.

Index

Printed in Great
Britain
by Amazon